AMERICAN OLIGARCHS

AMERICAN OLIGARCHS

THE KUSHNERS, THE TRUMPS, AND THE MARRIAGE OF MONEY AND POWER

ANDREA BERNSTEIN

W. W. NORTON & COMPANY
Independent Publishers Since 1923

Printed in the United States of America
First Edition

For information about permission to reproduce selections from this book, write to Permissions, W. W. Norton & Company, Inc., 500 Fifth Avenue, New York, NY 10110

For information about special discounts for bulk purchases, please contact W. W. Norton Special Sales at specialsales@wwnorton.com or 800-233-4830

Manufacturing by LSC Communications, Harrisonburg
Book design by Chris Welch
Production manager: Anna Oler

ISBN 978-1-324-00187-4

W. W. Norton & Company, Inc., 500 Fifth Avenue, New York, N.Y. 10110
www.wwnorton.com

W. W. Norton & Company Ltd., 15 Carlisle Street, London W1D 3BS

1 2 3 4 5 6 7 8 9 0

To Liz, Maya, and Jonah, who keep teaching me

the next mountain is always worth climbing.

No human being could have written this script.
Only God could have.

—CHARLES KUSHNER[1]

CONTENTS

ACT III

ACT IV

ACT V

AMERICAN OLIGARCHS

PROLOGUE

THE WEDDING

It had rained the day before, but by the morning of October 25, 2009, the weather had cleared. The sun brought the temperature to sixty degrees—mild, for late October in central New Jersey. By midafternoon, the only reminder of the previous day's rain was the pleasant smell of damp, newly fallen leaves, and the still-welcome faint whiff of composting plants that wafts over farm country in autumn.

A string of cars made its way down Lamington Road, past fields and woodlands, past vivid red and yellow oaks and maples, past a low semicircular stone gate with the words "Trump National Golf Club" written in gold script, below the Trump family seal, and above the subtitle: Bedminster.

The cars brought wedding guests from Manhattan and Atlantic City; from Newark and Livingston, New Jersey; from Harrisburg and Albany and Tallahassee; from Hollywood and Palm Beach; from Slovenia and the Czech Republic. Some arrived by helicopter.

The stream of limos and black SUVs ferried politicians and media moguls: Rupert Murdoch and his wife, Wendi; and Jeff Zucker and Mark Burnett from NBC. Barbara Walters, Regis Philbin, editors from *Vogue* and *Time* and *Town & Country* and the *New York Observer*. The chairman of Macy's was also among the guests, as were bankers, lawyers, and business partners; multiple rabbis; generations of people in real estate and finance; company employees. And, above all, the preeminent tribes, two patriarchs, their children, wives and an ex-wife; siblings and their spouses, aunts and uncles, nephews and nieces.[1]

All there to celebrate the marriage of two beautiful, impossibly successful, and wealthy young people: Jared Kushner and Ivanka Trump, twenty-eight and twenty-seven years old, with the world spread out before them like the gently undulating lawns of the golf course.

Jared Kushner rarely spoke in public, but when he did, his tenor voice betrayed the stretched-out vowels and thudding d's of New Jersey. He had become known, fleetingly, in 2006, as one of the subjects of Daniel Golden's book *The Price of Admission*, which chronicled how, despite an unexceptional academic record, Jared had been accepted at Harvard after large contributions from his father and a call from a US senator.[2]

By October 2009, Jared Kushner, just six years out of Harvard and two from his double business and law degree from New York University, owned a skyscraper on Fifth Avenue bought for nearly $2 billion and a salmon-colored weekly newspaper, the *New York Observer*.

Ivanka Trump had grown up, sometimes awkwardly, in front of the paparazzi; she was eight when her parents' public divorce swamped the front pages of the New York City tabloids; she'd done some modeling as a teen, and had appeared—clumsily—on television.

By her wedding day she had an undergraduate economics degree from the Wharton School at the University of Pennsylvania, was an executive vice president of the Trump Organization, had launched a jewelry line, had been named to the board of Trump Entertainment Resorts, and had published the book *The Trump Card*. She'd become a recurring character in the all-important gossip columns: in the *New York Post*'s "Page Six," and *New York* magazine's "Intelligencer." She had been pictured on the cover of *Harper's Bazaar* wearing a black bathing suit and wielding a jackhammer, her wrists encircled in elaborate diamond bracelets; and on the cover of *Town & Country* with the tagline "Smart, Successful and Sexy." But in 2009, Ivanka Trump was known, most of all, for her regular role as a judge on her father's television fantasy, *The Apprentice.*

By the time of his older daughter's wedding, Donald Trump had divorced two of his three wives and, putatively, cheated with two different women on the third (though no one knew that yet). He had defaulted on bank loans, sued his business partners and government officials with almost ritualistic rigor, and been sued, in turn, by vendors, customers, and financial partners. He had declared over a billion dollars in business losses and avoided a lifetime of taxes. His companies had gone into bankruptcy, he had survived multiple criminal investigations, and yet he was seen almost affectionately as the enfant terrible of Manhattan, Atlantic City, Palm Beach, and, sometimes, Beverly Hills. In those years, during the title sequence of *The Apprentice,* he would pronounce the lie, "My name's Donald Trump, and I'm the largest real estate developer in New York."

Unlike Donald Trump, Charles Kushner, the father of the groom—by then grey-haired, espresso-eyed, athletically lean and coiled—had not been able to avoid the consequences of his actions. The son of Holocaust survivors who had endured unimaginable conditions in Nazi-occupied Poland, Charles Kushner had once been the developer and manager of a New Jersey empire of 22,000 garden apartments and single-family homes, a don of suburbia. He had been, for years, a flagrantly generous philanthropist and the largest Democratic donor in New Jersey, showering the Democratic Party with donations the way the Enron Corporation had contributed to George W. Bush. For a while, he was on track to lead the Port Authority of New York and New Jersey, to be the chairman of a bistate transportation and real estate behemoth that has a larger budget than a fifth of US states.

Then he began to blur the lines between the family business and his own interests, so much so that his older brother—his business partner—sued him. The suit caught the attention of the new US attorney for New Jersey: Christopher J. Christie, who enlisted Charles

Kushner's sister and brother-in-law as witnesses. In a rage, Charlie retaliated by hiring a prostitute to entrap his sister's husband, William Schulder, at a diner in Bridgewater, New Jersey, and then lure him for sex to the Red Bull Inn, just a twenty-minute drive down Route 22 from the Trump golf course in Bedminster.

Charlie Kushner sent the secretly recorded video of the encounter to his sister, who brought it to the US Attorney's Office in Newark; after which Charlie was arrested for witness tampering. He was also ultimately charged with defrauding US taxpayers and violating campaign finance laws, pleaded guilty, and served a year in prison for his crimes. This period, in New Jersey, is referred to as "when Charlie went away."

By October 25, 2009, just three years after he was released from the Federal Prison Camp in Montgomery, Alabama, Charles Kushner had returned to real estate and moved his office to the fifteenth floor of the aluminum-clad skyscraper his company now owned at 666 Fifth Avenue. He'd bought an apartment abutting Central Park and moved his place of worship from the Suburban Torah Center in Livingston, New Jersey, to the prestigious Kehilath Jeshurun on Manhattan's Upper East Side. His son had acquired a newspaper whose province was "an Island paradise with fiefdoms, rulers, turf battles, borders and a brutal hierarchy," as its longtime editor, Peter Kaplan, once wrote. "Its voracious royals thought a great deal of themselves, bought a lot for themselves, dressed accordingly, traded in secret insults . . . brought their battles into private schools and charity balls with the idea that it was a game worth winning."[3] Peter Kaplan, too, was among the wedding guests.

The wedding ceremony was called for four in the afternoon, when the late day sun shone through the clear sides of a tent the size of a gymnasium, pitched on the Bedminster grounds. Donald and Melania Trump's then three-year-old son Barron (who shares a given name with a former business associate bested by Trump, Barron Hilton) was the ring bearer. Chloe and Grace Murdoch, the daughters of Rupert and Wendi Murdoch, were the flower girls. Strewing white petals, they walked up a broad aisle overhung with vines dripping with pendulous white flowers. The bridesmaids were Donald Trump Jr.'s then-wife, Vanessa, and Ivanka's half-sister Tiffany (who shares a name with the company from which Donald Trump had acquired the rights to build Trump Tower in New York City).

The wedding party congregated under an enormous chuppah, a canopy of white flowers covering the structure that symbolizes Jewish hospitality, the tents of Abraham, and the presence of God. Jared, grandson of Holocaust survivors, was raised to be a strict Modern Orthodox Jew: the family kept kosher, they went to shul, they observed the sabbath. Jared was supposed to marry a Jew. But then, at a business luncheon arranged by a young diamond dealer, he met Ivanka Trump, whose family was Protestant. Jared and Ivanka started dating. Their parents were not happy. For a time, the couple stopped seeing each other. Wendi and Rupert Murdoch intervened, reuniting the couple on a weekend trip. And then Ivanka began the arduous task of converting to Orthodox Judaism.

Ivanka and Jared's bond was sealed in front of a crowd of five hundred in traditional Orthodox fashion: the bride circling the groom seven times, a glass intentionally broken underfoot. All witnessed by family and friends, celebrities, movie stars, and a large coterie of influential people.

The guest list included the governors of Florida and Pennsylvania, Charlie Crist and Ed Rendell; the attorney general and comptroller of New York, Andrew Cuomo and Tom DiNapoli; the speakers of the New York State Assembly and New York City Council, Sheldon Silver and Christine Quinn; and the mayor of Newark, Cory Booker. The New York City police commissioner, Ray Kelly, and the city's schools chancellor, Joel Klein, were there. So were Jim McGreevey, the former governor of New Jersey, and Rudy Giuliani, the former mayor of New York. The guests included people who had regulated or could regulate the Kushner and Trump family businesses; had offered or could offer tax abatements or zoning relief; who could, in theory, investigate the family businesses if they ever ran afoul of the law.

One such person was not there: Chris Christie, who was then in the flat-out final days of a race for New Jersey governor. Christie was running on his image as a no-nonsense prosecutor, which included going after politicians and the people he thought corrupted them, including Jared's father, Charlie. But although Donald Trump had cultivated a friendship with Christie, and had initially put him on his list, Christie was not invited.

Jared did invite his employee David Wildstein, then the executive vice president of the Observer Media Group, who had a past as a political blogger, Republican elected official, and political dirty trickster. (Four years later, Wildstein would order the shutdown of access lanes to the George Washington Bridge in an act of political retribution against a Democratic mayor who did not endorse Chris Christie for reelection as governor. When he pleaded guilty and cooperated with prosecutors for a reduced sentence, Wildstein derailed Christie's own White House ambitions.)

The wedding was a lavish and elegant party, an event. The marriage of Jared and Ivanka was the joining of two famous real estate dynasties, each braided into the worlds of politics and media and celebrity. There was, also, the bad-boy allure of Donald Trump, the suggestion that something bold and exciting and maybe transgressive was about to happen. And that the people around him could be part of it, that Donald Trump was pulling back his curtain just for them. Even for this glittering crowd, Trump's promise cast the same spell it did on prime time at NBC for the nine million American fans of *The Apprentice*. That by entering into a corner of Trump's world they, too, could become (even more) rich or famous or successful.

There was also the sense of obligation. Trump had trained the political class to understand that their ever-ravenous political machines should compete for some of his purported billions lest he mete it out to their opponents. Years later, when he was running for president, Trump laid this out clearly, in an early Republican primary debate. "I gave to many people. Before this, before two months ago, I was a businessman. I give to everybody. When they call, I give. And do you know what? When I need something from them two years later, three years later, I call them, they are there for me."

"What did you get?" Trump was asked.

"Well, I'll tell you what," Trump replied. "Hillary Clinton, I said be at my wedding and she came to my wedding. You know why? She had no choice because I gave. I gave to a foundation."[4]

Hillary Clinton, in October 2009 the US secretary of state, did not attend Jared and Ivanka's wedding. But Donald Trump had created an implied command, and when he invited politicians to things like Jared and Ivanka's wedding, they came. The command also came from Jared, who ran a newspaper whose circulation, however tiny, captured the attention of Manhattan opinion makers in an era when social media was still a new toy for early adopters. And the command came from the couple of Jared-and-Ivanka, whose carefully cultivated red-carpet charity-circuit image made them sought-after potential donors.

The wedding itself had its own internal allure. The world of *The Celebrity Apprentice* was one of famous people who had seen better days: Dennis Rodman, Gary Busey, Dionne Warwick, Joan Rivers. There were actual movie stars at Jared and Ivanka's wedding: Princess Padmé Amidala of the *Stars Wars* movie franchise (Natalie Portman) and Maximus Decimus Meridius from *Gladiator* (Russell Crowe).

Among the old, dynastic families of New York real estate, when asked about Trump, people said, and still say, "Donald Trump is not one of us." They say they never saw Donald Trump at the Real Estate Board of New York, or the Partnership for New York City or the Alliance for a Better New York; they did not see him at civic events; they did not see him at charity balls or the ballet or the opera. With few exceptions, for example, the US Open tennis tournament in Queens, he stayed in his own homes, frequented his own clubs, and ate in the restaurants in his own buildings.

By contrast, Ivanka Trump had found acceptance in the Manhattan elite. She went to The Chapin School on the Upper East Side, and

Choate Rosemary Hall boarding school in Connecticut, she studied at the School of American Ballet and danced as a child extra in *The Nutcracker.* As an adult she was a sought-after supporter for causes from the World Wildlife Fund to the New York City Police Foundation. She was welcomed at the Met Gala and *Vanity Fair* parties and chatted about opera with Leonard Lopate on the public radio station WNYC.

Unlike her father and her husband, she had no hint of Queens or New Jersey in her measured speech. Somehow, through her, their accents were laundered.

Ivanka and Jared's wedding was Jewish in a Trumpian way. As women arrived they were given elegant shawls, to guard against the autumnal chill as the sun slid down the sky, but also to cover their shoulders. Ivanka herself wore a Vera Wang wedding dress, shoulders covered by white lace sleeves extending down to her elbows. In some dances, women were separated from men, in the Orthodox tradition. The food, served in a separate dinner tent, also enormous, was kosher. A rabbi had walked through the tent, koshering a caterer's knife by dipping it in water. There was pastrami, corned beef, turkey, a sushi station, and Peking duck. A thirteen-layer cake that was almost as tall as the bride and groom, ringed with cream-colored lisianthus, roses, peonies, lilies of the valley, and baby's breath.

Charles Kushner's speech was a variant of the one he gave at every family event, every *simcha*—Yiddish and Hebrew for "joy," a metonym for "joyous occasion"—about being the son of Holocaust survivors, about the miracle of survival, about Jews thriving and prevailing, about the values of family and *chesed*—Hebrew for "compassion," or "grace"—and Torah. He spoke about Ivanka, and how she had worked so hard to become Jewish, and how the family embraced her now.

Donald Trump had been bewildered by his daughter's conversion, but was gracious at his daughter's wedding. He spoke appreciatively, and uncharacteristically, of his first wife, Ivana, and all the work she had done to raise Ivanka, acknowledging he hadn't always been an attentive parent. The guests, who had come to the wedding with a mix of curiosity and anticipation and obligation and appreciation, were greeted warmly. They felt, for a fleeting instance perhaps, the gravitational pull of Donald Trump's personality.

That night, as guests left clutching their giveaway prayer books and a pair of Havaiana flip-flops that said "Jared" on one and "Ivanka" on the other, laced through with a string calling them a great pair, they were forced to embrace Trump's ostentatiousness even as they participated in his display; to pay tribute to this marriage of money and power; to acknowledge the authority of the patriarchs. From the vantage point of everything they had built, the families could say: We've arrived, you are complicit in our power, we are a force to be reckoned with, pay respect to us.

Foolishly, the world did not.

INTRODUCTION

In the early spring of 2017, I rode my bicycle to a block ten minutes from my own, to a stretch of four-story nineteenth-century brownstone town houses in Brooklyn. There were stoops sweeping up to grand doorways in the Italianate style, and long front gardens separated from the tree-lined sidewalk by low, wrought-iron fences topped with fleurs-de-lys. In the summer, these gardens are overwhelmed with flowers; roses scurry up the sides of the stoops, the smell of voluptuous pink and yellow honeysuckle wafts down the sidewalk.

The house I came to see—377 Union Street—was a type I knew well: elegant brown facade, tall windows on the parlor level, each with its own structured lintel, reaching up to an intricately chiseled black cornice. This building looked like thousands of homes I'd walked or ridden by over the years, like dozens I'd entered to visit friends and family. But this house wasn't, actually, a home.

This brownstone was the physical manifestation of an international money-laundering scheme. It had washed the wealth of Ukrainian oligarchs supporting the corrupt strongman President Viktor Yanukovych, through Cypriot shell companies, and into another shell company. This US shell company, MC Brooklyn Holdings, LLC, was in turn secretly owned by Paul Manafort, the international political consultant, who purchased the home for $3 million in cash at the end of 2012.

In those days, Manafort had a full head of brown hair, a perpetual tan, and a soothing deep voice. Then in his midsixties, he wore bespoke suits with Italian loafers, paid for by getting Yanukovych elected and propping him up as the Ukrainian president helped himself to billions from the national treasury. Manafort directed an illegal US lobbying campaign for Yanukovych, and evaded paying tens of millions of dollars in US taxes. His next gig was running the 2016 presidential campaign of Donald Trump.

For the past twenty-five years, I have covered politics, money, power, and influence: first for the *New York Observer* (a paper Jared Kushner bought after I'd left), then, for the past twenty years, for WNYC: New York and New Jersey Public Radio.

The first kinds of political corruption I documented were simple: jobs handed out to loyal party workers, contracts for campaign donors, a regulatory action snuffed for a large and powerful company. Over the years, as the laws loosened, the schemes became more complex: money sloshing from would-be government contractors to independent expenditure committees and back again through circles of accounts that became harder and harder to trace. Then money went to accounts so dark the money trail disappeared almost entirely.

In the spring of 2017, digging through New York City land records with my WNYC colleague Ilya Marritz for our story "Paul Manafort's Puzzling New York Real Estate Purchases,"[1] we didn't know yet about Yanukovych or Cypriot shell companies or the role of the Ukrainian oligarchs. Manafort hadn't been charged with any crimes, James Comey was still leading the FBI, and no one had even thought to hire Robert Mueller, the special counsel who went on to convict Manafort of fraud, money laundering, and conspiracy against the United States.

And yet, reporting the story of 377 Union Street, I caught a glimpse of the oligarchic wealth from the former Soviet Union surging like a flood tide into New York City's real estate, finance, and governing systems, inundating even my low-rise neighborhood in Brooklyn. And despite the fact that I'd covered money and politics and corruption for a quarter of a century, I had had no idea it was there.

In 1885, when Friedrich Trump arrived in New York harbor, just months after the Statue of Liberty did the same, America was racing towards the apotheosis of the Gilded Age. In 1860, the total national wealth was $16 billion. By 1900, it was $89 billion.[2] Railroads tracks were barreling across the country, fueled by 180 million acres of government land giveaways.[3] The very rich—the Carnegies, the Rockefellers, the Vanderbilts—were getting even richer. By the end of the century, the richest 4,000 families had amassed about as much wealth as the other 11.6 million families combined.[4]

Wealth was not only accumulating: it was on conspicuous display, celebrated. The very wealthy built enormous mansions: in New York City; in Newport, Rhode Island; in the Hudson Valley. They chose Delmonico's restaurant in Lower Manhattan for their extravagantly frivolous parties; one featured an artificial lake with real swans. [5] In at least one home, there was an actual gold toilet.

At the same time, the poor in New York City lived in filthy tenements, as famously documented by Jacob Riis, with thirty or more people sharing a single, fetid outhouse. Twelve adults would sleep in a room thirteen feet across. One of ten infants living in tenements died.[6] If you left the windows open at night, a feral animal might jump in.

This period, before the two World Wars and the Great Depression, was near the previous high point of global wealth inequality, as the French economist Thomas Piketty wrote in his book *Capital in the Twenty-First Century*. Ten percent of Americans owned 80 percent of the wealth.[7] But the United States was not the Old World—the Gilded Age was not the belle époque, its French counterpart. Channeling Honoré de Balzac, Piketty wrote that in Europe there was simply no way an individual, even working in a well-paid profession, like lawyering, could accumulate wealth as fast as inherited capital could.[8] By contrast, in America, with its egalitarian notions, vast tracts of land and growing population, and lower overall wealth, one could still transcend humble origins. "With a few years of work," Piketty wrote, "the new arrivals were able to close the initial gap between themselves and their wealthier predecessors."[9] This became harder as the nineteenth century wore on, but especially on the West Coast, where Friedrich Trump made his fortune, social mobility was still possible in 1885.

In Germany, Friedrich Trump had expected to inherit only a tiny, unusable piece of land—and to be forced into compulsory military service. In America, he was certain he could become rich. And he was right. First as a barber in New York City, then as a restaurant owner in Seattle, then as proprietor of the Arctic, a restaurant in the Yukon "where the bulk of the cash flow came from the sale of liquor and sex," as Gwenda Blair documented in her book *The Trumps: Three Generations That Built an Empire*.[10] Friedrich Trump was able to escape the gold rush—a fool's errand for most—with a sum equal to hundreds of thousands in today's dollars.[11] Back in New York, he converted that money to real estate; when he died in 1918, he passed that fortune on to his German wife, Elizabeth, and their son, Frederick Christ Trump.

As Piketty has demonstrated, capital had peaked not long before Friedrich died. The catastrophic world wars and the Great Depression equalized wealth by destroying vast swaths of capital. The Trumps suffered, too. But the same economic depression that for a while deprived Fred Trump of his real estate trade also triggered his ascent. Spurred by the federal government's New Deal, capital flowed to builders like Fred Trump, who constructed two thousand federal loan–backed single-family homes between 1935 and 1942, most of them in Brooklyn.[12] By 1946, just after the war ended, the Trump family was once again thriving. This is when Fred Trump's fourth child, Donald John Trump, was born.

At the same time Fred Trump was erecting homes, far away in northeast Poland, Rae and Joseph Kushner were losing theirs in unimaginably brutal conditions, first under the Soviets, then to the Nazis. "To a large extent," Piketty wrote, "it was the chaos of war, with its attendant economic and political shocks, that reduced inequality in the twentieth century. There was no gradual, consensual, conflict-free evolution toward greater equality. In the twentieth century it was war, and not harmonious democratic or economic rationality, that erased the past and enabled society to begin anew with a clean slate."[13]

Society *did* begin anew. In response to the darkness and destruction of not only of millions of lives, but also of the sense of responsibility of humans, one for the other, the western world set up multinational institutions: the United Nations, the Bretton Woods system, the beginnings of the European Union. Social safety nets were constructed. Taxes were so high at the upper end of the scale in some countries that it just wasn't worth it to become ultra-rich: you'd be giving most of the extra wealth back to society.

In was in this world-in-the-making that the Kushners arrived in New York. A frugal man, Joseph Kushner often slept in framed-out homes on construction sites in New Jersey to save the dollar bus fare to Brooklyn and back. He made ninety dollars a week, saving half of it. Four years after moving to New York, he used that savings to buy three lots in Clark, New Jersey, with two other Holocaust survivors.[14] So began the Kushner family real estate empire.

The timing was auspicious. In 1956, three years after Kushner went to work on his own, the federal government passed the Federal-Aid Highway Act. Through a variety of federal programs, most of them encouraging white flight out of cities, the government directly and indirectly poured money into suburban homes. By the time of his death, in 1985, Joseph Kushner had built some four thousand of them. Four of them, mansions in a part of New Jersey newly opened to Jews, were for his adult children: Linda, Murray, Charles, and Esther.

During the postwar years, Fred Trump kept growing his business. He built out huge rental tracts in Brooklyn: Beach Haven, Shore Haven, and the largest, in Coney Island, Trump Village. Rents came in, year after year. It was a sound and enriching business model. When his son Donald was inflamed by the desire to build in the riskier markets of Manhattan and Atlantic City, it was Fred's quiet guarantees that enabled him to do so. It was also Fred's determination to avoid taxes; he found almost three hundred ways to channel revenue to his children, largely untaxed, a billion dollars in all, the *New York Times* calculated.[15] The US taxpayers contributed hundreds of millions of dollars to Donald Trump's fortune.

The restructuring that tilted the postwar economy towards the suburbs drained capital and people from the cities. By the seventies, urban areas were teetering. After decades of unequal housing policies, "urban renewals" that forced middle-class African Americans out of their homes and into unwelcoming modernist towers, after the murder of Martin Luther King Jr. and rioting across the country (though not in New York), white flight accelerated. Even the area around Grand Central Terminal in Manhattan, a valuable transportation hub, was falling into disrepair. This was Donald Trump's entrée to Manhattan, a place where he could use his family's carefully cultivated political connections to convince state and city officials to write into law a special tax break just for him, based on an agreement where he lied to the bank about state approvals and to the state about bank approvals.[16] His reconstruction of what is now the Grand Hyatt hotel is the deal that launched him as a Manhattan developer; during the next decades of loosening financial regulations and lower taxes, it became the template for Trump's future negotiations.

Charles Kushner, equally, benefited from deregulation: in two decades he grew his father's four thousand units to twenty-two thousand. He expanded into commercial real estate. He bought a bank in New Jersey. He tried to buy one in Israel. It looked like he was trying to buy a governor, too.

Nineteen eighty-one, the year Jared Kushner and Ivanka Trump were born, was an inflection point in American history. Ronald Reagan had just become president. Financial and taxation policy in the United

States was about to take a dramatic turn in favor of the wealthy, allowing them to roll up assets, often untaxed and increasingly unfettered, faster than at any time since the 1920s.

According to a study by the economists Piketty, Emmanuel Saez, and Gabriel Zucman, between 1980 and 2014, incomes for the top 0.001 percent of Americans rose by 636 percent, while income for the bottom 50 percent stagnated. For the lowest 20 percent, incomes actually fell. In 1980, the richest Americans earned on average twenty-seven times as much as the bottom half of Americans. By 2014 that ratio was eighty-one to one, a level of income inequality comparable to Burundi and the Democratic Republic of Congo. It is still growing.[17] Through Jared and Ivanka's young adulthood, extreme wealth became folded into the zeitgeist in New York: a trade developed around $200,000 Birkin bags; apartments cost millions. No one batted an eye. Attracted by this wealth and the stability of New York, armed with the encouragement of new US laws, international capital began flowing to Manhattan at rates that alarmed the US Treasury: a full third of cash sales of high-end residential real estate involved buyers previously linked to suspicious activity.[18]

By the time Jared Kushner and Ivanka Trump, in their midthirties, joined the White House staff, it was getting harder and harder in the United States to transcend the social class of one's birth. As described by Matthew Stewart in a 2018 article in the *Atlantic*: "Contrary to popular myth, economic mobility in the land of opportunity is not high, and it's going down. Imagine yourself on the socioeconomic ladder with one end of a rubber band around your ankle and the other around your parents' rung. The strength of the rubber determines how hard it is for you to escape the rung on which you were born. If your parents are high on the ladder, the band will pull you up should you fall; if they are low, it will drag you down when you start to rise."[19] According to City University of New York economist Miles Corak, that rubber band was far weaker half a century ago: he rated it as 0.3 out of 1 then, and 0.5 now. The more unequal society gets, the harder it is to travel among the layers.[20]

Jared Kushner and Ivanka Trump live in the uppermost layer, the crust on the crème brûlée. In the year they became senior White House advisors, the two made at least $82 million in income. The next year they reported earning between $29 and $135 million. This is not an illustration of their net worth, but rather the money they were passively earning from their stakes in the Trump Organization, Ivanka Trump's merchandise, and (mostly) from Jared Kushner's family business—while at the same time working in the White House.[21]

Donald Trump ran for office with the slogan "Drain the Swamp!"—but when he became president, he used the vast financial resources of the donor class to prop up his power. At the end of his first year in office, following their record-breaking donations and acquiescence to his nativist agenda, he passed a law that limited their taxes. And he loosened a myriad of regulations that could have made them earn a little less money, a bit less fast.

Even before the Tax Cuts and Jobs Act of 2017, the wealthiest families could still pass along a healthy sum to their dependents—up to $11.2 million—free of the 40 percent estate tax. Under the new law, that number doubled: wealthy couples could pass on $22.4 million to their heirs tax-free. The law also benefited corporations, and in particular real estate companies, by cutting corporate tax rates from 35 percent to 21 percent. In just the six months after the bill passed, according to an analysis by the *New York Times*, corporate tax rates were at historic lows, contributing to a surge in corporate profits.[22] Donations to Trump's campaign and to the Republican Party soared commensurately.[23]

Twenty years into the twenty-first century, we live in age of oligarchs, where the very richest Americans hold vast sway not only over their elected officials—and by extension, the courts—but also the election process itself. The framers of the American republic feared this could happen. As constitutional scholar Zephyr Teachout delineated in her book, *Corruption in America*, they viewed the threat of corruption to the new American democratic experiment as being equal to that of war. She quoted founder Gouverneur Morris, who stated, "wealth tends to corrupt the mind & to nourish its love of power, and to stimulate it to oppression."[24] The framers' solution, rather than to outlaw specific acts, was to put in place structures that would limit temptations. It was human nature to respond to financial incentives, the framers thought, so instead of criminalizing that desire, they tried to construct the Constitution so it would remove financial incentives for corrupt acts. Failing to do so, the framers feared, would lead, as Teachout wrote, to "oligarchic or despotic rule."[25]

We almost got there anyway. In the 1880s, Joseph Keppler published a cartoon in *Puck*: it shows a band of enormous, rotund, top-hatted men looming behind rows of Lilliputian US senators. Emblazoned on the men's bellies are the names of trusts: Steel, Copper, Sugar, Coal. One wears a barrel that says "Standard Oil." These trust giants are marching into the US Capitol through a door that says "Entrance for Monopolists." The "People's Entrance" is barred shut. This was a defining image of US government in the late nineteenth century.

But the last time the United States approached entrenched oligarchic rule, it pulled back. The twinned predations of income inequality and corruption that thundered through the United States in the Gilded Age, publicized by journalists who came to be known as "muckrakers," were reined in during the Progressive Era that followed. In 1890, Congress passed the Sherman Antitrust Act to break up corporate monopolies. Two decades later, in 1913, states ratified the Seventeenth Amendment, allowing for the direct election of US senators. In 1920, the Nineteenth Amendment gave women the right to vote, further strengthening the levers of democracy.

Measures to limit financial inequality also kept corruption in check, by making it harder to amass vast stores of wealth that could be used to influence political systems. New Deal programs, despite glaring racial flaws, created housing and jobs, while at the same time limiting the power of banks through the Glass-Steagall Act. Progressive tax structures erected during the war remained in place afterwards; the GI Bill, the Highway Act, and other measures operated on the theory that collective investments could lift the common weal. Lyndon Johnson's Great Society brought measures to address those left out of the New Deal and postwar programs, including most of America's nonwhite population: the War on Poverty, the Voting Rights Act, Medicaid.

Even with strictures, big money kept wending its way into politics. President Richard M. Nixon's Watergate scandal was, at heart, about abuse of power and obstruction of justice. But the plot was propped up by hidden funds. "During their Watergate investigation, federal agents established that hundreds of thousands of dollars in Nixon campaign contributions had been set aside to pay for an extensive undercover campaign aimed at discrediting individual Democratic presidential candidates and disrupting their campaigns," Carl Bernstein and Bob Woodward wrote in the *Washington Post* in 1972.[26]

After Watergate, Congress enacted direct measures to curb the power of money in politics, based on the twin controls of caps and disclosures. The Federal Election Campaign Act was amended to limit single-campaign contributions to $1,000, with a total, per individual, of $25,000 to all federal candidates and committees. It also limited campaign expenditures, and—crucially—required disclosure: any contribution over $100 would have to be made public. A Federal Election Commission was set up to enforce the law.

In the 1976 US Supreme Court case *Buckley v. Valeo*, the Court ignored what the framers had tried to erect—a structure that would limit temptation—and created a system that encouraged it. *Buckley* held that laws could limit campaign contributions but not expenditures, creating a perverse incentive for candidates to spend all their time raising money.[27] This offered an opening for donors like Donald Trump and Charles Kushner to gain power by raising money beyond the limits, often by bundling donations, and for far wealthier donors to use their money to upend the American political system.

For forty years in the wake of *Buckley v. Valeo*, billionaires like the Koch brothers strategically flooded money into systems that could support their way of thinking, as Jane Mayer showed in her book *Dark*

Money. They backed political campaigns from state legislators to president, trained judges, and funded think tanks at elite universities. Their money supported gerrymandering, voter suppression, and partisan conflict. It undergirded the 2010 *Citizens United v. Federal Election Commission* US Supreme Court case that ripped through the tattered shreds of the campaign finance system, enabling larger and larger sums to secretly enter the political debate, undiluted and undisclosed. "In Trump," Mayer wrote of Charles Koch in her preface to the 2017 edition of her book, "he got the radical solution he had helped to spawn."[28]

Money flowing to lobbyists and big law firms had another effect: it dampened the zeal of prosecutors to investigate people who stole millions from the US taxpayers, or lied to banks, or gambled with the savings of millions for their own personal profit, as Jesse Eisinger showed in his book *The Chickenshit Club: Why the Justice Department Fails to Prosecute Executives.*[29] According to a study by researchers at Syracuse University, the number of white-collar crime prosecutions in 2018 hit a twenty-year low, with fewer than six thousand expected that year, compared to over nine thousand in 1998.[30] In 2019, it dropped again, to the lowest level in thirty-three years.[31]

With a judiciary increasingly influenced by the Federalist Society, funded by billionaires with the express intent of creating a pipeline of conservative judges, political corruption prosecutions also became more difficult. This was especially so in the wake of the US Supreme Court ruling in *McDonnell v. United States,* where the Court overruled a conviction of former Governor Robert McDonnell, who, with his wife, had accepted a Rolex watch, vacations, and other gifts in exchange for pressing the case of a donor. The Court said despite the gifts, merely attempting to sway the political system does not constitute a bribe. To be convicted of bribery, an official now had to precisely engage in "an official act," on behalf of a donor. Doing the things that governors do—making calls, having meetings, delivering hints about the way things should go—wasn't enough, even if the governor were motivated to do those things by the gift of a Rolex watch.[32]

Even before it became rare to prosecute white-collar crimes and political corruption, the Trumps knew how to escape legal consequences. As the late Wayne Barrett wrote in his prescient 1992 biography *Trump: The Deals and the Downfall* (later *Trump: The Greatest Show on Earth*), Trump "prided himself on never having met a public official, a banker, a lawyer, a reporter, or a prosecutor he couldn't seduce. Some he owned, and others he merely manipulated. As he saw it, it was not just that everyone had a price, it was that he knew what the price was. He believed he could look across a table and compute the price, then move on to another table and borrow the money to pay it. Yet he believed that a lifetime of such seductions . . . hadn't cheapened him."[33]

These seductions were generations in the making. Donald Trump's grandfather had fudged land claims; his father had been rapped by both the New York state and federal governments for self-dealing; and Donald Trump's own business deals had been repeatedly probed by prosecutors. Fred Trump and Donald Trump engaged in secret schemes to avoid paying taxes that the *New York Times* called "outright fraud."[34] The Manhattan district attorney seriously considered indicting two of Trump's adult children, Donald Trump Jr. and Ivanka Trump, for felony fraud, but dropped the case after a visit from Trump's lawyer, one of the DA's largest donors. All of this was before Trump's former lawyer Michael Cohen stood in a courtroom and said that he had committed two campaign finance crimes "at the direction of" Donald Trump, offering evidence Trump participated in a conspiracy to cover them up. All of this was before Special Counsel Robert Mueller said he "could not exonerate" Trump for multiple instances of obstruction of justice in connection with his probe of Russian interference in the 2016 election. But Trump appointed the attorney general, and the attorney general controlled the Justice Department, and the Justice Department had determined a sitting president could not be indicted.

At the end of the second decade of the twenty-first century, the wealthy, from the United States and abroad, can gain influence over politicians and elections in the United States through a myriad of means. They can make publicly reported contributions, or giant donations to inaugural committees, convention committees, and foundations associated with a particular candidate. They can donate undisclosed sums to dark money committees, or make direct payments to organizations or individuals secretly working to aid a campaign. Enormous corporations and foreign governments can hire lobbyists, who in turn make huge contributions. And under President Donald J. Trump, the first in recent history to profit from his private business and also serve as president, those wishing to ingratiate themselves with the leader of the Free World can stay or host a conference in one of his hotels or buy a membership in one of his golf courses, or buy a condo in India, or loan money to the business of his son-in-law. The ethics disclosure rules, laws, and regulations designed to rein in this sort of activity are woefully ill-equipped for the task.

In a 2014 article digesting Piketty's book, "Why We're in a New Gilded Age," in the *New York Review of Books,* Paul Krugman wrote, "The big idea of *Capital in the Twenty-First Century* is that we haven't just gone back to nineteenth-century levels of income inequality, we're also on a path back to 'patrimonial capitalism' in which the commanding heights of the economy are controlled not by talented individuals but by family dynasties."[35]

American Oligarchs: The Kushners, the Trumps, and the Marriage of Money and Power is the story of two such dynasties that have both benefited from and fueled a system of widening inequality and greater influence of money in politics, doing everything they can to lock us into this path for the foreseeable future. It is the multigenerational saga of two *emblematic* families of our time. But it is not a story of inevitable outcomes; it is not a story of *typical* families of our time. It is, rather a tale of specific choices—theirs, and the country's—about taxation, regulation, corruption, and campaign finance laws—that brought us to where we are today.

This book is also the inextricably intertwined story of how oligarchy washed up on our shores, how foreign capital flooded into our neighborhoods, into homes like Paul Manafort's brownstone at 377 Union Street in Brooklyn. And, when we weren't looking, threatened democracy, itself.

ACT I

1

THE ESCAPE

A few years before half of the family was murdered, the Kushners, as they usually did, took a summer vacation in the tiny town of Novoyl'na, then part of Poland. Amid the sharp scents of pine and spruce, and fresh water from the lake, the Kushner children played in the forest. On Friday evenings, as the late-setting sun angled through the woods, the family gathered for Shabbat dinner. Parents, grandparents, children, grandchildren, aunts, uncles, cousins sat in front of tall white candles to eat chicken soup, sweet kugel, the ever-present braided challah bread. "Summer camp" was how the surviving Kushners would later describe these trips. "Camping" and "going to camp" were among their fondest memories.

There's a picture that endures from one of these summers. The lower left corner is burnt, or chemically disappeared. But the image in the center is clear: a family of four children arrayed on a hammock around their father, tall trees standing like sentries in the background. The father is wearing light-colored, loose-fitting pants, neatly cuffed, a white shirt, dark tie. His hands are on his knees, his expression neutral. All the children look happy, relaxed; the younger ones, impish, even.

There's Esther in her late teens on the far left wearing a short-sleeved, close-fitting white button-down shirt, parted sharply with a dark tie.

Next to her is Lisa in a loose-fitting dress. In the photo, she's a preteen, skinny legs dangling over the hammock. On the other side of their father sits Chanon Kushner, not much older than Lisa, in short pants, a long-sleeved shirt, a goofy grin. And on the right, her hand draped behind her brother's back and resting on her father's shoulder: teenage Reichal "Rae" Kushner. Her thick black hair cut in a bob, Rae is smiling. Her face, like everyone else's in her family, is unworried, unlined. Her dark brown eyes gaze forthrightly into the camera, yet to witness any horrors.

Most of the year, the family lived in the commercial town of Novogrudok, Poland, population twenty-five thousand. There is a record of those years, left by Rae herself in two videotaped testimonies of her wartime experiences; other oral histories were supplied by her sister, Lisa, and fellow Novogrudok survivors.[1] Life in those years was good. Naum Kushner—the last name means "furrier"—sold hats and "beautiful ladies' coats" in his two shops to a mostly Jewish clientele. His wife, Hinda, helped with the business, and for household chores, the family had a maid. All four children went to private schools; Esther had completed college, and Rae had matriculated in a prestigious university in Kraków for part of her schooling. The Kushners attended the town's biggest shul, dressing in their finest on Fridays for the walk to synagogue. There was a robust civil society: Jews in Novogrudok funded a hospital, an orphanage, a Jewish home for the aged. There was commerce; there was culture, a regular diet of Jewish theater. "You were free," Lisa Kushner Reibel later said. "And everything was all right."[2]

Half a decade after the photograph was taken, three of six members of the Kushner family would be dead. Of hundreds of cousins, grandparents, sisters and brothers, uncles and aunts, only a handful, including Lisa, Rae, and their father, Naum, made it through—through the destruction of their home and the confiscation of their business; through family separations and multiple mass executions, starvation, lice, beatings, forced labor, German dogs, and Nazi bullets; past barbed wire; through months of hiding in the forest, braving the Polish winter, a trek across international borders, and years in a displaced persons camp. The Kushners lost everything. The photo survived.

Situated between three historic powers, 1930s Poland had endured a century of Prussian, Russian, and Austro-Hungarian incursion. The Treaty of Versailles redrew its borders once again, but through the agreement Poland achieved a tentative independence after World War I. Its Jewish population swelled. By the 1930s, Polish Jews numbered three million.

Novogrudok was in northeast Poland close to the Soviet border, in what is now Belarus. About half of the residents were Jewish. The rest were Poles, and Belarusians, or "White Russians." The national idea of "Poland" held little allure for Jews in Novogrudok, some of whom looked to a different country altogether, one that for the moment existed only in their imaginations: Israel. The Jews of Novogrudok spoke Polish, Russian, Yiddish, and Hebrew, but there was a popular Zionist saying: "Atah Ivrit, t'daber Ivrit" or "You are a Hebrew, speak Hebrew"—the language of the Holy Land.[3] There were even Zionist political parties in Novogrudok, including one for those who advocated taking over Palestine by peaceful means, by buying up land, and another, by the rifle. Still—in the 1930s, the state of Israel was just a dream, and getting papers to emigrate to the area arduous. A thousand kilometers away, in Berlin, Adolf Hitler was consolidating power. His anti-Semitic screed, *Mein Kampf*, was a bestseller. If you were a Polish Jew in the 1930s, there were barriers to migration to almost anywhere. Including the United States.

In Novogrudok, in those days, "we didn't know so much," Rae told an interlocutor from Kean University in 1982. "There used to come a holiday, they used to say to Jews, 'Go to Palestine, you don't have a place here,' but we didn't pay attention." Rae said this was a small group of people.[4]

On August 23, 1939, when Rae was sixteen, Adolf Hitler and Josef Stalin's foreign ministers signed a pact, once again carving up Poland. Novogrudok became part of the Soviet Union. But rather than run from their new conquerors, middle-class Jews met the Russians with bunches of flowers. "It is either to accept Russia, or to accept the Germans," Rae's fellow survivor Jack Kagan, the son of a saddle maker who resettled in London, said in his testimony. "The Germans we couldn't accept. So, whatever came as a substitute, for us it was a tremendous thing."

Soviet rule came with its compromises. The Soviets enrolled schoolchildren in the "Pioneers" program—a social group designed to encourage children to inform on their parents. Children who weren't members, maybe five in a class of thirty, were ostracized.

Sonya Oshman, another Novogrudok survivor, a former medical student who moved to New York, spoke in 1988 about being asked to serve as a "translator" for the Soviet secret police, the NKVD. "They wanted to, you know, to engage me into spying. I know you start with them with a little thing, with translations, and then I would go on and on and on and on and on. And this was very scary." Fearing she would be thrown in jail, Oshman declined. She was allowed to go free, but with strict instructions not to tell her parents. If she did, the Soviet officer speaking with her warned, "It's going to be like that": a finger pulled across the throat. "That's exactly what he showed me," Oshman said.[5]

The Kushners, too, soon chafed at Russian rule. The Soviets nationalized all the shops, including the Kushners' fur stores, and began to put the richer people on cattle trains to Siberia. At the time, this seemed the worst option possible. One Saturday, word spread among the wealthier families that the Soviets were coming that night. Rae's mother, Hinda, hid her children in different houses of poorer people. The Russians came that evening, as expected, but found no one at the Kushner home. It was the first of Rae Kushner's many, many escapes.

At the time, the Kushners exhaled. Later, Rae was sorry. She wished the Russians had taken her whole family. She considered those who were taken to Siberia to be the lucky ones. "But who knew there's going to come Germany?" Rae asked, in her Yiddish-inflected English. "And it's going to be so bitter for us."

They had been warned. Jews from South Poland came to Novogrudok. They said the Germans were killing Jews. But the Jews in Novogrudok didn't believe them. They asked themselves: What kind of people would do that?

Two years after the Hitler-Stalin pact, Rae would see for herself. In June 1941 Hitler launched Operation Barbarossa, his grand push to seize Moscow, for which he deployed an army of more than three million troops, six hundred thousand vehicles, and another six hundred thousand horses. Novogrudok was bombed, cratering homes, leaving bodies strung along downed electric lines. The Soviets quickly fled, abandoning the population of Novogrudok, and its thousands of Jews, to the Nazis.

At first, things didn't seem so bad. Yes, Jews were issued yellow stars; they were not allowed to use sidewalks and were instead relegated to the middle of the street. They could still go about their business.

In July 1941, the Nazis rounded up the town's intellectuals: the well-educated, the doctors—its professional class. Some thought the Germans were going to give them jobs. "So, some went, 'If they want me, I'll go,'" Lisa Reibel said. They were brought to the town square, where an orchestra was playing. But they did not get job assignments. Instead, fifty of these Jews were lined up in the market square and machine-gunned, face to face, "so I can see the way he is shot and he can see the way he is shot," as Lisa put it, betraying with her syntax that she had learned English after Yiddish, Polish, Hebrew, and German. All fifty were killed. One moved a little after he was shot, "so they killed him again."

Rae herself had been ordered to the square, along with the "fifty nicest looking girls," whom the Germans had enlisted for a grim cleanup duty. "The blood was running on the square on the stones," as Rae described it. The fifty girls were told to wash it off. "We helped to put the bodies on the wagon," Rae said. "Their heads were hanging, from the dead people, and we knew the people. And the music was playing and we washed the stones from the square." The Germans were having a dance in the square.

But Jewish witnesses to the killing were few, according to Sonya Oshman, who was herself in hiding. The next day a friend of hers was seized and gang-raped by Nazi soldiers, left for dead.

The Germans spread the story the Jews were murdered in the square because they had collaborated with the retreating Soviet army. The Jews thought the fifty were killed because they were the most likely to organize a rebellion against the Nazis.

Even after fifty people had been murdered, some Jews in Novogrudok rationalized what had happened. "There was no resistance," Jack Kagan recalled. "We could have escaped. We could have done whatever we wanted during this period of time. But at the same time we didn't know what was coming. We knew the time will be difficult. We knew it will be hunger; maybe it will be tough. Maybe we will be beaten or we will work in camps. . . . But we did not know that our lives will be at risk. Okay they will shoot fifty people out of a population of seven thousand. That's just bad luck and so on that they have been caught." The human mind resists accepting the possibility of awful outcomes. The Jews of Novogrudok had now seen atrocities; many would die because they could not imagine worse.

The denialism, too, soon ended. On December 5, 1941, one of the coldest days of the year, the Nazis put up handbills: there was an immediate curfew. No Jews were allowed to leave their homes. The next day, they were commanded to register at the town courthouse, bringing only what they could carry. Herded by Nazi soldiers, who baited the Jews with promises that the talented people and those who could work would get double portions of bread, some seven thousand were led to the courthouse, a white stone building with pane-glass windows, a sweeping staircase, and smooth octagonal floor tiles, "like the courthouse in Elizabeth," New Jersey, as Rae described it. Once there, they were forced to stand for hours in the frigid courtyard before eventually being let inside. All six Kushners passed that night together, huddled with their neighbors against the cold and brittle fear.

The trucks arrived. The Nazis entered the courthouse, with their crisp uniforms and white-gloved hands directing the crowds: "You to the right, and you to the left." To the right meant to die, to the left to live. Elderly people and children, toddlers, babies, were sent to the right. "They were screaming and children crying, little infants, you know, month old, two months, a year old . . . they took away the children and the mothers they told to go on the other side. Could you imagine the cruelty?" Oshman asked. Children were ripped from their parents' arms, tossed like rocks into the trucks. Some mothers refused to turn over their children. They were killed instantly.

A rumor went through the queues: these people were being taken to "special places" where they would work, get food, get clothing. "When you are very desperate or whatever and somebody tells you something, so maybe you believe it might be like that," Oshman said. "You could not imagine that they were going to take the people that they didn't do anything and just kill them," Oshman said. But it started to become clear. If a white-gloved Nazi hand pointed to the right, it meant you were going to die.

The Kushners were told to go to the right. Hinda Kushner, Rae's mother, started to scream. Rae went up to a German and told him "I'm young, I want to live, I want to work. Leave us on the other side." But the Nazi kicked her in the behind with his black boot and walked away as she tumbled down the stairs. The family was forced to throw into a pot all the valuables they had stowed in their pockets—"rings, jewelry, money"—before they themselves were ejected into the square into the din: "rabbis, young women holding babies by their breasts, old men and women screaming and praying to God." They were crying "Shema Yisrael"—hear me, Israel, the eternal is our God—the most central and holy of Jewish prayers. They watched as trucks left, loaded with Jews.

Rae's family was next. But it took time to load up the trucks. While they were waiting on line, Hinda exhorted her older daughter, "Run! Run! They're going to be killed all, maybe one from you is going to be alive." Esther, wearing a fur coat, ran into the building where the Nazis were gathering Jews who had not been immediately condemned. But a Polish police officer, a former school friend, saw her, stripped her of her coat, and dragged her back to the trucks.

While Esther was being detained, the Nazis came to the line and asked if there were any furriers. Hinda stepped out of the line and announced that her husband was a furrier. And so her family was saved, taken back into the courthouse. All except Esther, who was carted off in a truck to the edge of town. There, a mass grave had been dug, and the Jews were ordered to climb in it, so when the machine guns started firing, they would already be in the burial pit. Five thousand Jews died this way, among them Rae's older sister, Esther Kushner.

—

In the liquidation of December 1941, in Novogrudok, the Nazis killed the old and the very young, five thousand out of a population of seven thousand, sparing only those who they thought would be efficient workers—able-bodied men and women under forty who could be enslaved to the German war machine. They were forced, as Oshman put it, to clothe and "feed an army." To defy was to die. The Kushner family lost the wealth of generations: their home, their businesses, their candlesticks, their fur coats, their jewelry. They survived because of their tradecraft, because they could make hats for German soldiers mounting a winter campaign on the Soviet Union.

After the massacre, the Jews who had not been murdered remained in the courthouse for four days without food, during which time some of their number were ordered to build a fence around certain run down buildings at the edge of town. Their quarters thus encircled, the Jews were forced to move into Novogrudok's first ghetto. There were up to fifty people sleeping in a single building, with only the clothes they'd worn from their homes the morning before the massacre. The ghetto inhabitants received a ration of two hundred and fifty grams of bread a day and the occasional potato.

Weeks after the massacre, on New Year's Eve, the Germans came to the ghetto and demanded a small force of boys to keep a fire going in the governor's mansion, where German officers were celebrating the holiday. They needed the youths to keep the pipes from freezing. Lisa said there were three boys, Rae recalled there were twenty. But they both agree on the outlines of the story: That the boys, their sixteen-year-old brother Chanon among them, were tending the fire when a drunken German decided to entertain the party by demanding the boys raise their arms and say "Heil Hitler." Then he shot them. Chanon took a bullet in the leg and fell back on the fire, where he remained while the Germans checked the boys for signs of life. Burnt and shot, he was able to crawl out of the Nazi mansion, where he was found (Lisa said by some boys on a work assignment, Rae said by their mother) and smuggled back into the ghetto in a wheelbarrow full of straw. Hidden for months, he was able to recover.

In the ghetto, there was an active debate about how to respond. Some Jews began to escape into the forest. But others were convinced it was folly to brave the Polish winter. The Nazis needed them to support their army. They must be the elect, they reasoned, surely the Nazis couldn't kill them all. They would survive the war, they thought. The vast and frozen Russian territory had defeated Napoleon. Surely it would defeat Hitler.

They were also too terrified to leave. A friend of Rae's, who later moved to Saddle River, New Jersey, had a sister "so beautiful, that Miss America, you cannot find such a beautiful girl, intelligent," Rae said. She tried to run out of the ghetto with a non-Jew. But the Germans caught her, brought her back, and hung her from a tree. They cut off her breasts. Rae said, "They pushed in a stick, I can't tell you where, but you know where. And they made scared all the people, not to move."

The German army's demands were relentless. The ghetto residents were ordered to work on rebuilding the structures the Nazi bombs had destroyed, make clothing and saddles for Nazi soldiers and their horses, cook for the German army, and otherwise stoke the fires of the Nazi war effort. In May of 1942, Jews were brought in from the surrounding villages, temporarily swelling the population of the ghetto. Soon, they were killed, too.[6]

At four o'clock one morning, rousting the ghetto residents from their cramped sleep, the Nazis announced that they were taking the children to "kindergarten, they have a school, special for them." But the families didn't believe it. Mothers and fathers were kneeling on the floor, begging the Germans to leave the children alone. As Rae described it, one German stood with his white gloves on and pulled a child away from their mother, who was kneeling and begging. He told her she had to let her child go, or she was going with them. The Jews tried to hide some children behind stacks of newspapers, but the Nazis came back, with German shepherds, and poisoned them. Now, no Jewish children remained in Novogrudok.

In February 1943, the Germans came again, this time for older people they thought were too weak to work, Rae's mother, aged forty-two, among them. Rae and her family had tried to dig a hiding place for Hinda, but the Germans surprised them early in the morning. Through a window, Rae said, she, Lisa, Chanon, and their father watched their mother shot to death. At the end of this liquidation, there were only a few hundred Jews left alive.

By midsummer 1943, the Jews, the four grieving Kushners among them, had been relocated to some rough structures near the courthouse. There was a large fence, two rings of barbed wire, searchlights. All the residents had a number, and were counted every day. Oshman called it "a real concentration camp."

There were those who imagined that God had selected them to survive, but most of those who remained understood they faced certain death. By this time, word had reached the Jews of a partisan camp run by Tuvia Bielski some twenty-five miles away, in the Naliboki forest. Bielski, who was memorialized in the book and movie *Defiance*, offered haven to any Jew who could reach his camp. It was the largest organized Jewish armed resistance against the Nazis.[7]

The Jews in the Novogrudok ghetto sent word to Bielski: they wanted him to mount an attack to release them from the ghetto. Bielski smuggled a message back: he reiterated his offer of shelter, but he didn't have the resources to help them escape. With no other option, the last survivors of the Novogrudok ghetto, including Rae, Lisa, Chanon and Naum Kushner, Sonya Oshman, and Jack Kagan, began to dig day and night. They smuggled implements from their work sites: pieces of wood, spoons. After long hours of labor under Nazi overseers, they stayed up all night, removing bags of dirt from the tunnel and passing them along a human chain to be stacked behind the walls to hide their activity. They worked like this for three months, at one point assigning the Jewish electrician to wire the tunnel with lights. The initial plan was to build a 150-meter tunnel to terminate in a cornfield, but the harvest came, and they had to more than double the length. Chanon Kushner, by now eighteen, was among the dozens of Jews who dug out the earth. As the tunnel neared completion, one of their number became frightened, saying the Nazis would surely catch and kill them all. The others worried he was going to inform on them to the Nazis, so they took him into the tunnel and choked him to death.

On a rainy night at the end of September 1943, as the Rosh Hashanah holiday was beginning, the residents of the ghetto decided conditions were right. With rain pounding down, they loosened a sheet of tin on the roof to add to the din. The electrician shorted the electric wires to dim the searchlights. The two hundred and fifty or so remaining residents lined up, the youngest and strongest in the front. The tunnel was claustrophobic, only large enough for one person to crawl through at a time. The lineup ensured that if anyone elderly fainted and blocked the tiny tunnel, there'd be fewer stuck behind. Rae and Lisa, though they were young, decided to stay back with their father. Lashed together with ropes and belts so they wouldn't lose their way, wriggling through a sixty-centimeter-wide dirt tunnel with another human's feet in their faces, all two hundred fifty Jews escaped Novogrudok.

At the end of the tunnel, connected by a belt to Lisa and Rae, Naum Kushner faltered. "I told my children: 'You are young, go save yourself, leave me here,'" he was quoted in Nechama Tec's *Defiance* as saying. "One of my daughters had an onion and an apple. She smeared the onion over my face and I felt better."[8] The sting woke him up. He kept moving.

Chanon Kushner was not so lucky. He and the other leaders of the escape became disoriented when they exited the tunnel in the driving rain. There was delirium in being free, out beyond the ghetto walls. The boys became confused and started to run in different directions. The next day, the enraged Nazis found Chanon and the others, and shot them. This was the second time the Nazis had shot Chanon and left him for dead. This time, he did not survive.

But Rae made it. As she, Lisa, and Naum were leaving the tunnel, Rae latched on to a Jewish youth who was from that area, who knew the countryside. She grabbed his pants and told him he was not going without her family. "We're gonna die all together or we're gonna live all together," Rae said. The boy started to cry. He had someone, a gentile woman, who would take him in. But if he brought Rae, and Naum, and Lisa, he feared, she would call the Germans and they would all die. Rae told him that if she called the Germans they would all die together.

The country boy led the Kushners to the farmhouse, where the owner recognized them from the fur store. She gave them bread, water, and onions, but ushered them on their way, afraid the Germans would kill her if she was discovered hiding Jews. Another group, coming after Rae and Lisa and Naum and the farmer boy, prevailed on the woman to let them stay. All eight of them, including the Polish woman and her husband, were killed when the Nazis discovered them.

For the next ten days, from Rosh Hashanah to Yom Kippur, the Kushners and the country boy hid in the bushes in the pouring rain. Lisa almost gave up, "What kind of life is this?" she asked. "Let them kill us already." Eventually, they found a farmer to take them in. After two days, wagons pulled up. At first, Rae thought it was the Nazis. The men had machine guns. But soon they recognized the Jewish partisans. Tuvia Bielski had heard of their escape and dispatched a group to look for survivors.

For nine months, from the fall of 1943 until the summer of 1944, Rae lived in the woods with the Bielski partisans, in a highly organized camp of over a thousand Jews. At night, small armed groups would make their way silently to farms owned by gentiles for potatoes, onions, bread—and if they were lucky, an egg or a piece of meat. The partisans' tactics could be brutal: when they believed Belarusian farmers were turning Jews over to the Nazis, the partisans would kill them, sometimes slaying whole families. Then the food was collected, and the ammunition, and brought back to the camp for defense and more raids.

Inside the camp there were artisan shops, a central kitchen, even a theater. Amid the death and destruction, men and women took "forest wives" and "forest husbands." There were even a few children, doted on by the whole group, especially loved, because so many children had been murdered by the Nazis.

Sometime during this period, Rae Kushner met Yossel Berkowitz—Joseph. The accounts vary slightly in their facts but not in their import. In her testimony to Kean University, Rae told her interlocutor that she knew her husband before the war, that he had lived in a small town near hers. The version told in *The Miracle of Life*, a history written by her four children, goes like this: Yossel had escaped from a Nazi work camp, and lived in a hole in the forest before joining the partisans, where he met Rae. Joseph's brother Chaim had wanted to marry Rae before the war, but wasn't permitted to because of class differences. But the Holocaust erased those differences. "In the woods, escaping from the Nazis, there were no social class distinctions. All were simply Jews."[9]

By the spring of 1944, the Soviets had repulsed the Nazis from Leningrad and started to march west. Germans began to escape to the forest, shooting Jews as they retreated. The Jews struck back, beating Nazis to death. The forest, which had been a place of refuge, was becoming a battleground. In July 1944, the Soviets ordered Tuvia Bielski to lead the group back to Novogrudok. As Nechama Tec told it in her book *Defiance*, the Russians feared the forest would become the base for anti-Communist sabotage, and ordered the Jews to destroy the camp. Early on the last morning they wrecked bunks, filled wells with soil, and buried utensils. The next day, Bielski assembled the twelve hundred camp residents in a line extending a full mile. "First came the scouts on horseback, followed by marching fighters, then came the carts pulled by horses, followed by all the walking survivors. Only the sick and very weak were allowed to ride in the carts."[10] Their march back to Novogrudok took two days. "There was no joy in our hearts," one partisan told Tec. "As we neared the areas of Jewish settlements, we realized the extent of the disaster that had befallen us. It looked as if our very lives had been consumed by flames, we were walking into a wasteland."[11]

Novogrudok was an inhospitable place. The Soviets pressed the Jews to join their army. The Jews had lost their homes and their businesses, all their capital, all their documents. All that was left was destruction and mass graves.

"You cannot imagine, I fainted twice," Rae said. "We all wanted to run away from our town. We wanted to run any place—but like, Russia took us in. We were afraid to move. We couldn't move. You needed a passport. You needed papers. It's not so easy." They organized and they made passports. They asked themselves, "Where should we run? Nobody wants to take us in."

Still, there was a Jewish underground, helping to plot their escape. Nine months after their return to Novogrudok, telling Russian soldiers they were Greeks, Rae, her sister and father boarded a train to Czechoslovakia, and then made their way to Hungary, where she met up with Joseph. After so much destruction and loss, the desire to couple was irresistible. Single boys and single girls wanted to get married. They all felt lost, alone. No families from Novogrudok were left intact. Every one had lost someone. In a synagogue in Budapest, alongside some twenty other couples, Rae and Joe were married by a rabbi.

There is a record of this moment, a *ketubah*, or Jewish wedding contract, normally a carefully prepared document, but in this case hastily scrawled on yellow paper with different pens, written before they fled again. According to *The Miracle of Life,* the couple then "illegally crossed the Alps and several borders by foot, train and any other available mode of transportation," ending up in a displaced persons camp near Rome. There, they were stuck for four years.[12]

Their daughter, Linda, was born in the refugee camp, as the Kushners frantically pleaded for papers from South Africa, Australia, the United Kingdom, the United States. "We would go anywhere where we could live in freedom but nobody wanted us." Rae said. "Nobody opened their doors to us. Nobody wanted to take us in."[13] A picture from those years shows Rae, her lipsticked mouth a perfect bow, her shoulder-length hair still lush and brown, brushed up and back, her once forthright gaze now indelibly marred with worry and pain.

Finally, with the help of the US refugee aid group HIAS (the Hebrew Immigrant Aid Society), Rae, Joseph, and baby Linda, along with Rae's sister Lisa and their father Naum, received visas to travel by ship to the United States. Their passage on the SS *Sobieski*, from Genoa to New York, took two weeks. Joe was seasick the whole time. The Kushners were anxious, unsure of what was ahead. But they had faith it would be better than where they came from.

Gaunt, bedraggled, speaking very little English, Rae and Joe, Naum, Lisa, and baby Linda were greeted on the docks on March 29, 1949, by the refugee workers. The organization sheltered them and helped Joe find work. Rae took English classes and managed the family's money.

After Linda, Joe and Rae had three more children. First Murray, then Charles, then Esther. Linda was named for Rae's mother, shot by the Nazis as Rae watched from the window. Charles was named for Rae's brother Chanon, who had survived fire and bullets to help build a tunnel that saved hundreds of lives, only to die when he reached the open air outside the ghetto. Esther was named for Rae's older sister, who made a futile run for her life at the Novogrudok courthouse in December 1941, before perishing in a mass grave on the edge of town.

Over fifty years later, on the occasion of their mother's seventy-fifth birthday, Chanon and Esther's namesakes, Charles Kushner and Esther Schulder, along with their siblings Murray and Linda, pulled together their parents' stories in the book *The Miracle of Life*. It began by quoting Proverbs, Chapter 1, Verse 8: "Hear, my child, the instruction of your father, and do not forsake the teaching of your mother."

Five years after that, their families stopped speaking, for good.

2

THE AMERICAN DREAM

During the war, Joseph Berkowitz—Yossel, in Yiddish—lived in a hole in the ground. A "grave," the family sometimes called this trench—*ziemianka*, in Polish—covered with branches, designed to conceal his existence from the Nazis. At night, he snuck out for food, but otherwise his life was confined to this tiny carve-out in the dirt. Everything he needed to live—potatoes, matches, salt, flour—had to be begged or stolen from wary villagers. In the winter, these provision runs became nearly impossible because of the tracks he would leave in the snow. Ziemiankas were dark; typically the only light came from bits of burning wood stuck in the walls emitting a stinging smoke. The days passed slowly. Yossel lived in constant fear that he would be caught and killed or sent back to the Nazi labor camp from which he'd escaped.

By the time of his death, forty years later, Joseph Kushner, still doing calculations in his native Yiddish, had built thousands of homes for middle-class families in New Jersey, including four large homes for his children. All of them above ground.[1]

Yossel Berkowitz was the son of poor tailors from the small village of Korelitz, not far from Novogrudok. Novogrudok was an actual town, but Korelitz was a shtetl, like the one in *Fiddler on the Roof*, tight-knit, contentious, vulnerable. Unlike his future wife, Rae, who had attended one of the area's most prestigious universities before the Nazis closed in, Yossel had little education. He could read and write, but only in Yiddish.

But—he could hustle. As a boy of twelve, as the story was passed down, he would buy run-down horses, then place hot potatoes in their rectums so they would jump around and look frisky. Then he would sell these young-looking horses for a lot more than they were worth. When he was fifteen, Yossel's father died of pneumonia, and Yossel apprenticed himself as a carpenter. This lasted only four years.

In June 1941, the Nazis marched into eastern Poland. The next summer, young Yossel was forced to watch as the Nazis murdered his mother, three of his six sisters, their husbands and children. Then he was sent to a labor camp. Before the Nazis could march him to the Novogrudok ghetto for a massacre, Yossel escaped to the forest, where he dug his "grave," hiding out with some siblings until he moved again, to join Tuvia Bielski's partisans.[2] "To save a Jew is much more important than to kill Germans," Bielski would say, and the camp took all comers.[3]

Yossel found a compatriot in Bielski, a strapping young Jewish man who had grown up in a farmhouse. During the war, in the middle of the forest, the once-privileged intellectuals and the bourgeoisie had less to offer the band of Jews than working-class youths like Yossel. He found purpose in the camp, where his carpentry skills were much in demand. Sometime during the war, he and Rae found each other.

Nechama Tec compiled a number of accounts of relationships in her book *Defiance*—forest liaisons were both life-affirming and an act of survival. "A connection to an 'appropriate' man could ease the move from the ghetto to a safe place in the forest," Tec wrote. "Men who could do that were usually the more resourceful, lower-class youths. . . . A simple, common youth had no trouble getting a socially superior girl, someone he could have only dreamt about before the war."[4]

Whatever their social positions prior to the fighting, Joseph and Rae had nothing after the war. "I was rich man," Joseph later joked. "I spent my honeymoon in Budapest."[5] After that, he and Rae embarked, without passports, on a perilous journey of over a thousand kilometers, much of it on foot through the mountains. At one point, Rae was stricken with grave appendicitis. They traveled from Budapest, two countries away from their native Poland, through Hungary and on into Italy, sneaking across international borders as they went, until they arrived at the refugee camp outside Rome. They were known as DPs—displaced persons.

"The misery of the DPs was indescribable," Mark Wischnitzer wrote in the 1956 book *Visas to Freedom: The History of HIAS*, about the Hebrew Immigrant Aid Society, which helped resettle refugees before, during, and after the war. "Failing a miracle, only an act of Congress could resolve the problem. But for this, public opinion had to be roused. A nation-wide organization was required to bring home to the American people the plight of the victims of Nazism and Fascism and their need to find a home."[6]

Joseph and Rae and their family were not wanted in America. "Nearly every surviving Jewish family in central and eastern Europe had been broken up by the war and Nazi atrocities," Wishnitzer wrote. "Obtaining the documents required for emigration presented almost insurmountable difficulties." Joe and Rae were stuck. In 1948, three years after the war ended, aid organizations were only able to settle 847 Jews in the United States.[7] That June, President Harry Truman signed a flawed Displaced Persons Act, one that sharply limited Jewish immigration. Joe, Rae, Naum, Lisa, and Linda could not leave the refugee camp, ensnared between the horrors of the past and a future they could not reach.

In Italy, Joseph made money selling scarce goods—sugar and tobacco—on the black market. But he was caught and arrested and sent to jail. Perhaps, his family whispered, a jealous relation had turned him in. His father-in-law was unable to prevail upon the authorities to let him go. So Rae, nine months pregnant with Linda, traveled to the neighboring town where her husband was being held. She too, begged for his release. Then, she bribed the guard. Her husband was freed.

Not long after that, her husband took on his wife's last name. The Kushner family histories offer many reasons for assuming the matriarchal name. One version suggests it was to elide Yossel's arrest record.[8] Another, from Rae herself: "We were relatives."[9] A third: even when they were penniless, the name "Kushner"—furrier—connoted wealth. But almost certainly, the reason Yossel Berkowitz became Joseph Kushner was because US immigration laws were written so that, as Naum's son, Joseph could get a visa. As his son-in-law, he could not. "Because sons and fathers were given priority to get visas," the Kushners wrote in *The Miracle of Life*, "Yossel assumed his wife's maiden name, being that he traveled with his father-in-law."[10]

Shortly before he moved to America, Yossel Berkowitz became Joseph Kushner, son of Naum Kushner. No records remained in Europe to demonstrate otherwise.

In America, HIAS began a new set of records, which remained buried for seventy years. In those papers, Joseph Kushner was born. On March 16, 1949, "Josef Kushnier, 26," as his name was recorded, boarded the SS *Sobieski* in Genoa, with aid workers in Rome cabling caseworkers in New York to let them know the Kushner family was on its way. The migration department worksheet prepared by aid workers listed "Naum, 51," as the family patriarch, with "Josef, 26," as his son. "Raja," also twenty-six, was listed as the daughter-in-law. Raja's—Rae's—"maiden name" was given as "Sloninski," a version of the last name of Joseph's maternal grandfather. Lisa was listed as nineteen, Linda as two. For all of them country of birth was listed, not as Poland but as "Germany,"[11] which, under the Displaced Persons Act of 1948, raised fewer eyebrows.

There was also the name of a sponsor: a Dr. H. Bussel, of the Bronx. On the back of the migration worksheet there's a notation by an aid worker that on March 25, while the Kushners were en route, a Miss J. Schwartz of the New York section had investigated. The notation said, "Dr. Bussel does not know family, assumes no responsibility." When HIAS aid workers met the family at the port of entry, the Kushner family had a total of $2 in its pockets, and nowhere to go.

HIAS put the Kushners in a shelter. The family was allotted $1.80 per person a day, with $4 a week for baby Linda. Two weeks later, during Passover, the Jewish celebration of the Exodus from Egypt, the Kushners received an extra HIAS allowance for food for their holiday.

Joseph kept up the ruse that Naum was his father and Lisa his sister. "Josef came to inform me that his father was still ill and could not keep his appointment," an aid worker noted in the file. "Josef, who assumed a great deal of responsibility for the family, indicated he would like to initiate discussions around planning although he recognized that final discussions would of necessity involve his father as well." Nervous about the family's resettlement, Joseph "expressed some anxiety about the ability of the agency to assist him because there were so many jobs to be obtained for the family."

Under the Displaced Persons Act, all of the family had to be "suitably employed." Joe was a skilled carpenter, he pointed out, "doing 'white work' of a finished nature." The aid worker told him HIAS could help, but that the work could be anywhere in the United States. Josef asked to stay in New York, saying that a "landsman from Novogrudick in White Russia" had recently reunited him with his "father's"—that is, Naum's—sister. But now, Josef had a new challenge: convince the aid worker that he was Polish (which he needed to do in order to stay in New York) and not German, as the HIAS forms had listed (which could have helped when entering the country).

"I was ready to accept his statement concerning their origin, especially because of the marked Russian accent of his Yiddish." the aid worker wrote. But more proof was needed for the family to stay in New York. Caseworkers asked for documents from the claimed American relatives, called references, and met with them all in person. "The documents fully supported the statements," the caseworker noted. "There is also a marked facial resemblance." The Kushner family was accepted for authorization in New York.

They were a large group. Housing was tight. They couldn't find anyone to take them in. They stayed on at the shelter. They met with aid workers a few times a week. "Work with the K. family was complicated by the size of the family and above all by their attitude towards the agency," one caseworker wrote. "They seemed to believe that they could get what they need or want by exercising pressure on us. They have a tremendous drive to establish themselves and start off again and were extremely active in trying to locate an apartment or to utilize the community resources. They also tried to obtain everything at once as if they would not get everything they were entitled to."

After two months, the Kushner family was given a time limit. They located two furnished rooms at 102 West Eighty-Seventh Street, a narrow five-story brownstone. The family eventually found its way to a one-bedroom walk-up on St. John's Place, Brooklyn, near Eastern Parkway, in Crown Heights. On February 27, 1950, Rae's twenty-seventh birthday, the United Service for New Americans, which had worked with HIAS, sent the Kushner family a bill, as was standard practice, for their passage from Italy, their shelter, and other costs, for a total of $1,435.32, worth about $15,000 today. The bill was sent to the address of Dr. H. Bussel, the American "sponsor" who had disavowed responsibility for the family. It's not known if the letter was ever properly routed, or if the sum was paid back. The HIAS paper trail stops there.

As GIs returned home after the war, they faced an acute housing shortage for their growing families. The federal government began fueling home construction, especially in New Jersey. Sandwiched between New York and Philadelphia, the first and third largest cities in America at the end of the war, New Jersey was an epicenter of middle-class growth on the East Coast. It was also a magnet for immigrants: as far back as 1910, a quarter of the state was foreign born. "The forces of suburbanization were as great as anywhere in the country," James Hughes, the former dean of the Bloustein School of Planning and Public Policy at Rutgers University, said in an interview. "New York City and Philadelphia were manufacturing dynamos."[12] Tube radios were manufactured in Camden, black-and-white televisions in Jersey City, apparel in New York City. From the 1950s to the 1970s a thousand homes were built each week in New Jersey, for a thousand straight weeks.

There was plenty of work for a carpenter. "My grandfather came here on a Tuesday, got a job on a Thursday and he just worked very very hard and he was able to create the American dream," is how Jared Kushner later described it.[13] Nicknamed "Hatchet Joe," Joseph Kushner made ninety dollars a week, sometimes sleeping at job sites to save the one-dollar bus fare home and back. He worked this way for four years, through the birth of his second child, Murray. During that time, Rae and Joe saved half his salary. But Joseph was finding it increasingly hard to reconcile his long days in New Jersey, and sometimes evening shifts in Brooklyn, with being an observant Jew.

In 1953, after a supervisor questioned his taking days off on both Rosh Hashanah and Yom Kippur, the Jewish high holy days, Joe decided to work for himself. He entered into a real estate deal with the sons of a fellow Holocaust survivor he met on the commuter bus to New Jersey, Harry and Joseph Wilf. With five thousand dollars he had saved in weekly increments, Joe Kushner became a minority owner of three lots in Clark County, New Jersey. "We made a couple dollars from the three houses," Rae later said.

Their second son, Charles Kushner, was soon born, as well. Since all of their cash was tied up in real estate, Joe and Rae had to borrow money to pay for his bris, the religious circumcision ceremony that takes place when a Jewish boy is eight days old.

Not long after, on his way home from work, Joseph saw Murray, then three years old, sitting on the stoop of their building in Brooklyn "with a little black boy," as described in *The Miracle of Life*. "As he approached the children, he heard Murray teaching his 'friend'"—the quotes exist in the original—"the 'Shema Yisrael,'"[14] the same prayer Jews had shouted in the courtyard in Novogrudok as the Nazis were hauling them away on trucks.

Climbing the stairs to their walk-up apartment, the words of the prayer in his ears—"Hear, O Israel, God is One!" Joe decided to leave Brooklyn, to move his family "to a Jewish neighborhood." Through her Jewish immigrant network, Rae had heard about a small Orthodox Jewish community in Elizabeth, New Jersey. Because Orthodox Jews don't travel on the sabbath, there had to be a shul—a synagogue—in walking distance. There had to be yeshivas—Jewish schools—for the children. There had to be a life, like the one in Novogrudok in the early 1930s, where Jews could observe their religion, and study, and pray, and eat, and do business together, and be safe.

The family moved to Elizabeth, New Jersey, to a rental home on South Jersey Avenue. Four years later, they moved to a house Joe built, on Summit Road, a tidy brick two-story on a small lot, with Murray and Charlie in one bedroom and Linda and the new baby, Esther, in another.

—

Joe founded his homebuilding business at an opportune time. It benefited not only from a suburban housing boom, but from two decades of federal legislation and largesse. In June of 1934, President Franklin Delano Roosevelt had signed into law the National Housing Act. For the first time, mortgages were to be insured by the federal government. Before the NHA, banks would typically only loan half a home's value; worse, loans were structured so buyers were typically left owing a lump sum which they were often unable to pay back, leading to foreclosures, evictions, and countless family tragedies.

The NHA created the structure of home mortgages as we know them now: long-term loans, requiring a standard 20 percent down payment. The act stabilized the housing market, stanched the flow of foreclosures, and pumped money into the economy two ways: by fueling housing construction and by giving middle-class renters a toehold onto home ownership. As described by Richard Rothstein in his book, *The Color of Law*, it also codified racial segregation; early FHA rules explicitly said that issuing loans for homes in racially mixed neighborhoods was a financial risk the federal government was unwilling to take.[15]

The GI Bill, passed in 1944, stimulated housing construction even further, providing even lower down payments and longer loan terms for millions of returning World War II veterans. But redlining by banks and explicitly racist covenants—private agreements enforced by public courts—meant that the housing construction boom in the suburbs overwhelmingly supported and attracted white buyers.[16]

Suburbanization got another boost, in 1956, from the Federal-Aid Highway Act, the largest public works project in American history, which came with an initial authorization of $25 billion. As with the federally backed railways of a century earlier, interstate highways modernized American transportation, allowing people and things to move rapidly, and for money to be made more efficiently. If the National Housing Act encoded racially segregated housing, the Highway Act made it easier for white families to leave cities, because it was relatively cheap to commute to urban centers, where most jobs in factories and offices were still located. This was the tailwind that helped Joe and Rae's real estate business get off the ground: federal funds and laws undergirding housing construction, suburbanization, and segregation.

Joseph Kushner's history as a builder in New Jersey is largely written in the land records of Union, Middlesex, and Essex Counties, a stack of mimeographed deeds, mortgages, and land transfers. To each was affixed a revenue stamp with the image of William H. Crawford, a former secretary of the treasury, assigned a corresponding dollar value. One of the earliest such records, from September 12, 1956, is a deed of sale for the lot on Summit Street. Rae Kushner's name is spelled "Rej." Six months later, Joe and Rej "also known as Rae Kushner," took out a $10,000 mortgage on the lot, just eight years after they had arrived in New York, penniless.[17]

A year after that, the Kushner real estate business began in earnest. By early January 1958, Joseph Kushner and Harry Wilf formed Vineyard Homes Inc., to develop lots in Edison, New Jersey. The small two-story houses they built looked much like Joe and Rae's own home: bungalow-style with a second story jutting up in the middle. That top floor, under the eaves, housed the children of growing American families.

The Wilfs had spent the Holocaust years in Siberia, traveling to American-occupied Germany after the war. Their family arrived in America virtually intact: all but one sister had survived. The Wilfs had a little bit of a running start on the Kushners.[18] In this early venture, Joe Kushner was the secretary, but Harry Wilf was the vice president. More crucially, Harry guaranteed the loan, for $458,300, an amount worth over four million dollars in 2019.[19]

Joe worked constantly: out of his car, using pay phones for his calls. To the extent he had an "office," it was in the small house on Summit Road, underneath the bedrooms of the two boys and the two girls. In 1957, they were all under ten. Rae did the paperwork, Rae selected the partners, Rae figured out how to set up corporations under the laws of the State of New Jersey in a way that would redound to the family's financial advantage. In the summers, she took the four children to the beach or the mountains: to Far Rockaway, or to the Catskills, where the five of them would live in a single room. Joe would visit on weekends. Sometimes, he would even work on Shabbat.

By 1963, Joe was the president of his own company, able to guarantee his own loan, for three hundred thousand dollars. Savings and loans were the typical banks of the era, small and stable, making a profit by taking in savings accounts on which they paid a few percentage points in interest, and issuing mortgage loans for a little more: a rate of 5 or 6 percent interest. The next year, Joe Kushner bought two new lots, which were owned by two new companies, and took out another $400,000 mortgage, and another for $310,000. On these lots, Joe Kushner began building garden apartments: long, motel-style two-story apartments that offered inexpensive housing for young postwar couples, who moved to these homes in a voracious, seemingly endless stream. The companies, and complexes, had names like Scotch Plains, Cherry Pines, Martha Bell.

In this era, the mid-1960s, the Kushner family real estate business became more complex, and Joe Kushner, under Rae's tutelage, began placing his companies into a series of complicated, interlinked trusts, the vehicle that in those days insulated people from corporate liability. It was the trusts that acquired, held, improved, leased, and mortgaged the properties to homeowners, that sold the properties, and that made the money for their beneficiaries.

By 1966, the Kushners were doing very, very well. They flew to Israel for a vacation.[20] Some of Joe's relatives had moved there after the war. Nineteen-sixties Israel had an ineffable pull for Jews. "If Israel would have existed, maybe we could have rescued some Jews, and not killed so much," Rae said. "A million and a half children—"

The year they traveled to Israel, Rae and Joe bought a new lot at the corner of Wilder Street and Westminster Avenue in Hillside. There were unwritten codes that kept Jews confined to certain areas, but Hillside was by then a town of Jewish enclaves, a place where Jews who were coming up in the world, like the Kushners, could live. Joe finished building the house on Wilder Street in 1967, a 9,000-square-foot white brick home on a 17,000-square-foot corner grassy lot, with a large center staircase, the master bedroom downstairs, the kids' bedrooms upstairs. Nineteen sixty-seven was the year Charles turned thirteen; his bar mitzvah year, the year, in Jewish tradition, that boys become men. Murray was in high school; Linda was already married. On Shabbat there were candles and challah, and people would gather in the living room in Hillside: family, business associates, guests.

After the move to Hillside, there were more real estate developments, more corporate configurations, more partners. Joe built generous, expansive homes for his children, in West Orange and Livingston, affluent New Jersey towns newly opening up to Jews. As the sixties turned to the seventies and then the eighties, and white flight from New York and Newark accelerated, the Kushners moved, too. Hillside was slowly becoming less white. Livingston was whiter, and conspicuously affluent.

In 1970, Joe and Rae began to act like truly wealthy people. They set up trusts for each of their children: "The Linda K. Laulicht Trust Number I," "The Murray Kushner Trust Number I," "The Charles Kushner Trust Number I," and "The Esther Kushner Trust Number I." These, unlike the previous trusts, were not a way to ward off liability. These trusts were a way to transfer wealth, untaxed, to their children and grandchildren, in a family that had risen from the ashes.

By the 1970s, the Kushner family had celebrated many *simchas*, or joyful occasions: two brises, two bar mitzvahs, a wedding. There were many more in their larger community, occasions to drink and eat and wear brightly colored dresses and, for the men, suits or black tie. They would celebrate among ice sculptures and large cuts of meat at the kosher banquet facility in Short Hills, New Jersey, noshing and hugging and telling one another, "Mazel Tov!"

Yet the past never left them. "There could be a party of a thousand people, all American. There comes a European, we stay on one side. And what are you going to talk? Where were you? Where you lived, how you got out," Rae said. The conversations always led back to the concentration camps and the ghetto.

The Kushner children, Esther and Charles and Murray and Linda, absorbed these conversations. Rae's children lived her life, as well as their own. "I don't know if it is so healthy for our kids to have the same mind. They are more serious kids, our kids," Rae said. "To live a little bit of our lives, with our past. . . . Our youth went away, our junior years went away, and the middle years went away. When you live a new life in a country without language, to start from the beginning, it's not easy." In America, the Jews from Europe put their all into every party, to make up for lost time. At the *simchas*, the younger generation was warned: never forget where you came from. "People should know what happened to us," Rae said. "If we not gonna tell now, in twenty years I don't know who's gonna be to tell. And now we have still the strength and the power to do this, and to warn the rest of the world to be careful: who is coming up on top of your government?"[21]

3

LAND OF OPPORTUNITY

When it comes to telling his family origin story, Donald Trump is, uncharacteristically, a man of few words. Perhaps that's because, while Donald Trump's family story is a uniquely American one, it is not the kind of family story that typically underpins one's case to be elected president of the United States. It's the tale of a hustling entrepreneur immigrant grandfather who made money satisfying the appetites of Western lumberjacks and miners for food, liquor, and prostitutes; of a builder father whose career included several run-ins with government investigators, and decades of hiding a massive fortune from the IRS. It is memorable but not uplifting, a story of men and their money, a gleaming shadow edifice, rooted in fraud.

At the turn of the last century, Friedrich Trump, Donald Trump's grandfather, found himself in the Yukon, in Canada, chasing the last major North American gold rush, the Klondike. On July 17, 1897, the *Seattle Post-Intelligencer* greeted with three extra editions the arrival of a steamer called *Portland* carrying $700,000 worth of gold from the Yukon. Sixty-eight "ordinary" people were the proprietors of this gold, suggesting to everyone struggling with Seattle's wet, rainy weather and manure-covered streets that they too, could strike it rich.[1]

Much of the West Coast was raw, virtually lawless country in those days, smelly, rough-hewn. Its energy was fueled by the verve of immigrant laborers, massive streams of European capital, and land giveaways—of territory taken from Native Americans—that underwrote the transcontinental railroad. Each new discovery of precious metals produced a torrent of interest: even a Canadian government requirement that prospectors needed to carry a year's worth of food, weighing more than 1,100 pounds, did not deter more than a hundred thousand gold-seekers from slogging over mountain passes, consuming meat from the horses who died along the way, swatting away swarms of fierce Northwest mosquitos.

Tall and lean, with a sharp nose undergirded by a bushy mustache, Friedrich did not follow the gold rush to mine, but to profit from the masses of prospectors heading north. To do so, he ran three incarnations of a venture called the Arctic Restaurant. The Arctic served a startling array of meats, from salmon to duck to sheep, as well as raspberries and red currants. One version of the Arctic was "a small oasis of luxury" on the town's main street. "The bulk of the cash flow," wrote Trump family biographer Gwenda Blair, "came from the sale of liquor and sex." Indeed, the "Arctic was open twenty-four hours a day and had private boxes for ladies—facilities that here included not only a bed but a scale for weighing the gold dust used to pay for services." This was the origin of the Trump family fortune: selling food, liquor, and sex.[2]

Friedrich Trump had arrived in America in 1885, pushing away from a militarizing Europe where inheritance laws gave him few financial prospects. For about twenty dollars, he purchased a space in steerage on the SS *Eider*, soon pervaded by the stink of "ship," as Blair wrote.[3] In New York, Friedrich lived with his older sister, Katherine, and her husband, and worked seven days a week as a barber. But cutting hair was a slow way to make money. So Friedrich Trump took a long train ride to Seattle, a place where a young man could make money fast.

His first venture was a restaurant, the Dairy, in Seattle's red-light district. As Blair described it, the establishment was "thick with the smells of wet cloth, hot meat, sour beer and unwashed human flesh." By noon, "the sawdust he sprinkled on the floor every morning lay in muddy, manure-dotted clumps."[4] Blair, whose book was written with the cooperation of the Trump family and who provided a detailed account of Friedrich's story, suggested that the Dairy was also a whorehouse. She wrote, "for Friedrich Trump to offer anything else . . . would put him at a punishing competitive disadvantage."[5]

Friedrich soon moved on from Seattle to Monte Cristo, a forbidding Cascade Mountains mining camp, where feet of snow and sucking mud made passage almost impossible. But the possibility of finding a rich lode of silver ore was fueled by the endorsement of John D. Rockefeller, whose investment convinced Trump and others of the soundness of the bet. Friedrich Trump identified a prime piece of land next to the future train depot, exactly the place where miners would arrive and congregate, hungry to satisfy their appetites. He couldn't afford this land, so he claimed that he intended to mine it, which would give him access, effectively for free. In April 1893, Friedrich recorded his claim, swearing he was making a "placer" claim—that is, that he would mine it—because he had found "color"—that is, ore. "Not one of these statements, it seems, was true," Blair wrote.[6]

Indeed, Friedrich Trump's actions suggest he had other plans for the property. Even before filing his claim—despite the fact he was not allowed to build on the site—he had purchased five thousand board feet of lumber from the Monte Cristo Mining Company. He constructed a two-story boarding house that enabled him to profit from the risks the miners were taking, without taking that risk himself. He took his earnings and moved up to the Yukon. "Once again," Blair wrote, "in a situation that created many losers, he managed to emerge a winner," leaving the Yukon with "a substantial nest egg."[7]

Friedrich moved back to New York with this nest egg, and on a trip back to Germany, met his future wife: Elizabeth Christ, a blond and blue-eyed neighbor from a poor family with whose classic beauty he became instantly smitten. Friedrich and Elizabeth took another ship across the Atlantic Ocean, and moved to an apartment in the South Bronx, but Elizabeth was desperately homesick. Friedrich, now wealthy, tried to move back to his native country. But because he had not done his military service, Germany wouldn't have him. In 1905, Friedrich Trump returned to New York City, with Elizabeth five months pregnant with their son, Frederick Christ Trump.

In New York, Friedrich Trump entered the real estate business, settling in Queens, a small borough by population and the largest borough by land. Queens was then known as the "cornfields" borough; farmers still brought their wares to Manhattan by horse and cart. Unlike Brooklyn, which had been connected to Manhattan by bridge, Queens was accessible only by ferry or a circuitous route through Brooklyn.

That was about to change—the city was building the Queensboro Bridge, and the Pennsylvania Railroad was digging a tunnel under the East River from Manhattan to Queens, infrastructure improvements that would create massive value for Queens real estate at just the time Friedrich Trump was buying in. In September 1908, Friedrich used some of his Yukon nest egg to buy a two-story frame house on Jamaica Avenue in Woodhaven. Soon, the city began constructing the elevated train there, leaving great mounds of excavated dirt along the side of the former wagon path. The Trumps moved to a quieter street nearby in what was fast becoming a German immigrant enclave, and Friedrich continued his real estate business, conducting much of it in German with other German immigrants, dealing with a German mortgage broker, dining at the Triangle Hofbrau, a restaurant whose wooden barrel heads came from a village just a few miles from Friedrich's hometown of Kallstadt. Friedrich Trump spoke German at home to his children, too.[8]

The senior F. Trump prospered in early-twentieth-century Queens for almost a decade. But the upward trajectory was abruptly halted: in 1918, at the age of forty-nine, Friedrich went for a late spring walk with his older son along Jamaica Avenue, stopping to chat with brokers along the way. During the walk, according to Fred, Friedrich turned to his son and said he felt sick. He climbed into bed and died the next day, felled by the influenza epidemic of 1918 that claimed as many as a hundred million victims. By the time of his death, he had accrued a substantial fortune: after taxes, it came to over $31,000 in mortgages, properties, lots, bank accounts, and insurance, equivalent to more than half a million dollars today.[9] Friedrich's occupation, noted on his death certificate, was "the real estate business."[10]

Freidrich's untimely death came amid a wrenching turn in global history: two world wars, sandwiching a global depression. Even with their comfortable lives built on Friedrich's proceeds from the gold rush years, the value of Friedrich's land holdings shrunk, battered by postwar recession. Elizabeth took over the attenuated family business: hiring a contractor to build homes on the lots she'd inherited, selling the houses, providing mortgages, and living off the mortgage income, plus what she could make by sewing. After his 1923 graduation from high school, Fred Trump found work as a "horse's helper," pulling construction materials in wagons along icy roads that mules couldn't navigate. He also worked as a carpenter, eventually building homes. As described in Nina Burleigh's *Golden Handcuffs: The Secret History of Trump's Women*, Elizabeth's "business model was an embryonic form of the debt-leveraging, borrow-build-borrow style that remains a hallmark of the Trump Organization today." In April 1927, a local newspaper announced the incorporation of E. Trump & Son, the prototype of Fred Trump's real estate business.[11]

That same year—on Memorial Day, 1927, as reported by the *New York Times*—"1,000 Klansmen and 100 police staged a free-for-all battle in Jamaica." Seven men were arrested, among them "Fred Trump of 175–24 Devonshire Rd. in Jamaica." Fred Trump's exact role at the rally is unclear, but a contemporaneous report in the *Daily Star* said that the arrest was for "refusing to disperse from a parade when ordered to do so."[12]

Elizabeth's industrious use of Friedrich's nest egg didn't insulate the

Trump family from the Great Depression. But it kept the family from sliding into the oncoming abyss. Nevertheless, E. Trump & Son could not support Fred; by 1934, he was running a supermarket in Queens.

Still a young man, tall, with a broad forehead and a trim-reddish brown mustache topping a dazzling smile, Fred received two breaks at the height of the Depression that launched his career as a New York developer. He got his first big break from the collapse of the House of Lehrenkrauss. The family-owned company had issued $26 million in mortgages over fifty years,[13] but as Julius Lehrenkrauss testified in court, he had sold shares in the same mortgages over and over to different buyers and used other methods to pressure buyers to make investments in nonexistent assets.[14] The company went into involuntary bankruptcy, but there were still extant parts of the business to run: namely gathering fees for collecting the payments on the outstanding mortgages. Moreover, Fred Trump saw another angle: getting the lists of mortgage payers. "The real value in the business . . . was in the information they gleaned from the Lehrenkrauss operations," Michael D'Antonio noted in his biography, *The Truth About Trump*.[15] If Fred was able to get the appointment to service the mortgages, he would find out who was behind in their payments and who faced foreclosures, enabling him to get a jump on offering to buy the distressed properties. This was valuable intelligence.

In order to be able to get the assignment to take over this part of the Lehrenkrauss business, however, Fred needed to get his bid in contention, which meant submitting it to a Brooklyn court. Fred Trump had little experience servicing mortgages, only the one-offs he'd put together in his early business with his mother. In letters to the court, he bragged that he had ten years in the building business, even though he'd only had five.[16]

Fred showed up alone the first day in court as six inches of snow blanketed the city. He was "solicitous and self-assured. He had an erect, almost military bearing, musclebound and purposeful," as Trump biographer Wayne Barrett described it. "He made a brief oral statement to the court in a thick German accent."[17] The other bidders had counsel. Fred represented himself. He fought for his bid. When it looked like he might lose, he teamed up with another Queens businessman. A third bidder complained, calling them "two individuals who there is no doubt in my mind, do not run a servicing company at all; and are trying to make a bid to buy something for nothing."[18]

Fred had reason to be confident; he had learned something important about the way the system worked. To be seriously considered in the Brooklyn bankruptcy court, he had to be seen as having the endorsement of the party bosses. Around the time of the Lehrenkrauss bid, Fred opened up communications with a Brooklyn boss: Frank V. Kelly. The two were seen lunching at Park Slope's Montauk Club, the ornate private social club near Prospect Park, said to be modeled on a palace on Venice's Grand Canal. Exactly what Fred did to get the court's approval isn't entirely clear. But as Barrett noted, "the vigorous support he received from the Democratic Party players suggests that he was their designated winner, making Lehrenkrauss the introductory venture for an alliance between Trump and the Brooklyn organization that would last a lifetime."[19] Fred Trump would at times be among the very largest donor to Brooklyn Democrats, in some years raising tens of thousands of dollars for the party. Fred hired the party's lawyer to be his own. He became a regular customer of an insurance broker favored by the party. And year in, year out, he showed up at the annual gala of Brooklyn's Madison Democratic Club, eating rubber-chicken dinners, glad-handing the political bosses who held the power behind the scenes. The public might not have known their names; Fred Trump did.

He used those connections to secure a second, crucial break: an enormous infusion of federally backed funds. Fred Trump was one of the earliest and largest beneficiaries of the National Housing Act of 1934, the law that regularized mortgage lending and later contributed so much to the 1950s growth of suburbia.

To build a sturdy edifice of debt, the Federal Housing Administration created a series of strictures for home lending: for example, homes had to have readily accessible bathrooms in order to hold their value, that is, in order to be a good lending bet. But it wasn't just sound principles of construction and markets that guided the FHA, as documented in Richard Rothstein's *The Color of Law.*[20] In its earliest iterations, the FHA institutionalized racial discrimination and segregation by requiring, in so many words, that lending should only go to properties "occupied by the same social and racial classes."

In the FHA, Fred Trump saw opportunity. And once again, his club connections paid off. The first director of the New York State FHA Office was Tommy Grace, who Wayne Barrett described as "a bouncy little Irish politician."[21] While working at the FHA, Grace later acknowledged, he was also a partner in his brothers' law firm, which made most of its money from clients who wanted help getting approval *from* the FHA.[22] In 1936, with Grace's backing, Fred Trump was able to get one of the first major FHA commitments for a New York project: $750,000 in mortgage insurance for the development of 450 homes in East Flatbush, Brooklyn.[23]

In 1938, Fred Trump got federal backing for another Brooklyn development, this one valued at $1 million. The loans allowed a transformation in construction practices. No longer building house by house, Fred Trump could now build hundreds of homes at a time, sometimes setting up scaffolding that spanned a city block.[24] The Brooklyn *Eagle* wrote that "among the real-estate fraternity he is known as the 'Henry Ford of the home-building industry.'"[25] By 1943, Fred Trump—who a decade earlier had to abandon the real estate industry to run a supermarket—was a millionaire, in 1943 dollars. He was becoming one of the largest recipients of FHA loans in the country.[26]

Fred Trump's mother was an immigrant, and so was his wife, Mary Anne MacLeod. MacLeod was born in the village of Tong on the Scottish island of Lewis, in a two-bedroom home with her parents and nine siblings, warmed by a smoky peat fire. When she was six, two hundred of the island's young men, returning from war, were drowned in a shipwreck on New Year's night, 1919. Eleven years later, listing her occupation as "domestic," MacLeod arrived in New York City, declaring on her immigration papers she intended to seek US citizenship, and did not intend to return to Scotland.[27] Indeed, Mary MacLeod found work as a maid at the East Ninety-First Street mansion of the widow of the richest Scotsman in the world, Andrew Carnegie, a baron of the Gilded Age, who had made his fortune from steel. According to Nina Burleigh's *Golden Handcuffs*, "her live-in maid's position meant she spent her days—and presumably nights (she is listed in the census as a household member)—in an American palace, rubbing shoulders with the closest thing Americans had to royalty, during the depths of the Great Depression."[28]

A half decade after she arrived in America, Mary Anne MacLeod attended a dance in Queens and met a builder who, like her, spoke with an accent, but who was tall and neat and fast becoming rich. "The most eligible bachelor in New York," she later called him. The two were wed at the Madison Avenue Presbyterian Church in Manhattan, with a reception at The Carlyle, a hotel on the Upper East Side, a newly built symbol of elegance just a block from Central Park.

A decade later, in an exclusive Queens enclave, Fred built his new wife and family a twenty-three-room, nine-bath, red-brick colonial fronted by six white columns, a Queens version of Manhattan wealth, exuding a whiff of royal aspirations. Mary Anne MacLeod Trump had given birth to Maryanne, then Fred Jr., then Elizabeth. Fred Sr. dressed impeccably, even at home. His rules for the house were strict: curfews, no cursing; for the girls, no lipstick.

During the war, Fred stopped speaking German, and went silent on his German roots. He began telling people he had Swedish ancestry. And with a growing prominence of Jews in real estate, politics, and finance in New York, Fred also started to generously donate to Jewish philanthropies. In 1941, he was on the dinner committee of a fundraiser for the New York and Brooklyn Federation of Jewish Charities.[29] Some people assumed he was Jewish. He let them.

In 1946, at the very outset of the baby-boom era, Mary Anne Trump gave birth to her fourth child, Donald John Trump. Donald's three older siblings were children of the Depression and the war; Donald was what biographer Blair calls a "faux firstborn," part of a post-war generation that became the repository of post-war parental dreams, hopes, and optimism.[30]

In 1946 New York—lifting its wartime blackout curtains, adjusting to newly plentiful foods like eggs and meats—the subway still cost a nickel. And out at the end of the subway line in Brooklyn, in Coney Island and Brighton Beach, land was still cheap. Backed with $26 million in federal loans, Fred Trump erected unlovely brick complexes with nice names like "Shore Haven" and "Beach Haven."[31] The buildings were drab but practical. After the war, families wanted to nest and to grow, and Fred Trump built affordable homes that served both needs. His complexes were some of the largest in the country. Woody Guthrie lived in an apartment in Beach Haven and wrote a song about it. "Beach Haven is a heaven where no black folks come to roam" was one of the lines. "No, no, no! Old Man Trump! Old Beach Haven ain't my home," was another.[32]

As Fred built, with tens of millions of dollars in federal help, he began to shield his fortune. In a series of moves that the *New York Times* called "dubious tax schemes" and "outright fraud," Fred Trump would move wealth eqivalent to a billion dollars to his children without paying the proper taxes, including $413 million to his son Donald.[33]

One of the earliest such schemes was at Beach Haven. Fred Trump transferred the title of the land under his buildings to a trust benefiting his children, then leased the land *from* the trust, in effect making his children his landlords. This meant Fred Trump could take money that he, Fred Trump, was collecting from rents on units he built with federal help—and transfer those profits to his children, without returning money to the government as taxes.

In this way, almost immediately upon his birth, Donald Trump started making money. As documented by the *New York Times*'s David Barstow, Susanne Craig, and Ross Buettner, as a toddler, Donald Trump was making, in today's dollars, $200,000 a year from the wealth transferred from his father. By the time he was eight, he was a millionaire. At seventeen, he was part owner of a fifty-two-unit apartment building, and as a young college graduate, Donald Trump was making the equivalent of $1 million a year.

Among the methods the *Times* documented: Fred Trump would undervalue his properties when transferring them to his children, thereby minimizing or eliminating gift taxes. (The Trumps would later inflate the value of those properties when seeking bank loans.) Sometimes, Fred Trump would simply transfer properties through a web of companies, "without public trace," as the *Times* put it, and pay no taxes at all. Once, he sold Donald a $15.5-million property stake for $10,000; in effect, a $15.49-million untaxed gift.

There were other routes: Fred Trump set up a sham corporation, All County Building Supply & Maintenance, which he placed in his children's names. All County wasn't a real company; it didn't do anything; it simply bought supplies, like appliances, at prices negotiated by Fred Trump's employees, then marked them up and billed Fred Trump's properties for them. Fred's children collected the difference, again evading taxes.

A young Donald Trump was also paid to manage his father's buildings, even though there were Trump employees to handle day-to-day management. At one point, Fred Trump helped his children buy mortgages on his own properties, making them, in effect, his bankers, again paying them money while avoiding taxes.[34]

There were 295 such revenue streams, in all. "I think they took delight in the tax games that they played," Susanne Craig, one of the journalists who spent eighteen months on the investigation, said in an interview for the *Trump, Inc.* podcast. "Any dollar that they could keep away from the tax man was a victory for them. They delighted in these transgressions that they played, both of them."[35]

Fred Trump was doing something that all Americans, all parents, like to do: pass on what they've earned to their children. This tendency, as Thomas Piketty wrote in *Capital in the Twenty-First Century,* fuels the intergenerational transfer of wealth, allowing younger generations of wealthy families to accumulate money faster than their counterparts who earn their livings through wages. Postwar America tried to correct for that, by imposing relatively high taxes on the top brackets of income, as well as a hefty real estate tax. This meant rich Americans could pass along their wealth, but had to give some of it back to create a more egalitarian society. Fred Trump simply evaded those laws, insuring that greater and greater portions of his wealth (which had been generated with huge assists from the US government) were kept away from tax authorities.

In 1954, Fred Trump was subpoenaed before the US Senate banking committee in a widespread probe of corruption and abuse in federally backed housing loans. Investigators had found that local Federal Housing Administration officials, who had sometimes been given gifts like television sets by area developers, would then give FHA approval for bigger FHA mortgages than their properties warranted, thereby restricting the pool for other possible developments.[36] This is what the committee wanted to ask Fred Trump about. So, after being subpoenaed late on a Friday afternoon in July, Fred boarded a 9:30 a.m. plane Monday from New York to Washington to take their questions.

During the hearing, Fred Trump conceded he'd paid just $180,000 for the land underlying Beach Haven, but had, a few years later, got the FHA to appraise it at $1.5 million. When he transferred the land to his children, Fred Trump acknowledged, he'd valued it at the lower amount, $180,000, thus paying taxes at the lower rate. He further acknowledged that the higher appraisal allowed him to take a higher mortgage, and that he'd used the difference to finance other projects, paying no taxes. This was, he said, what he was entitled to do under the regulations.[37]

The senators extracted more admissions: that Fred Trump had inflated his building costs by working into the budget a "building fee," that he paid to himself. "You don't want to be misunderstood, testifying under oath, that you paid that money out, do you, Mr. Trump?"

the general counsel on the FHA investigation, William Simon, asked him. "No, I will explain this to you, Mr. Simon," Fred Trump said, maintaining that "whether we supervised the work ourselves or paid someone to do it," he still considered himself entitled to the fee. There were other ways Fred shaved money from the FHA, including inflating architectural fees in his FHA application. Fred Trump defended himself, saying he'd built thousands of high-quality homes.[38]

But a federal report found the inflated cost estimates that had enriched Fred Trump and other developers were "outright misrepresentation," and they had "saddled tenants with the burden of meeting not only legitimate costs" but also the portion of the loans the developers were keeping for themselves. And it condemned another Fred Trump tactic: "fictional division of single projects into two or more projects" to sidestep federal loan insurance limits.[39]

This was not Fred Trump's last appearance before a government investigative committee. In 1966, the New York State Investigations Commission called Fred Trump and his Madison Club friend Bunny Lindenbaum before a televised hearing on the construction of Trump Village, a seven-building project in Coney Island. Fred Trump, it emerged, had again engaged in a pattern of double valuation: he secretly set up an equipment-rental company and paid his own company padded fees—$21,000, for example, to lease a truck worth $3,600, and $8,280 for two tile-scrappers each worth $500."[40]

At the hearing, Fred Trump erupted. "This is peanuts what you are talking about compared to $60 million!" But the state commission wasn't finished: there was $1.2 million he'd pocketed by overestimating land costs, and returned only when the hearings loomed. He'd overstated construction costs by $6.6 million, and used that figure to claim a higher fee from the state. Even his lawyers charged $650,000, compared to a $70,000 fee for legal work on a similar, non-Trump project.

After the hearings, the case was formally referred to the Brooklyn District Attorney's Office, "a cemetery for public corruption probes," as biographer Wayne Barrett put it. As the commission's attorney later acknowledged to Barrett: "These people were untouchable."[41]

—

Two decades later, the government was once again investigating Trump business practices. In 1973, the US Justice Department brought a race discrimination suit against the Trump Organization, alleging the Trumps had systematically refused to lend to blacks. According to the suit, several people working for Trump confirmed that rental applications were coded by race. Doormen were told to tell black applicants there were no vacancies. Some employees said instructions came straight from Fred.[42]

In a deposition in the case, Donald Trump, by then in his twenties and working for his father, claimed ignorance of the Fair Housing Act of 1968, which required nondiscrimination in rentals. He claimed both that he had no idea of the rental composition of his complexes *and* that some were all white and some were all black. When asked if he, personally, had "anything to do with rental decisions," he said, "No, I really don't." Yet, while applying for his brokerage license application he had said the opposite: that he "supervises and controls the renting of all apartments owned by the Trump organization."[43]

To defend himself in this lawsuit, Donald Trump made a fateful alliance at Le Club, where he'd talked himself into a membership. Le Club "was the hottest club in the city and perhaps the most exclusive," Trump wrote in his first memoir, *The Art of the Deal*, "and its membership included some of the most successful men and the most beautiful women in the world. It was the sort of place where you were likely to see a wealthy seventy-five-year-old guy walk in with three blondes from Sweden."[44]

Once inside, Donald met a short man with a high forehead and a nose that looked like it had been smashed in a fight. A man who had become known to the nation as the young prosecutor who in the 1950s sent alleged Soviet spies Julius and Ethel Rosenberg to the electric chair, and then became chief counsel to the Senate Permanent Subcommittee on Investigations, chaired by Senator Joseph McCarthy.

The lawyer's name was Roy Cohn.

By this time, McCarthy, with Cohn's eager assistance, had led a relentless series of probes into suspected Communists in government, leaving a trail of ruined careers, damaged reputations, and suicides. Cohn had organized the hearings in 1954 where McCarthy met his match. The senator tore into Joseph Welch, the lawyer for the US Army, insinuating that a young Harvard grad who had briefly been a member of the National Lawyers Guild was a Communist, an accusation that could have ruined the young man's career. McCarthy would not let it go. Welch interrupted. "Have you no sense of decency, sir? At long last, have you left no sense of decency?"[45]

After those hearings, Roy Cohn quit government and formed a private practice that he ran out of his Upper East Side town house. Cohn would display his power by doing business in his bathrobe. At events, his suits changed from black and grey and the occasional tan to yellow and lavender. A closeted gay man, his client list came to include Mafia figures including Tony Salerno, Carmine Galante, and John Gotti.

Around the time he met Trump, Cohn had been under investigation or indictment in both New York and Illinois for, among other things, jury tampering and perjury. (He was never found guilty.)[46]

"I don't like lawyers," Trump told Cohn when they met at Le Club, telling Cohn the government "has just filed suit against our company . . . saying that we discriminated against blacks." Or so Trump described the encounter in *The Art of the Deal.*

"My view is tell them to go to hell and fight the thing in court and let them prove that you discriminated, which seems to me very difficult to do," Cohn replied. "I don't think you have any obligation to rent to tenants who would be undesirable, white or black, and the government doesn't have a right to run your business."[47]

Donald Trump hired Roy Cohn.

He would never love any lawyer as much, again.

ACT II

4

THE FALL OF NEW YORK

On September 24, 1975, fourteen mayors traveled to the US Congress Joint Economic Committee in Washington, DC, to make a desperate plea for help. One of them, a diminutive man wearing a maroon tie, pink shirt, and thick black glasses, craned his head toward the banks of senators and representatives. This was the New York City mayor, Abe Beame. "The state has done all it can," he said, chopping his hand against the table. "The city has done—and is committed to do—in the months ahead, more of what we've done." Beame paused, sucking in his lips. "And if the federal government does not help us, I think it will find the problem afterwards, which it would have to help us with, much more serious."[1] "Afterwards," in Beame's Lower East Side accent, came out "afta-woods."

Seated next to Beame, New Orleans Mayor Moon Landrieu, in silver aviator glasses with pinkish photosensitive lenses, blue coat, and brown tie, made his own plea for New York City. "New York is not here as a supplicant, it is not here for a hand-out. It's not asking for anything that we haven't done repeatedly for private enterprise." If New York could fail, Landrieu was arguing, any American city could fail. By the mid-1970s, almost all of them were under stress.

In New York City, the manufacturing jobs which had surged during the 1940s and 1950s had dropped off precipitously, from over a million following World War II to half that amount by the 1970s.[2] New York City, like the other cities, was deeply in hock: for decades, the state, banks, and financiers had encouraged the city to borrow to solve its debt problems.[3] As documented by Kim Phillips-Fein in her book *Fear City*, the two largest ratings agencies, Moody's and Standard & Poors, concerned about a potential slowdown in borrowing, actually upgraded New York's bond rating in the early 1970s, continuing to prime a cycle of borrowing and debt.[4]

At the same time, urban populations were rapidly declining. Whites were moving out. Practices like blockbusting, though illegal, were common throughout New York—where realtors would convince whites to sell in a hurry at under-market rates because blacks were purportedly moving in, then sell to blacks at inflated prices—accelerating the cycle of foreclosure and the rate of white flight.

From 1970 to 1980, the population of New York City shrank by nearly a million, from 7,894,862 to 7,071,639. Like a business that had lost its customer base, New York was retrenching. It couldn't pay its debts. It risked default. But instead of helping the city—and all cities—through lean times, the federal government backed away.

Urged on by his chief of staff, Donald Rumsfeld, President Gerald R. Ford had chosen not to help. "The people of this country will not be stampeded," Ford told the world a month after the mayors' appeal, in a speech at the National Press Club in Washington. "They will not panic when a few desperate New York City officials and bankers try to scare New York's mortgage payments out of them." The *New York Daily News*, as tabloids do, turned Ford's statement into shorthand: "Ford to City: Drop Dead."[5]

Beame, an accountant, had run for mayor on the slogan: "He Knows the Buck."[6] As a young man, five foot two at full height, Beame became an avid election-day captain for Brooklyn's Madison Democratic Club, for which he was rewarded in 1946 with an appointment to be assistant budget director for the city. He ascended to budget director, then was elected comptroller, then mayor. But his knowledge of numbers couldn't help him in 1975, when the federal government turned its back.[7]

Under Beame, New York City took unpopular measures, pushing the economic pain onto its residents. It raised transit fares from thirty-five cents to fifty cents, charged the first-ever tuition fees at the City University of New York, and cut services while laying off employees. But it was the teachers' union that saved the city. After a tense night of negotiations, the union allowed its pension fund to cover the city's shortfall, thus keeping the city solvent—doing what the federal government could have done, but chose not to.[8]

The same month that Gerald Ford didn't precisely tell New York City to "Drop Dead," October 1975, a twenty-nine-year-old Donald Trump—"the kid," as government officials and real estate executives referred to him in those days—launched the deal that would make him a Manhattan real estate mogul. From a broke and broken city, Donald Trump siphoned off tax breaks worth $4 million a year. These abatements would last forty years into the future, well into the new millennium, to help finance a hotel that was profitable the day it opened.[9] Nineteen seventy-five may have been one of the worst years in the life of New York City. It was one of the best years ever for Donald Trump.

By then Donald had joined his father at the Madison Club dinners, eating the chicken entrées, providing a steady stream of donations, often through companies they controlled.[10] They hired the Madison Club lawyer, Bunny Lindenbaum, and later his son Sandy. The ties proved lucrative: Governor Hugh Carey came out of the Madison Club, as well as Beame. When it came to city government, it was hard to tell where Beame's staff ended and Trump's began.

Like his father, who had his first big break in a bankruptcy court, Donald Trump saw opportunity in the carcass of Penn Central railroad, which had recently declared the single largest bankruptcy in the nation's history.[11] Railroads had begun dying a slow death after the war, a victim of the Federal-Aid Highway Act's support for autos over mass transit. Penn Central was looking to sell off large parcels of land and properties in Manhattan. Donald Trump was buying. He had his eye on the increasingly decrepit Commodore Hotel: a clunky and small-windowed brick behemoth on Forty-Second Street next to Grand Central Terminal. The man in charge of the sale for Penn Central, Ned Eichler, was both attracted by Donald Trump's brashness and energy and worried about his youth. Unsure if he was making the right bet on Trump—as Wayne Barrett told the story—Eichler asked Donald for proof of his political ties.

"I'll have to see the mayor," Eichler said.

"When do you want to see him?" Trump wanted to know.

"Tomorrow at two P.M." Eichler told him.

There was no hesitation, no checking to see if two o'clock in the afternoon was convenient for the mayor. Donald sent his limo to pick up Eichler at one-thirty. At two, they met with Mayor Beame, at City Hall.[12]

In the mid-1970s Donald Trump was still working out of Fred's office on Avenue Z in Brooklyn. He served as a manager of his father's outer-borough apartment complexes, collecting rents himself and handling maintenance contracts. But he had the verve and hunger to build in the center of Manhattan—and the contacts to get the approvals and zoning changes a large developer needed. "It was uppermost in our minds that . . . the developer . . . be very high in his political position. Trump is doing what, in our judgment, if anyone can do, he can do,"[13] Eichler said in court papers explaining why the company had cast a favorable eye on an untested developer. Donald Trump's political ties meant something; they were cashable chits, and in the Commodore deal, he would show just how much those connections were worth.

Trump contrived with an obscure city bureaucrat to develop the plan: Trump could buy the hotel from Penn Central, donate it to the city, and then lease it back for ninety-nine years, thus avoiding property taxes. The deal would become more favorable still: it would be run through a New York State agency, the Urban Development Corporation, or UDC, that had wide powers to condemn land and seize properties, powers that could be used to give Trump leverage removing tenants from the Commodore.[14]

Trump had a case to make: that a troubled city needed development, that he was willing to take a risk, and that his risk-taking would draw more economic activity to the city. But the deal he worked out was riven with fraud, self-dealing, and outright lies.

To announce the hotel deal, city officials billed it, falsely, as a new state program that was designed to stimulate the ailing city economy, not a gesture to aid one particular development project for one particular developer. Handwritten notes on a City Hall memo revealed the deception. "Rather than announce the project, announce the program with this as the first project." There was no program, only the project.[15]

There wasn't even, really, a project. Donald Trump didn't have a commitment to the financing. He didn't actually own the option for the property, either. In his book *The Art of the Deal*, Trump boasted that he fooled people about that too: "A city official had requested that I send along a copy of my option agreement with the Penn Central," Trump wrote. "I did—but it was signed only by me, and not the railroad, because I had yet to put down my $250,000. No one even noticed that until almost two years later."[16]

This is the period when the mythmaking around Donald Trump began in earnest. In 1973, Fred Trump corralled a *New York Times* reporter to take stock of his "empire," complete with a prominent photo in front of Trump Village with Fred, wearing a tall black hat, standing next to a hatless, wind-tousled and very blond twenty-something Donald. "Donald is the smartest person I know," Fred was quoted as saying in the article. "Everything he touches turns to gold." The reporter wrote that Donald was first in his class at the Wharton School of Finance at the University of Pennsylvania.[17] Donald Trump was not first in his class in the undergraduate program, which he'd entered as a third-year transfer student. The commencement program from Wharton in 1968 does not name Donald Trump as having graduated with honors of any kind.[18] (When he ran for president, Donald

Trump went so far as to threaten lawsuits if his grades or SAT scores were ever released.[19])

A few years after the *Times* profile with his father, as he was beginning to formulate his plans to build in Manhattan, Donald Trump invited another *Times* reporter to spend a day with him, riding around in his silver Cadillac, chauffeured by an ex-cop. "He is tall, lean and blond, with dazzling white teeth, and he looks ever so much like Robert Redford," the reporter wrote of Trump. "He is 6 feet, 3 inches tall and weighs 190 pounds, and he was wearing a three-piece burgundy wool suit, matching patent-leather shoes, and a white shirt with the initials 'DJT' sewn in burgundy thread on the cuffs." He told her he was worth more than $200 million. He said, contra the truth, that the Trump Organization had 1,000 employees and properties in Washington, DC, Maryland, Virginia, Las Vegas, and California. He told her, falsely, "I'm Swedish." He did not tell her he'd been unable to get financing for the Commodore deal.[20]

No option, no financing—but Trump had convinced an array of people to commit moral compromise to get the deal done. In the "Tax Break Hotel" chapter of his Trump biography, Barrett tallies them up. There was Mayor Beame and Governor Carey, to whom the Trumps had given tens of thousands of dollars in campaign contributions. There was a state attorney who had also worked as a fundraiser for the city comptroller, to whom Trump also donated. There was Louise Sunshine, a fundraiser for Governor Carey who became a registered Trump lobbyist and oversaw the final terms of the Commodore deal. These included a provision that allowed Trump to define his "profit"—a portion of which was supposed to go to the city—in a way that allowed him to overstate expenses and understate revenues.[21]

And then there was Deputy Mayor Stanley Friedman, who also had a high-level political post in the Bronx County Democratic Party, an organization controlled by Trump's lawyer: Roy Cohn. As deputy mayor, Friedman allowed Cohn to siphon off cash from city parking lot contracts. For his part, Cohn held out the promise of a job for

Friedman. Working for the city, Friedman pushed through the Commodore deal on terms almost entirely favorable to Trump.

"Cohn's exploitation of Friedman to secure the Commodore booty was an unforgettable lesson for Donald, exposing him to the full reach of his mentor's influence and introducing him to the netherworld of sordid quid pro quos that Cohn ruled," Barrett wrote. "This almost ritualistic initiation not only inducted Donald into the circle of sleaze that engulfed Cohn, the bountiful success of it transferred the predatory values and habits Cohn embodied to his yearning understudy."[22]

—

In the summer of 1976, the bicentennial of the Declaration of Independence, a group of fashion models from Montreal came to New York City to promote that summer's Olympics, which Montreal was hosting. As Ivana Trump told it in her book *Raising Trump,* she was wearing a "red minidress with three-quarter sleeves and high heels. My blond hair was long and straight, swinging all the way down to my waist." She was a beautiful young woman, with seven other beautiful women, but they could not get a table—until "a tall, smiling, blue-eyed, handsome blond man," offered to intervene.[23] He paid for dinner, sent her one hundred red roses the next day. He drove her in his Cadillac, took her to Le Club. He traveled to see her in Montreal; she came to New York. On one early trip, she met the whole Trump family, at Tavern on the Green: Fred Trump, Mary, and the four other children. Fred ordered steak. Mary ordered steak. The five Trump children ordered steak. It was eleven in the morning. Ivana ordered filet of sole. Fred interjected with the waiter, "She'll have the steak." After Ivana insisted on the sole, there were three minutes of silence at the table.[24]

Still, Donald and Ivana set a wedding date: April 7, 1977. Roy Cohn, representing Donald, wrote the prenuptial agreement, and an associate of his served as Ivana's lawyer. Ivana was promised just $20,000 a year if their marriage broke up immediately, and $45,000 if she made it to thirteen years, which she did.[25] Donald asked that the agreement include an additional lump-sum bonus payment for each potential child. He wanted five, Barrett quoted him telling a friend, so "I know that one will be guaranteed to turn out like me."[26] Ivana rejected the bonuses.

Donald and Ivana were married in the late afternoon at the Marble Collegiate Church by the Reverend Norman Vincent Peale, the author of *The Power of Positive Thinking.* It was an event studded with business associates and powerful officials: Abe Beame, Bunny and Sandy Lindenbaum, Roy Cohn. But in the spring of 1977, the Commodore deal still wasn't complete.

Three months later, in July 1977, a three-day blackout led to widespread looting all over the city and nearly 4,000 arrests. In August, there were bombings inside New York office buildings by the FALN, a Puerto Rican separatist group. The Son of Sam, a serial killer, was terrorizing New York, shooting six people dead and wounding seven others. Mayor Beame's grip on the unruly city was loosening.

"Beame Finishes Third" was the *New York Times* headline on September 9, 1977, in the wake of a seven-way Democratic primary for mayor.[27] Beame would soon depart City Hall, leaving fewer than four months to wrap up the Commodore deal. Trump, Cohn, and Friedman began to sprint. The plan still needed approvals from nine city and state entities. One of the last was a permit for a "Garden Room" for the new Commodore, a restaurant overhanging Forty-Second Street, a flashy new attraction for a city that might be putting its worst days behind. On December 29, 1977, the last working day of the Beame administration, Stanley Friedman, at Cohn's direction, got the final approval for a twenty-five-year consent for the restaurant. In return, Donald Trump's restaurant would pay the city $24,000 per year, less than what the Garden Room could gross in a day.[28] Within days, Friedman went to work for Cohn's law firm. (Friedman was later convicted by an ambitious US attorney, Rudy Giuliani, on unrelated charges of mail fraud, conspiracy, and racketeering, and sentenced to twelve years in prison.)

In May 1978, the Commodore deal finally closed. But Donald Trump alone could not secure the financing. That could only be had with the guarantee of Fred C. Trump, whose Trump Village Construction Corporation also loaned Donald a million dollars during the construction.

The next month, on a sunny and blue-skied June day, Governor Carey called a press conference with Trump to celebrate the hotel's ceremonial groundbreaking. "When he looked into cameras it was as if he was eyeing himself in a mirror, admiring the triumph he'd become, and, at the same time, laughing haughtily at the world," Barrett wrote. "He had seen the amoral hunger of more men during this breakthrough deal than most people saw in a lifetime."[29] As Barrett put it, "the debut project of this bold entrepreneur, was, in truth, a breakthrough example of the new state capitalism—public risk for private profit."[30]

By 2018, city records show, the hotel had amassed a $393,245,999.55 "tax expenditure." That is, taxpayer money the city had allowed Trump and his partners to keep, an unusually generous government gift by any standards, and the longest ever granted by New York City.[31]

A year after his blue-skied Commodore groundbreaking, a cloud blew in. Federal prosecutors were examining Trump's early dealings with Penn Central, and whether, at one point in the bankruptcy negotiations, Trump had improperly offered a lawyer for the company's shareholders' lucrative legal work to secure his support for Trump's bid for the property.[32] By 1979, the US attorney for the Eastern District was investigating the transaction and sought to question Donald. Rather than conduct the interview in his office on Fifth Avenue, Trump met the investigator in his father's bare-bones office on Avenue Z, accompanied by Ivana and his toddler son, Don Jr. No charges were filed.

That November, Ronald Reagan, who'd risen to national prominence while attacking "welfare queens," came to midtown Manhattan, to the New York Hilton, to announce his candidacy for president.[33] Some fourteen hundred diners, at five hundred dollars a head, were invited to hear Reagan say of the federal government at the Hilton that night:

"It has overspent, overestimated, and over-regulated." It's unclear whether Donald Trump attended the event, though one source of dubious veracity has placed him there: Roger Stone.[34]

By 1979 Stone had already built the résumé of a dirty trickster. During the Nixon administration, at age nineteen, Stone—with his then-brown hair, Roman nose, and unsettlingly penetrating gaze—had joined the Committee for the Re-Election of the President, or CREEP. Stone's first dirty trick for the Nixon campaign had been to travel to New Hampshire to make a donation to Nixon's primary opponent in the name of the "Young Socialist Alliance."[35]

After Nixon resigned, Stone was a founder of the National Conservative Political Action Committee, or NCPAC. At a time when reformers in Washington had cracked down on the lax campaign-finance rules that contributed to Watergate, NCPAC pioneered a loophole that allowed unlimited contributions to pay for big-money attack ads that trafficked in "the half-truth, the innuendo, the distortion," as Democratic Party activist Pamela Harriman described it in a press conference as NCPAC was emerging as a political force.[36]

In 1980, Stone was twenty-eight, and working as Reagan's director for New York, New Jersey, and Connecticut. For the duration of the campaign, Stone lived in an apartment in Roy Cohn's town house.[37] "Roy was a Democrat, but he was an anti-Communist and a master of public relations, and he wanted to help me with Reagan," Stone told the *New Yorker* in 2008.[38] Stone, like Trump, learned from Cohn. No maneuver was too low, no offense was too offensive, no bonfire too consuming if it helped your side win. In a 1982 interview on the WNYC radio show *Insight*, Roy Cohn was asked who was the "smartest political sage" he'd ever met. Cohn didn't hestitate. He named his law partner, the former Bronx boss and Trump fixer Stanley Friedman. Also, President Lyndon Johnson, though he was "full of baloney." Also on the list was "a young guy named Roger Stone who isn't 30 years old yet who managed the Northeast Reagan campaign."[39]

Reagan carried forty-four states in 1980. With NCPAC's help, Republicans not only seized the Senate, they also sank many of the

Democratic Party's rising stars. Weeks after his inauguration, on February 18, 1981, speaking to a joint session of congress, Reagan called for aggressive tax cuts and the defunding of social safety nets, research, and education.[40] Democrats, who still held a fifty-three seat margin in the House, nevertheless agreed to a "compromise" bill that had a 25 percent individual tax cut, a cap on income taxes at 50 percent (down from 70) and a capital gains top rate down from 28 to 20 percent.

Despite bipartisan support, the new law drew criticism. *New York Times* White House correspondent Steven R. Weisman warned that "broad social consequences—intended and unintended—flow from changes in the tax system." More than a third of the benefits were expected to go to less than 6 percent of the population. "The underlying philosophy seems to be a throwback to the nineteenth century view that any attempts to tamper with the free accumulation of wealth are likely to be counterproductive," Weisman wrote.[41]

Even Weisman's prescient analysis missed another twist: the tax bill of 1981 gradually raised the amount that an estate could exempt from tax from $175,000 to $600,000. The estate tax had been, for decades, a way to balance America's egalitarian ideals with its entrepreneurial notions. Success was valued, but so was a communitarian spirit. You could pass on your wealth to your children, but you had to give some of it back to society. In 1981, the balance began to shift. It would become easier and easier to transfer wealth, unfettered, from generation to generation.

The Senate passed the bill 89–11. The Democrat-controlled House passed it, 238–195.[42] Reagan signed the bill on August 13, 1981, while vacationing in California. Most of the questions at the news conference following the signing weren't about taxes. They were about the Professional Air Traffic Controllers Organization, or PATCO, whose members Reagan had just fired for what he called an "illegal strike."

Like the tax bill, the PATCO strike had lasting effects. "More than any other labor dispute of the past three decades," historian Joseph McMartin wrote, the dispute "undermined the bargaining power of American workers and their labor unions. It also polarized our politics in ways that prevent us from addressing the root of our economic troubles: the continuing stagnation of incomes despite rising corporate profits and worker productivity."[43] From the New Deal until the 1980s, income had risen along with union membership, with 70 percent of the rise in income going to the poorest 90 percent of workers.[44] Since PATCO, unionization rates have halved.[45]

Five years later, after another landslide victory, Reagan pushed through a second tax cut. The Tax Reform Act of 1986 cut the top marginal rate for individual taxes to 28 percent, corporate tax rates to 34 percent, and reduced the number of income brackets to two. At the outset of the decade, a rich person could pay over two-thirds of her top income in taxes. By decade's end, that person would never pay more than a third.

In 1986, in the latter part of his presidency, Reagan held a news conference in Chicago to announce aid to farmers. "I think you all know that I've always felt the nine most terrifying words in the English language are 'I'm from the government and I'm here to help,'"[46] Reagan told the assembled journalists. In the decades that followed, the speech would become an iconic conservative rallying cry, and a new idea took hold: government was an instrument of harm.

If you were the victim of centuries of discrimination, or were trying to knit together a fraying social compact, or relied on government assistance or mass transit or public education, the message was clear: Drop Dead.

If you were from a well-to-do family, like the Trumps, this party was for you.

5

THE BUSINESS OF DONALD TRUMP

In the early 1980s, when Donald Trump began to put together the deal for the building that would become Trump Tower, New York City was still limping its way out of the fiscal crisis. But the long construction drought into which Donald Trump had pitched his plans to renovate the Commodore Hotel was over. Developers, who view the city's timeline in decades, not individual years, were starting to build again. AT&T, IBM, Citibank—all were putting up large, new midtown towers.

Encouraged by his success with the Commodore, Trump wanted to build the tallest residential tower in the city, at the chicest address he could find. In real estate terms, the "Tiffany location" is used to mean a city's best, most lucrative site, in whatever city it's in. In Manhattan, Trump coveted the actual location of Tiffany & Co., on Fifth Avenue, right below Central Park.

The land belonged to the Equitable Life Insurance Company. Bonwit Teller, the luxury department store specializing in high-end women's clothing, held the lease. Like many urban department stores in the 1970s, Bonwit's faced stiff competition from suburban malls. Trump convinced Bonwit Teller to sell their lease for $25 million. But the building wasn't nearly tall enough for Donald Trump.

In New York, floor space is value. Because Manhattan is an island, developers need to push upward to increase their properties' worth. Value is based on floor area ratio, which naturally increases as a building stacks more floors above the same piece of land. Typically, there are zoning limits, but they can be surpassed by buying up the so-called "air rights" of nearby buildings that aren't as tall as the law allows. This is what Trump wanted to do, and to do it, he needed the approval of the New York City Board of Estimate, a body that included the mayor, the comptroller, and the five borough presidents.

Trump had already contributed tens of thousands of dollars to these people, and his lawyer, Roy Cohn, had given more.[1] The Board of Estimate approved the plans. Once again, Trump had used his ties to convince the city's political leaders to put their thumbs on the scale. By the onset of the Reagan era, Trump had amassed the rights to build the tallest residential tower in the city at one of the most valuable intersections in the world. The apartments—"apahtments," he said in those days, his Queens accent more pronounced—were to be among the most expensive in the city.[2]

To begin work, Trump hired a demolition team to tear down the old building. The contractor, who had little demolition experience, bid a bargain-basement price. To make his bid profitable, the contractor hired undocumented Polish workers, off the books, for $4 an hour. Sometimes they weren't paid at all. They worked twelve-hour shifts, seven days a week, with neither overtime pay nor asbestos protection.[3] Trump himself, the workers later testified, visited the job site, and knew about the illegal workers.[4] The contractor eventually faced repercussions, and Trump paid a $1.375-million settlement.

Cheap labor wasn't enough. Trump wanted a tax abatement, too. In 1971, New York State had passed a law designed to encourage developers to build affordable housing in places where they wouldn't otherwise build, like the South Bronx. The law offered developers tax breaks to help make such properties profitable, even in low-rent neighborhoods. Fifth Avenue and Fifty-Sixth Street wasn't a marginal neighborhood, but Donald Trump wanted the tax abatement anyway. He argued the future Trump Tower should receive a $25-million subsidy from the taxpayers.

In March 1981, Trump and Louise Sunshine, the former Democratic Party fundraiser and Trump lobbyist who was by then a senior Trump Organization executive, attended a breakfast with Manhattan borough president Andrew Stein, another well-coiffed son of a wealthy New Yorker and a friend of Roy Cohn. Stein's family connections, like Trump's, had launched his career: for him, Democratic politics. Stein had asked the city housing commissioner, Tony Gliedman, an appointee of Mayor Ed Koch, to attend the breakfast. Gleidman was in his thirties, a graduate of Amherst College, a loyal Democrat. Unlike most city commissioners, Gliedman lived in Ditmas Park, Brooklyn, then an unfancy neighborhood of freestanding Victorian homes. Gliedman kept a listed telephone number. His children played Little League in Prospect Park.

By contrast, Trump and Stein were members of what Mayor Ed Koch called in his book *Mayor*, "The Old School Tie Network."[5] They didn't do business in cramped, overheated, fluorescent-lighted city offices. They did it over drinks, or breakfast, in Park Avenue apartments, like Andy Stein's.

Sunshine and Trump and Stein and Gliedman met to discuss the use of 421a tax abatements, so named for the portion of the 1971 state law that created the breaks. Like most laws of this nature, 421a required developers to show that the existing building was "functionally obsolete" or "underutilized," terms that developers could massage to their favor. "I'd probably succeed with Trump Tower even if I didn't get a tax exemption," Trump acknowledged in *The Art of the Deal*.[6] Nevertheless, he asked Gliedman to approve 421a status for Trump Tower. Gliedman listened, but made no promises. Back in his office in Lower Manhattan, Gliedman asked two associates, both women, if they thought the Bonwit Teller site was underutilized. There was laughter all around.

Mayor Ed Koch, who had been generous with developers in general, drew the line at affordable housing tax abatements for Trump Tower. Gliedman denied Trump's application. At which point, Trump phoned Gliedman, called him "dishonest" and said "Tony, I don't know whether it's still possible for you to change your decision or not, but I want you to know that I am a very rich and powerful person in this town, and there is a reason I got that way. I will never forget what you did." Gliedman memorialized the call in a memo to Koch.[7]

A year later, Gliedman got another phone call. It came to his home in Ditmas Park from a man named "Vinnie," at seven in the morning. Though Gliedman's phone was listed, not many people thought a city commissioner would have his name in the phone book, or would live in Brooklyn. His wife handed him the phone. "Uh-huh," Gliedman said. "OK." Then he left for work.

The contents of that call weren't publicly reported until more than thirty-six years later, in 2017. According to FBI records first obtained by Jason Leopold of *BuzzFeed News*, Gliedman "received a telephone call at home at approximately 7:00 am on 4/20/82 threatening his life over a tax abatement issue concerning DONALD TRUMP. The caller . . . became very abusive and profane regarding GLIEDMAN's inability to approve Mr. TRUMP's request for a tax abatement."[8]

Gliedman did not immediately tell his wife. But that afternoon he called her at work, and told her he was coming to pick her up, and that they would be under twenty-four-hour police protection. A team of police officers, a couple, shadowed them days and nights, in their living room for family meals and at the park for Little League. A police cruiser parked on their blocks for months.

The day after Gliedman got his call, someone else called the FBI: "DONALD TRUMP of the Trump Organization." He delivered his own message, conveying that he had "received a telephone call from a [redacted] (LNU) who indicated that he [redacted] was going to 'kill' Commissioner GLIEDMAN." The caller "advised TRUMP that [redacted] had been 'shafted' by GLIEDMAN and, for that reason, was going to retaliate." Trump reported he heard again the next day from the caller "who indicated that he was going to 'kill' TRUMP if Mr. TRUMP told the authorities anything concerning their prior conversation." Trump added that his dealings with Gliedman "are strictly business and that he harbors no ill feelings towards Gliedman."[9]

The NYPD investigated, but closed the case with no action.

Trump did attack Gliedman—through the courts. Trump sued the city, claiming he had been unfairly denied the tax abatement. He also sued Gliedman, personally. Trump called the city's decision "a purely political act," suggesting Mayor Koch had denied the tax abatements in an election year to prove he wasn't soft on developers. It was "the most discriminatory thing I've seen in my life."[10]

Trump won in the lower court. The city appealed, and an appellate court overturned that decision, ratifying Gliedman's "rational basis" in denying the tax break. "Trump Tower's enormous bulk (760,000 square feet) was achieved by means of multiple zoning variances," the appeals court wrote, "including the transfer of air rights and the use of a special Fifth Avenue District (C5–3) zoning bonus given solely for the continued high-quality retail use of Fifth Avenue. This has nothing to do with encouraging residential housing by means of a tax exemption."[11] Indeed, the court ruled, if Trump got the tax give-back, the argument could be made that every lot in Manhattan would be eligible for one, since it could always be argued that a larger or taller building would better utilize the site, even at what the court, quoting Trump, called "the best [site] in the world."

Trump appealed, again.

"My lawyer, Roy Cohn, did a brilliant job," Trump wrote in *The Art of the Deal*, "arguing before seven justices without so much as a note."[12] At one point in the litigation, Cohn showed up for a meeting with a city lawyer in a white T-shirt, purple suit, and loafers with no socks.[13]

Ultimately, the state's highest court ruled for Trump.[14] The law might have been intended to create an incentive to build housing in high-poverty neighborhoods. But the court said the law had been inartfully written, that legislators had drawn it so broadly that even construction at Fifth Avenue and Fifty-Sixth Street was eligible. The decision was unanimous.

"By this time," Trump said, "Trump Tower was an unqualified success."[15]

The Trump Organization was so confident of its new building that it had already asked President Ronald Reagan to send a presidential telegram for the Trump Tower opening ceremony, in a letter claiming, "The Trump family have been long time supporters of the President."[16] The White House Counsel's Office declined, and an official noted on Trump's request that the White House couldn't endorse a commercial project.

Two years later, his personal lawsuit against Gliedman still going, Trump invited Gliedman to breakfast at the 21 Club. Gliedman, still a commissioner, refused, and the two had lunch at a modest restaurant in Little Italy, in Lower Manhattan. Gliedman paid. In those days, Trump kept appearing on television and on the covers of magazines, all of them touting how rich and appealing he was. Trump said he had exciting projects for Gliedman to work on, including renovating the city-owned skating rink in Central Park. He promised to drop his lawsuit. Gleidman, struggling with his weight, his high forehead betraying the combover that was to come, was making $82,000 as a city commissioner in a downtown office. "At this point in my career, the offer of a very exciting position as Executive Vice President of the Trump Organization is a challenge and one which will allow me the opportunity to continue in my chosen profession, housing and real estate," Gliedman told Mayor Koch in his resignation letter.[17]

Gliedman worked for Trump for about five years, managing the speedy renovation of Wollman rink in Central Park, which Trump used for years as an example of the superiority of the private sector. In public, the Trump-Gliedman relationship seemed mutually beneficial. "Tony has a tremendous sense and a feel for the politics of what's going on," Trump told the *Washington Post*.[18] In private, Trump heaped abuse on Gliedman, who lost 120 pounds while he worked there. After Gliedman left the company, Trump, incensed at what he saw as Gliedman's disloyalty, refused to speak to him, or his family. Gliedman suffered a debilitating stroke a few years later. He died in 2002, at age fifty-nine, of heart failure.

From the moment Trump Tower opened in 1983, it symbolized the excess that defined the decade. Inside the building, the pinkish marble surfaces, the golden escalators, the sixty-foot waterfall—all were indicia of aspirational wealth. Trump's own penthouse triplex—inspired by the apartment of Saudi billionaire Adnan Khashoggi, who lived nearby—had fifty-three rooms, an eighty-foot living room, and massive columns meant to look like classical relics, but newly carved because actual antiquities looked too old.[19]

Trump had promised to donate the beaux-art friezes on the old Bonwit Teller building to the Metropolitan Museum, but instead pulverized them so he could apply for his tax abatements without delay. The new tower's exterior black and gold surfaces, its terraced balconies, its three-foot tall lettering proclaiming the building's provenance; all projected wealth and gaudy newness.

The business structure was new, too. Trump Tower was a condominium building in a city of cooperative apartments, which had been organized around the turn of the last century to apportion ownership of New York's newly rising apartment buildings. In a co-op building, units are sold as shares in a corporation, and are thus subject to a great deal of oversight. By contrast, condos, which were only allowed as a form of home ownership in the United States beginning in the 1960s, require far less scrutiny. In Trump Tower, three-quarters of the initial condo buyers were wealthy nonresidents and out-of-town corporations.[20]

Trump Tower was a pioneer of a new form of structural wealth in New York. Limited liability companies, also known as LLCs, were only invented in the late 1970s, and were then just emerging as a favored form of real estate ownership for the wealthy.[21] An LLC, often a shell company with no business purpose, could easily hide its true owner or owners, and the business partnerships they represented. The use of LLCs made it easier for foreign and questionable money to find its way into New York real estate. For Trump—whose business relied on favors and secrets—this was the perfect business model.

Some of the earliest owners of Trump Tower apartments were associates of criminals or soon-to-be criminals. There was Verina Hixon, the friend of John Cody, the Teamsters boss and Roy Cohn friend who, when work began on Trump Tower, had already been arrested eight times and convicted thrice. (Hixon was not accused of wrongdoing.) Before Trump Tower was completed, Cody was convicted of racketeering charges for which he was sentenced to five years in prison.[22] But Cody made sure Donald Trump had a continuous supply of concrete even during the citywide concrete worker walkout in the summer of 1982. Hixon, an Austrian divorcée with no obvious source of income, was allowed to design her own apartment right below Trump's, complete with a (rare) swimming pool. At one point, Trump arranged for her to obtain a mortgage to cover a $3-million financing shortfall.[23]

Then there was David Bogatin, flush with money from a gas-tax scam run by the Brighton Beach Russian mob, where they siphoned off cash that was supposed to go to gasoline taxes and pocketed it themselves. Bogatin stored some of his money in the form of five apartments in Trump Tower. Donald Trump himself attended the closing.[24] Bogatin later received a sentence of up to eight years for his role in the scam, but not before turning over his mortgages to a Genovese crime family associate and fleeing to Poland, as detailed in Robert Friedman's book *Red Mafiya*.[25]

There was Joey Weichselbaum, who paid rent to Donald Trump for an apartment partially in cash, partially in in-kind helicopter services. Weischelbaum was charged and pleaded guilty to drug trafficking charges in Ohio. Donald wrote a rare letter asking for leniency. "Mr. Weichselbaum has been conscientious, forthright and diligent in his business dealings with us," Trump wrote in a letter to Weischelbaum's lawyer to be filed with the court.[26] Weichselbaum received three years in prison, of which he served about half. Upon release, he moved to apartments 49A and B in Trump Tower, purchased by his girlfriend for $2.35 million in cash.[27]

By 1983, Roy Cohn had played an essential role for Trump in his two signature deals, the Commodore and Trump Tower. That year, the State of Israel Bonds organization feted Cohn at the Commodore—now the Grand Hyatt—for his "deeply-rooted commitment of purpose on behalf of his fellow man," according to the dinner program. Senator Alfonse D'Amato was there, and Rupert Murdoch, and Alan Greenberg, the chairman of Bear Stearns, and Donald Trump. Within a year, Cohn was dying of AIDS, which he told everyone was liver cancer. As Cohn got sicker, Trump began to withdraw his business. When Cohn wanted a room for a former boyfriend, also dying, at Trump's Barbizon Plaza Hotel, Trump assented, but then Trump started to send him bills. "Donald pisses ice water," Cohn said. At Cohn's memorial service, Trump stood in the back, not asked to speak.[28]

6

THE GAMBLE

On a June night in 1990, bunches of grey fog clung[1] to the faux-minarets of the Trump Taj Mahal casino, Donald's third, and biggest, casino, then the tallest tower in Atlantic City. The Taj featured seventy onion-shaped domes, nine stone elephants, staff that wore ostrich feathers, and a 135,000-square-foot betting floor.[2] The casino had opened in April in a sea of chaos: the Taj's managers didn't know how much cash they had on hand, and some of the slot machines had to be shut down because they weren't working. Trump went on the *Larry King Show* to claim that these slot machines "blew apart" from demand.[3]

Despite the troubles, or perhaps because of them, Trump arrived that June night for a forty-fourth birthday party to promote his new casino. Police officials in Atlantic City had watched anxiously as Donald Trump's helicopter landed in the fog, but there were no problems. At the ceremony, a huge model of the Trump Shuttle—Trump's newly acquired airline—rolled onto the stage, past other large models of Trump's mini-empire of Atlantic City casinos: the Trump Taj Mahal, the Trump Castle, the Trump Plaza. The door of the "Trump Shuttle" opened and out stepped Robin Leach, host of the 1980s hit television show *Lifestyles of the Rich and Famous*, and the borscht-belt comedian Freddie Roman. "Don't count him out," Leach said, of Trump. "He's the very best there is. Made a career out of doing what people said couldn't be done." Comedian Joe Piscopo took the stage, singing "Happy Birthday" to Trump, Frank-Sinatra style. There was a President George H. W. Bush impersonator, a marimba line, and chorus-line dancers in skin-tight outfits singing about Donald Trump's money. Confetti dropped from the ceiling ducts. The middle-class crowd, lots of older men with younger women, clapped wildly. There was a video clip about Trump, which ended with an image of him holding a check. Then the real Donald Trump appeared on the dais, flashing a victory signal, accompanied by two women in gold lamé dresses.

The Trump Organization had invited the entertainment press to witness all of this, issuing large yellow plastic-encased press credentials. But one reporter—a tall man with a mustache and a long forehead and shaggy brown hair—was not allowed in: the *Village Voice*'s Wayne Barrett. Dogged and irascible, Barrett had been covering Trump for over a decade by this time. Sometimes, Barrett spoke to students wearing a trench coat and a fedora, calling himself "the people's detective." He dug up documents, worked sources, described the levers of power that Trump had pulled to make his deals. While Barrett was investigating the Commodore's forty-year tax abatement, a state employee tipped off Trump that Barrett was at the headquarters of the state agency, examining documents. Trump called Barrett, and offered an interview. During their conversations, Trump, who had done some investigating of his own, learned Barrett lived in a shabby apartment in Brownsville, Brooklyn. "Wayne," Trump told him, "You don't have to live in Brownsville. I have plenty of apartments." When Barrett's questions got harder, Trump told him about a reporter he'd ruined, by suing him.[4]

By 1990, a decade's worth of Trump reporting behind him, Barrett was barred from the Taj Mahal birthday party event. A hotel executive read from a card that said, "Wayne Barrett is banned for life." Lurking at the door, Barrett saw Fred Trump and other family members depart. When Donald left for the after-party, Barrett approached, but Trump's bodyguards surrounded him and shoved him aside. Barrett was promptly detained by off-duty Atlantic City cops working as Trump security guards, his notes fished out of his pocket, his tape recorder briefly confiscated. Then Barrett was taken to a real police station, where other police officers, who also had work as part-time Trump security guards, handcuffed him to a wall in a blood-stained holding cell, and charged him with "defiant trespass."

A little over a week later, Trump's casino empire started to unravel.

New Jersey had passed a referendum in 1976 allowing for legalized gambling. Not long after, Trump began to think about building there. In New Jersey, Trump wasn't the son of Fred, the outer-borough apartment guy. Donald Trump was a flashy New York developer. His sister was first a federal prosecutor, then a judge. Her husband, John Barry, was a well-connected New Jersey lawyer. "What they saw was a very self-assured young man," a former Trump associate told Barrett, referring to the New Jersey officials who regulated gambling and real estate development. "He obviously showed he came from a family. It was like dealing with a Vanderbilt."[5] Trump represented New York, and to New Jersey, New York was always going to be an object of desire.

By contrast, Michael Checchio of the *Press of Atlantic City* described the city this way: "Since the dawn of casino gambling in Atlantic City, organized crime has been entrenched. Before the hotels and gaming halls went up, the mobsters were here. They were dabbling in real estate. They were buying bars and transferring liquor licenses. They were distributing cigarettes to vending machines throughout the Atlantic City area and setting up cleaning companies and laundries that could handle future casino contracts." The casinos are free of organized crime, Checchio wrote, but "the periphery is under invasion."[6]

This was the environment Donald Trump entered around 1980, driving down to Atlantic City, taking in a Frank Sinatra concert, strolling on the Boardwalk later that night, laying his eyes on a desirable parcel of land.[7] Around this time New Jersey regulators were signaling they were serious about barring casino operators with potential mob ties. They'd indicated that business partners, too, were subject to vetting, and at one point prevented the Hilton Hotel chain from opening a business in Atlantic City because one of the Hilton lawyers had also worked for Mafia figures in Chicago.[8] Trump had a similar liability, because his own lawyer, Roy Cohn, was working for several New York mob figures. When Trump got to Atlantic City, he made additional problematic connections.

Some of the land Donald Trump coveted belonged partly to Kenneth Shapiro and Daniel Sullivan, who journalist Timothy O'Brien described in his book *TrumpNation* as, respectively, "a street-level gangster with close ties to the Philadelphia mob" and "a Mafia associate, FBI informant, and labor negotiator."[9] Sullivan was a six-foot-five former truck driver who had been arrested on weapons and assault charges and been incarcerated for larceny.[10] Trump drew him close: according to Sullivan, Trump asked him to handle the problem with the underpaid, undocumented Polish immigrants working on Trump Tower, and to serve as a "labor consultant" for his newly renamed Grand Hyatt hotel on Forty-Second Street in Manhattan.[11]

In Atlantic City, this could have posed a problem for casino regulators. Since Trump was negotiating a lease deal with Sullivan, that made Sullivan subject to the state's licensing requirements. So, Trump pulled off a neat trick: he met with two FBI agents who knew Sullivan "to express his reservations about building a casino in Atlantic City," as described in a memo written by the agents in a form called a 302.[12] "TRUMP advised Agents that he had read in the press media and had heard from various acquaintances that Organized Crime elements were known to operate in Atlantic City." Trump, under the guise of inquiring how to fight the mob, brought up his Mafia associate with the FBI. Then he told the casino regulators in New Jersey that Sullivan had introduced him to the FBI, so everything must be okay.

The agents were taken aback at this. "Writer and Case Agent have repeatedly told TRUMP that they were not references for source and cannot speak for source's business dealings. The TRUMPs have advised writer and Case Agent that source is involved as a labor consultant to their firm. They are aware that this is a very rough business and that source knows people some of whom may be unsavory by the simple nature of the business."

But Trump's trick worked. The New Jersey Division of Gaming Enforcement issued a report laying out a trail of troubling information about Sullivan, including a meeting with a labor lawyer in 1966, after which the lawyer disappeared "and neither he nor his body were ever located." But the DGE relied on Trump's representations that "he had been in contact with a law enforcement agency in New York regarding Sullivan and that he had obtained no derogatory information." It concluded: "During the course the Division's investigation, it has ascertained that the matters related herein do not impact in a negative manner upon the credentials of Trump."[13]

For a long time, Trump continued to nurture his relationship with both Sullivan, the "Mafia informant," and Walt Stowe, one of the FBI agents who'd handled Sullivan's case. Stowe later told the *Washington Post* that Trump had invited him to play golf and took him to lunch at the 21 Club in his chauffeur-driven limousine. Trump even raised the idea of hiring Stowe. "Here I am, like I said, I'm 31 years old or so, and I can see people looking all around to see who is this guy having lunch with Donald," Stowe said. Being associated with Trump could help an FBI agent on the way up. He "was a guy who knew people," Stowe said.[14]

For the next decade, and even after his crash, Donald Trump continued to operate with regulatory favor, continued to build connections to local officials, both insignificant and important. In October 1980, in a rendezvous arranged by lobbyist Louise Sunshine, Trump met with New Jersey Governor Brendan Byrne, who sat atop all the New Jersey regulatory structures. Byrne told Wayne Barrett he was insulated from the regulatory process, and viewed the visit as "a courtesy call." Afterwards, Sunshine went shopping with Byrne for a present for his wife's birthday.[15]

Trump hired the local fixers, too, the lawyers who had grown up across the street from the city commissioners who would be making key decisions about his casinos, like decorated veteran Patrick "Piano Wire" McGahn, so nicknamed because he was reputed to have used a piano wire as a weapon against his enemies in hand-to-hand combat in the Korean War.[16] McGahn, the son of an Atlantic City saloonkeeper, was a South Jersey Democratic Party leader with an outsize personality and a reputation for getting things done—for the right people. McGahn was "Paddy" to friends, and soon, to Donald Trump. At one point, when purchasing land for a Trump casino from a particularly blatant mob associate, McGahn had the parcel transferred to his secretary's name, before turning it over to Donald Trump.

Trump had another in with New Jersey politicians: Roger Stone. After the 1980 Reagan campaign, Stone had offered his political consulting services to Tom Kean, the patrician politician made famous by his advertisements, "New Jersey and you, perfect together," pronounced "puh-fect," in blue-blood New Jerseyese. Rare is the politician who doesn't burn a special candle for the consultant who helped them win their first significant political victory, just as a dying patient venerates the surgeon who saves their life. Those consultants' opinions always carry a little extra weight; their calls get returned extra fast. Roger Stone understood he could introduce business associates to politicians he'd worked for, and influence their decisions. Trump understood this, too. They struck up a relationship.

In 1980, Stone had co-founded a corporation in the state of Virginia—a lobbying firm: Black, Manafort, and Stone. Charles Black had been a long-time political strategist and advisor to Reagan's campaigns going back to 1976. Paul Manafort Jr., the son of a Connecticut builder and local politician, had transformed himself into a smooth Washington operative. As Franklin Foer wrote in the *Atlantic*: "Whereas other firms had operated in specialized niches—lobbying, consulting, public relations—Black, Manafort and Stone bundled all those services under one roof, a deceptively simple move that would eventually help transform Washington."[17] They worked for politicians during the campaign season, performing their political strategists' magic. In the off-season, they worked for business clients who paid them to call the very politicians they'd helped elect.

This was Stone's relationship with Kean: he helped him get elected, and reelected, and could call him about anything. Even if Kean were perfectly—puhfectly—upright in all of his transactions with Stone, Stone's proximity to Kean was a selling point. Especially to Donald Trump.

In 1983, Stone helped the Trump family in a different way: he and Roy Cohn both recommended to the White House that Trump's sister, Maryanne Trump Barry, be named a federal judge in New Jersey. There was then, as now, a paucity of women judges, and so for Kean, picking a young woman prosecutor was a deft political move. But Trump Barry was an assistant United States attorney in those days, a position which rarely led straight to a federal judgeship. The American Bar Association gave her a tepid rating of "qualified." She told Trump biographer Gwenda Blair: "There's no question Donald helped me get on the bench. . . . I was good, but not that good."[18]

Trump continued to charm the regulators. On one occasion some years later, as Matt Katz of WNYC has reported, Trump flew by helicopter to Trenton to take then-State Attorney General David Samson—the man ultimately in charge of casinos—out to a steak lunch. Days later, Trump sent a thank-you note to Samson that included a picture of Trump's then-girlfriend.[19] Trump showed up at every regulatory hearing, even if it was only a staff hearing, in person.[20] He took local council members to dinner.

There was something else. Legislators from New York and New Jersey would regularly hit the casinos, where they were comped with all manner of freebies.[21] But their every transaction was recorded and memorialized for regulators, and was caught by the unblinking eyes of the video cameras placed around the casinos. In an interview, one former New Jersey legislator said he was warned to be careful about activities he didn't want anyone to know about. He was told, "never do it within sixty miles of Atlantic City." The legislator further clarified, "'It' was not gambling or drinking, 'it' was sex."

By the late 1980s, Trump was a notably large political donor. He made the *New York Times* as one of a small group of $100,000 donors to the Republican Party.[22] He and his father were among the largest donors to the Manhattan district attorney, Robert Morganthau[23] (whose favored charity, the Police Athletic League, the Trumps also generously supported.)

Trump had given so much money in campaign contributions that regulators in two states had taken note. For July 1985 through September 1986, the New Jersey Division of Gaming Enforcement tallied the number at $200,000.[24] The New York State Commission on Government Integrity called Trump to testify about why he'd been so generous; about what he wanted.

"According to the Board of Elections records that the Commission has examined, you contribute quite heavily to local campaigns?" his examiner asked.

"That's correct. Yes," Trump responded.

"In fact, in 1985 alone, your political contributions exceeded $150,000, is that correct?"

Trump suggested his contributions were so large, from so many sources, that he couldn't keep track. "I really don't know, I assume that is correct, yes."

He was asked to identify, from elections records, which "enterprises are either Trump-controlled or have significant Trump interests." The list was long: "Shore Haven Apartments No. 2, Inc., Shore Haven Apartments No. 6, Inc."—also Number 3 and Number 1. There was Trump Village Construction Corp., Sussex Hall, and Garnet Hall, Inc.: a vast interlocking network of companies.

"Why," he was asked, "aren't these political contributions just made solely in your name?"

"Well," he replied, "My attorneys basically said that this was a proper way of doing it."[25]

—

As the Reagan era came to an end, Donald and Ivana Trump traveled to the USSR to explore the idea of partnering with the Soviet tourist agency, Intourist, to build and manage a hotel in Moscow. Their trip was arranged by the Soviet ambassadors to the United States and the United Nations. During what would turn out to be the final years of the USSR, Donald and Ivana stayed in the National Hotel, under twenty-four-hour surveillance by the KGB. Within months of his return, counseled by Roger Stone, Trump took out full-page ads in the *Boston Globe*, *New York Times*, and *Washington Post*, calling for the United States to stop spending money to secure Japan and the Persian Gulf.[26]

Immediately the question came up: Is he running for something? In October 1987, prime test-the-waters time, Trump flew to Portsmouth, New Hampshire, where he was enthusiastically greeted with signs that said "Trump for President." Trump did not run. George H. W. Bush did.

For New Year's of 1989, Donald Trump decided to bring both his wife and his girlfriend to Aspen, with his children, Ivanka, Don Jr., and Eric. The day before Don Jr. turned twelve, the family was lunching at the ski resort, when a leggy blue-eyed blonde walked up to Ivana and said, "I'm Marla and I love your husband. Do you?"[27] Back in New York, Donald and Ivana Trump carried out a marital dispute via the tabloids.

Then it was spring, in Atlantic City. For a decade Trump's biggest success had been working his contacts to convince regulators that they should allow him to borrow more and more money. After his first casino, the Trump Plaza, Trump added the Castle, which he picked up from the hotelier Barron Hilton, and the Taj Mahal, which he acquired after a shareholders' fight that involved the television magnate Merv Griffin. Having three competing businesses on the same strip was unsustainable, but each time Donald Trump asked to expand and borrow, the regulators said Yes. "The Casino Control Commission is like the Catholic Church: you can make all kinds of sins as long as you make confession," one Trump business associate told Wayne Barrett.[28] Some regulators that approved Trump projects were later given judgeships. But Trump's bankers were starting to look more closely at their loans.

"Donald Trump is driving 100 miles per hour toward a brick wall, and he has no brakes," a banker told then–*Wall Street Journal* reporter Neil Barsky while sitting at a poker table. "He is meeting with all the banks right now."[29] Four banks had large Trump exposures. Trump had personally guaranteed $830 million of debt, "which was reckless of him, but even more so for the banks," as Barsky later wrote. The bankers were furious with Trump. They faced losing tens if not hundreds of millions from their association with him. Trump, divorcing his wife—and trying desperately to keep his finances from her, the tabloids, and the bankers—was facing insolvency, and, worse, for Trump, ignominy.

He tried to stave it off. At one point, Barksy reported, Fred Trump sent an attorney to buy $3.5 million worth of gambling chips at one of Trump's casinos and then leave, essentially making an unregistered $3.5-million loan to his son, which enabled Donald to make a bond payment. Not long after, a Trump attorney offered Barsky tickets to a boxing match in Atlantic City. Barsky accepted them, "an act of bad judgement," he later called it. A story appeared in the *New York Post*, saying Barsky had extorted the tickets. Barsky was made to give up the Trump beat.

Not long after, Trump very nearly lost everything. On June 15, 1990, the day before Trump's birthday party at the Taj Mahal with the faux-shuttle and the scantily clad dancers, Trump's Castle casino failed to make its bond interest payments. First Fidelity Bank sent the casino a notice of default. Personal loans from Manufacturers Hanover and Citibank were also coming due, and there was no apparent way for Trump to pay them. Singularly for an Atlantic City casino, the newly opened Taj Mahal earned less than 50 percent of its revenues from slot machines. The Castle had undergone costly renovation to attract high-end gamblers that were never really a market for Atlantic City. Only the Plaza made money.[30]

There were days of tense negotiations. Some bankers simply wanted to pull the plug, to offer Trump no further loans and no restructuring deals and end their business relationship. A banker named Wilbur Ross argued otherwise. He convinced the other bankers that "Trump" was too big to fail, and that Trump should continue operating his properties, with the Trump name.

"We believe that part of the assets of the casino, albeit one that we don't have a mortgage on, is Donald Trump," Ross told reporters at the time.[31] Trump had to give up some assets—the airline he'd acquired, the yacht he'd bought from Adnan Khashoggi—and he had to live on a $450,000-a-month "budget," but the bankers let him keep going, as Trump.

From then on, however, mainstream American banks all but ceased doing new business with Trump. He would have to look elsewhere for money: abroad.

In 1989, right before Donald Trump's Atlantic City crash, real estate financial analyst Abe Wallach went on PBS's *MacNeil-Lehrer News-Hour* to criticize Donald Trump. With short, reddish brown, curly hair, round gold banker's glasses, a charcoal suit and yellow paisley tie, Wallach looked the part of sober financial analyst, the kind of guy who scrutinizes rows of numbers and sees buildings. Wallach couldn't stand the glitz and the glamour and the stretch limos. He couldn't understand how banks had loaned Trump huge sums for a West Side property when there was no demand for residential or office space. Or how Trump owed banks hundreds of millions of dollars at a time when tourists and businesses were trimming real estate expenditures. Wallach saw a braggart entangled in scores of legal disputes who had left a trail of broken promises, and he wanted the world to know it.

A week after the show, Wallach said, he opened the door at his Chelsea loft to a process server, who handed him papers for *Trump v. Wallach*, asking for $250 million in damages for defamation. Wallach enlisted his firm's lawyer (also, as it turned out, Trump's lawyer) to defend the case. Not long after, Trump invited Wallach to his offices, where the analyst stepped off the elevator. "I did get taken in by the beauty of the views from the 26th floor out to Central Park," Wallach later said in an interview in his Southampton home.[32] There were the magazine covers and the nonstop phone calls coming into Donald's office. There was the forceful personality, turned solely, fleetingly, on him. Donald offered him a job. Despite his distaste, there was a sense of beckoning possibility. Anything could happen if he went to work for Donald Trump. Wallach said Yes. "Donald was a name to be reckoned with, even if he was having hard times." And it was exciting. Trump would call up Wallach and invite him and his boyfriend for last-minute helicopter rides and a night in Atlantic City, sometimes with Marla Maples.

Wallach became Trump's executive vice president for acquisitions and finance. As it soon became clear, Wallach was not going to find financing for Donald Trump among US banks. Trump had burned them too badly.

So, Wallach went in search of foreign money. As Wallach told the story, he was turning the pages of a newspaper one day when he read that sovereignty of Hong Kong was going to revert to mainland China. He figured some Hong Kong financiers would be in a rush to export their money, so he asked Donald for his Rolodexes, the 1980s-style rotating spindles that contained lists of contacts, each written out on a three-inch card. The basic unit was about six inches in diameter. Donald Trump had two of them, each about two feet high. Wallach was only allowed to look at them one at a time.

Wallach found some names, people with whom Donald had discussed starting a casino in Macau. Wallach made calls, flew to Hong Kong, and convinced investors to finance a proposed Trump project on the Upper West Side, which Donald was about to lose for lack of financing. While Wallach was in Hong Kong, he learned that Trump had simultaneously signed a deal on a napkin with a broker to pay her $10 million to introduce him to the very people Wallach was meeting with. "And I said, 'Donald why would you do this?'" Wallach said. "You know he doesn't really give you an answer for anything. But that was the nature of what went on." The project did get financing, with both the US broker and Wallach claiming credit.

—

During the decade he was with Trump, Wallach found financing in many unusual places. After Wallach's intervention, an elderly German man who, Wallach said, was afraid the Russians were going to invade and come for his money, extended Trump a 250-year lease for 40 Wall Street. Wallach obtained financing from a South Korean conglomerate for Trump World Tower, across from the United Nations. In a meeting in South Korea, the idea was casually raised that the financiers could name a building they were working on the Trump Tower Seoul. The bankers' agreed, launching Trump's foreign licensing business.

As with Gleidman and his weight issues, Trump had something he could use to manipulate Wallach: Wallach was gay, and also, he was a convicted shoplifter. Trump began to push Wallach to cross lines on his behalf. Wallach used a secret side room off the Astor Suite at the Plaza Hotel to listen in on Saudi-Chinese negotiations over the fate of the Plaza. Once, seated next to a business adversary on an airplane, Wallach put a tranquilizer in the man's drink so he could secretly rifle through his briefcase to understand his negotiating tactics.

Despite these techniques, the tacit embargo on loans from US banks crippled the Trump Organization. It scaled back and shrunk its staff. Two-foot-high Rolodexes or no, Trump's active list of important contacts had ebbed to a few dozen. Trump became practiced at not paying full fees to people who did work for him.

During this period Wallach bought a new home in Westchester, and Donald offered to renovate the bathroom for free. "So after maybe a month of hassling me about the bathroom I finally said 'Okay. Do it. Do it.' And it wasn't just redoing a bathroom. He brought his people up from Mar-a-Lago and they put in walls of granite. Not tiles of granite but slabs of huge granite and after a month I had the most gorgeous bathroom I had ever been in and I didn't like the gold fixtures but, you know, I could live with it."

At the end of the year, when it came time for bonuses, Trump shifted stances. "Didn't I pay for your bathroom?" he asked. Wallach had a check at the ready, to pay for renovations. Trump tore up the check, gave him a bonus anyway.

This had become standard business practice. Everyone, Trump seemed to think, was making extra money by working with him so no one got paid full price. They owed their success to him and had to pay a tithe for it. Trump stiffed the contractor who molded the seventy minarets and domes for the Taj Mahal.[33] One lawyer who had worked for Trump said in an interview that Donald told him, after paying him thirty cents on the dollar: "You don't know how much business you get by telling people you're my lawyer." Premier New York broker Barbara Corcoran had to sue him to get her brokerage fee. There was the bill Trump sent a dying Roy Cohn for his boyfriend's accommodations. Trump tried to extract a million dollars from Louise Sunshine when she left to work with financier Tom Barrack.[34] He even tried to rewrite his own father's will in a way that would have put Fred's assets at risk to Donald's creditors. (Fred found out and had Maryanne Trump Barry put a stop to it.)[35]

It was Wallach's job to deal with people who tried to collect on their invoices. Wallach said they "would come into my office and say, 'Hey, can you get them to write me a check for the thirty thousand you know he owes me?' And I would say to these people, 'Why do you keep coming back for more? Why don't you stay away from him because you know he's not going to pay or it's going to be a struggle?'" None of them quite managed to quit Donald Trump. "Everybody wanted to be around Donald Trump," Wallach said. "I mean, even though you know he had had his financial problems, he is a very dynamic individual."

In 1996, on a gorgeous spring evening, Wayne Barrett and I were trying to cover the New York GOP's high-roller fundraising gala at the Waldorf Astoria from the eighteenth-floor elevator lobby. We were told we would be arrested if we didn't leave. We did not leave. Minutes later, a police officer stationed in the Waldorf's basement was upstairs, ready to issue pink desk appearance tickets for trespass. Before we were taken away by the police, we caught a glimpse of the blond hair and kinetic energy of Donald J. Trump.

The charges against us were dropped on a technicality.

Despite all of Donald Trump's courting and threatening of politicians, by the 1990s, regulators did begin to penalize Trump entities. In 1988, the Federal Trade Commission sued Trump for buying stock via the brokerage house Bear Stearns but keeping it in Bear Stearns' name so competitors wouldn't know what his interest was; the case was settled for $750,000.[36] In 1991, New Jersey's Casino Control Commission penalized Trump's casinos $200,000 for removing black and women dealers from the table when a high-rolling gambler patronized the Trump Plaza.[37] And the Castle had to pay $30,000 after Fred Trump was caught buying $3.5 million in chips from his son's casino, which was an unregistered loan.[38]

In 1998, the US Treasury caught up with Donald Trump, sort of. Because it's so easy to turn money into chips, and then back into cash, casinos are required to report any large transactions to authorities so they can screen for money laundering. That year the Treasury Department's Financial Crimes Enforcement Network, or FinCEN, found 106 occasions where the Trump Taj Mahal had failed to report large currency transactions to regulators. The casino settled, admitting no wrongdoing, and was assessed a civil money penalty of $477,000.[39] At the time it was the largest fine in FinCEN history.

Two years later a Republican named David Grandeau, with thick black hair and a perpetually neat look, even in casual dress, had a job nobody wanted, as head of the New York Temporary State Commission on Lobbying. The unpopularity of the job stemmed from its torpor: anyone who took it seriously would immediately become a pariah in the company town that is Albany. At first, Grandeau's job consisted largely of looking out for illegal lobbying by sitting and reading the paper all day, and listening to the radio.

In early 2000, Grandeau started to notice certain advertisements in those media. Some of them attacked the governor at the time, George Pataki, for trying to bring casino gambling to Monticello, in the Catskills. Some of them made disparaging, racist claims about the Saint Regis Mohawks, the Native American tribe trying to start the casino. One showed a picture of a hypodermic needle and portrayed the tribe as drug dealers and smugglers with connections to organized crime. The ads were signed by a group in Rome, New York, which is 150 miles from Monticello: the "New York Institute for Law and Society."[40]

"I didn't think any organization in Rome, New York, called the Institute for Law and Society, would have the necessary resources to run an ad in *The New York Times*," Grandeau said in a 2016 interview. He called up the executive director of the "Institute for Law and Society," Thomas Hunter, who turned out to be a magazine salesman. Hunter quickly folded and told Grandeau he worked for Roger Stone.

Grandeau demanded phone records, bank statements, and invoices. Those documents showed that Stone had hired Thomas Hunter to be the front man, and together they invented the group, including its fictitious 12,000-person donor list, which they described as conservative New Yorkers opposed to gambling.

Stone had hired the lawyer who incorporated the group. He wrote and handled payments for all the ads. He scripted the robocalls, the mailgrams, even the talking points that Hunter used when speaking to reporters. It eventually came out that Hunter didn't even understand some of the words that Stone put in his mouth. "Panacea" was one of them.

Grandeau summoned Stone to Albany, to be deposed under oath. He got Stone to admit that the Institute for Law and Society was a sham.

"Everything they did you completely controlled?" Grandeau asked Stone in the deposition. "Yes," Stone acknowledged.

But Stone was himself a marionette. During the deposition, Stone admitted that the Institute for Law and Society was a front group for Donald Trump.

"It didn't exist. Only reason it existed was so you could hide the actions of Trump?" Grandeau asked, in the deposition.

"Yes," Stone said.

"From the public?"

"Yes."

"And you did that?"

"Yes."

"Over and over again?"

"Yes."

Stone and Trump had concluded, correctly, that the Institute for Law and Society's conservative anti-gambling message would be muddied if people knew it was being funded by Trump. But Trump personally approved every aspect of the campaign.

They had "two sets of documents," Grandeau said. One was from Trump, the other from Stone. There was, for example, an invoice for a media buy. "On the document we got from Trump, the invoice had the amount, the date, everything, but no other writing on it. The invoice we got from Stone, was the identical invoice but it had a note on its side, clearly in Mr. Trump's handwriting. I've seen quite a bit of it, that bold, up-and-down stroke."

A copy of the ad with hypodermic needles, blaming the Mohawks for bringing drug dealing to the Catskills, also had Trump's writing on it. It said "Roger—this could be good." On another, it said: "Roger, do it—Donald." Trump signed off on the bills for the television and radio ads and the anti-Pataki ads. Stone spent tens of thousands of dollars on a private investigator to dig up dirt on the Pataki administration, which Stone shopped around to reporters. Trump signed off on that, too.

The documents show that Trump also bankrolled and controlled a lawsuit against Pataki brought by two New York State Democrats. On one of the documents, Stone explained that the two were Trump's lawyer's plaintiffs, and described the Institute for Law and Society as a "pass-thru." Trump wrote on those documents, too. He spent over a million dollars in all.

Grandeau said Stone seemed bursting to share his deviousness. "It was actually a very easy deposition to get Roger Stone to convict Roger Stone because he wanted to—in some weird way he wanted to take credit for the whole thing."

Grandeau fined Trump $250,000 for running an illegal lobbying campaign, which was then the largest fine in the history of the New York State lobbying commission. He fined Stone $100,000.

The next year, Trump offered Grandeau a job, which the regulator did not take.

In 1997, Trump was furious with rival casino owner Steve Wynn, who wanted to build a tunnel from the expressway to his own proposed casino, bypassing Trump's. The tunnel was supported by a New Jersey state senator and power broker, William Gormley. As a casino owner, Trump wasn't allowed to donate to New Jersey legislative races. But according to the *Press of Atlantic City*, Roger Stone ran a candidate against Gormley, and much of the money for it came from lobbyists, law firms, and consultants who had worked for Trump.[41] Gormley won anyway. Wynn got his tunnel.

Two years later, Trump decided he actually needed Gormley on his side, and marshalled his full support for Gormley when the state senator decided to run for the US Senate. Whatever the outcome of the federal race, Trump could ply Gormley with donations that he was not allowed to directly give to Gormley's state senate campaign. If Gormley won the US Senate seat, he could help Trump; if he lost and stayed in the state senate, he could help him even more. So Trump held a fundraiser for Gormley at his Trump Tower triplex, attended by a number of Trump employees. Trump invited a hundred guests, acting "in my individual capacity and not in my representative capacity as Chairman Trump Hotels & Casino Resorts, Inc.," supplying his guests with "food and beverages," according to an affidavit that Trump filed in connection with a complaint that had been made. Charged with having illegally pressured subordinates to make donations, Trump fought back, specifically delineating the ways his contributions had *not* been illegal corporate contributions, had not come from undue pressure on his employees, had not been handed over personally by him or his subordinates, but were collected at "a table in the foyer inside the entrance to my residence which was staffed by Gormley for Senate personnel."[42]

Gormley's campaign was later fined for campaign finance violations in a conciliation agreement that did not mention Trump.[43] Gormley lost the Senate primary and remained a New Jersey state senator, where, aligned with Trump, he fought forcefully against a new tax on casinos.

In his state senate post, Gormley also had oversight over a bistate transportation agency, the Port Authority of New York and New Jersey. His committee had to approve the incoming Port Authority chairman, a position that typically goes to a financial benefactor of the governor. Because there was no statewide elected official in New Jersey other than the governor, use of this oversight authority was one way an opposition party could put the brakes on a governor's power. In the early 2000s State Senator Gormley sought to do exactly that, by focusing on one such political patron. The new appointee at the Port Authority was an ambitious real estate developer with seemingly bottomless pockets.

Charles Kushner.

7

THE DON OF SUBURBIA

The brown and red brick house on Summit Road in Elizabeth, New Jersey, had one bedroom for Joe and Rae, one for the girls, and one for the boys. Charlie and Murray's room was small, divided up, as were their roles: Murray was the oldest son, the smarter one, the protector; Charlie was younger, and scrappier. They tussled, as American boys do, yet they got along. Yiddish was their first language.

It was a modest house, on a small lot, purchased in 1956 for $20,625, closely abutting the next house over. Elizabeth was one of the towns in New Jersey where Jews could live in those days. It had been so since the 1930s, when Summit Road was not dissimilar from the fictional Summit Avenue where Philip Roth set his novel *The Plot Against America*. In the counterfactual historical fiction, President Charles Lindbergh makes an alliance with Adolf Hitler, slowly tightening a noose around American Jews, Roth's fictional family included. Summit Avenue, as Roth described it, "rises a hundred feet above the level of the tidal salt marsh . . . and the deep bay due east of the airport that bends around the oil tanks of the Bayonne peninsula and merges there with New York Bay to flow past the Statue of Liberty."[1]

As in *The Plot Against America*, Jews in 1950s Elizabeth were not welcome in the rest of Union County. When restrictions fell in the late

1960s, the Kushners transplanted themselves, moving to a big white brick house in Hillside where each Kushner teenager could have their own bedroom.

At home, Joe chain-smoked, wore wife-beater undershirts, and insisted on certain rules. If someone with jeans or long hair entered his home, he would kick them out. Rae would entertain, cooking large quantities of meat and soup. The children were close. Their family home was a hub of activity. It smelled like burnt *potatonik*, a giant latke fried in chicken fat, a recipe Rae had made as a teenager before the war and brought with her from Poland. The Holocaust was never far away, but rarely discussed. For a while, Rae said, she couldn't talk about it. She wanted to establish a normal life and leave the horrors of the Holocaust behind.[2] Gradually, as the children matured, Joe and Rae began to share their stories.

As the boys grew into their teens, they talked business with Joe, in Yiddish, but he was rarely home; they competed for his attention. Joe drove the new network of roads in New Jersey, overseeing his growing empire of suburban garden apartments, working from his car, checking on the construction, the maintenance, the management. He would buy up empty lots, almost always with partners, keeping his debt low, then build and sell dozens of homes on those lots for $50,000 or $60,000, $73,000 by the 1970s, the prices tracking the decades.[3]

Linda, the oldest, married young. Murray grew more distant from his younger siblings, Charlie and Esther, who were just fifteen months apart. Charlie and Esther grew tighter. Joe conveyed an ethos: the siblings were to take care of each other, the boys should watch over the girls.

Before Nixon resigned, Joe and Rae sent Murray to the University of Pennsylvania, where he graduated summa cum laude, and then to the University of Pennsylvania Law School. He studied at the London School of Economics, where he met Jack Kagan, who had crawled through the tunnel from the Novogrudok ghetto with Rae and Lisa and Naum. Charlie attended New York University in the years after Watergate.

Murray married his first wife, Ruth Dunietz, at the New York Hilton in June 1974, while he was still in law school. Ruth was from a large, wealthy, observant family. She'd gone to Boston University and worked in an ad agency.[4] Within months of Murray's marriage, though three years younger than Murray and still an undergraduate at NYU, Charlie was married as well, to Seryl Stadtmauer, a Modern Orthodox Jew who had gone to Stern College for Women, a branch of Yeshiva University. In February 1979, while Charlie was matriculated at both the NYU Stern School of Business and Hofstra Law School, Seryl gave birth to their oldest child, Dara.

In 1979, a few months before fifty-two Americans were held hostage in Iran, Charlie graduated from Hofstra Law and NYU Business, wanting to be neither a lawyer nor an accountant. But he took a job in accounting at Price Waterhouse, at the newly opened, triangle-topped Citicorp building in midtown. He hated it. After about a year, he walked into a New Jersey real estate law firm and sat down with one of the firm's partners. The partner told Charlie he had no job for a new associate. But by the time the men stood up, Charlie Kushner had talked his way into a job at the law firm.

Unlike his father, Charlie was not, at first, a builder. His specialty was spotting real estate parcels, acquiring them, obtaining necessary approvals to develop the land, and selling them. To do so, Charlie needed other people's money—financial partners, willing to invest. One of the lawyers in Charlie's firm introduced him to George Gellert, already a successful food importer, accustomed to profits of pennies on the dollar. Charlie and Gellert invested in a sod farm near Princeton and got approvals to build. When they sold it a few months later, they doubled their money, clearing over $10 million. The two became lifelong business partners. Charlie was soon making so much money on his deals, the law firm made him a partner.

On January 10, 1981—ten days before Ronald Reagan was inaugurated—Seryl gave birth to a son, Jared. The couple soon took title to a lot on Fawn Drive in Livingston, New Jersey, on February 27, 1981,[5] down the street from Murray, and close to Esther and Linda.

Their families were all growing by then: Esther and her husband Billy had a daughter, Jessica, and a son of their own, Jacob, born nine days after Jared. Linda and her husband Murray Laulicht had four daughters. Murray Kushner's first wife, Ruth, had died of breast cancer at age twenty-nine, but had first given birth to two sons, Jonathan and Aryeh. In 1982, Murray remarried, to Lee Serwitz, a divorcee with two children of her own: Marc and Melissa. All the cousins were raised together. Rae and Joe did not approve of Lee, however, who was glamorous and free-spirited and liable to get her nails done on Shabbat. Also, she was not Ruth.

Livingston, New Jersey, population 28,000, had become a town of conspicuous consumption. "Everybody was trying to impress everyone else with what they had. They had to have the best," one former town official said in an interview. The median income was well above the national average. Housing prices were increasing at more than two times the rate of inflation.[6] Charlie owned a large house on a large lot. Down the hill, in a small home on a small lot, a young high school boy, captain of the baseball team, was getting involved in politics: Chris Christie.

The 1980s were a good time to be investing; markets were rising. There was a bicoastal real estate frenzy; the average home price in the northeast in 1980 was $69,500. By the end of the decade it had more than doubled.[7] "It's morning again in America," went Reagan's reelection television ad, optimistic music swelling as a farmer steers his tractor, a man passes a paperboy on his bike, and a family carries building materials into a suburban home. The ad continued: "With interest rates at about half the record highs of 1980, nearly 2,000 families today will buy new homes, more than at any time in the past four years. This afternoon 6,500 young men and women will be married, and with inflation at less than half of what it was just four years ago, they can look forward with confidence to the future."

As Reagan started his second term, Charlie decided to form Kushner Companies with his father. Charlie acquired Oakwood Village, with some six hundred homes, with the intention to build six hundred more. But before the deal closed, Joe died. He passed during the Jewish High Holy Days of 1985, a wealthy man, his original $5,000 land investment now worth tens of millions of dollars, most of it placed in tax-avoiding trusts he'd set up for his four children. Charlie, distraught, had little experience hiring contractors, or framers, or plumbers. He had started a huge building project, and his father wasn't around to help him.

Joe's will divided his properties among his children, subject to the newly reduced estate taxes of Reagan's 1981 tax bill. Joe specifically wrote Murray's adopted children out of his will: "It is my intention that the terms 'issue' and 'children' shall include only natural-born children and natural-born issue, and shall exclude any legally adopted individual and his issue," the will said.[8]

Though Charlie and his brother Murray both worked in real estate, the two brothers did not work together. For a while, Murray and Charlie continued on parallel tracks. Murray operated as a standard developer and builder, while Charlie expanded his father's business model from development to one that relied on acquisition and debt. At one point he was on track to acquire more properties than anyone in New Jersey, ever.[9]

At the end of the 1980s, the real estate market tilted into recession. Deregulation of banks that began under Carter and continued under Reagan had propped up a lot of shaky debts. When those debts collapsed, many smaller real estate companies went bust. But Charlie had grown his company enough that it survived the shakeout. In 1986, with George Gellert and others, he made his first foray into Manhattan, buying into a partnership that purchased the Puck Building in SoHo for $19 million. The building, named for *Puck* magazine, is a Gilded Age Romanesque revival. A golden statue of the character Puck from Shakespeare's *A Midsummer Night's Dream* adorns the entrance.

In one picture from this era, Murray and Charlie, in black bow ties, stand around Rae, who is wearing a black square-necked dress with slightly puffy sleeves; a dramatic, dazzling necklace frames her neck. Murray and Charlie are both dark-haired; Charlie wears a mustache.

The photo accompanies an announcement; they are going to be honored, together, by Morristown, New Jersey's Rabbinical College of America. Tutored by Rae, both Charlie and Murray donated to Jewish causes: the Kean College Holocaust Resource Center, the United States Holocaust Memorial Museum, MetroWest Federation-United Jewish Appeal. One cause, Operation Exodus, resettled Soviet Jews in Israel. When Joe died, the brothers endowed a yeshiva, renaming it the Joseph Kushner Hebrew Academy.

Nothing is more important for the Jews, Rae had argued, than the survival of the State of Israel. The Holocaust could happen again. "We must have a country of our own," Rae said—that was the only way to ensure the survival of the Jewish people. She taught her kids to be Zionists, to support Jewish organizations and Israel. On social policy, her views sometimes lined up with Reagan's. Too many people wanted welfare, she said. "We lived through Hitler, we wanted a piece of bread and water and wanted to build."[10]

Charlie became known during these years for his generous gestures: showing up at shivas, sending flowers and letters, and appearing at hospital bedsides when his associates' children became ill. If people asked him for money to support causes, he wrote checks many times larger than they asked. His temper was volatile: he could berate an employee for a minor infraction, but when her child was sick, he sent them on a private plane to Denver for treatment.

During the 1980s and 1990s, Charlie regularly hosted the *ganze mishpacha*, the whole family, at his house on Fawn Drive in Livingston. Charlie was the fun one, athletic. At these gatherings the family played basketball and baseball in the backyard. The girls played in the basement. On Shabbat, Charlie's home was the hub. Rae brought over matzoh ball soup, which she made with a tomato.

At Murray's son Marc's bar mitzvah, held at Short Hills Caterers, Rae stood and said, as she did at all her grandchildren's b'nai mitzvah, "Marc is my favorite grandchild." Charlie held Marc's hand and gave a version of the speech that he made at all the gatherings: that they came from a family of Holocaust survivors, they will never forget, they will be forever vigilant, they will watch out for those who would destroy the Jews. They will always transmit the values of family, *chesed*—kindness, mercy, compassion—and Torah, the values that had been transmitted to them from Rae.

Murray and Charlie set up a new series of formal business partnerships, but there were tensions. Both Kushners were aggressive in business, in a way that made Rae proud. Like the rest of the so-called "Holocaust builders," the Jewish family dynasties such as the Wilfs, Joe's first partners, who built the Jersey suburbs, Murray was a private man; he kept his business to himself. Charlie had a much more public profile. He was written up in *The Record*[11] in 1993 as "the main principal in the business started by his father, Joseph." One of Charlie's associates bragged: "The family has been able to anticipate population movements and build homes in those locations before people migrated."

Murray and Charles were both long-distance runners. Charlie ran the Midland 15K run year after year. One year, Charlie came in at 1:22:10.4, and Murray was next, twelve seconds behind Charlie. Charlie tended towards endurance sports, once telling the *Star-Ledger*, "Kids from Elizabeth didn't play golf. We didn't know from golf sticks."[12]

During all the *simchas* and Holocaust commemorations and galas for Jewish and Israeli organizations, Charlie met some Jewish politicians: Robert Abrams, the New York attorney general, who was a relative by marriage; and New Jersey US Senator Frank Lautenberg, a philanthropist himself, who was impressed with Kushner's charitable giving. Lautenberg likened the Kushner family to the Rockefellers or the Kennedys.[13] Following Lautenberg's example, Charlie and Seryl started to make political donations, too.

Two hundred and fifty dollars. Five hundred dollars. A thousand dollars. Charlie made donations through his children: eleven-year-old Jared, with his occupation listed in federal records as "student," made two one-thousand-dollar donations to Senator Lautenberg. Three years later, at fourteen, Jared gave another two thousand. In 1996, Rae gave ten thousand dollars to the Democratic Senatorial Campaign Committee, the soft-money account that supports US senators.[14] In the mid-

1990s, before a set of IRS and court decisions allowed for huge inflows of money into politics, $10,000 was a substantial sum. The Kushner family donations caught the attention of President Bill Clinton, who called up Charlie and asked to come by his office for a private lunch. The president came for a public event, too, where he was presented with a shofar, a ram's horn, while paying a visit to the Kushner Companies' low-slung suburban office building in Florham Park.

"I think we're closer to a time," Bill Clinton said in Charlie's cavernous office as Charlie and his family looked on—"in which we can reach across all the racial, the ethnic, the cultural, the religious lines that divide us, and stand in stark contrast to what is going on in so much of the world today and to the terrible story that Charles told us that had such a wonderful ending—of his family—by being a country that really can embrace all this diversity, celebrate it, respect it, honor it, and say, 'We're still bound together as one America.'"[15] Clinton kissed Rae Kushner, and she told him, post–Monica Lewinsky, to "be careful." A saucy joke.

This was the period that Charlie started to run through stop signs: He bought a bank but did not properly report its ownership to bank regulators, making representations that were "inconsistent" with the facts.[16] He used funds from his real estate partnerships to pay then-former and future Israeli prime minister Benjamin Netanyahu $400,000 to make speeches in Livingston.[17] He and Netanyahu grew so close that Bibi stayed at the Kushner home on Fawn Drive. And Charlie began donating sizable sums to a New Jersey mayor then considering a run for governor.

Despite all the attention and money Charlie lavished on national politics, in New Jersey, there was and is one real power: the governor. The state executive ultimately oversees permits, contracting, regulation, even law enforcement, by appointing the attorney general. The US senators have modest, indirect sway on key economic decisions: local tax breaks, zoning variances, land use. There is no elected statewide comptroller, no elected attorney general. Even the local sheriffs can be elected with the backing of the political apparatus installed by the governor. The only statewide power position independent of the governor is the US attorney, a figure appointed by the president, usually at the recommendation of the local senators. As a result, the paths to power are few. Aspiring governors can go the route of US attorney, like Chris Christie. They can be very rich, like Tom Kean, Christine Todd Whitman, John Corzine, and Phil Murphy. Or they can find an exceedingly generous patron, which is what Democrat Jim McGreevey did in 1997 when he began his association with Charlie Kushner.

In September of that year, according to reporting by *The Record*, McGreevey, a state senator and the mayor of Woodbridge, a relatively diverse town, population 100,000, met with Charlie. A day later, five people—all with the last name Kushner, all listing their employer as a Kushner company—donated a total of $10,000. The same day, various Schulders, Laulichts, and Kushner business partners gave at least another $40,000.[18]

McGreevey narrowly lost the 1997 race to Christine Todd Whitman, but immediately started planning another campaign. Over the course of thirteen days at the end of 1997, Charles Kushner gave a total of $554,000 for this new race. In the next three years, Charlie gave another $140,000 to McGreevey's soft money account, which paid the salaries of McGreevey's top advisors, and for McGreevey to travel to Israel, a necessary prerequisite for those seeking major office in New Jersey and New York. Charlie also bought an insurance company from a key McGreevey advisor for over $3 million.[19]

By this time, Charlie, moving to solidify his role as the center of the family, built an addition for Rae at the house on Fawn Drive. He bought her a Rolls-Royce. She hated it, yet used it to tool around Livingston, driving to visit her children and grandchildren.

None of this was enough. "Charles Kushner is a big fish in the small pond of the New Jersey multifamily real-estate industry" the *Wall Street Journal* reported in September 2000.[20] "His family owns more than $1 billion of apartment buildings and commercial property, a small bank, an insurance concern and a construction business. . . . But

Mr. Kushner wants to swim in the ocean, and when real-estate stocks plunged in 1998, he began to make his move."

Charlie's ambition was naked: "I would like to be one of the largest owners in the country in the next 10 years," he told the *Journal*. In 2000, he was on the cusp of purchasing the WNY Group for $280 million. WNY controlled 8,000 units in Pennsylvania, Maryland, New Jersey, and Delaware. This would bring the total number of apartments Kushner Companies controlled to over 20,000, up from 4,000 when Joseph had died a decade and a half earlier. But the WNY deal papered over another, larger deal that had gotten away, a $1.3-billion portfolio owned by Berkshire Realty Company, for which Charlie had been ready to put up $100 million in equity from his family trusts. That deal would have been the Kushners' biggest yet. According to Berkshire's proxy statement, Charlie had the winning bid, but never supplied the necessary letter of credit. Murray had reined it in.

The-deal-that-never-was became a needle in the eye for both Murray and Charlie.

Around this time, the Kushners built a new campus for the school named for his father, less than a mile from his office, and just a few miles from his home. It sits on a hill, adorned with a dome that looks like a tourist photo of Jerusalem, with three flags out front, one American, one Israeli, and one that says JKHA. Giant Trump-sized letters announce to drivers on the suburban road below, past the grassy lawn and tiered parking lots, that this is the JOSEPH KUSHNER HEBREW ACADEMY. At the center of the school there is a "Holocaust garden." Itzhak Perlman once performed at the school.

While Jared was in high school the students were tracked; classmates in the highest-level classes could not recall ever being in a class with Jared. Charlie, who did not go to Harvard, pledged $2.5 million to the Ivy League school in 1998, the year before Jared graduated from high school. Jared got in.[21]

On Fawn Drive, things had been getting rougher. Charlie started insisting that everyone adhere strictly to religious rules. He began to drink heavily, and when he did, he could be verbally abusive. Like

Joseph before him, he would not allow any of the younger generation in his house to wear jeans—dungarees, he called them. He insisted on formal dress for Shabbat. Infractions incurred a tongue-lashing bordering on bullying. He became more and more disapproving of Murray's second wife, Lee.

In business, Charlie and Murray became suspicious of each other, each accusing the "other of taking more than his fair share out of their common businesses," according to a later court opinion.[22] Murray accused Charlie of misappropriating their partnership funds by using partnership money to pay for charitable contributions and political campaigns and personal items. In 2000, $186,000 went to organizations including Charlie's synagogue, the Suburban Torah Center; a consulting firm researching the comeback prospects of then-former Israeli prime minister Bibi Netanyahu received $10,000; $25,384 went to private-school tuition for the children of Kushner Companies employees; $7,027 to "holiday alcohol"; more money bought Yankees, Mets, and Nets season tickets. The practice of using corporate money for personal and political reasons was discussed openly at the family business's regular Tuesday morning meetings. Charlie used a phrase to describe it: "losing a bill."[23]

"It didn't matter," Charlie said, "because it was all family."

To Murray, and to Esther, it mattered.

Murray and Charlie started to have flare-ups. Rae intervened, or prevailed on Linda's husband to be the peacemaker. But, thanks to Joe, Murray Kushner and Charlie Kushner's business interests were inextricably intertwined. If Charlie was breaking the law, Murray, who, like Charlie, was a lawyer, an officer of the court, could be liable, too. Esther was the youngest, and a woman, the person with the least power in the family. She wanted to stand up for what was right. Her husband Billy, who worked for Charlie, had an inside view of what was going on at Kushner Companies. So did Bob Yontef, Charlie's accountant.

For Passover 1999, Rae gathered the entire family at the Fontainebleau in Miami Beach, Florida, an arc of high-rise of white concrete embracing multiple pools and decks and palm trees. They had spent

Passovers this way for over a decade. Rae would pay for the whole family, and they would rent a row of adjoining rooms, more than a dozen cousins bouncing on the beds, running from room to room, clutching the twenty-dollar bills that Rae had given each of them for the arcade, hanging out on the balconies together and by the pools as they grew into their teens.

By April 1999, Murray was simmering at Charlie; at the political contributions to Bill Clinton, Benjamin Netanyahu, and Jim McGreevey; at the personal expenditures that had been paid without Murray's consent out of their joint partnership accounts and in violation of tax and campaign finance laws. And Charlie was simmering because he felt Murray's caution had blown the multimillion-dollar deal with Berkshire.

At the Fontainebleau that spring, Charlie told Murray that maybe they couldn't do business together.[24] And Murray angrily responded, according to court papers Charlie later filed, "If we can't be partners, we can't be brothers!"[25] Charlie told Murray that Murray didn't appreciate all the ways Charlie had elevated the family's business, its prestige, its cachet. Lee joined the fray. Of her son, Marc, at whose bar mitzvah he'd extolled the value of family and *chesed*, Charlie said: "You think your son got into Penn? I got him in!"

Lee took her family and left. The Murray Kushners did not return to the Fontainebleau.

At work, according to a complaint filed by his former accountant, Charlie became more strident, even to his sister. "Esther was verbally abused by Charles in front of the entire office and left his employ," accountant Bob Yontef said in a court filing.[26] Around this time, Esther's husband, Billy, stopped working for Charlie. (Charlie denied Yontef's allegations, and countersued. The suits were privately settled.)

Passover at the Fontainebleau got worse. Charlie was even more belligerent. The Passover seder is the celebration of the Exodus of the Jews, the escape from slavery, the passage out of Egypt through the *Mitzrayim*, the narrow place, through which they must cross before they get to the promised land. It is resonant for all Jews, more so for

Rae, whose passage through a narrow tunnel had given rise to this enormous brood.

The Fontainebleau seders were formal affairs: suits and ties for the men and boys, blazers and skirts for the women and girls. Forty people or so sitting around a square of four long tables, with wine and matzoh, bitter herbs and shank bone, salt water and sweet *haroset*, each item reminding Jews of the bitterness of slavery, of the agony of the struggle for liberation, the sweetness of freedom.

But Charlie began drinking, and lobbing insults, still feeling slighted by Murray's claims against him, and his perception that his sister Esther and her husband Billy were siding with Murray. Murray and his family were not there, but Charlie was set to boil. He began to hurl obscenity-laden abuse at Esther's children—his nieces and his nephew, Jacob—who had grown up like a brother to Jared. At one point he said, "You're so pious. Go on, Billy, and tell your kids how pious you are."

Billy, the adults knew, many associates in New Jersey knew, had a weakness. He'd had an affair with one of Charlie's employees, in the office where they all worked. Esther knew.

"You're a fucking putz!" Charlie yelled. "How can you be so rude?"

"They're not worth it," Jared said. "They're not worth fighting about."

This was the last time the Schulders celebrated Passover with Charlie Kushner's family.

8

ICARUS

The summer of 2000, Al Gore, vice president of the United States, arrived in Livingston with his motorcade. He didn't want to stop at Charlie's office, and asked aides why he had to. He was told, *it's part of the package.* If the vice president wanted to go to the fundraiser on Fawn Drive, he had to go to 26 Columbia Turnpike first. So he did.

But that summer, as the Gore-Lieberman ticket was running against Bush-Cheney, Charles Kushner was more focused on a race that would be run the next year, in which Jim McGreevey would run for governor of New Jersey.

The Kushner-backed Committee for Working Families paid for Jim McGreevey's travel to Israel on a Metrowest-United Jewish Appeal tour. There, McGreevey met Golan Cipel, a young communications aide to the mayor of Rishon LeZion, a small city outside Tel Aviv. McGreevey was smitten. He offered Cipel a job on his campaign.

Not long after, McGreevey formally announced his candidacy, with the endorsement of Charles Kushner, who praised how McGreevey's "energy, his vision, and his heart were committed to running for Governor."[1] Kushner's statement was a signal that McGreevey would have the money to compete in the expensive media markets of New York and Philadelphia, whose television stations beam into New Jersey. By this time, Charles Kushner was already a donor to both Hillary Clinton, who was running for the US Senate in New York, and Senator Robert Torricelli of New Jersey.

That year, the National Conference for Community and Justice, a group founded in 1927 to fight anti-Catholic bigotry that later expanded to address "all issues of social justice including race, class, gender equity, sexual orientation and the rights of people with different abilities," named Charlie Kushner "The Humanitarian of the Year."[2] Charlie gave a one-million-dollar contribution to the Democratic National Committee, a gift that, at the turn of the century, was more than ostentatious. Kushner donations to Democrats had now exceeded $3 million, matching the amount that Enron contributed to President George W. Bush.[3]

Around this time, Charlie got himself introduced to the incoming president of New York University, John Sexton, according to two people familiar with the meeting. Charlie "wanted to do a significant philanthropic gesture," one of the people said. "We all understand the desire to move into the glitterati, the chattering class of the oligarchy of New York." There was no better way to do this than to serve on the board of NYU. Charlie talked about a donation of $10 million. He offered space in the Puck Building to the university for significantly reduced rent. At one point, he offered to give the building entirely to NYU, but the deal fell apart because Charlie wanted to overvalue the contribution by tens of millions of dollars in a press release. Still, Charlie got a seat on the NYU Board of Trustees. The law school has a Seryl and Charles Kushner Student Lounge and there's a "Seryl Kushner Dean of the College of Arts and Science."

In September 2001, at the height of the McGreevey campaign for governor, the World Trade Center towers were attacked. Thousands were incinerated in the blast or crushed in the collapse, or died jumping from windows. The New York City mayoral race was upended as the towers descended to a pile of rubble, and ash filled the streets, which smelled of burning for months. The Friday after the attacks, rain drenched the city. President George W. Bush climbed a pile of rubble and spoke, barely audible, through a bullhorn. "I can't hear you!" a worker shouted. "I can hear you!" Bush yelled back, megaphone to mouth. "The rest of the world hears you! And the people—and the people who knocked these buildings down will hear all of us soon!"

In November, Charlie's candidate for New Jersey governor, Jim McGreevey, sailed to an election victory. One of McGreevey's first acts upon taking office was to name Charlie to the board of the powerful, sprawling Port Authority of New York and New Jersey—which controlled the World Trade Center site—with the intention of making him chairman. If approved, Charles Kushner would lead the Port Authority during one of the most critical periods in its history, as it oversaw the rebuilding.

Later, McGreevey wrote, "All my financial contributors were vying for payback. . . . You can't take large sums of money from people without making them specific and personal promises in return. People weren't shy about saying what they expected for their 'investments'—board appointments to the Sports Authority or the New Jersey Economic Development Authority, for example, which were coveted not just for their prestige but because they offered control over tremendously potent economic engines, with discretionary budgets in the tens of millions. The plum was the Port Authority of New York and New Jersey; directors there controlled a multibillion-dollar budget." But McGreevey maintained that Kushner's appointment was all good government. "Kushner refused my appointment three times before finally accepting," McGreevey wrote.[4]

The chairmanship would give Charlie two things he very much wanted: actual power, and the ability to draw attention in New York. To accompany this, Charlie needed a premier apartment. He bought a co-op at Fifth Avenue and Sixty-Seventh Street on the Upper East Side of Manhattan, priced at $5.4 million. He now had a prestige job, an apartment at a location with cachet, a seat on the board of NYU, and a son at Harvard.

At 26 Columbia Turnpike, things got worse. The accountant, Bob

Yontef, was noting spending irregularities: Super Bowl packages, playoff tickets, landscaping bills, political contributions charged inappropriately to Kushner real estate partnerships that included Charlie and his siblings and all of their children. "Most of these substantial contributions—well into millions of dollars per year—were made mostly in Charles' name even though the funds came from the Entities," Yontef said in a sworn statement attached to the employment lawsuit he later filed in federal court.

"In thinking about everything that went on at the Kushner Companies, I became more and more upset," Yontef wrote. "I began to tell Esther how Charles was making massive political and charitable donations from the Entities and the other ways he was misallocating and misappropriating the funds of the Entities in which she and her family were partners." Yontef gave Murray some samples of the documents "which demonstrate these wrongdoings."[5] Murray filed his own suit against Charlie in state court in Hudson County, claiming that Charlie was siphoning money from the real estate partnerships.[6]

In Trenton, Jim McGreevey made another appointment, a fateful one: he elevated Golan Cipel, the communications aide he had met in Israel, to advise him on New Jersey's homeland security efforts, and blurted out the arrangement in a meeting with *The Record*'s editorial board. To reporters on staff, the appointment instantly seemed odd; aside from five years in the Israeli Defense Forces and stints as a communications aide for the Israeli consulate in New York and the mayor of a city in Israel, Cipel had few credentials. Journalists from *The Record* began investigating Cipel. They found he had a job at a PR company when he moved from Israel, and that his visa was sponsored by that company. They traced the corporate ownership through a network of limited liability companies, and found that the PR firm belonged to Charlie Kushner.[7] "Cipel's ascent occurred without routine background checks or any kind of official announcement from the governor's office, standard procedure for high officials in state government," *The Record* reported. "I didn't feel that kind of check was necessary," McGreevey told them. "He's a super-bright and supercompetent individual who brings a great wealth of knowledge on security. . . . He's someone who thinks with a different set of eyes." Months after 9/11, the rubble from the World Trade Center site not yet removed, Cipel, as a foreign national, couldn't get the necessary security clearance. Prompted by the connection to McGreevey, *The Record* began to take a closer and closer look at Charles Kushner's LLCs and real estate partnerships.[8]

In May of 2002, Charlie received a legal notice from the Federal Election Commission, telling him that "the Office of the General Counsel recommends that the Commission find reason to believe that Kushner Companies, Charles Kushner as Chairman" had violated campaign finance law, including by "directing subordinates to plan, organize, or carry out a fundraising project as a part of their work responsibilities using corporate resources."[9]

Since 1976, campaign finance laws had been guided by the US Supreme Court decision *Buckley v. Valeo.* Contributions, the Court ruled in *Buckley,* could be limited, because unlimited contributions were likely to corrupt the democratic process. But the Court said expenditures could not be limited, because that would violate the First Amendment freedom of speech of donors. Individual donors—like Charles Kushner—who could "bundle" contributions became more and more important. But it had to be done according to a strict set of rules.

The FEC report delineated at least eight laws that it believed Kushner and his company had broken. It named business associates, his family, and his children, including Jared, then attending Harvard. In a routine audit, the legal notice said, auditors from the FEC found forty checks in the same handwriting, all but one with the same date, most even with the same typo, identifying the fundraiser to whom the checks were directed as "Japoch" rather than "Sapoch." The actions, the auditors said, violated a well-known overarching principle of campaign finance law; that corporations cannot contribute to federal campaigns, and that individuals cannot use different names to multiply the amount of money that they can otherwise legally donate. Without that, campaign finance limits would be meaningless.

One of things Charlie did, the FEC said, was to make contributions in the name of his family members and business partners without notifying them. Forty-one thousand dollars in contributions were attributed to Jared Kushner, who had just turned twenty-one.[10]

That summer, Charlie confronted Yontef, the accountant, about his turning over information to his siblings. According to an affidavit Yontef swore out on June 25, ninety minutes after the confrontation happened, Charlie said to him: "Why did you do this? You just ruined me. I am going to ruin your life. You made a big mistake. Get out of here and never come back into my Company again."[11]

In September 2002, Charlie's lawyers filed his response to the FEC's investigation. His lawyers first gave some biographical data. "The late Joseph Kushner was a Holocaust survivor who emigrated to the United States in 1949, became a construction worker, and in the post-war 1950s began developing real estate," the lawyers wrote, by way of introduction. They argued that Charles Kushner had not violated any laws against corporate contributions to federal elections because "'The Kushner Companies, Inc.' is not an operating corporation. 'Kushner Companies' is a name used for public marketing purposes only. The Kushner Companies, Inc. was originally incorporated in 1988 as a New Jersey corporation. However, its corporate charter was declared void by the State of New Jersey in 1995. The charter was not reinstated until April of 2001. Accordingly, in 1999, when the contributions at issue were made, Kushner Companies was not a legal entity."[12] Charles Kushner had not filed certain legal documents with the state, his lawyers argued: therefore, technically, no laws against corporate contributions had been broken.

Charlie's overarching claim was that his partnership agreements with his siblings vested in him the authority to make political donations on their behalf. "Charles Kushner's activity, both charitable and political, has raised his name and reputation in the broader real estate community as a prominent real estate developer and an individual who dedicates his success to the well-being of his community," his lawyers wrote. "Charles Kushner and the Partnerships did not have this recognition ten years ago. Because the various Partnerships are identified with Charles Kushner, the properties developed, administered and maintained by these Partnerships have become some of the most desirable and profitable properties in the Northeast community. Thus, Charles Kushner's reputation and the charitable and political contributions made by the various Partnerships have been beneficial to each of the partners."[13] All of these donations and expenses were making the whole family money, Charlie and his lawyers were arguing. His siblings should be grateful.

They were not.

In November of 2002, Esther filed a declaration with the FEC. She told the regulatory agency that political contributions had been made in her name without her knowledge. Her lawyers had already informed the FEC that in the summer of 2001, two years after the contributions had been made, a Kushner employee had contacted her, asking for her retroactive approval. "Over the next several weeks," the lawyers wrote, "Esther received significant financial pressure to execute the letters. At the same time, Esther was under substantial emotional strain. As a result of this pressure, Esther signed the attribution letters on her own behalf and on behalf of her children as well, believing that doing so was appropriate" based on the Kushner employee's representations. Jessica, Jacob, and Ruth Schulder, then twenty-four, twenty-one, and twenty, signed declarations too.[14]

Murray filed his own declaration, asserting that Charlie had made contributions in his name without his foreknowledge or approval, "I, Murray Kushner, declare under penalty of perjury that the foregoing is true and correct," Murray wrote at the bottom of the statement, still on file in an obscure corner of the FEC website.

At the Port Authority, things were also going badly. The *New York Observer* was paying attention, and not in a good way. As a member of the Port Authority board, Charlie was able to vote on budgets, contracts, and proposals before the bistate agency. But as reporter Tom McGeveran wrote, Charlie had personal financial interests that could conflict with the agency's public interest. According to one article, Charlie had invested in a $165-million real estate partnership for the Monmouth Mall with a developer who was making a bid for the tower atop the Port Authority Bus Terminal.[15] While serving on the board of the Port Authority, which was involved in a large-scale operation to dig up dredge spoils from deep in the New York Harbor, Charlie had also entered into negotiations to do a real estate development in the Meadowlands with a company looking to use those same dredge spoils in a construction project, according to another report.[16] At each turn, Charlie promised to recuse himself, but at the Port Authority, where the board exerts enormous control, recusals are widely understood to be a ruse.

To join the Port Authority board, Charlie needed the approval of the state senate, and specifically of Senator William Gormley—the one against whom Trump had fought when Gormley supported a tunnel for a rival casino owner, and who then became the beneficiary of Trump's own fundraising efforts. Gormley was a Republican, and the chairman of a powerful state senate committee, and Charles Kushner was one of the most important Democrats in New Jersey. Gormley started to examine Charlie's ownership of NorCrown Bank—state law said bank owners can't make political contributions to candidates for state office. Charlie's lawyers said that NorCrown was owned by a trust, in which Charlie didn't have a majority interest. Gormley wanted Kushner to come and testify about the bank ownership. At a wedding for a top Jim McGreevey aide, Charlie confronted Gormley, telling him he would not come testify in front of Gormley's fucking committee.

While Charlie was under scrutiny in New Jersey, the Port Authority board was preoccupied with an enormous project, selecting the design for the World Trade Center site. On February 26, 2003, as reporters staked out board members to discern which architect would design the master plan, Charlie withdrew his nomination for board chair. It was the day before Rae's eightieth birthday. In the frenzy of news coverage over the World Trade Center site's master plan, Charlie's retreat hardly made news. But one person did notice. The US attorney for New Jersey, Chris Christie.

—

Chris Christie was only a year into his position, a political creature positioning himself as a corruption fighter, a Bush fundraiser who placed himself ostensibly outside of the world of politics. The law firm Murray hired was led by Herb Stern, who Christie had sometimes looked to for advice. And Christie caught wind of Murray's lawsuit, *Kushner v. Kushner.* Prosecutors often find the seeds of criminal probes in civil litigation, but the Kushner suit, directed as it was at Democratic Governor Jim McGreevey's chief financial patron, was irresistible. Precisely as Charlie Kushner was resigning from the Port Authority, Christie's office was launching a grand jury investigation.

Christie was brash and plainspoken, definitively a Jersey boy and not an Ivy League grad (he went to the University of Delaware and Seton Hall Law School). While many politicians hire trainers to stay in shape for the cameras, Christie embraced his overweight physique. It gave the impression he was on the people's side. He was a fat guy who would fight the fat cats.

The Kushner case was a paper case; it involved the tedious prosecutorial work of using corporate records, the murky trails left in interlocking LLC ledgers, to make out the crime of tax evasion. It is illegal to cheat the US Treasury by using nondeductible expenses—charitable contributions, political donations, personal entertainment expenses—to reduce business income, and thereby, taxes. This is what Charlie had done. Christie's team also had an eye on the FEC campaign finance investigation, and on the FDIC's investigation of Charlie's ownership of his bank. Kushner's entire business empire seemed rife with irregularities.

Charlie fought back. He hired an aggressive team of New Jersey lawyers. The lawyers worked to discredit Bob Yontef and Billy and Esther Schulder, making "regular efforts" to demonstrate that Esther, Billy, and Yontef were "inciting the federal investigation and were generally untrustworthy."[17] Charlie made an audio recording of Billy, with the goal of showing that Billy had obstructed justice in Murray's civil suit.

None of this worked to dissuade Christie from his criminal

probe. Christie's team became increasingly convinced that Charlie had engaged in a massive tax fraud. Members of the New Jersey bar noticed what they saw as Christie's unusual, personal interest in this case. Often, in white-collar cases, a team of lawyers working for the defendant—ex-prosecutors, frequently—persuade prosecutors that the crimes they are investigating are not serious, that no one was really hurt, and subtly, that they won't be worth the trouble. When this tactic didn't work, Charlie Kushner took matters into his own hands.

Charlie met a running buddy, an East Orange police captain on the verge of retirement named Jimmy O'Toole, and offered Jimmy an unusual gig. Jimmy was a high school grad, without many post-retirement job prospects. In his large office, Kushner seemed to be offering a brass ring to O'Toole: a six-figure private security job. But first, Charlie had a one-off task for him. Sitting at his desk, he passed O'Toole an accordion file stuffed with cash. Charlie suggested that Jimmy and his brother Tommy O'Toole, a Utica, New York–based private investigator, hire a prostitute to have sex with Billy, secretly videotape the tryst, and use the tape to "cause problems and personal difficulties" for Billy. Charlie promised to pay them $25,000 for their efforts. But for the next three months, the scheme stalled as Jimmy and Tommy could not find a prostitute to do the job.

Jimmy, still working as an on-duty cop, had been raised a strict Irish Catholic, an altar boy. He decided to call it quits. He took the accordion file with the cash back to 26 Columbia Turnpike. Charlie wouldn't take no for an answer. He handed Jimmy a phone number. "I want you to call this number and say you're a friend of John's," Charlie told Jimmy. It was a phone number for a Manhattan prostitute named Susanna, "a high-priced, European-born call girl on Manhattan's Upper East Side," as Christie described her in his book, *Let Me Finish*. Jimmy called Susanna. He said he was settling a family dispute. He told her not to worry—it wasn't blackmail. Susanna said she trusted him. He was a friend of John's.

As the charging documents laid out: "In or about November 2003, in New York City, defendant CHARLES KUSHNER personally recruited a woman (W1) known by defendant CHARLES KUSHNER to be a call girl—to seduce and have sex with CW2 on videotape. Defendant CHARLES KUSHNER told W1 that he would pay her approximately $7,000 to $10,000 if she would have sex with CW2 on videotape. Defendant CHARLES KUSHNER further told W1 that he wanted to make the videotape so that he could have leverage over CW2."[18] W1 or "woman 1" is the prostitute; CW2, or "cooperating witness 2," is Billy.

The next month, during a snowstorm, Susanna traveled from Manhattan to the Red Bull motel in Bridgewater and checked into a room that the O'Toole brothers had secretly wired with a hidden camera. She'd been told that Billy frequently ate at the Time to Eat Diner, which was a short drive from the Red Bull and from Murray's real estate offices, where Billy was by then working.

The Time to Eat is a classic New Jersey diner: blue leatherette counter stools, red leatherette booths, a menu that goes on for pages offering enormous plates of eggs and potatoes, triple-decker sandwiches, and gooey Italian specialties. When Billy walked out, Susanna approached and asked him for a ride back to her motel, telling him her car had broken down. She invited him in, but that day he said no. She gave him her number. Jimmy and Tommy drove her back to Manhattan as the snow kept piling up. The next morning, early, they brought her back to the Red Bull. She waited. Billy called. He drove over to the motel, where the secret video camera recorded their activities.

Tommy O'Toole retrieved the tape and drove it over to the Kushner Companies headquarters in Florham Park, about thirty minutes away. Charlie and Richard Stadtmauer—Seryl's brother—covered up the walls of the Kushner Companies conference room with paper, and laughed as they watched the tape of Billy and the prostitute having sex. In the words of the criminal complaint, Charlie "expressed satisfaction with" the video to Tommy.[19] Charlie then asked Tommy to make copies of the tape, with the woman's face pixelated, and to make 8 1/2-by-11 still photos from the video. For a while, Charlie did nothing with them.

Charlie tried the same entrapment plot on Bob Yontef, but Yontef did not take the bait.

Charlie's lawyers continued to mount an aggressive defense. Charlie refused to comply with subpoenas for documents, and ordered his accountants to refuse as well. Prosecutors were getting more and more suspicious. In mid-December, the day of the Kushner Companies' Hanukkah party, federal agents executed a raid at Kushner headquarters, seizing boxes of ledgers and documents.

The next month, Murray and Charlie settled their civil suit in Hudson county. The *Star Ledger* wrote up the settlement: "Ultimately, they went to court to trade allegations of betrayal, deceit and corporate espionage in an extraordinary public airing of dirty laundry. It was the most acrimonious family quarrel ever in the cloistered world of New Jersey's ultra-rich and powerful."[20]

Settling a civil suit is a classic tactic for defendants who want a corresponding criminal case to go away. But Christie did not let go. He was making a campaign finance and tax evasion case in an era when the laws were becoming more and more lax, at a time when his own party was hastening their demise.

In 2001 and again in 2003, George W. Bush continued the Reagan tradition and cut taxes for the wealthy. By one analysis, the wealthiest households received an average tax cut of $50,000 a year, increasing their post-tax income by almost 7 percent.[21] Meanwhile, the poorest households saw only a 1 percent increase. The "tax cuts are not simply a matter of returning unneeded or unused funds to taxpayers, but rather a choice to require other, future taxpayers to cover the long-term deficit, which the tax cut significantly exacerbates," the Brookings Institution wrote.[22]

On March 31, 2004, just before Passover, Rae died at the Mount Sinai hospital in Miami Beach after a long bout with Parkinson's. She had outlasted her mother and brother and sister in Nazi-occupied Poland, crawled through a narrow tunnel, and survived a Polish winter in the forest. She had walked across borders as a refugee, and bent the visa rules to gain entry into the United States. She had given birth to four children who gave her fifteen grandchildren, anchored a family business, and outlived her husband from the shtetl by twenty years. She'd met a president and vice president of the United States of America and once lit candles in the US Capitol to commemorate the Holocaust, testament to her will that no one should ever forget what happened under the Nazis.

Rae left her considerable estate to be divided up among her four children, and all her grandchildren, including the adopted ones. By then, the tax laws had made it easier and easier to pass along her wealth, untaxed, to her heirs. She left "ONE MILLION ($1,000,000) DOLLARS divided into four shares" to the children of each of her children, but the true value of her estate went far beyond that. That number was not made public in the will.[23]

Rae's funeral was held at the Joseph Kushner Hebrew Academy. Two thousand people came. At the shiva, guests noticed the strain: Murray and Esther staying to one side, Charlie and Linda to another. Charlie and Murray were supposed to be co-executors of Rae's estate. They filed papers with the court, turning over that function to their sisters.

After Rae died, with Christie's prosecutors circling, Charlie became unmoored. On May 7, prosecutors sent out a series of letters notifying potential targets of a grand jury probe. Christie's office was "locking in" testimony. This is typically the final stage of a criminal investigation, the last step after prosecutors have collected and analyzed documents and before they file charges.

On May 8, Charlie reached out to Jimmy O'Toole and asked him to meet the next day, Mother's Day, his first without Rae. Charlie's directions were precise: Jimmy was to have four separate packages of the VHS video of Billy having sex with the prostitute, her face pixelated, and the 8 1/2-by-11 stills, mailed to his sister from Canada, timed to arrive on the eve of the engagement party of Jacob Schulder, Esther's son, then twenty-three, almost exactly Jared's age. There should be one package for Esther, and one each for Jacob, Jessica, and Ruth, close in age to Charlie's own daughters Dara and Nicole, who had all celebrated *simchas* at the house on Fawn Drive, vacationed together in Florida, attended each other's bar and bat mitzvahs. Jimmy refused to send the video to the kids. He "convinced defendant CHARLES KUSHNER that he should not send the video to the children of CW1 and CW2," the charging documents noted.[24]

When Esther saw what was in the package, she quailed. Then she called her lawyer. Jacob and his fiancée's celebration went on as planned. It was a beautiful day for an engagement party.

Not long after, Esther and Billy drove over to the US Attorney's Office in Newark, in a brutalist plaza of grey rock, dominated by a sculpture of an enormous blindfolded head—and handed the VHS and the envelope with the still photos to federal agents. Emotions ran high.

Outwardly, Charlie pursued business as usual. Israeli newspapers considered him a serious bidder for the Israel Discount Bank. Owning a bank in Israel had been a longtime professional dream of Charlie's. He was expected any day to submit a letter of intent, for a takeover that would have to be overseen by Kushner's friend and recipient of Kushner's largesse: Finance Minister Bibi Netanyahu, once again rising in Israeli politics.[25]

Charlie never made the bid.

The next month, the legal consequences began rolling in. There was a Federal Election Commission fine at the end of June, penalizing Charles Kushner and forty real estate partnerships he controlled a sum of $508,900, one of the largest fines in the commission's history. According to the FEC press release, "The FEC investigation found that the Kushner partnerships violated Commission partnership contribution regulations by failing to obtain the agreement of the partners to whom the contributions were attributed. Charles Kushner . . . selected the political committees that would receive contributions and determined the aggregate amount of these contributions. He signed the contribution checks and directed management personnel of Kushner Companies to forward the checks on Kushner Companies' letterhead to the recipient committees."[26]

On July 13, a sultry midsummer day, twenty-three-year-old Jared, on his way to his summer internship at the Manhattan District Attorney's Office, got a call from his brother Josh, an incoming freshman at Harvard. Charlie had not shown up at the Tuesday morning Kushner Companies meeting, an inviolable tradition. Jared called his father, who told him he was about to be arrested. "For what?" Jared said, as he later related it to Gabriel Sherman in *New York Magazine.* "Is it because of the tape? I thought your lawyers knew about that. I thought it's not illegal."[27]

It was illegal. Charlie turned himself over to federal authorities in Newark, where he was placed in leg irons and handcuffs, his belt and tie removed, leaving the collar of his blue-and-white-checked button-down shirt hanging slightly open.[28] Kushner posted a $5-million bond secured by his homes in Livingston and Long Branch, and was ordered to surrender his passport and to wear an electronic bracelet. He was charged with witness tampering, obstruction of justice, and promoting interstate prostitution under the Mann Act, a statute that no one in the District of New Jersey could ever remember invoking. (It was later used to investigate the governor of New York, Eliot Spitzer.)

Chris Christie announced the charges in the muted, sober tones of a prosecutor, flanked by investigators from the FBI and the IRS and the US Attorney's Office.[29] He said Charlie had hired prostitutes "to entice witnesses who were cooperating with the federal investigation into engaging in sex acts with those prostitutes and to have those sex acts then videotaped" to discourage the witnesses from testifying. As Christie detailed it, Charlie paid $25,000 for the successful enticement, and $12,000 for the unsuccessful one, against Bob Yontef, the accountant.

"This office sent out target letters to a number of associates of Mr. Kushner's," Christie said, and "two days after those target letters were received, Mr. Kushner instructed his co-conspirators to mail the videotape to the cooperating witness's wife—she was also a cooperating witness." Christie noted, pointedly, that Kushner had to be talked out of sending it to the potential "witnesses' children."

"This Department of Justice, and this United States Attorney's Office with our partners at the FBI will not tolerate the obstruction of federal grand jury investigations," Christie said, his voice level. He added, "There is nothing, nothing more sacrosanct in our rule of law than the integrity of the federal grand jury investigative process. When people under investigation decide to take the law into their own hands, to obstruct justice, to attempt to impede the rule of law, it is our obligation to act swiftly and surely to end the obstruction."[30]

The reporters jamming into the conference room on the seventh floor of Newark's federal building lobbed Christie with questions, but he kept cool, his voice only sharpening when he berated the assembled journalists for dwelling on Governor McGreevey, who was not named in the criminal complaint. But then, Christie was asked a question that made the corners of his mouth turn up, a smile he could not suppress.

"Will the tape ever be made public?"

"I have no idea," Christie said, trying to maintain control of his lips. "I assume that if there were a trial in this case that that is something that would be considered."

As Charlie moved through the courthouse that day, appearing before a judge, his face was frozen, locked. His lawyer, Ben Brafman, was livid. "Charles Kushner is one of the most successful, well-respected business leaders in America and one of the greatest philanthropists of this century," Brafman said. "The charges in this case are entirely baseless. When this matter is resolved in court, he'll be completely exonerated."

But over the next month, it became clear to Charles Kushner and his team that Christie had more cards to play against him. It wasn't a coincidence that Charlie had told Jimmy O'Toole to call Susanna and tell her he was a "friend of John's." Prosecutors had learned that for years, Charlie had been living a double life, using the pseudonym "John Hess," to travel to Manhattan and avail himself of Susanna's services, according to seven people with knowledge of Charlie's activities. To tell the story of how Charlie ensnared his brother-in-law in a web of sex and vengeance—that is, to gain a conviction at trial on the witness-tampering charges—prosecutors would need Susanna's testimony, as well as that of the woman who had tried and failed to catch Bob Yontef in a similar plot. They were prepared to put both of them on the stand. They were prepared to let the world know about "John Hess."

In his book, Christie alluded to his own knowledge. "I'm burdened with facts about your father that even you don't know, that I can never tell you, because if I did I would break the law," Christie said he later told Jared Kushner.[31] In an interview, Brafman said, "All of this was drilled down by me and my investigator fifteen years ago, and there was zero evidence to suggest any of that to be truthful."[32] But New Jersey journalists were unearthing Charlie's exact relationship to Susanna; they already had her cell phone number. Charlie and his lawyers decided to avoid the embarrassment of a trial. They took a plea deal. In an email, Brafman said, "Mr. Kushner recognized the poor, isolated judgement that led to his arrest and his decision to quickly plead guilty and accept responsibility for his conduct was made to address these allegations and then move on with his life as quickly as possible."[33]

There was one last power play. Charlie had been set to plead guilty to an additional charge of conspiracy, but at six in the morning, his lawyers showed up at Chris Christie's house in Mendham while Christie was still in bed, and convinced him over bowls of Cheerios that if he wanted his plea deal that day, he would have to drop the conspiracy charges, which implicated Seryl's brother. Christie ultimately agreed, lest he lose the whole deal. The plea deal was finalized a few hours before Charlie appeared in court.[34]

On August 18, Charles Kushner pleaded guilty to sixteen counts of tax fraud, one of witness tampering, and one of lying to the FEC. Among the crimes to which he pleaded guilty was using three partnership entities to pay a total of $13,768 for "an individual's private school tuition expense."[35] That same year, Charlie had given $250,000 to Harvard. That latter amount was legally deductible from Charlie's personal taxes.

All of this was indeed sensational news, but less so because five days earlier, something even more spectacular had happened. Governor Jim McGreevey, recently married, father of a toddler, went on live television to declare, “I am a gay American.” He had been having sex with Golan Cipel, the man he had appointed to be his national security advisor. At the time, he was the highest-level politician in America to say he was gay. Then he offered his resignation. “I am also here today because, shamefully, I engaged in an adult consensual affair with another man, which violates my bonds of matrimony,” the governor said. “It was wrong. It was foolish. It was inexcusable.”

For Charlie, the criminal case was not the final legal consequence. The repercussions continued, more quietly. In February, he and the trust through which his family owned NorCrown Bank, were assessed the unusually steep fine of $12.5 million to settle allegations of lying to bank regulators and for setting up the trust without getting approval from the FDIC.[36]

More than six hundred people wrote letters for the defense to give to the federal judge in advance of Charlie's sentencing: employees who were grateful for his tutelage; mothers whose sick children he had helped; business partners who had worked successfully with him for years; people with multiple sclerosis to whose cause Charlie had donated. Leaders of Jewish and Holocaust remembrance groups, rabbis, educators, politicians he'd supported, including Bob Abrams, Robert Torricelli, and Cory Booker. This bulging file of letters was not kept, according to clerks, pursuant to judicial discretion.

In the end, Charlie served just over a year in prison. His legal team had researched which prisons offered accommodations for Orthodox Jews, and the best odds of allowing early release for inmates with alcoholism, a benefit for which Charlie Kushner successfully applied. The prison was in Alabama. After serving his year, Charlie was sent to a halfway house in Newark, from where he resumed his business dealings.

In the coming years, six associates would also be convicted for their roles in Charlie's tax evasion scheme, including Seryl's brother, Richard Stadtmauer, who was sentenced after trial to three years in prison. Most of the others received no prison time.

Upon his release from prison, Charlie sat down with the *Real Deal*, a New York–based real estate industry magazine in which he began, once again, to build his own image. "My parents were poor immigrants when they came to this country. My mom didn't really speak English, so when the nurse, who happened to be African-American, asked what my name was going to be, my mother answered with a Yiddish name, Chanon. I was named after her brother, who was killed in the Holocaust. The nurse said they don't name children like that in America. The nurse named me Charles. Chanon is the Hebrew name I kept."[37]

Chanon, Charlie's namesake, had been a leader of the group that carved out the tunnel out of Novogrudok. He had been shot by the Nazis, but not before his cohorts had strangled a Jewish teen they feared might collaborate with the guards. The Nazis often offered Jews small perks to inform on their fellow ghetto residents, as a means of keeping control, Rae once explained.[38] The residents, on the verge of escape, could not take the risk. For Charles Kushner, nothing was worse than what he saw as collaboration.

"If you had to start all over again, what would you do differently?" Charlie Kushner was asked in the November 2007 *Real Deal* interview.[39] "I don't think I would change much," Charlie replied. "I probably would have heeded my father's advice not to take my brother in as a business partner, which my father always urged me to do."

Had he reached any resolution with his sister and her husband?

"I mean, it's a family tragedy what happened. I believe that God and my parents in heaven forgive me for what I did, which was wrong. I don't believe God and my parents will ever forgive my brother and sister for instigating a criminal investigation and being cheerleaders for the government and putting their brother in jail because of jealousy, hatred and spite. On my worst day in prison, I wouldn't trade places with my brother and sister, and yet I know what I did was wrong."

No one who lived through this story, and especially not Charlie, or Jared, or Chris Christie, would ever leave it behind.

ACT III

9

"A BRIDGE TO THE FUTURE"

A few days before the 1989 New York City mayoral election, the Republican candidate, Rudy Giuliani, thin and long-faced with square-cut black hair, took the podium at a breakfast at the New York Hilton. He was there to make his closing argument in the race against the Manhattan borough president, David N. Dinkins, who was running to be New York's first African-American mayor. The podium was in the middle of a long table, where women with feathered hair and well-padded shoulders were seated on either side of forty-five-year-old Giuliani, who was wearing a black suit and a black tie, looking like a G-man teleported from the 1950s. In his speech, Giuliani mentioned the Soviet Union.[1]

The race had not gone quite as planned: Giuliani had thought his opponent would be Mayor Ed Koch, running for a fourth term, whose years of presiding over a city government riddled with municipal corruption had offered a wide and public target. But Koch unexpectedly lost the primary, and Giuliani hadn't been able to consolidate support among Republicans. At the women's breakfast, he plowed gamely on. "As United States Attorney I got to see up close the inner workings of this city," he said with his slight lisp, more pronounced in those days. "I saw the invisible government of drug dealers who are taking over our neighborhoods. The mobsters who infiltrate legitimate businesses and make our housing even more unaffordable, the white-collar criminals who think they can get away with not paying their taxes and the traders on Wall Street who think they can escape the rule of law."

Giuliani's speech gained steam, his eyebrows popping up when he thought he'd hit a high note of logic. "I saw the corrupt politicians who take money from our seniors and our children to line their own pockets. . . . I've met older New Yorkers trapped in their homes in fear of the violence on the streets of this city." I am the one who can fix this, Giuliani was arguing. I understand it as no one else. Elect me.

This was Giuliani in his purest form. His US Attorney's Office had broken the spine of "The Commission," the group that ruled the Mafia, also known as La Cosa Nostra. Giuliani personally led the prosecution of Bronx boss and Roy Cohn law partner Stanley Friedman for racketeering. But as a candidate, he was not above making specific promises to specific communities. "Wherever I've travelled during this campaign, I've heard the concerns, and I've responded," Giuliani said at the breakfast. "When I met with the people on the Upper West Side, I told them I oppose the Trump project and the extra congestion and density it would bring to the area."

Giuliani and Trump already had a history at this point. In 1988, Trump had been investigated by an FBI agent working for Giuliani, a man named Tony Lombardi, who had looked into whether Trump had done anything improper when he sold an apartment to a man named Robert Hopkins. As reported by Wayne Barrett in the *Village Voice*, Hopkins's 1984 closing—where Trump made a personal appearance—involved two dubious tax returns, faked diamond appraisals, and up to $200,000 in cash in a suitcase delivered to a New Jersey bank favored by Trump in a Trump limo.[2] Hopkins was later convicted of running a mob-backed gambling ring out of Trump Tower. Trump wasn't charged.

In 1988, a witness who was himself under investigation approached Lombardi, offering up dirt on Trump. But instead of quietly investigating, as law enforcement agents usually do, Lombardi went straight to Trump. "The guy met me without an attorney, he answered all my questions," Lombardi told Barrett. "I amazed myself that I was able to talk to him for an hour without being interrupted."

In an article about the incident, Barrett laid out evidence that Lombardi, instead of trying to investigate Trump, was secretly feeding Trump information, and ensuring that Trump wouldn't be prosecuted. "The best indication," Barrett wrote, of Lombardi's "continuing ties to Trump involve this reporter." At one point, Barrett had asked Lombardi about a tip he'd received, a tip he'd discussed with no one else. "An outraged, well-informed Trump was telling a lawyer about it right after my meeting with Lombardi," Barrett wrote. Later Barrett confronted Lombardi about the tip. Lombardi denied passing along the information, though he acknowledged he would have liked to work for Trump, telling Barrett the men had "chemistry."

Not long after the investigation fizzled, Trump announced that if Rudy Giuliani ran for mayor, he, Trump, could raise two million dollars for him in half an hour. The following year, Trump served as co-chair of Giuliani's first major fundraiser, sitting on the dais at the Waldorf Astoria. According to Barrett, Trump, "his family, and his staff raised and gave at least $41,000 to the campaign."[3] But by the time of the women's breakfast at the Hilton, the developer's ties to Giuliani had begun to attenuate. No matter which political party occupied Gracie Mansion, the Democrat-led committees would still oversee the approvals and abatements Trump needed. Backing an untested Republican for mayor was a risk. Giuliani lost.

Four years later, in 1993, Rudy, as everyone now called him, made another run at Dinkins, this time as a changed man. (I directed the communications team for the last six months of the Dinkins campaign. It was my final job in politics before switching to journalism.) Giuliani had come to a truce with the Republican kingmaker, Senator Alfonse D'Amato, and hired Ed Koch's strategist, but most of all, he came back with a new and highly nonspecific message: one of cutting government, cutting taxes, cutting benefits, cutting "red tape" for businesses, and most of all cutting crime.

Though crime rates had already started to fall from their peak, under Dinkins, homicides were still at intolerably high levels, over two thousand a year.[4] The recession that hit the country in 1990 had taken hold in New York City fifteen months prior; it cut across every sector, hundreds of thousands of jobs were lost, 10 percent of the city's jobs base.[5] Rudy's answer was to cut city workers, privatize city services, and generally limit the ways the city provided for its citizens: fewer teachers, less government-provided healthcare, less money for the subways. Rudy eked out a victory, becoming the first Republican in a quarter century to ascend to the mayoralty.

Just two weeks after the mayoral election, the US House voted to approve the North American Free Trade Agreement (NAFTA); the Senate followed suit three days later—in both cases Republicans made up the majority of yeas.[6] The bill had been negotiated and signed by President George H. W. Bush, but it was Bill Clinton who steered it through Congress. In his first year in office, Clinton had reversed some of Reagan's tax cuts, reinstating a 39.6 percent top tax rate, a hike expected to affect only the top 1.2 percent of wage earners. NAFTA was, among other things, a rapprochement with Republicans.

"When you live in a time of change the only way to recover your security and to broaden your horizons is to adapt to the change, to embrace, to move forward," Bill Clinton said at a signing ceremony in the East Room of the White House in September 1993.

"Nothing we do—nothing we do in this great capital can change the fact that factories or information can flash across the world; that people can move money around in the blink of an eye."[7] By 1993, the American middle class was visibly struggling. Bill Clinton's solution was NAFTA.

Speaking in California, Donald Trump disapproved. "It's a no-brainer," Trump said, as reported by the *Long Beach Press-Telegram* in 1993. "The Mexicans want it, and that doesn't sound good to me."[8] Giuliani, weakly, opposed NAFTA. "I continue to be concerned about the effect it would have on the job situation in New York City," he told reporters the week after his election. "It is somewhat a narrow perspective, but it's my most important narrow perspective, which is the people of New York City."[9]

On January 1, 1994, Giuliani was sworn into office, and NAFTA took effect.

A few weeks later, Bill Clinton, in his State of the Union address, was making more promises: "to guarantee health security for all, to reward work over welfare, to promote democracy abroad and to begin to reclaim our streets from violent crime and drugs and gangs, to renew our own American community."[10] Of those goals, two aligned with Giuliani's and real estate developer Trump's interests: reforming welfare and reducing crime through heavy policing. Those two reforms were enacted. The other major pillar—health care for all—failed spectacularly, and created as a by-product the image of a monstrous, power-hungry, and secretive Hillary Clinton, an image that would plague her for the next quarter century.

In New York City, Rudy pushed his interpretation of the "broken windows" theory of crime fighting, based on the idea that visible signs of crime and disorder breed more serious crime and disorder. If the NYPD focused on arresting the turnstile-jumpers, the pot-smokers, and people with open beer cans on their stoops, the theory went, it would discourage more violent, disruptive crimes. Broken windows policing translated to the criminalization of daily behavior, which dovetailed with the Clinton-supported Violent Crime and Control Act of 1994. Both fueled the era of mass incarceration, disproportionately affecting black and brown Americans, and a surge of new police officers on a local level.

While funding the police, Rudy made deep cuts elsewhere: city workers, health care costs, and, above all, welfare. "Reinventing Government," Rudy called this shift in priorities. "Instead of fearing change we should lead the way," he said in his 1995 State of the City Address. In Washington, Bill Clinton, the Democrat, had been pushing a similar agenda.

Clinton, born to a widowed mother in Hope, Arkansas, had promised in his 1992 campaign to "end welfare as we know it," taking his cue not from Franklin Delano Roosevelt but from Ronald Reagan. The Personal Responsibility and Work Opportunity Act, which Clinton signed in 1996, ended six decades of social policy that ensured federal guarantees of assistance.[11] The Rose Garden ceremony was protested on Pennsylvania Avenue by women's groups and advocates for the poor. As the *Washington Post* wrote, a "cloud of controversy" settled over the signing.[12]

Then Clinton flew to Chicago for the Democratic National Convention, where he averred, "We do not need to build a bridge to the past, we need to build a bridge to the future, and that is what I commit to you to do. So, tonight let us resolve to build that bridge to the twenty-first century, to meet our challenges and protect our values."[13]

Though Trump had drifted from Giuliani during the 1989 campaign, they were again closely aligned by the mid-1990s. Trump and his wife, Marla, had given well over $10,000 to Rudy's campaigns.[14] Trump, who knew better, tried to send two checks totaling $6,900 to Rudy Giuliani at City Hall, plus another $3,100 to the Liberal Party of New York, run by lobbyist and Trump friend Ray Harding. There was a scrawled note with the contribution: it said, "Rudy—Marla thinks you're GREAT!" next to the sharpie-signed initials, DT. Rudy's deputy mayor, Randy Mastro, sent the checks back with a note that Trump needed to send them to "Friends of Giuliani," the campaign committee. But by then the City Hall administration had been made pointedly aware of Donald's largesse.[15]

In 1995, around the same time Giuliani was talking about work requirements and fraud prevention measures for welfare recipients, Giuliani's Department of Housing Preservation and Development wrote a letter to its Washington counterpart, endorsing a Trump proposal seeking $356 million in federal mortgage insurance intended for low-income housing. The money was for a Trump project named Riverside South, a proposed suite of massive silver towers along the Hudson River on Manhattan's Upper West Side. Candidate Rudy Giuliani had predicted during the 1989 mayoral race that it would bring "congestion" and "density."

A coalition of Upper West Side elected officials, including a portly, bespectacled second-term congressman named Jerrold Nadler, went ballistic. They accused the city of "colluding with Trump." They said the "tainted" application was a "speculative scheme to subsidize luxury housing in an already largely affluent area."[16]

The federal mortgage insurance relied on the site's getting an official "blight" designation under Section 220, a 1954 federal program backing housing in so-called "urban renewal areas," that is, slums. The Riverside project "would not eliminate slums and blighted conditions," Representative Jerry Nadler wrote in a letter to the federal Department of Housing and Urban Development, because the site lay "in the heart of one of the wealthiest, fastest growing, thriving areas of the City, if not the entire nation."[17]

Still, the Giuliani administration argued that the site was indeed "blighted" and the Trump development was part of a "coordinated" plan for the area. But though the Giuliani administration could argue that a major developer deserved $356 million in federal mortgage insurance to build luxury condos at the same time that it was arguing welfare recipients should be stripped of their monthly grants (maybe $2,500 for a family of four), it could not, in fact, produce the loan.

By the time HUD was ready to make a ruling, the federal agency was run by a curly haired, espresso-eyed cabinet secretary, Andrew Cuomo, who had done legal work for Trump while his father, Mario, was governor. Andrew Cuomo was not inclined to approve the project, which his counsel, Howard Glaser, later described on Twitter as "an attempt to siphon fed $$ for his luxury housing."[18] What Trump was doing, Glaser said, was a "scam" to "skim $350 million" that was "typical Trump": attempting to inflate the value of the federal subsidy by including the value of adjacent city parkland. Cuomo determined it would have been illegal, according to Glaser.

Trump was furious. As he described it in his book *How to Get Rich*, in a chapter called "Sometimes You Have to Hold a Grudge," he leaned on Andrew Cuomo's father, former governor Mario Cuomo, to sort out the problem. "I called Mario to ask for a perfectly legal and appropriate favor involving attention to a detail at the Department of Housing and Urban Development, which at the time was being run by his son Andrew."

Trump continued: "Mario told me that this would be hard for him to do because he rarely calls the 'Secretary' on business matters. I said to him, 'Mario, he is not the Secretary, he is your son."

Mario demurred.

Trump wrote: "I began screaming, 'You son of a bitch! For years I've helped you and never asked for a thing, and when I finally need something, and a totally proper thing at that, you aren't there for me. You're no good. You're one of the most disloyal people I've known and as far as I'm concerned, you can go to hell.'"

"My screaming was so loud that two or three people came in from adjoining offices and asked who I was screaming at. I told them it was Mario Cuomo, a total stiff, a lousy governor, and a disloyal former friend. Now whenever I see Mario at a dinner, I refuse to acknowledge him, talk to him, or even look at him."[19]

What Trump did not put in his book, according to Glaser: Mario Cuomo's firm was working for Trump at the time. Trump went to the firm's senior partners and threatened to fire the firm, Glaser wrote, unless "M. Cuomo got A. Cuomo to approve the fraudulent use of funds. M. Cuomo declined of course."

Though Rudy Giuliani was unable to secure federal subsidies for Trump's luxury housing project, the mayor was able to help the developer out in other ways. Trump hired the lobbying firm closest to Giuliani, that of Liberal Party boss Ray Harding, once described by the *New York Times* as "his own smoke-filled room."[20] Harding's firm helped Trump World Tower, across from the United Nations, get approvals from three separate levels of the Giuliani administration, despite vociferous opposition to the height of the tower from figures including fossil-fuel billionaire David Koch and Walter Cronkite, the former CBS news anchor.[21] (Giuliani's administration did draw the line at offering Trump a 421a "blighted" tax break for the luxury tower across from the United Nations. Trump sued, and eventually settled for an abatement worth $119.5 million over ten years.[22])

In June 1999, Fred Trump, who had suffered from Alzheimer's in his later years, died at age ninety-three, after contracting pneumonia. His funeral was attended by senators and entertainers and real estate developers, written up in the *New York Post* under the headline, "Trump Patriarch Eulogized as Great Builder." Mayor Rudy Giuliani gave a speech. "Fred Trump not only helped to build our city, but helped to define it," Giuliani said, standing near the coffin draped with white roses. "He helped make it the most important city in the world." The *New York Post* described Fred C. Trump as "the son of a Swedish immigrant father."

"This is by far the toughest day of my life," Donald Trump said when it was his turn to speak. "My father was a great builder. I learned everything from him. He was a master builder, but also a very hard worker. He would be very upset if his kids weren't working today. . . . He was a great husband for sixty-three years to my equally incredible mother, something I'll never be able to catch him on and he knew that."

Concluding his remarks, Donald Trump said: "I love you, Pop."[23]

By the time he stood before the crowd at Marble Collegiate Church for his father's funeral, Donald Trump and his siblings had already spent the better part of the decade implementing strategies to avoid the tax on Fred's estate, some of them legal, and some of them, according to the *New York Times*, that were "legally dubious and, in some cases, appeared to be fraudulent."[24] The legal part involved a special type of trust, called a GRAT, an acronym for grantor-retained annuity trust, that allowed dynastic families like the Trumps to pass parts of their wealth from one generation to the next, paying zero dollars in estate taxes.

"The details are numbingly complex," the *Times* wrote, "but the mechanics are straightforward. For the Trumps, it meant putting half the properties to be transferred into a GRAT in Fred Trump's name and the other half into a GRAT in his wife's name. Then Fred and Mary Trump gave their children roughly two-thirds of the assets in their GRATs. The children bought the remaining third by making annuity payments to their parents over the next two years. By November 22, 1997, it was done; the Trump children owned nearly all of Fred Trump's empire free and clear of estate taxes."

The benefits were not equally distributed. Fred Trump wrote the heirs of Fred Trump Jr.—an alcoholic who had died in his forties—largely out of his will. Fred Jr.'s heirs sued. At one point in the legal battle, Donald Trump terminated Fred's children's health insurance, even though one of them had an eighteen-month-old son who suffered from a rare neurological disorder. "When [Fred 3rd] sued us, we said, 'Why should we give him medical coverage?'" Donald Trump told the *New York Daily News* during the legal battle. "Asked whether he thought cutting their coverage could appear cold-hearted, given the baby's medical condition, Donald made no apologies," the *News* wrote. "I can't help that," Donald Trump said. "It's cold when someone sues my father. Had he come to see me, things could very possibly have been much different for them."[25]

By the time Fred Trump died, the summer of 1999, Rudy Giuliani was already thinking about his next move, a run for US Senate. Rudy had a story to tell: He had presided over a halving in violent crimes, and a reduction of the unemployment rate, from over 10 percent to a little less than 7 percent.[26] He had pushed economic development in places like Times Square, that transformed the neighborhood from the gunshot and prostitute-wracked war zone of Tom Hanks's 1988 movie *Big* to a haven for families and tourists. And Giuliani had created an enormous amount of wealth for people who owned real estate. A Manhattan apartment worth $100,000 in 1993 was worth $197,000 in 2000, Giuliani's penultimate year in office, according to New York University's Furman Center.[27] This success story was to be the basis for his US Senate campaign against the person everyone believed would be his opponent: First Lady Hillary Rodham Clinton, who was already preparing a run.

While Clinton was conducting a "listening tour" in upstate New York, three hundred miles to the south, in Washington, DC, her husband was helping to maneuver through Congress the Gramm-Leach-Bliley Act, aka "The Financial Modernization Act," which repealed the Glass-Steagall Act.

In 1933, after widespread bank failures, four thousand bank suspensions, hundreds of millions of dollars in depositor losses, and a week-long shutdown of the entire banking system, President Franklin Delano Roosevelt signed the Banking Act of 1933, which included key provisions known as Glass-Steagall. These were designed to create a firewall between commercial banks—the ordinary banks where people make deposits and get loans—and investment banks, which oversee the issuance of riskier investments, like stocks and bonds. The idea was that unsophisticated customers should be shielded from the risk more-sophisticated investors might make, and that if there was a problem in the investment banking world, the contagion would be contained.

By the 1980s, regulators and judges began eroding the law. In 1991, the first Bush administration called for its outright repeal. Eight years later—and after a campaign that involved hundreds of millions of dollars in lobbying and political contributions[28] to a bipartisan group that included New York's junior senator, the banking committee chairman Alfonse D'Amato, and the man that succeeded him, Charles Schumer—President Bill Clinton struck a deal "to maximize the possibilities of the new information-age global economy, while preserving our responsibilities to protect ordinary citizens and to build one nation here."

It was, Bill Clinton argued, a victory for freedom and free markets and consumer protection. "The Glass-Steagall law is no longer appropriate for the economy in which we live," Clinton said, at the bill signing. "It worked pretty well for the industrial economy. But the world is very different." The president thought, wrongly, that he was preparing the country for the economy to come. "Today what we are doing is modernizing the financial services industry, tearing down these antiquated walls and granting banks significant new authority. This will, first of all, save consumers billions of dollars a year through enhanced competition. It will also protect the rights of consumers."[29]

At a desk, Clinton picked up a dozen black and gold pens one by one in his left hand and signed the bill to delighted applause from a mostly male group of members of Congress, who clustered around him in a triangular tableau.[30]

Three months later, in a vaulting student gym at the State University of New York in Purchase, in the suburbs of New York City, the president joined his daughter and the two US senators from New York as his wife, Hillary Clinton, wearing a black pantsuit and pearls, her hair short, her face unlined, formally announced her campaign. "I don't believe government is the source of all our problems or the solution to them," she told two thousand onlookers, an unusually large crowd for a US Senate launch in New York. "But I do believe that when people live up to their responsibilities, we ought to live up to ours to help them build better lives. That's the basic bargain we owe one another in America today."[31]

In 1999, before he even declared for US Senate, Rudy raised an astonishing $11.6 million, including $100,000 raised from the Florham Park offices of New Jersey real estate developer Charles Kushner. Until then, Charlie had not been a Republican donor. He was introduced to Giuliani by friends in the Orthodox Jewish Community. Raising money for a law and order candidate, Kushner ran afoul of federal campaign finance rules. "Errors Turn Fund-Raising Coup Into Embarrassment for Giuliani," a *New York Times* headline read. Fifty-seven thousand of those dollars had to be returned.[32]

In December 1999, the Center for Public Integrity's Knut Royce raised more questions about Rudy's fundraising:[33] from 1994 to 1999, Rudy had accepted more than forty thousand dollars in contributions, an unusually large amount, from the family of a Russian émigré named Semyon (Sam) Kislin.[34] Kislin was a commodities trader who the FBI had once suspected of being tied to the Russian mob and to various money-laundering schemes. Kislin denied the allegations and was never charged.

At the time Kislin donated to Rudy, he'd been working at a business made lucrative by the soaring real estate values under Rudy. In 1998, the ruble crashed, Russian banks started to collapse, and newly valuable New York real estate was a particularly good place to park foreign capital. Kislin began issuing mortgages for apartment buyers in the Trump World Tower. According to a report by *Bloomberg*'s Caleb Melby and Keri Geiger, "It's highly unusual for individuals to issue formal mortgages for U.S. luxury real estate, and the tower loans are the only ones Kislin ever made in New York, public records show."[35] One of those loans, for $674,000, was to Vasily Salygin, a Ukranian politician, for an eighty-third-floor apartment in Trump World Tower.[36] Kislin and Trump had done business before. Around 1980, Kislin and a partner, ex-Soviet cab driver turned electronics entrepreneur Tamir Sapir, had sold Donald Trump two hundred television sets for the Commodore Hotel.

Trump also gave money to Rudy Giuliani at the start of his campaign. But that came before a dramatic four weeks in the spring of 2000, when Giuliani announced in rapid succession that he had prostate cancer, was having an affair (with his future third wife, Judith Nathan), and was separating from his second wife, Donna Hanover, which news he made known to her via a press conference. Hanover, in turn, accused Rudy of having another affair, with a mayoral staffer. Giuliani dropped out of the US Senate race.

The next month, ten people with the last name "Kushner" contributed to Hillary Clinton's campaign, among them nineteen-year-old Jared, who had just finished his freshman year at Harvard.[37]

Clinton won her race against Rudy's replacement, Long Island Representative Rick Lazio, early in the evening of November 7, 2000. "We started this great effort on a sunny July morning in Pindars Corners on Pat and Liz Moynihan's beautiful farm," she said in her victory speech. "And sixty-two counties, sixteen months, three debates, two opponents, and six black pantsuits later, because of you, here we are," Clinton said.[38] The crowd cheered particularly hard when she pledged to defend a woman's right to choose.

The next morning, the presidential race was still unsettled. Al Gore had been poised to concede, then pulled back. Bush led by a few hundred votes out of millions cast in the swing state of Florida. During the protracted court battle that followed, a group of well-dressed young men disrupted an attempted recount in what became known as the "Brooks Brothers riot." One of its instigators was Roger Stone.

"When three Democratic commissioners took the box into a room by themselves and closed the door then I said, 'Yes, break that door down, you're breaking the law.'" Stone said in a 2004 interview with Wayne Barrett. "I don't think the people that rioted did anything wrong," Stone added.[39] The count was halted.

There was another way Stone bolstered Bush's post-election efforts.[40] He secretly organized the "Committee to Take Back Our Judiciary" to run campaigns against judges who might rule in favor of Gore. There was, actually, no such committee, a judge ruled, just a front group created by Roger Stone. It never emerged who had provided the funds for Stone's efforts.

The recount of Miami-Dade's votes was never completed. Bush won Florida, and the presidency, by just a few hundred votes. (He won the electoral college but lost the popular vote nationally.)

Almost right away, as senator, Hillary Clinton began building an operation that would allow her, someday, to run for president.

10

ESCAPE FROM NEW JERSEY

On a warm May afternoon in 2014, when he was thirty-three years old, the owner of a New York newspaper, already having negotiated ten billion dollars in real estate deals, Jared Kushner received an honorary degree from Hofstra University. The degree was a Doctor of Humane Letters, *honoris causa*. His father, Charles Kushner, had graduated from Hofstra Law School thirty-five years prior and subsequently donated enough money that the university installed him on its board of trustees, renamed the law school building Kushner Hall, and established the Joseph Kushner Distinguished Professorship in Civil Liberties Law.

"I want to dedicate this speech . . . to my dad," Jared Kushner said. "Growing up, my father told me about his experience on the day of his graduation and how his father, who was an immigrant and a Holocaust survivor, pulled him aside under a tree and said, 'You know, son, as I learned in my life, you know, I saw with the Nazis—they took everything from me. They took my family, they took my money, but nobody can ever take away your education.' And I think that's a lesson that obviously is very important for all of you today." In Kushner's Jersey accent "today" came out as "t'da-eey."

"We grew up with a very hard-working mentality in our family, the immigrant mentality really went its way down," he continued. "And my father was always working, and if we wanted to spend time with my dad we'd go to work with him. So, from when I was four years old, a lot my friends were going to football games with their dads on Sundays, I'd be in the back of his car with him going to construction sites and job sites."[1] Jared liked to tell this story and told it often. "I'd be in the back of my dad's car with my pair of mini construction boots," was how he described it in a 2009 interview.[2]

Real estate, he said at Hofstra, "really got into my blood."

—

Born on January 10, 1981, Jared Corey Kushner was the firstborn son of devout Modern Orthodox Jews, in a religion with strict gender roles. Nine days later, on the eve of Ronald Reagan's inauguration, Charlie's younger sister Esther also gave birth to a son, Jacob Schulder. When they were born, Iran had not yet released its American hostages, Reagan had not yet declared government the enemy. In New Jersey, a smiling Joseph Kushner, in his late fifties, posed for a photo with his two grandsons, baby Jared and baby Jacob, on his knees.

The enormous house in Livingston, New Jersey, where Jared lived as a child, stood on a quiet suburban street behind a thatch of trees and a stone wall surrounded by elegant landscaping. The house, which would eventually grow to comprise eighteen rooms and seven thousand square feet, contained an enormous glass atrium and a floor-to-ceiling fireplace.[3] When Jared was born, Chris Christie and David Wildstein had recently graduated from Livingston High School.

When Jared was one, his uncle Murray, widowed with two young boys, remarried Lee Warshow Serwitz and adopted her two young children. Until he left for Harvard, Jared lived around the corner from four cousins, the children of Murray and Lee Kushner—Jonathan, Aryeh, Marc, and Melissa—and a ten-minute drive from his other cousins, Jessica, Jacob, and Ruth, the children of Esther and Billy Schulder. Linda's children were older, but they all spent Shabbat together, walked to synagogue on Saturdays, attended the Joseph Kushner Hebrew Academy together. Their sports jerseys said "Kushner" on the front and "Kushner" on the back.

By the time Jared was thirteen both he and his father, Charlie, were feeling the siren pull of Manhattan, where Rudy Giuliani had just been elected mayor. Jared's black-tie bar mitzvah was held at a midtown Manhattan hotel. Hundreds of people attended, including members of the New York Giants football team. A central part of the bar mitzvah is reading a portion of the Torah. Jared's portion was Beshalach, the part of the Exodus story where God parts the Red Sea for the Israelites and then allows the waters to flood the pursuing Egyptian army.

Afterwards, Rae Kushner was proud. "Jared is my favorite grandchild," she said at the reception. A week later, Jacob Schulder's bar mitzvah was held in New Jersey, also black tie, but with no members of the New York Giants in attendance. "Jacob is my favorite grandchild," Rae said.

For high school, both boys attended the prestige school for Modern Orthodox children: The Frisch School in Paramus, a thirty-minute drive from Livingston. Frisch was highly regimented. Students were put into tracks: "H" was the lowest, "K" was honors, "L" was highest honors. In a class of a little over one hundred, students were keenly aware of the rankings. Jared claims he was in honors classes and AP classes, but in interviews, people in the K or L classes could not recall ever sharing classes with him.

Jared was tall in high school; tall for a Jew, classmates said. He played basketball all four years, he was popular with girls, in the way a Modern Orthodox boy can be. Sometimes he would slip into Manhattan to socialize with high schoolers from Ramaz, a Modern Orthodox school on the Upper East Side. Jared was polite to a degree that some of the people who knew him in high school called "performative," especially around his father. The Frisch School stressed *derech eretz*, or acting decorously and with respect, particularly towards parents, elders, and teachers. Modern Orthodox boys had rules to observe, and Jared observed them: the food he ate, the clothes he wore, which prayers he said at which time of day. At one get-together with his cousins, before the family blew apart, Jared was pictured wearing a white button-down shirt and tie; everyone else is wearing sweaters.

According to federal records, eleven-year-old Jared was already making political contributions: two thousand dollars to Senator Frank Lautenberg, twelve hundred and fifty to New York Attorney General Bob Abrams, who was running for US Senate from New York. In 1997, Jared (misspelled "Gared" in *The Record*) was photographed with his cousin Jacob, sophomores by then, when Senator Robert Toricelli visited their school.[4] By the time he'd graduated from Frisch, Jared Kushner, "student," had made thirteen thousand dollars in political contributions,[5] as orchestrated by his father.[6]

At Frisch, the politics were distinctly Zionist. Palestinians were "Arabs." There was no discussion of the legitimacy of their land claims. Yasser Arafat, the Palestinian leader, was presented as an evil, one-dimensional caricature. When Jared was a teen, once and future Israeli prime minister Bibi Netanyahu was paid by Charles Kushner's bank to speak at Charlie's office. Jared was tapped to introduce him. Bibi was out of power at the time but planning a comeback, cultivating ties with wealthy Americans who could help his campaign. Netanyahu, the story goes, stayed on Fawn Drive that night, playing basketball with Jared in the driveway.

In 1998, during the fiftieth anniversary of the founding of Israel, Jared Kushner joined "The March of the Living," an annual trip to Israel and Poland founded by two Israeli benefactors. The trip included a two-mile march, with Israeli flags, from one concentration camp to another: Auschwitz to Birkenau. Joel Katz, Jared's trip leader, described Kushner to the *Forward* as "a quiet, down-to-earth, intellectual teen already 'extremely steeped in Holocaust education and *yiddishkeit*' or Jewishness. 'He was understanding the severity of our journey, the commitment he had to his family and his legacy.'"[7]

In the fall, there were college applications to fill out. At Frisch, the students and the teachers were acutely status-conscious, strivers. It was understood that at a school like Frisch, only a few students would get into each Ivy League school, only one or two would get into Harvard. Typically, to keep their acceptance rates high, schools like Frisch maintain their prestige by constricting the number of students that apply to each of the top schools. You had to be at least a Level K to be eligible to apply to Harvard, the thinking went—and yet, Jared got in. Other kids, who had achieved more, in more difficult classes, did not. They thought Jared had taken their spot. As the investigative journalist Daniel Golden wrote years later in his book *The Price of Admission*, "Jared was not in the school's highest academic track in all courses, and his test scores were below Ivy League standards." A former Frisch official told Golden, "There was no way anybody in the administrative office of the school thought he would on the merits get into Harvard. His GPA did not warrant it, his SAT scores did not warrant it."[8]

The Harvard class of 2003 had at the time the lowest admission rate in school's history.[9] But Charles Kushner had circumvented that hurdle. In 1998, the year before Jared applied, Charlie pledged $2.5 million to Harvard, which named Charlie and Seryl to its Committee on University Resources. For good measure, Charlie called Senator Frank Lautenberg, to whom he'd been making tens of thousands of dollars in political donations beginning in the early nineties, and asked him to prevail upon Senator Ted Kennedy to call Harvard on Kushner's behalf. (Kennedy denied any memory of this to Golden.) Charlie, through his attention-getting donation, had scored a double victory: his son got a coveted slot at Harvard, and he was able to write off the cost as a charitable contribution. Legal records filed with the Federal Election Commission show Charlie began to make the payments only after Jared matriculated.[10]

Before he left for college, Jared hosted a graduation beach party at his family mansion in Long Branch, a grand stucco home with a terracotta-tiled roof, rounded balconies, and a forbidding wall separating it from the beach. Because Orthodox boys and girls weren't supposed to dance together, he also hosted an unofficial "prom" at the Puck Building. He was leaving New Jersey behind.

—

At Harvard, classmates viewed Jared as affable, nice. He wore preppy clothes, played junior varsity squash, was tapped to join an exclusive Harvard "final club," The Fly.[11] He also became an instant mogul. "I bought my first few buildings: call it a bad idea with follow through." Jared said later. "Whatever it was I saw a good opportunity and I went for it."[12] It was, actually, an opportunity created and backed by his father, an intergenerational transfer of wealth obscured by a pleasing family story.

In November 2000, when Jared Kushner was a sophomore at Harvard, records show that a series of Kushner-related companies purchased $5,250,000 worth of properties in Somerville, a small city abutting Cambridge. A few months later, Jared's limited liability companies received $9 million in credit from Citicorp. The paperwork was signed by Richard Stadtmauer, Jared's mother's brother, who at the time worked for Charlie in a role described by associates as "consigliere." The next year, a Charlie Kushner LLC signed on as the mortgager, borrowing another $1,050,000 for his son's real estate education, this time from Bear Stearns.[13]

Jared bought, renovated, and managed apartments during the school year, riding back and forth from his Harvard dorm in the cab of his contractor's Dodge pickup. Jared once described the contractor as "a six foot five Guatemalan guy." In a moment of self-awareness, Jared recalled in his Hofstra speech how he would tell the contractor, " 'We're going too slow, this work's not good enough, you're too expensive'—and then I'd sheepishly ask him if he'd give me a ride back to my dorm."[14] Eventually, Jared got a Range Rover so he could drive himself.

From Harvard, Jared negotiated rents, fielded complaints about uncollected trash, smells, pests, and in one case, lack of heat for a whole season. The *Boston Globe* reported that on one occasion he told a set of tenants that he'd be renovating their apartment while they lived in it. When they asked for a month's rent as consideration, Jared counter-offered $100. They rejected it, and the work was cancelled. As the *Globe* reported, Jared "managed 40 apartment units across a run-down but rising Somerville market. He converted another 16 units into condominiums that he would sell individually. And his efforts paid off—the properties he bought for $8.3 million sold four years later for $13 million."[15]

Jared's Somerville investment, his first foray in the family line of work, came as the family, and family business, were coming under increasing strain. By 2002, as he finished his junior year, Jared had already been subpoenaed by the Federal Election Commission in its investigation of illegal donations; his uncle had sued his father for stealing; and Jared had already denounced his cousins at the family seder at Fontainebleau, saying of Esther's children—Jessica, Ruth, and Jacob, who'd grown up like a twin brother—"they're not worth fighting about."

At Harvard, Jared implanted himself in an institution that offered community in exchange for strict adherence to a set of religious rules: Chabad, the evangelical branch of Orthodox Judaism. Jared gave eighteen thousand dollars to the Harvard Chabad.[16] "It's very, very rare that college students contribute on any level," E. Hirschy Zarchi, the rabbi of Harvard Chabad, later told the *Harvard Crimson*. Zarchi, whom the *Crimson* described as a "close friend" of Jared's, also said: "He was almost like a partner [to Chabad]. . . . He was a great friend. At a very young age, he brought a certain wisdom and strategic thinking about building an enterprise."[17]

In his senior year at Harvard, Jared Kushner was given the honor of speaking at the unveiling of a new Chabad center on campus. Jared stepped to the podium that day looking extremely young, his cheeks pink and soft, like he had barely started to shave. His syntax was clunky. "Going away to college or graduate school can be a time when young adults begin to challenge the teachings of their past while setting the course for their futures," he said. "People are encouraged to find personal significance and meaning in whatever it is that one is looking for." He quoted Margaret Thatcher. He said a-day-jes, for "adages."[18]

In his time in school, Jared sometimes flew home on the shuttle from Boston to New York. In the shuttle lounge, there were stacks of free newspapers, including a salmon-colored news weekly, the *New York Observer*. The *Observer* obsessively covered the inside workings of New York's key industries: real estate, politics, finance, entertainment, media. "The Rudy Team has '04 Dream: Bush-Giuliani" was one headline at the end of Jared's junior year. There was a cover story about the casual use of the F-word gaining currency in polite society.[19] An article about "power seders" caught Jared's eye.[20]

After graduating from Harvard in 2003, Jared Kushner was twenty-two and about to make more than five million dollars from selling real estate in Massachusetts. Later that summer he moved to the Manhattan neighborhood of NoHo, near Greenwich Village, to begin a double degree program in business and law at New York University, to which Charlie had given three million tax-deductible dollars. That same month, Jared's father asked an East Orange cop to hire a prostitute to ensnare Jared's uncle.

In July of the next year, while interning for the Manhattan DA, Jared learned of his father's arrest. Jared took a cab to Newark, and his plan—to finish law school and business school and work in a nonprofit—was permanently derailed. "My first year in law school I had a little bit of a set-back," he later said to the Hofstra Law grads, "which forced me at that point to get into the family business . . . sooner than I would have liked to."[21]

Jared's father had sent the videotape of his uncle Billy with the prostitute to his aunt Esther on the eve of his cousin Jacob's engagement party. Charlie had wanted to send it to Jacob, too. Jared's relationship with his one-week-younger cousin was over.

In April 2005, Charlie Kushner began his federal prison term in Alabama. Most weekends, throughout law school, Jared flew down to visit him, sometimes on the private plane of Howard Jonas, a Jewish businessman and a partner of Charlie's who founded the tech company IDT. In prison, Charlie ate cottage cheese, bought his own sneakers. He gave Jared a wallet that he made while behind bars.

A family narrative of resentment was nurtured during these trips.

"His siblings stole every piece of paper from his office, and they took it to the government," Jared later told *New York* magazine. "Siblings that he literally made wealthy for doing nothing. He gave them interests in the business for nothing. All he did was put the tape together and send it. Was it the right thing to do? At the end of the day, it was a function of saying 'You're trying to make my life miserable? Well, I'm doing the same.'"[22]

As the years went on, Jared's views set. Christie "tried to destroy my father," Jared later said, as described by Christie in his book *Let Me Finish*. "There was a dispute inside the family," Christie quoted Jared as saying. "My father made those people rich, and they did nothing," Jared said. "They just benefited from my father's hard work. And those are the people who turned him in. It wasn't fair." And then, the crescendo. "This was a family matter," Jared said, "a matter to be handled by the family or by the rabbis"—not prosecutors.[23]

In 2006, Jared Kushner had a year to go at The Stern School of Business and New York University School of Law. He became increasingly involved in the family business, while also interning at a start-up private equity firm.[24] Jared noticed that the *New York Observer* was for sale, and at age twenty-five, called up the paper's owner, Arthur Carter, whom, he later said, "I had met a few times through my father." Carter put him off; he was already negotiating with a group that included actor Robert De Niro.

Founded in 1987, the paper fostered a generation of journalists willing to, as editor Peter Kaplan put it, "get up inside the pipes" of the wealthy and powerful, to expose their foibles, their New York-i-ness, and sometimes, their corruption. There was a running cast of characters: Rudy Giuliani and Tina Brown; Martin Scorsese and Rupert Murdoch; Alfonse D'Amato and Michael Bloomberg; Hillary Clinton and Donald Trump. Candace Bushnell's character "Mr. Big" was invented on the pages of the *New York Observer*, which launched the column Sex and the City.

By 2006, Arthur Carter, a real estate magnate himself, was tiring of the business. Publishing was never a sure way to make money in New York, although it was almost always a way to have influence. De Niro's group had been circling and circling, asking detailed questions about everything down to the postage bill, but had not committed to sustain the paper if it didn't start making money in three years.

Jared kept wooing Carter and, equally as important, the *Observer's* visionary editor, Peter Kaplan. Himself a Jew from New Jersey who had gone to Harvard, Kaplan had thick, greying hair and tortoise-shell glasses. A loosened tie typically held together his button-down shirt as he sat behind his messy desk, stacked high with newspapers, his own and others.

Jared was charming, solicitous. Carter and Kaplan were wary that De Niro's bid was a prelude to a shutdown. Kaplan knew the history of the Kushner family; he was editor when the series of stories uncovered Charlie's conflicts of interest at the Port Authority and helped end Charlie's bid for the chairmanship of the bistate agency. Colleagues warned him that "the family was no good," but Kaplan thought that Jared was young, malleable, someone he could shape and mentor. The De Niro bid wasn't closing and the future of the paper was in doubt. Kaplan backed Jared.

Jared met with Carter at his apartment and, to counteract his own youth, brought along one of his father's lawyers, who was grey-haired and bow-tied. Jared was deferential, loving almost, about the *Observer*, promising to be the caretaker of an institution, committing to preserve Carter's vision. He clicked through a PowerPoint presentation showing how "I can improve circulation, I can improve ad sales, I can make this thing great, I can make it hip, I can do this." Later Jared would admit, "I didn't know what I was talking about, I'd never done any of these things before."[25]

Then, in a display of *chutzpah*, before any terms had been worked out, Jared wrote out a check for ten million dollars. Carter was impressed. He sent Jared a term sheet, which Jared worked on through the night. In the morning he called his boss at the private equity firm where he was interning and told him he had to quit because he'd bought a newspaper.[26]

The following Monday, the *New York Times* published pieces on the sale by the legendary media columnist David Carr and the longtime political reporter Katherine Q. Seelye. "I love my father," Jared Kushner told Seelye, "but I have worked to develop a separate and distinct identity in different projects I have worked on. The only difference is that this is far more public." Thinking optimistically, but betraying his anxiety by raising the subject, Kaplan told Seelye that "Mr. Kushner had no agenda," adding, "he told me that he will not interfere with the paper, that editorially, the paper is ours."[27]

Almost immediately, this proved false. Jared had promised to retain staff and seek advice from Arthur Carter. He soon shut that off. Jared criticized the previous version of the paper as too long and too boring and too dry, "unbearable to read."[28] He was heard boasting in the newsroom that he hadn't really read the paper in the past, other than picking it up in the shuttle lounge at the airport, that he didn't read books, that he didn't read magazines, that he barely read journalism at all, only the *Wall Street Journal* and *New York Post*, both owned by one of his mentors, Rupert Murdoch. To the newspaper's staff it was clear he cared deeply about Israel and the right-leaning politics of its prime minister, Bibi Netanyahu, but that few other topics stirred his passions. Jared pressed for shorter articles, more churn, more clicks.

Kaplan told people he was being pushed to assign a story on Chris Christie—whose star had risen since he sent Jared's father to prison—that Jared wanted a "hit job." Though Jared denies this, those words would be bruited about Kushner Companies and the *Observer* offices for many years. "Hit job" is a textbook example of malice, and not a phrase that most editors or publishers typically use when assigning stories. It's a political phrase, imported into the *Observer* to describe an article Jared apparently desired, on the person he believed had destroyed his family.

Kaplan resisted. "Jared's killing me," he told associates. "There was a constant grinding lack of understanding of what a publisher's role was, of journalism and journalism ethics," said an *Observer* staffer who was there at the time. Jared questioned why the *Observer* had to pay for a restaurant critic's meals, wanting to know why the critic couldn't be comped, saying he had a friend from Harvard who could do the job.

In those early days, Jared also ran his company's business out of the *Observer*'s offices. It was hard to see where one concern began and the other ended. Jared took more and more cues from Rupert Murdoch. He increasingly followed Murdoch's model of using his publications to achieve a set of political and business aims. On Mondays, Jared discussed his social interactions with Rupert and his wife, Wendi Murdoch, with *Observer* colleagues.

Kushner and Kaplan fought about budgets and editorial control; for Jared, the Harvard grad with the JD and the MBA, getting the paper to live within its means was an existential play. "I knew that the paper needed big changes and it had to start with the product, which had become dull from the uncertainty and lack of direction surrounding the business," he said later.[29] From Jared's perspective, Kaplan's editing style meant they couldn't print the paper on time, couldn't get into the Starbucks stores that had promised to carry it. Kaplan's vision, as Jared saw it, would inevitably lead to a well-crafted enterprise that no one would see. "The paper had become stuck, in the sense that the articles were way too long, it wasn't visually stimulating, and I thought that people today are more responsive to shorter, easier pieces like they get on the Internet," Jared said.[30] He saw himself as a disrupter; his very ignorance of the industry gave him the ability, in his view, to be clear-eyed about what needed to be done. "When I was 25 years old and I bought a newspaper with no experience in media, I came into a group of people who were very ingrained in the ways that they did their business and I noticed that the industry was changing very rapidly and for me it was very important to drive change."[31]

One of those changes was to acquire *PoliticsNJ*, a website widely read and followed by New Jersey's power elite, owned and run by an anonymous blogger with the pseudonym "Wally Edge," who collected emails and phone numbers and tips. Statehouse power brokers lived in fear and awe of "Edge," and almost all of them fed to him, including the young and ambitious prosecutor Chris Christie. "Wally Edge" was a nod to Walter Edge, an advertising magnate, publisher, and banker, who as governor and US senator from New Jersey had dominated the state's GOP for half a century.

"Wally Edge" was actually David Wildstein, a hefty man with close-cropped dark hair from Livingston, New Jersey. Wildstein had begun his career as a Republican Party activist at age twelve. By the year 2000, when he formed *PoliticsNJ*—under a pseudonym to obscure the fact that a political activist was running a news website—Wildstein had already, as a twenty-one-year-old campaign volunteer, stolen Senator Frank Lautenberg's suit jacket, leaving him in his shirtsleeves for a public debate, and, while mayor of Livingston, thrown out nominating petitions to thwart a candidate in local elections. There were maybe ten people who knew that Wally Edge was Wildstein, a blogger whose output was "fairly harsh, very blunt, very direct . . . going directly at people and challenging candidates," as Wildstein later put it.[32]

Jared Kushner, in elementary school when Wildstein was mayor of Livingston, was drawn to *PoliticsNJ*'s style, to the political currency it could give him, as owner. He wanted to take the model national. It was only after he'd made an approach that "Wally Edge" revealed himself as David Wildstein. Wildstein became executive vice president of the Observer Media Group. The blog's name was tweaked to *PolitickerNJ*, and spun out to seventeen state-specific sites, including *PolitickerNV* and *PolitickerNH*, but Jared soon closed nine of them. Only *PolitickerNJ* ultimately survived.

Most of the *Observer* staff still didn't know David Wildstein was Wally Edge. In conversations at the *Observer* offices, he made no mention of his inside knowledge of New Jersey politics. Wildstein held his post at the *Observer* for three years, until 2010, when he left Jared's employ to work for his father's nemesis: Chris Christie, then the newly elected governor of New Jersey. Christie named Wildstein the Director of Interstate Capital Projects for the Port Authority of New York and New Jersey, a post from which Wildstein insisted billions of dollars in government resources be spent in ways that bolstered the reelection campaign of Governor Christie, including masterminding the Bridgegate scandal. Though Jared never forgave Wildstein for going to work for Christie, after Wildstein was forced out for his Bridgegate role, Jared offered him his old job back at the *Observer*. "For what it's worth," Jared Kushner wrote, referring to the politically motivated lane closures on the George Washington Bridge, "I thought the move you pulled was kind of badass."[33]

A few months before Jared closed the deal on the *Observer*, in the spring of 2006, Charlie Kushner was released from prison in Alabama to a halfway house in Newark. At 7:45 in the morning, men in work boots and blue jeans poured out of "a gritty collection of dormitories squatting near the tracks that cut through the industrial remains of Newark's South Ward," as Jeff Pillets described it in *The Record*. The men, former prison inmates, were headed to "mostly minimum-wage jobs as cooks and busboys and day laborers. Many stop just for a second to light a cigarette as they rush to catch the bus," Pillets wrote. "Into the scene comes a deep blue Cadillac DeVille, whose white-haired chauffeur steps out on the sidewalk long enough to pull on his sport coat, brush out the wrinkles and make a brief cellphone call. Almost an hour later, another former inmate, dressed in a navy blue blazer and pressed dress slacks emerges from a building with bars on the windows and steps into the Cadillac, which whisks him to downtown Newark. This man then spends his day working on real estate deals and lunching at the Savoy Grill, a restaurant frequented by federal judges and politically connected lawyers."[34]

While residing at the halfway house, Charlie Kushner was arranging two enormous real estate transactions that, if timed to land in the same calendar year, could save him an enormous amount of money. Under section 1031 of the Internal Revenue code, one may avoid paying capital gains taxes on a sold property if one reinvests the money in new property within the year. Charlie was looking to sell off much of his suburban real estate empire, more than seventeen thousand units. He was simultaneously hiring a broker to find him a building "in the one- to two-billion-dollar range," as a person involved in the deal later described it. This is not the way one usually buys a building; most often, a buyer has a location and size in mind, not a specific price. The specific price, a record one in Manhattan at the time, was a tell: the Kushners wanted to be noticed.

Soon, Kushner Companies began to negotiate to purchase 666 Fifth Avenue, a tall aluminum-clad tower just blocks from Trump Tower, for $1.8 billion. The building had been erected in 1957, its blocky stippled silver exterior projecting power and strength, its interior lobby, with undulating ceiling art and a floor-to-ceiling silver "waterfall" sculpture by Isamu Noguchi, connoting Manhattan sophistication. By the time Kushner Companies purchased the building, it was hard for people working with the company to see where Charlie ended and Jared began: the two operated as one. The Kushners' desire to enter the Manhattan market in a splashy way, to purchase their own "Tiffany location," was palpable.

In 2007, on January 10, Jared's birthday, the Kushners closed on the sale. Charlie, a convicted felon, wasn't able to sign the mortgage documents. Instead they were signed by Jared and a Jersey billionaire, the food entrepreneur and long-time Kushner business partner and family friend George Gellert, who had profited so handsomely on an early deal with Charlie, flipping sod farms in Princeton. There was a closing party at The Modern restaurant overlooking the Abby Aldrich Rockefeller Sculpture Garden at the Museum of Modern Art. The participants (almost all men) were given cufflinks designed to resemble the distinctive aluminum cladding on the outside of 666 Fifth Avenue. A last-minute glitch in the financing had led Charlie to wire the money in multiple increments to Tishman-Speyer, the building's seller. The broker chided Charlie for acting "like pikers from Jersey." But the money went through. At the party at the Modern, Charlie was heard to say, "Am I still a piker from New Jersey?"

Piker or not, his first name was not on the building documents—

Jared's was. In January 2007, at twenty-six, the younger Kushner owned a building valued at almost two billion dollars and the *New York Observer* publishing group.

Three months after he bought 666 Fifth Avenue, Jared Kushner hosted an event with Peter Kaplan to officially present the *New York Observer*'s website relaunch. It was held at the Four Seasons, the chic mid-century haunt of the rich and powerful designed by Philip Johnson and Ludwig Mies van der Rohe, characterized by sweeping windows and dramatic light fixtures. The power lunch had been invented at the Four Seasons, which was described in the *New York Times* as a place where "powerful people eat in order to be seen with other powerful people."[35] On April 18, 2007, many powerful people showed up to herald the arrival of the Kushners in New York: former *New Yorker* editor Tina Brown was there, as was Tom Wolfe, the novelist, and *New York Post* gossip columnist Cindy Adams. Members of old real estate families of New York, the Tisches and the Rudins, joined the city council speaker, Christine Quinn, and the police commissioner, Ray Kelly, along with old Kushner family friends like George Gellert and Rosemary Vrablic, the Kushner's personal banker. Jim McGreevey, the former governor of New Jersey, was there, with his partner, Mark O'Donnell. Also there: Ivanka Trump, photographed on Jared Kushner's arm.[36]

The Kushners had formed their real estate empire in New Jersey. To some Manhattan real estate families, that meant they were not rich or smart enough to make it in New York. These were the people "that looked down their nose at Donald Trump, dismissed the Kushners as hicks," one person who attended Jared Kushner's party at the Four Seasons said in an interview. "To them he could now say, 'We've arrived.'"

11

ENTRÉE

There's a story that Ivanka Trump once liked to tell, about her six-year-old self—brown-haired, puffy-cheeked, gap-toothed—given a Christmas gift she didn't like. Chrismas 1987 capped the year of peak Donald Trump. It came a month after the publication of *The Art of the Deal,* but before Trump's marriage to Ivanka's mother Ivana flamed out in a blaze of tabloid headlines and his debt threatened to swallow his empire.

"I remember one of my earlier Christmas gifts was a Barbie and I was devastated, because my brothers had gotten Legos and Erector Sets, so to me this was traumatic," Ivanka told Conan O'Brien in a 2007 interview. "So I ended up taking my younger brother's Legos, bringing them into his room, to add insult to injury, locking him out, taking my mother's super-glue from the 1980s—there was plenty for her nails—and gluing the Legos together in a model of Trump Tower."

When she told this story on national television at age twenty-five, a bronzed and glowing Ivanka recalled the incident with great specificity and confidence. Wearing a large gold necklace and a black halter top over black flowing pants, Ivanka said, "So my father, in scolding me, also, was never so proud. So you know my little brother is crying—he's saying, 'Ivanka, that's terrible,' but at the time he looked very proud."

Conan and Ivanka riffed on this for a while, “So your father comes in the room and he sees that you've built a skyscraper—” Conan said.

“A skyscraper of Legos,” Ivanka jumped back in, gathering steam, “ruined the Christmas present completely,” her voice nearly breaking with glee, “but one of the most amusing things that I think is so typical of him and his parenting style and just how he is, is that four days later he actually came up to me and goes, ‘You know, Ivanka, this has been bothering me’—keep in mind I'm six years old—and I go, ‘What, Dad?’

“ ‘You know the other day when you made a model of Trump Tower with these Legos? You made five setbacks in the architectural facade of the building, there are only four.’ So this had been bothering him for four days,” Ivanka continued. “He was thinking how to tactfully tell me that there were four instead of five setbacks. He could not let it go. He could not let it go.”[1]

Except, there never was a Lego tower, no super-glue, no setbacks, no praise from her father. In her 2009 book *The Trump Card*, Ivanka Trump described a confrontation with her brothers, well into her professional life, who told her she had it all wrong, that *they* were the ones to glue the Legos together. Ivanka took the matter to Donald for adjudication, who told her they were all wrong; the story was his.[2] He'd told it to the world in his best-selling book *The Art of the Deal*. It went like this:

“My brother Robert likes to tell the story of the time when it became clear to him where I was headed. . . . I wanted to build a very tall building, but it turned out that I didn't have enough blocks. I asked Robert if I could borrow some of his, and he said, ‘Okay, but you have to give them back when you're done.’ I ended up using all of my blocks, and then all of his, and when I was done, I'd created a beautiful building. I liked it so much that I glued the whole thing together. And that was the end of Robert's blocks.”[3]

Tony Schwartz, the person who actually wrote *The Art of the Deal*, said that, too, was likely made up. He wrote in an email: “There is considerably less than a fifty percent chance that anything like that ever happened.”[4]

In her own book, Ivanka grappled with her apocryphal tale, acknowledged its falsity, and excused herself for telling it. "It's not the story itself that rates a mention," she wrote. "It's not even the tug and pull over our family legacies that I find so interesting. It's the way my brothers and I seemed to grab at this memory as emblematic." It reinforced the idea that "the fuzzy, uncertain eye of memory can sometimes take us to a deeper, more fundamental understanding of how things really were." She concluded: "Mostly, though, the story stands as one of the first and best examples of how we work together as a family."[5]

Years later, in October 2013, Ivanka posted a photo on Instagram of her own pajamaed two-year-old daughter, Arabella, next to a beautifully constructed multicolored plastic Magna-Tiles edifice. "She's a builder!" the post read. "I think it's safe to say some things are genetic."[6]

Ivana Marie Trump—"Ivanka" is the diminutive form of her mother's name—was born on October 30, 1981, after President Ronald Reagan, still in his first year in office, had already enacted tax cuts for the rich and budget cuts for the poor, after Donald Trump had applied for his first casino license in Atlantic City and been (temporarily) denied his tax abatement for Trump Tower by Tony Gliedman. Both the casinos and Trump Tower would be built during her young childhood.

Ivanka's mother was, like Donald, an object of gawking press attention: for her Czech accent, her blond beehive, her extroverted personality, her work renovating the Plaza Hotel and as president of one of Trump's casinos, but mostly for her proximity to her husband.

Ivanka likes to remember her childhood as one where her mother would allow her the run of the Plaza Hotel and where she danced a child part in New York City Ballet's *The Nutcracker.* She was, she said, introduced by her parents at an early age to construction, hotel, and casino management, in an upbringing bolstered by two Irish nannies, Bridget and Dorothy, and by Ivana's parents on their visits to the United States.[7] She recalled a childhood in which her father would always "stop whatever he was doing, at least for a few precious moments, whenever I called."[8] Other than that, former Trump Organization employees said in interviews that Donald showed little interest in his young children.

When Ivanka was eight, the *New York Post* featured one of its most infamous covers: "Marla boasts to her pals about Donald: 'BEST SEX I'VE EVER HAD.'" During her parents' raucous divorce, Ivanka went with her mother, Ivana, and her brothers to their vacation home in Palm Beach, Florida—Mar-a-Lago. Her brother Donald Trump Jr., aged twelve, wouldn't speak to his father for a year.[9]

Not too long after, Ivanka began appearing frequently in public at Donald's side. Paparazzi spotted her, aged nine, wearing a gold dress to the black-tie "Maybelline Look of the Year" party, surrounded by models and movie stars; joining her father at the US Open; wearing a white lace dress at the opening of the Galeries Lafayettes. Magazines showed Donald and eleven-year-old Ivanka, brown-haired, leaning against a Harley at the grand opening of the Harley-Davidson Cafe.

Ivanka Trump attended The Chapin School on the Upper East Side, then boarding school at Choate Rosemary Hall in Connecticut, which had also graduated, years earlier, John F. Kennedy, the future president. "It was a given, in our house that we would reach for the very top rungs of the private school ladder and, looking back, I suppose my father assessed the accompanying tuition bills in much the same way he looked at construction costs. He always used the finest materials," Ivanka wrote in *The Trump Card*. "Not that we couldn't get a perfectly fine education in a public school setting. . . . But he wanted the best for his children so that we might realize our full potential."[10]

This was a running theme for Ivanka: that her parents were strict, that they made her and her brothers work for their money; that, unlike the other rich kids, they were neither bratty nor spoiled. Contra their image, Ivanka said in interview after interview, both her parents had a meticulous attention to detail and one of those details was to instill in their children the value of earning what you have.

As a teenager, proud of her Trump name, Ivanka became a model, a career she pursued from boarding school in Connecticut. She was on the cover of *Seventeen*, walked down catwalks, appeared in ads for fashion lines like Tommy Hilfiger. Ivanka was green in those days; she cohosted the 1997 Miss Teen USA contest in a cringeworthy performance. ("I can guarantee my brothers were loving that," she said after the bathing suit contest.)

At the end of the decade, Ivanka left for college, first Georgetown, then Wharton. During college, she was interviewed for the documentary, *Born Rich*, a film that challenged the premise that America is a meritocracy. Ivanka comes across as one of the more sane of the young elite, even as she introduced what would soon become her old saws. "My grandfather . . . built more housing units than anyone else has ever done in New York" (which was not true). She also told of preferring Legos to Barbies, and another story, which would become familiar, about her father instructing her in the meaning of debt, after seeing a homeless man sitting outside Trump Tower. "I remember my father pointing to him and saying, 'You know that guy has $8 billion more than me,' because he was in such extreme debt at that point." (The number was more like $800 million.) Ivanka said she didn't understand it until she thought about it around the time she was leaving for college. "It made me all the more proud of my parents, that they got through that."[11]

At Wharton, Ivanka, was, by all accounts, a serious student. A little aloof, perhaps, but no one really expected otherwise, given her exceedingly public life. She graduated, cum laude, in May 2004, not summa cum laude, as it said on her book jacket, and as she would frequently affirm when asked by reporters.[12]

In her final semester of college, Ivanka appeared on Oprah, bubbling over appealingly about her plans for a post-college life. "Ivanka will graduate this spring, and what do you get the girl who has everything?" Oprah asked.[13]

"A great gift that my dad gave me recently is an apartment because I'm graduating and I don't want to live at home anymore," Ivanka, said, leaning forward slightly, with an open laugh. Later she would recalibrate. In her book, she wrote: "I own a two-bedroom apartment in a Trump building, but no one gave it to me. Nor did I benefit from an insider price. I bought my first apartment in one of our buildings because I believe in the Trump brand." She continued: "I'm paying a mortgage on my apartment, just as my brothers, Don and Eric, pay mortgages on their apartments in other Trump buildings. Admittedly, I pay my mortgage directly to my father instead of to a bank, but it's a mortgage just the same, and I've never missed a payment."[14] Though New York City property records do show the sale of an apartment to Ivanka from her father for $1.5 million shortly after she graduated, they do not show a mortgage.[15]

Ivanka did not go straight to work at the Trump Organization; her father called a fellow developer, Bruce Ratner, and asked him to give her a job at his firm, Forest City Ratner. Ivanka wrote in *The Trump Card* that she did not know how to take the subway to Brooklyn, and did a trial run on Labor Day, getting hopelessly lost. The next day, she showed up at work two hours early.[16]

Ivanka worked hard at Forest City. She was not given a plum assignment: she had to deal with the least glamorous aspect of real estate, commercial retail. But she was collegial. Her co-workers liked her. She did not come off as arrogant. She worked hard and was eager to learn. "Lovely," one co-worker described her, admitting a disinclination to like a Trump. "She pulled her weight."

In 2005, a twenty-four-year-old Ivanka went to work for the Trump Organization. This was a time of sharp transformation for the Trump family business: away from real estate development, from actually building buildings, and towards licensing, branding, selling products, and generally capitalizing on the hit television show *The Apprentice*, which had debuted in January 2004 and immediately rocketed to the top of the ratings.

By the time Ivanka arrived, her older brother had been at the company a few years already. Don Jr. had grown up hunting with his Czech grandfather—to whom he spoke Czech—avoiding his father, joining a fraternity in college.[17] After college, he lived in Aspen, Colorado, skiing, hunting, and tending bar, before returning to New York to work for the Trump Organization. He was assigned at first to work as an assistant to his father's employees. He was thought of as a "good kid."

By the time Donald Trump launched *The Apprentice*, he had come very near to personal default and his casinos had already filed for bankruptcy protection. But in the show opener, featuring a shot of the Trump International Hotel and Tower at Columbus Circle, at the southwest corner of Central Park, Trump proclaimed that he was "the largest real estate developer in New York," and that, after being "billions of dollars in debt" he "fought back, and I won, big league." He continued, "I've turned the name Trump into the highest quality brand," over a shot of "Trump Ice" water (the only brand allowed on set, people who worked on *The Apprentice* said). "As the master, I want to pass along my knowledge to somebody else. I'm looking for The Apprentice." The bassline thrummed, the O'Jay's intoned "Money, money, money, money."

"He is not the largest developer in the New York, nor does he own Trump International Hotel and Tower," *New York Times* real estate correspondent Charles V. Bagli wrote in the story "Due Diligence on the Donald," greeting the show's debut. The opening sequence didn't include the lyrics of the O'Jays song that went, "I know that money is the root of all evil / Do funny things to some people," morphing it, as Bagli wrote, "from a warning about greed, gold, and celebrity into a paean to them."[18]

Donald Trump was furious and threatened to sue Bagli, complaining falsely to his editors that Bagli had once tried to shake Donald down for US Open tickets. The *Times* responded that Bagli had attended the tennis match as part of his coverage of a story. The matter was eventually dropped.[19]

But far beyond the reach of the *New York Times*, *The Apprentice* beamed an image of Trump: successful entrepreneur, deal maker, patriarch. Its first season finale hit number one in the Nielsen ratings.[20] "I like it when critics slam a movie and it does massive box office," the show's founder, Mark Burnett, once said. "I love it."[21] *The Apprentice* would set indelibly in the minds of customers and voters. What Trump had, they wanted. If he was involved, it was going to be exciting; it was going to be good.

—

In 2004 and 2005, as *The Apprentice* phenomenon was taking hold, and as Ivanka was joining the company, foreign wealth surged into New York real estate. NAFTA and the repeal of the Glass-Steagall Act had enabled money to move without friction around the globe. A loophole in the USA PATRIOT Act, passed in the wake of the September 11 attacks, made it even easier. The PATRIOT Act had several measures designed to curb money laundering, which was viewed, correctly, as a key aspect of international terrorism. But real estate was exempted, as Franklin Foer wrote in his *Atlantic* story "How Kleptocracy Came to America." "Every House district in the country has real estate," Foer wrote, "and lobbyists for that business had pleaded for relief from the PATRIOT Act's monitoring of dubious foreign transactions. They all but conjured up images of suburban moms staking FOR SALE signs on lawns, ill-equipped to vet every buyer." The result: "for all the new fastidiousness of the financial system, foreigners could still buy penthouse apartments or mansions anonymously and with ease, by hiding behind shell companies set up in states such as Delaware and Nevada."[22]

By the time Ivanka Trump was elevated to the post of vice president of development and acquisitions, powerful financial incentives were pushing Trump's business to become increasingly international in scope, increasingly dependent on customers, financing and business partners from overseas, particularly from the former Soviet Union, where Russians made rich by denationalizations were looking for safe places to store their money.

Calling herself a "deal junkie,"[23] Ivanka began forming limited liability companies during this period. She received check-writing privileges and joined the board of the Trump foundation. People would call—journalists, politicians, potential partners—and Trump would put Ivanka on the phone. "Talk to Ivanka," he would say. "Here's Ivanka." Just as his own father had done for him.

Ivanka made her professional Trump-world debut in December 2005, just a few months after starting at the Trump Organization. She glittered on the red carpet at *The Apprentice* Season 4 after-party at Planet Hollywood in New York, wearing a black and white–striped chinchilla jacket. The awkwardness of her teen years was gone, replaced by a noticeable polish.

When not appearing on red carpets, Ivanka was traveling the world. In *The Trump Card*, she told of some of the places she'd gone for work: Dubai, Colombia, Panama, Jordan, Israel, and Kazakhstan, where she was presented with a meal of boiled horse meat and fermented camel's milk, neither of which she could abide. "I'm determined not to be one of those ugly Americans who leaves her hotel only for meetings and eats only room-service hamburgers," Ivanka wrote, "so I dug right in . . . I took pains to disguise my lack of interest from my hosts."[24]

She also traveled, quietly, to Moscow.

The winter of 2006, Ivanka and her brother, Donald Trump Jr. flew to the Russian capital where they were photographed—Ivanka wearing the same chinchilla coat—with a broker and a business partner for Trump properties in Sunny Isles, Florida.[25] Moscow was a growing market for the Trumps by 2006: the Trump World Tower, and Florida's Sunny Isles—known as "Little Moscow"—were propped up by Russian buyers.[26]

During this trip to Russia in 2006, Ivanka and Don Jr. were squired around Moscow by a business associate of their father's: Felix Sater, a deep-voiced, sharply dressed Jewish Soviet émigré who by then was working at Bayrock Group, a real estate developer with offices in Trump Tower just below Trump's own. Sater grew up in Brighton Beach, Brooklyn, with a father who was convicted of small-time mob activity.[27] He was friends as a teenager with another young Jewish boy, from Long Island, the son of a Holocaust survivor, named Michael Cohen. Sater tried to make a career for himself on Wall Street, but this line of work was derailed when he got into a bar fight with a man in Manhattan, slashing his face with the broken stem of a margarita glass. Sater served time in prison; got out, and was then convicted for his role in a $40-million pump-and-dump stock scheme. Rather than go to prison, Sater began cooperating with various US intelligence and law enforcement agencies. For over a decade, much of which time he was working as a Trump business associate, he turned over information to the US government on five Italian mob families and the Russian mob.[28] He started going by the name Satter to avoid detection, and tried to reinvent himself as a Trump business associate.

In Moscow, in 2006, Sater took Ivanka and Don Jr. on a tour of the Kremlin. As *BuzzFeed News* reported, "Sater, as would be the case over and over in his life, had an inside connection. He phoned an old friend, a Russian billionaire, whom he knew through his Bayrock connections. The billionaire sent a fleet of cars and guards to escort them through the Kremlin, and when a tour guide pointed out Putin's office, Ivanka Trump asked if she could sit in his chair at an antique desk. One of the guards said, 'Are you crazy?' "

As Sater later described it, he said " 'C'mon, she's a girl, what is she going to do, steal his pen?" Ivanka "sat behind the desk, spun in the chair, and that was that."[29] Later, they went to the extravagant home of the man who had set up the Kremlin visit: Russian-Azerbaijani businessman Telman Ismailov. They ate white caviar, produced by albino sturgeons, orders of magnitude more valuable than regular caviar. Ivanka Trump did not discuss her Moscow trip until 2017, when asked about it by the *New York Times*. "In a statement," the *Times* wrote, "she said that during the 2006 trip she took 'a brief tour of Red Square and the Kremlin' as a tourist. She said it is possible she sat in Mr. Putin's chair during that tour but she did not recall it. She said she has not seen or spoken to Mr. Sater since 2010. 'I have never met President Vladimir Putin,' she said."[30]

Not long after she returned from Moscow in 2006, Ivanka Trump joined her father at a press conference in Trump Tower to promote one of their earliest foreign licensing deals: the Trump Ocean Club Panama. "I really think the time for Panama has come," Donald Trump proclaimed. According to a newsletter unearthed by ProPublica's Heather Vogell, Donald Trump "said the Trump organization does have a financial interest in the project but he would not disclose the amount."[31] But the Trumps did not have equity. Their purported stake was a ruse to reassure buyers and investors that it was such a good financial deal, the Trumps were putting their own money in.

The false claim was part of the Trump's financing strategy. Trump's licensing deal in Panama was written so he would get a cut if he procured the financing, a construction bond from Bear Stearns. But in order to get the financing, the investment bank had to be assured Trump's partners had presold over 60 percent of the units. The press conference and its attendant sales pitch were designed to drum up those sales.

A few months after the Trumps announced the Panama project, they used the last episode of *The Apprentice* Season Five to advertise another new building, the Trump SoHo.[32] Felix Sater had put together the group to build the Trump SoHo. It included Tevfik Arif, a Kazakh-Turkish investor, and Tamir Sapir, the Soviet émigré who had once sold televisions to Donald Trump, but who by then had become an ostentatiously wealthy developer.

By early 2007, selling units in the Trump SoHo was a key family priority. That January Ivanka Trump appeared in an advertisement for the Trump SoHo in a low-cut white cocktail dress, draped on the floor of an empty room with New York's skyline pictured on three sides, under the tagline "Possess Your Own SoHo." The *New York Observer*, her future husband's newspaper, called it—in January—"the Real Estate Image of 2007 (so far)."[33]

In September of that year, the Trumps held a launch party for the Trump SoHo at the Tribeca Rooftop. According to the *New York Daily News*, "guests were greeted by doormen in 18th-century French costumes complete with powdered wigs. Ushered into elevators draped in blood-red velvet curtains with gothic mirrors, guests walked onto two floors with five open bars that dished out every flavor of Grey Goose ever made." There were nine food tables serving "racks of lamb, filets of beef, crab claws, shrimp cocktails, dim sum, sushi and oysters all night. Iced bottles of Perrier Jouet Rosé Champagne rested on blood-red silk tables, waiting to be popped."

"This party was not thrown to pump sales," Donald Trump told the *Daily News*. "We already have a 3,200-person waiting list to see the units. It was thrown to celebrate a new kind of luxury downtown."[34] There was no such waiting list. Ivanka told the *Daily News* that the "sales office had been flooded by calls from potential international buyers."[35]

Not too long after this party, the *New York Times*'s Charles Bagli got a tip that Felix Satter, Trump's associate on the Trump SoHo, was actually Felix Sater, convicted felon. "I'm not proud of some of the things that happened in my 20s," Sater told Bagli. "I am proud of the things I'm doing now." Trump claimed the news surprised him: "We never knew that. We do as much of a background check as we can on the principals. I didn't really know him very well."[36] By this point, Trump and Sater had been on marketing trips around the country, including one in Colorado, where they rode in a limo together.[37] One former high-level Trump Organization official said in an interview that Sater's past was known to Trump: a tipster had called the company to inform them. After internal discussion, the Trump Organization decided to accept Sater's argument he was on the road to reform.

He continued to work with the Trump Organization well into 2016.

Right after *The Apprentice* introduced the Trump SoHo, Donald Trump ousted the Trump Organization employees who had acted as judges and replaced them with Ivanka and Don Jr. On season six, episode one, Donald introduced "my daughter, Ivanka. She'll be working with me and she went to the Wharton School of Finance, she was a terrific student so she will be my eyes and ears for this and I think you'll all get along very well with Ivanka."[38]

The Apprentice, through all its mutations, had a formula: two teams were assigned a business task, the cameras followed them as they tried to complete it; at some point the judges—in later seasons Ivanka and Don Jr.—would appear to evaluate each team's progress. One team would win, and the losing team would be called into the "boardroom" (actually, a set in Trump Tower, or for part of the show, in a Hollywood mansion), where Donald Trump, eventually accompanied by his children, encouraged the contestants to call out each other's weaknesses, to lay blame for specific failures on specific individuals.

On her *Apprentice* debut Ivanka pressed the losing team. "Was there a strategy?" she asked. "Because when I got there it didn't seem like there was any clear direction." Her voice rising, she queried the "Project Manager": "Where were you in the first hour?" Her father jumped in. "Who do you blame for losing?" he asked the contestants. "If you were me, who would you fire?"

During Ivanka's debut, Martin Clarke, an African-American graduate of George Washington University Law School, and Frank Lombardi, an Italian-American real estate developer from the Bronx, had been called to the boardroom. Frank, the project manager, had made some key errors in judgment, but soldiered on. "I'm fighting for my life to stay here, I want to prove myself to you, sir," he said to Donald Trump.

It was at this point that Ivanka was asked to weigh in. "Martin," she said, "I don't see you fitting in with our company, I don't see you working side by side with me and my father." Martin disputed this conclusion, as *Apprentice* contestants were encouraged to do, but Ivanka pushed back. "Martin," Donald Trump said, "you're fired."

Ivanka's debut was a marketing coup. "The Trump Organization was already the world's most recognized development company before the show, but *The Apprentice* has raised our visibility as a family and as a development company to a whole new level," Ivanka wrote in *The Trump Card*. "That's been especially true for Don and me. By appearing on my father's show . . . my brother and I have become almost instant celebrities."[39]

The Trumps fed this celebrity machine. As with her father, who was described in his 1976 *New York Times* profile as displaying "dazzling white teeth" and looking "ever so much like Robert Redford."[40] Ivanka's own sex appeal was soon on full display, not only to market Trump real estate, but also to sell her growing list of Ivanka-branded products. In each interview, Ivanka was celebrated as young and brilliant, a savvy businesswoman *and* a knockout. It became a canon.

She was featured in a low-cut bustier-topped dress on the cover of *Stuff* magazine in the fall of 2006 with the cover line "Ivanka Trumps All! The Apprentice's Red-Hot Taskmaster," and inside, in an even lower-cut slip-style dress, lying on a desk with her knee brushing up against a placard that said "Vice President."[41] Just as she was launching Ivanka Trump Fine Jewelry,[42] she appeared on the cover of *Harper's Bazaar* in a black bathing suit with high-cut legs, wrists encircled with enormous Ivanka Trump–brand bracelets and ears adorned with prominent Ivanka Trump–brand drop earrings, all while wielding a jackhammer with a backhoe for a backdrop. The cover line touted "The New Queen of Diamonds."[43]

In a profile in *Marie Claire*, Ivanka embraced every part of her image. "On her desk is a copy of the September issue of *Trump* magazine, and she's on the cover, flaunting cleavage."

"I would never have done this a year ago," she told *Marie Claire*. "I would have said, 'Oh, I should be buttoned up' and whatnot. But once I realized that, ultimately, I'm never going to blend in, and I don't need to be a guy to succeed in this world, I decided it's OK to be 25 and have a little bit of fun with it, and still unabashedly walk into a meeting with any banker and not be embarrassed. Because I am in a strange position, and I've been enjoying it."[44]

—

In early 2007, Ivanka Trump was invited to a luncheon by a young businessman, Moshe Lax, who, like Ivanka, worked in both diamonds and real estate. "I was pursuing a lead on a piece of land in Fort Myers, Florida. I didn't like the deal when it was laid out for me, but I looked closely," she wrote in *The Trump Card*.[45] The Laxes' primary business wasn't real estate, it was diamonds. Though the deal didn't work out, it launched a lasting business relationship. (Years later, the US Justice Department sued the Laxes for tax fraud, charges they denied.[46]) Ivanka Trump's business luncheon with Moshe Lax launched another lasting relationship: Jared Kushner had been invited too. Ivanka told friends she was smitten.

In April 2007, spotted at the *New York Observer* relaunch party by the *New York Post,* Ivanka looked "radiant." Both she and Jared told the *Post* they were "buddies" and "close friends."[47] The next month, they were spotted kissing at the Bowlmor.[48] In September, the "lovebirds"[49] were shot strolling hand in hand through SoHo.[50] By December, they were being written about in the *New York Times*.[51] "Introducing the Ivanka," the article was titled.

In 2008, Jared and Ivanka's relationship hit a sand trap. Donald Trump didn't understand why his daughter wanted to marry an Orthodox Jew, and Charlie and especially Seryl Kushner did not want their son to marry a non-Jew. Ivanka pushed back. "I'm a New Yorker, I'm in real estate. I'm as close to Jewish, with a *'i-s-h'* naturally as anyone can start off," she later told *New York* magazine's Gabe Sherman.[52] Jew-i-s-h was not enough. The couple broke up. In mid-2008, Rupert Murdoch and his wife, Wendi, by then one of Ivanka's closest friends, contrived to get Jared and Ivanka back together by inviting each separately to spend the weekend—together—on their yacht.

The next month Jared and Ivanka were spotted by the *New York Post*'s Page Six, entering Congregation Kehilath Jeshurun on East Eighty-Fifth Street in Manhattan.[53] Ivanka began studying the Torah. She consented to observe the sabbath, which meant not driving, not checking her cell phone, not working on Friday nights and Saturdays. She learned Kosher cooking, was tested by a religious panel, and took a ritual cleansing dip in a *mikvah*. By the fall of 2008, Ivanka Trump was undergoing the arduous task of converting to Judaism. The *New York Post* ran a gossip item with the headline "Shiksa No More."[54]

Inside Trump Tower, Ivanka's role in the family company was growing. "I'm involved in every aspect of our new construction projects," she told *Portfolio* in 2008. In her capacity as vice president, she pointed out, "a lot of what I do is get involved in the acquisition process, from sourcing the potential opportunities and then the initial due-diligence process, but then, of course, I follow the deals through to predevelopment planning, design, interior design, architectural design, sales and marketing, and, ultimately, through operations. One of the things that I've done and been very active with since joining the company four years ago is get involved with the ramp-up and the development of our hotel-management company, called the Trump Hotel collection." When she paused for breath, she added that she'd sold forty units at Trump Ocean Club Panama.

"You did?" the interviewer asked. Well, she answered, "We did, our project," before adding that the building was 90 percent sold, and that it was selling at a 500 percent premium. The building was not 90 percent sold out, it never sold at a 500 percent premium, and those involved in selling the project couldn't remember Ivanka selling a single unit herself.[55]

In the early summer of 2008, Don Jr., Ivanka, and Eric called a press conference for the foreign press at Trump Tower to promote the Trump SoHo. Ivanka told the assembled reporters the Trump SoHo was 60 percent sold. This too, was a lie.

There was another sales promotion event around this time, in San Diego, to sell units for a project in Baja California. Ivanka allowed buyers to believe that the Trump family were developers (they were licensors), that they had equity in the project, and that she was so sure of the resort that she herself was buying a unit. (She did not say she had a special, undisclosed discount.)[56] "Market conditions simply do not apply to the Trump Ocean Resort—or to any *other* Trump development," Ivanka Trump wrote in one communication with buyers, court records show.[57]

But market conditions did apply, the project was never built, and buyers were threatened with a total loss. When that happened, Ivanka backed off the story that the Trumps had been all in on the development. She told CBS News: "We were never the developer of this project, and that was made clear. We never took anyone's deposit, we never had access to the escrow accounts, we lived up to our obligation under our license agreement." She added, "I am sorry for everyone but we are in the same boat," before going on to insist, "the Trump organization has really never been stronger."[58] This, too, was a misdirection.

A few months later, Ivanka announced her engagement on Twitter: "truly the happiest day of my life!!!"[59] In mid-October, she published *The Trump Card* with an attendant burst of publicity. There was an interview with WNYC's Leonard Lopate, the ultimate arbiter at the time of a certain kind of society taste, in which she discussed opera. "Peter Gelb told me that you're a big opera fan," Lopate said, referring to the general manager of the Metropolitan Opera. "I am, I am," Ivanka answered. "I've been a bit remiss over the last year, and I haven't had the fortune to go last year, but the previous year, I went probably around ten times." Lopate approved. Then they talked about her book.[60]

A week and a half later, she was married.

Unlike her father, Ivanka Trump, at twenty-seven, was a true child of Manhattan. Donald Trump was gauche, Ivanka Trump was polished; he was unruly, she was disciplined. He was fun, but always a bit of a spectacle, Ivanka had become, to the Manhattan elite, *one of us*.

Less than a year later, Ivanka Trump was under criminal investigation for felony fraud for lying to buyers of the Trump SoHo.

12

A FLOOD OF MONEY

In November 2006, a limited liability company called "John Hannah LLC" bought Apartment 43G in Trump Tower from David Barger, one of the founders of JetBlue Airways. The purchase price was $3,675,000, and the entire sum was paid in cash.[1] There was, and is, nothing unusual about such a transaction: thousands, if not tens of thousands, of similar transactions take place every year in New York City. American laws, largely written by lobbyists and supported by both Republicans and Democrats, have long been friendly to anonymous shell companies, and by 2006, New York City was vacuuming in money from around the globe.

There is, actually, a human being named John Hannah, a former national security advisor to former vice president Dick Cheney. But the real John Hannah has nothing to do with "John Hannah LLC," a limited liability company named by combining the middle names of Paul John Manafort and Rick Hannah Davis,[2] two business partners who, even in 2006, had conducted a number of business transactions with oligarchs in Russia, Montenegro, and, increasingly, Ukraine.

By 2006, Manafort had worked as a strategist on four Republican presidential campaigns, beginning with Gerald Ford. When he wasn't working on campaigns, Manafort sold high-level access to politicians with the busisness model he'd invented with Roger Stone, hiring himself out as a strategist and lobbyist for some of the most brutal strongmen on earth: Ferdinand Marcos of the Philippines; Mobutu Sese Seko, of Zaire; Angola's South Africa–supported rebel leader, Jonas Savimbi, known for perpetrating a bloody thirty-year war.

In early 2004, Manafort made a new business contact: the Russian oligarch Oleg Deripaska. Deripaska had become a billionaire by emerging a victor of "the aluminum wars" in the former Soviet Union, where people were killed in the struggle over who could control the newly privatizing Russian aluminum industry. Deripaska's role in the aluminum wars and possible ties to organized crime led the US State Department to refuse to issue him a visa for years.[3] (Deripaska's "official spokesperson" said in a statement that "any suggestion he acted improperly in so-called aluminum wars is false," and denied any ties to organized crime.)

If becoming a billionaire in Russia in the post-Soviet era required a deadly sangfroid, keeping that money meant staying on the good side of Vladimir Putin, and indeed, an email released in the early days of WikiLeaks claimed that Deripaska had boasted of making himself "indispensible to Putin and the Kremlin." (Deripaska denies saying this.)[4] As the *Atlantic*'s Franklin Foer reported in his Manafort masterwork, "The Plot Against America," Manafort soon went to work for a Deripaska friend, a Georgian politician and former KGB agent who'd previously been accused of plotting to assassinate that country's president.[5]

The political campaign was unsuccessful, but Manafort and his partner Rick Davis mounted a successful referendum for independence in Montenegro, "an effort that Deripaska funded with the hope of capturing the country's aluminum industry," Foer wrote.[6] (Deripaska disputed this.) By 2005, Manafort and Davis felt emboldened enough to make another pitch to Deripaska, to "influence politics, business dealings and news coverage inside the United States, Europe and former Soviet republics to benefit President Vladimir Putin's government," according to documents uncovered by the Associated Press.[7] (Deripaska's spokesperson said that he had "never received, nor requested, any such proposals.")

But Manafort soon went to work on another Deripaska proxy battle: to thwart a movement for the renationalization of steel mills in Ukraine. The privatizations had led to massive job loss and widespread hunger. In 2004, a candidate named Viktor Yushchenko was running for president, and the oligarchs feared he would renationalize the steel mills. During that campaign, Yushchenko was poisoned; the poisoning caused his face to be disfigured by permanent lesions. Yet he ultimately won. According to documents and testimony in the later trial of Manafort, the oligarchs then hired Manafort to counter Yushchenko.[8] In the US political system, wealthy people have to contribute to candidates, who then hire the strategists. In Ukraine, the route is direct: the oligarchs just paid Manafort to install a compliant politician to maintain their control of the steel mills. In this case, the politician was a former prime minister named Viktor Yanukovych, an apparatchik from Eastern Ukraine who was jailed twice in his youth for violent crimes. (His official bio said the convictions were quashed.)[9]

Manafort began his work by taking a poll for one of the oligarchs, steel magnate Rinat Akhmetov. The poll laid out the sharpness of the challenge: 87 percent of Ukrainians "said that they would not like to see Yanukovych as Prime Minister ever again."[10] But, with Manafort's help, Yanukovych led his party to victory in 2006, and four years later, he was elected president. Akhmetov paid Manafort handsomely, and in 2005–2006, according to a document released by prosecutors from the Special Counsel's Office, so did Russian oligarch Oleg Deripaska.[11] (Deripaska disputes paying Manafort for Ukraine work.) Eventually, tax filings showed that a ten-million-dollar loan traceable to Deripaska was made to John Hannah LLC. At the end of 2006, John Hannah LLC purchased apartment 43G in Trump Tower, just an elevator ride down from the penthouse triplex of Donald J. Trump, for $3,675,000 in cash.

The apartment was a smart investment. According to an analysis by the Furman Center at New York University, from 2006 to the time

Manafort went to work as campaign manager for Donald Trump in 2016, Manhattan apartments increased in value by fifty percent.[12] In Washington, Albany, and New York City during the aughts, government policies were making it easier for wealthy men like Manafort and Trump to get even richer.

There were, first, two George W. Bush tax cuts. The initial one, in 2001, had been conceived during the 2000 presidential campaign as a way to dispose of a surplus accumulated during the Clinton years. Yet it was pitched as a populist measure. "Let's start where the need is greatest: with social mobility for hard-working American families," Bush said during the campaign. By mid-2001, with recessionary storm clouds hovering on the horizon, Bush recast the same proposal as a stimulus package. The Economic Growth and Tax Relief Reconciliation Act of 2001 cut the highest tax bracket from 39.6 percent to 35 percent, erasing a tax on the wealthy that Bill Clinton had enacted. Bush's law cut taxes for everyone—though reducing percentages at the bottom of the scale provided de minimis relief for those making less than $20,000, a fact Bush advisor Larry Lindsay acknowledged to Jonathan Chait, then writing for the *New Republic*. "If you don't pay taxes," he told Chait, "it's very hard to get a tax cut."[13] Most significant, the tax cuts of 2001 phased out the estate tax and the generation-skipping tax, eliminating them entirely for 2010.[14]

In New York, too, the wealthy were getting an assist from their new technocratic, billionaire mayor, Michael Bloomberg, who had won election months after the 9/11 attacks after spending $73.9 million of his own money, more than double the cost of any previous self-financed campaign in American history. Bloomberg was a rationalist, a great believer in his own ability to manage his way out of any crisis. His early years were characterized by a share-the-pain approach—budget cuts, tax hikes, borrowing—but all of that was overshadowed by the overweening need to rebuild a city in which the smell from the rubble of the World Trade Center still pervaded the blocks around City Hall.

That rebuilding effort soon transmogrified: Bloomberg was remaking the city. In 2003 and 2004, with a fervid eye on securing the

2012 Olympics (which went to London), Bloomberg's administration pushed through a frenzied set of rezonings in Greenpoint, Williamsburg, and downtown Brooklyn, along the East River in Queens, and on the West Side of Manhattan, giving developers the right to build up and up, instantly doubling and tripling and quadrupling the value of their land.

—

In Washington, Bush cut taxes again. The cumulative result of his two tax cuts, according to economist Joseph Stiglitz, writing in *Vanity Fair*, was that by "2012 the average reduction for an American in the bottom 20 percent will be a scant $45, while those with incomes of more than $1 million will see their tax bills reduced by an average of $162,000." There was another, ancillary effect, Stiglitz argued: with the presidential administration preoccupied by tax cuts, "the job of economic stimulation fell to the Federal Reserve Board, which stepped on the accelerator in a historically unprecedented way, driving interest rates down to 1 percent."[15]

Cheap borrowing meant not only that it was easy for consumers to get money, but also that international investors would soon be prowling for higher-yielding places to put their money than US Treasury bonds, as Adam Davidson and Alex Blumberg reported for *This American Life's* "Giant Pool of Money" episode. "Among the many things they put their money into," Davidson said, "there was this one thing that they fell in love with": mortgage-backed securities.[16] These were investment instruments that packaged and resold and repackaged again a mix of mortgages. So long as the housing market went up, the whole system worked.

New York City real estate beckoned to international oligarchs like Lev Leviev, an Uzbek-Israeli diamond magnate and self-described friend of Putin who was a major backer of Chabad in Russia—Putin's favored Jewish group.[17] In late 2004, Leviev began growing his New York business. His companies bought properties as diverse as the $170-million 20 Pine Street, a thirty-five-story office tower near Wall

Street[18] (it would later figure centrally in a Russian money-laundering scheme, in which Leviev was not implicated[19]) and, for $8 million, a plot of land along the well-situated but heavily polluted site known as the Gowanus Canal in Brooklyn.[20] There were soon more purchases, in SoHo and Tribeca in Lower Manhattan, and eventually, in 2007, Leviev bought the former New York Times Building on West Forty-Third Street in Manhattan for $525 million.[21]

In 2003, Donald Trump and his siblings had decided to make, uncharacteristically, a quiet real estate deal. Before the success of *The Apprentice*, needing cash for his casinos, Donald Trump urged his siblings to liquidate their father's real estate assets. Fred's empire was still producing profits, but as the *New York Times* reported it, Donald's siblings didn't object. On May 4, 2004, the family sold off all of Fred's real estate for $737.9 million, hundreds of millions of dollars less than it had been appraised."[22]

This meant that, as the housing market softened, Trump had some cash. He rooted for a crash. "Well first of all, I sort of hope that happens because then people like me would go in and buy. You know, if you're in a good cash position—which I'm in a good cash position today—then people like me would go in and buy like crazy," he said in an audiobook released in 2006. "If there is a bubble burst, as they call it, you know, you can make a lot of money."[23]

This was the period when he was positioning himself as a guru of real estate. Two years earlier, Trump had been approached by a golf buddy, a senior managing director at Bear Stearns, Jonathan Spitalny. Spitalny introduced Trump to a man named Michael Sexton, who had an idea: he wanted to license the Trump name to sell real estate advice in the form of online seminars. The initial concept was that actual experts from actual universities would hold online "classes" in business and real estate. And though it wasn't actually a university, and though they were warned by New York State not to advertise it as such, they named it "Trump University." This seemed, like so many ideas that came to Trump in the mid-aughts, like a way to get free money: he could sell his name and take no risk. Soon, though,

Trump decided that he wanted to invest and took a 90 percent stake in the company.

The idea of webinars had yet to catch on, and the web class approach was further complicated by the target audience: adults in their mid-forties and older, who were the least likely demographic to pioneer online learning. About a year after, Trump University pivoted from a web-based service to live events.

This is when Trump University became pure sales pitch, a way to separate middle-class people from their money and divert it to the Trump family business. Trump University offered an initial free ninety-minute session, which served mainly as a hard sell for a three-day event costing $1,495. But that event, hundreds of victims told the New York Attorney General's Office, was actually "an upsell to increasingly costly 'Trump Elite' packages starting at around $10,000 and ending with what was supposed to be a year-long personal mentorship program at a cost of $35,000."[24] Victims told the AG that they were pulled out of sessions and encouraged to call their credit card companies to increase their credit limits so they could afford these sums. They were driven around by unprepared "instructors" who had simply pulled real estate listings off the internet. One woman spoke of how she had been induced to buy a Florida property for $35,000, only to realize that the wiring wasn't up to code, the roof was faulty, and there was no washer-dryer.

Trump University launched as *The Apprentice* was hitting its stride. Donald Trump was not a successful real estate magnate at that moment; he only played one on TV. He never actually divulged any of his "personal real estate secrets," as the Trump University students were assured he would. They were told Trump had "handpicked" the instructors. But, the complaint said, "not a single one was 'handpicked' by Donald Trump." Most "instructors" weren't actually instructors, didn't have a background in real estate and "some came to Trump University shortly after their (own) real estate investing caused them to go into bankruptcy." The students were promised they would "recoup the cost of the courses in a few months, with access to 'insider' financing and close mentoring by Trump instructors." Consequently, "relying on these representations, individuals spent thousands of dollars of their savings or took on thousands of dollars in debt—while Trump University brought in over $40 million in revenue."

This was not an arm's-length licensing scheme. Trump University's operations were managed day to day by the Trump Organization. Though there were nesting LLC companies set up to shield the Trump Organization from liability, "almost none of the formalities of a separate corporate existence were observed by Trump University or the limited liability companies through which Donald Trump purported to hold his stake in it. Trump University could not even issue its own checks, and it never held a board meeting," the charging documents said. Check-writing privileges were reserved for Donald Trump; his three adult children Don Jr., Ivanka, and Eric; and his chief financial officer, Allen Weisselberg.[25] In the course of its investigation, the New York AG found that Donald Trump had written himself such checks, personally withdrawing the sum of five million dollars.

In 2008, Trump sold a house in Palm Beach for $95 million, one he'd bought out of bankruptcy a few years earlier for $41 million. Maison de L'Amitié, it was called, French for "house of friendship."

"I sold the house in Palm Beach about fifteen seconds before—for a hundred million—fifteen seconds before the depression came," Trump told journalist Deborah Solomon in a 2009 interview. "That's the highest price—I consider that to be the high-water mark or the low-water mark depending on your definition of this country, because that's the only time a house ever got 100 million dollars." Trump explained to Solomon that he purchased the home to fix it up though, he said, he spent only "twelve dollars to fix it up," just to have it painted, before putting it on the market, when he sold it to "a Russian."[26]

The Russian was a forty-one-year-old billionaire named Dmitry Rybolovlev. As described by *Politico*, "with a net worth that *Forbes* estimated at $13 billion, Rybolovlev had made his fortune in the wild west of 1990s post-Soviet Russia. He'd spent a year in prison on murder charges (he was later cleared) and wore a bulletproof vest when his own life was threatened."[27]

When Trump sold the mansion to Rybolovlev, the financial markets were crashing. The freely issued, shakily backed subprime mortgages that had been scooped up and packaged together as the miracle financial instrument of the new century began to unravel, symbolic of banking's disturbing comfort with backing investments built on quicksand. Bear Stearns fell. Then Lehman Brothers. Its employees, wearing jeans and pastel-colored polo shirts, were filmed leaving their offices, brown cardboard file boxes in their hands.

That very day, an article appeared in a real estate industry publication, *eTurboNews*. The headline was "Donald Trump Jr. Bullish on Russia and Few Emerging Markets." Don Jr. had been interviewed during a real estate conference that had taken place from September 9 to 12 in New York City. As Wall Street was collapsing, the Trump family was looking abroad. "The emerging world in general attributes such brand premium to real estate that we are looking all over the place," Don Jr. said in the interview. "There is a lot of new money in the emerging markets which appeal to certain brands whether ego-driven or having the life-jacket effect that we feel gives added-value to our investment."

There was one place in particular where this seemed particularly true. "In terms of high-end product influx into the US, Russians make up a pretty disproportionate cross-section of a lot of our assets," Don Jr. said, adding that Russians were buying Trump real estate "in Dubai, and certainly with our project in SoHo and anywhere in New York. We see a lot of money pouring in from Russia."[28]

The American real estate world was sinking. Flight capital, particularly from Russia, was keeping the Trumps afloat.

The Trumps weren't the only real estate business drawing Russian money before the crash. Attracting foreign money to New York was a deliberate policy of Mayor Michael Bloomberg; both in his governing and in his business, he encouraged the flow of global capital through New York. His administration's construction of bike lanes and pedestrian plazas, his espousal of congestion pricing to fund mass transit, all were deliberate and successful attempts to make New York an attractive investment prospect for global business and investors.

The foreign capital parked in New York real estate had a transformative effect on the city, particularly midtown Manhattan. "In a large swath of the East Side bounded by Fifth and Park Avenues and East 49th and 70th Streets, about 30 percent of the more than 5,000 apartments are routinely vacant more than 10 months a year because their owners or renters have permanent homes elsewhere, according to the Census Bureau's latest American Community Survey," Sam Roberts reported in the *New York Times* at the decade's end. "In one part of that stretch, between East 53rd and 59th Streets, more than half of the 500 apartments are occupied for two months or less."[29] On a map, this is the area radiating out from Trump Tower.

The flow of foreign capital in many ways protected New York City from the worst effects of the Great Recession. But it also drove up prices at an astronomical rate: a Manhattan apartment costing $1,000,000 in 2001 would be worth $1,872,000 a decade later.[30] Wages did not keep pace. For the middle class, housing ownership slipped beyond reach, pushing rents even higher. Though the city built and built and created more supply, the demand was insatiable. In Harlem, property values jumped 222 percent and in East Harlem, median market rents went from roughly $1,200 in 2002 to $1,900 in 2011.[31]

Housing was just one measure of rising income inequality in New York City. According to the city's own poverty measure, roughly 46 percent of New Yorkers were poor or "near poor" in 2011. For a family of four, that meant earning under $46,416 annually.

Mayor Bloomberg testily defended this social order. "If we can find a bunch of billionaires around the world to move here, that would be a godsend, because that's where the revenue comes to take care of everybody else," Bloomberg told *New York* magazine as he wrapped up his years in City Hall. "Who's paying our taxes? We pay the highest school costs in the country. It comes from the wealthy! We have an $8.5 billion budget for our Police Department," Bloomberg continued. "We want these people to come here, and it's not our job to say that they're over- or underpaid. I might not pay them the same thing if it was my company—maybe I'd pay them more, I don't know. All I know is from the city's point of view, we want these people, and why criticize them? Wouldn't it be great if we could get all the Russian billionaires to move here?"

13

THE INITIATION

In June 2008 Don Jr., Ivanka, and Eric Trump called a press conference at Trump Tower to discuss what they said was a hot property: the Trump SoHo hotel and condominium. Ivanka Trump had recently joined the board of the New York City Police Foundation and that of Trump Entertainment Resorts; that month she'd been named number fifteen on the *New York Post's* list of the 50 Most Powerful Women in NYC.[1] The seventh season of *The Apprentice* had wrapped, Ivanka and Don Jr.'s second as regular judges in the series. The show had that season debuted its *Celebrity Apprentice* formula. Piers Morgan had prevailed over country singer Trace Adkins, model Carol Alt, and reality TV star Omarosa Manigault.

A few months after the season finale beamed live from Rockefeller Center, the Trumps entered the board room at Trump Tower—the real boardroom, on which the television set had been modeled—and sat at a long table, facing the press. "It was 2008 but I still quite clearly remember thinking 'Wow, this is the next dynasty of the Trumps,'" reporter Dominic Rushe, then of the *Sunday Times* of London, said in a later interview.[2]

The Trump SoHo hotel/condo was already troubled: there had been a grisly death after a worker stepped on to a wooden platform forty stories up and fell to the street below; a local zoning fight; protests against the plan to build a forty-three story tower in the low-rise neighborhood of SoHo; and the discovery of the architectural remains of an abolitionist church which was being paved over by the project. Six months before the press conference, the *New York Times* had run its story about Felix Sater's criminal past.[3]

But the Trump SoHo, Ivanka Trump told the assembled group of foreign press, was doing extremely well. "We are in a very fortunate position," she said. The Trump SoHo was to be the triumphant return to Manhattan real estate for the Trump family. "Everyone was very excited about it," Rushe said. There were "all the usual Trump superlatives, like the biggest, the best, his and hers Turkish baths." Ivanka told the reporters: "We have enough sales and now we are very strategically targeting certain buyers." And despite the building's troubled history, despite the collapsing national economy, she said, the building was already 60 percent sold.

It was a stunning number. And it was false. Prosecutors thought it might be criminally false.[4]

Named for one of Manhattan's trendiest neighborhoods, the Trump SoHo wasn't really in SoHo, but located just west of it. Local activists and politicians were caught by surprise when Trump announced the project two years earlier on *The Apprentice*. As strings swelled and the camera panned up a rendering of a gleaming tower, Donald Trump proclaimed, "located in the center of Manhattan's chic artist enclave, the Trump International Hotel and Tower in Soho is the site of my latest development." He called it "an awe-inspiring masterpiece."[5]

There had already been a licensing agreement and a new company formed called Donka SoHo Member—a composite of the names Don Jr. and Ivanka—rolled into the Trump SoHo's corporate structure, but New York regulations did not permit a tall residential tower at the site. So the hotel/condo hybrid was a work-around: a way for Trump to be able to build the tower "as of right," meaning it would need no special approvals, so long as unit owners never actually lived in their units. This made it nearly impossible to sell.

Despite the Trump's assurances that their properties were somehow immune to the gathering economic thunderhead, the market for high-end condos was beginning to crack. Not only were units in the Trump SoHo a pricey product, buyers were prohibited from personalizing their units in any way, and they were not allowed to stay in their units more than twenty-nine days at a time. If they wanted to come on the weekends—peak hotel guest times—they wouldn't even be guaranteed they could stay in their own unit. There were no kitchens, just a sink and a microwave. Even in pre-construction days, when apartments typically go for cheaper rates, the Trump SoHo was priced expensively at $2,500 or more a square foot, which didn't include the elevated monthly costs unit owners would have to pay to maintain the hotel facilities. And the building was situated on heavily trafficked Varick Street, where New Jersey–bound commuters idled as they endured the wait for the Holland Tunnel. It was not what realtors considered to be "prime SoHo."

The Trump team of brokers, under Ivanka's oversight, spread out across the globe to woo buyers from Russia, Venezuela, Colombia, Spain, Dubai, the United Arab Emirates. For broker Ruedi Sieber, the Trump SoHo was a tough sell. "Very, very much so!" he said in an interview. If the brokers got over all the other hurdles—the price, the rotating living arrangement, the location—there was still one question on the minds of potential buyers. "Every client is going to ask: 'How well has the building sold?' Why? Because they want to have certainty or reassurance that they are going to get into something that other people have obviously done as well. That they're not the only ones dumb enough to want to buy."[6]

Sales had never gone well for the Trump SoHo. When Donald Trump proclaimed at the launch party with the bewigged eighteenth-century doormen and the blood-red curtains that there was a waiting list of 3,200 buyers and Ivanka told reporters that phones were ringing off the hook, only 2.4 percent of units were actually in contract.

The sales team, with the Trumps acting as chief marketers, let out a stream of positive numbers to buyers and the press: 31 percent sold, 53 percent sold, 60 percent sold. This is not entirely unheard of in the world of high-end real estate, where it's widely understood that everyone is inflating figures to some extent. For example, a claim of 60 percent sold is understood to mean a project is actually 40 percent sold. But the Trump SoHo, documents later filed with New York's attorney general showed, wasn't anywhere near 60 percent sold in 2008. It was less than 15 percent sold.

This was more than a marketing problem. Under a New York law designed to protect consumers, the Trumps and their partners weren't allowed to close any sales unless they had verified contracts signed for at least 15 percent of the units. If they didn't achieve that threshold, the Trumps and their partners would have had to return the buyers' down payments. To avoid that, the Trumps kept pumping out false sales statistics.

In October 2009, the month of her wedding, Ivanka Trump appeared on a segment on ABC's *Nightline*, at one point displaying a three-hundred-thousand-dollar Ivanka Trump necklace to the crew, at another, taking them to the highest floors of the Trump SoHo construction site. "Ivanka Trump has replaced her high heels with construction boots," correspondent Cynthia McFadden noted. As the two walked through the site in hard hats, McFadden said, "The project is her latest baby, a 46-story, $450 million baby." (It's only forty-three stories.) Ivanka led McFadden up in a construction elevator, apologizing for the cloudy day and limited view. But McFadden still gushed, "Oh my goodness! Whoa!" when she walked out onto the upper-floor balcony.[7] Yet sales did not ignite.

The Trump SoHo project was approaching a deadline: if it didn't achieve the 15 percent threshold by March 2010, the project would fail. Developers in New York State have to go through a complicated certification process to be able to close sales; the procedure involves filing reams of paperwork with the real estate unit of the Attorney General's Office, described by attorneys there as a "Gringotts bank."

Then assistant attorneys general review the files to ensure the condo projects meet state requirements, including having met the 15 percent threshold. For the developers and brokers, it's a fraught time. An entire subspecialty of real estate law focuses on convincing the attorney general to certify condo and cooperative projects.

In October 2009, while the Trump SoHo project was under review, Ivanka Trump and Jared Kushner sent a wedding invitation to the New York Attorney General Andrew Cuomo and his girlfriend, "semi-homemade" television chef and author Sandra Lee. The Trumps also opened up their wallets during this period. After the Trump SoHo "offering plan" had been filed with Cuomo's office but before it was approved, the Trump family made a series of generous donations to the campaign coffers of Andrew Cuomo, who was then pondering a run for governor. The donations totaled $39,000 in all, including a one-time contribution of $25,000 from Donald Trump in June 2009, then Trump's largest-ever contribution to Cuomo—the man whose father he'd called "a total stiff, a lousy governor, and a disloyal former friend." It was accompanied by a $1,000 contribution that month from Ivanka.[8] (When asked about the donations, a Cuomo spokesperson did not address the propriety of their timing.)

At least once in the past, Trump had found himself under the microscope for a similar series of contributions. In 1989, the New York State Commission on Government Integrity found that Trump had made similar overtures to then–Attorney General Bob Abrams, who had a self-imposed rule of not accepting contributions from developers when their proposals were under review. However, in 1985, when Trump had as many as six projects before Abrams's office, Donald Trump met Abrams for breakfast, and donated $20,000. Abrams said he had been unaware the proposals were being reviewed by his office at the time.[9]

In March 2010, days before the deadline, the Trump SoHo offering plan was certified. At a ribbon-cutting party the next month, a relieved-looking Donald Trump Jr. took the microphone. "It really is a special place that we're proud of," he said. "Unfortunately, there's not really that much more to say. I probably would rather let the product speak for itself and let you see that what we've been saying for all these years actually is true and has really come to fruition."[10]

Four months later, the Trumps were sued for "an ongoing pattern of fraudulent misrepresentations and deceptive sales practices."

According to the civil complaint, Ivanka Trump, Donald Trump Jr., Donald Trump, and their Trump SoHo business partners were "engaged in a coordinated pattern of falsely overstating the number and percentage of Trump SoHo Units sold," the complaint alleged, "because robust sales are a strong indication of the development's value and that the Units are well priced in the marketplace." The lawsuit accused the defendants of "a consistent and concerted pattern of outright lies."[11]

On August 3, 2010, there was a short article buried on page twenty-four of the *New York Times*: "Fifteen Buyers File Lawsuit Against the Trump SoHo Project." The plaintiffs contended the Trumps and their partners "inflated sales figures in the first year and a half of marketing the project," adding that the Trumps and their representatives said the project was "'30, 40, 50, 60 percent or more sold'—both in individual sales pitches and statements to the press—but after the offering plan became effective in May, buyers learned that just over 15 percent of the building, 62 of the 391 units, had been sold."

"They never would have signed contracts if they knew only 10 percent of the units were sold, instead of the 50 or 60 percent they were told," lawyer William Geller told the *Times*.[12] The Trump Organization called the lawsuit "a simple case of buyer's remorse."

Over in his office at One Hogan Place, a building made famous for being the setting of the District Attorney's Office in *Law and Order*, a prosecutor from the Major Economics Crimes Unit, reading the *New York Times* story, was piqued. It looked like this might be more than civil fraud. He thought crimes might have been committed. Felonies. He started looking closer.

Prosecutors are often wary of getting involved in a dispute between wealthy litigants. But, in this instance the lawyers in the Major Economic Crimes Bureau quickly concluded that there was enough to warrant an investigation. They believed that Ivanka and Don Jr. might have violated the Martin Act, a New York statute that bans any false statement in conjunction with the sale of securities or commodities, including real estate. Prosecutors also saw potential fraud and larceny charges, applying a legal theory that, by overstating the number of units sold, the Trumps were falsely inflating their value and, in effect, cheating unsuspecting condo buyers.

By the time Manhattan District Attorney Cyrus Vance Jr.'s office launched a criminal inquiry into the Trumps' work on the Trump SoHo project, Donald Trump had been sued, repeatedly, for cheating buyers, shareholders, customers, and vendors. One of his casinos had been cited by the US Treasury for failing to enforce money-laundering controls. He had been given the biggest fine for violating lobbying laws in New York State history. He had been interviewed by FBI agents on multiple occasions about multiple criminal schemes. And yet neither he nor his family had ever been charged with a crime.

The DA's office issued subpoenas and conducted interviews. The Trumps, it turned out, had left an email trail, according to people who saw the emails, one that showed a coordinated, deliberate, and knowing effort to deceive buyers. In one email, the Trumps discussed how to coordinate false information they had given to prospective buyers. Because the sales levels had been overstated at the beginning of the sales process, any statement showing a lower level could reveal the untruths.

In another email, according to a person who read them, the Trumps worried that a reporter might be on to them. In yet another email chain that included Don Jr. and Ivanka, the younger generation of Trumps issued the email equivalent of a knowing chuckle, saying that nobody would ever find them out, because only people on the email chain or in the Trump Organization knew about the deception. There was "no doubt" that the Trump children "approved, knew of, agreed to, and intentionally inflated the numbers to make more sales," one person who saw the emails said. "They knew it was wrong." "It couldn't have been more clear they lied about the sales and knew they were lying," another person said. Yet another said, "I was shocked by the words Ivanka used." Was there any doubt the Trumps knew they were lying and that it was wrong? "Ten thousand percent no."

In the DA's office, Peirce Moser, an assistant district attorney known for his methodical, comprehensive investigations, soon took over the case. The Trump side lawyered up, too, hiring an all-star team of white-collar defense attorneys, one of whom was a former law partner of the district attorney, Cyrus Vance Jr., and the brother-in-law of the legendary prior district attorney, Robert Morgenthau. By the fall of 2010, not long after the civil suit was filed, the Trumps and their partners had amassed around a million dollars in legal bills, internal billing records showed. They refused to pay the full bill, offered sixty-eight cents on the dollar, and retained new counsel.

Moser had prepared an elaborate PowerPoint presentation, featuring dozens of emails that prosecutors believed showed that Ivanka and Don Jr. had repeatedly lied to buyers. "You couldn't have had a better e-mail trail," a person familiar with the investigation said.

In November 2011, fifteen months after he'd filed the case, the lawyer representing the buyers in the civil suit, Adam Leitman Bailey, settled, receiving almost a complete refund of the buyers' deposits. In exchange, Bailey made two unusual agreements. First, he agreed on behalf of his clients that they would not cooperate with the criminal investigation unless they received a subpoena. This in itself was a potentially significant obstacle; while emails can tell a story in a prosecution, actual victims are usually required to turn those emails into a coherent narrative and convince juries to convict defendants of a crime. But there was another extremely unusual provision. After the settlement, Bailey wrote a letter to Vance, which said, "We write to advise you we have amicably settled the litigation under a settlement in which we acknowledge that the Defendants haven't violated the criminal laws of the State of New York or the United States. For this reason, in the offering of the Trump SoHo Hotel Condominium units to our clients none of the defendants have engaged in any conduct that has violated the criminal laws of New York or the United States."[13] The Trumps' attorneys had insisted on this language, a person familiar with the negotiations said.

In an interview, the district attorney, Cyrus Vance Jr., said that he had never before seen a letter where plaintiffs in a civil case asserted that no crime had been committed. "I don't think I'd ever received a letter like it," Vance said. He called it a "significant and important" communication. Prosecutors could still subpoena the buyers of Trump condos. But they feared the witnesses would undercut the criminal case by claiming they weren't victims of a fraud.

The night of the settlement, the plaintiff's lawyer, Bailey, celebrated with Trump's lawyers at Per Se, that year proclaimed the city's best restaurant by Sam Sifton of the *New York Times*. It was certainly one of the most expensive. A few months later, Ivanka's husband's newspaper, the *New York Observer*, ran a glowing profile of Bailey.[14] Jared Kushner had not seen the story before it was published, three people familiar with the story said, and became furious when he did. He said Bailey's name was never to appear in the paper again. (Bailey had worked for the Kushners prior to the Trump SoHo suit and was fired during it; years later, the company hired him again.)

Despite Bailey's letter saying his clients would no longer cooperate with the criminal inquiry, Peirce Moser pressed on, recommending the empaneling of a special grand jury. That would have represented a significant escalation in the case, because it is often a prelude to indictments. With a grand jury in place, defense lawyers knew the risk of indictment would be high.

The defense team offered a deal to stave off this possibility, floating a settlement of some kind, including a deferred prosecution agreement, which would have meant the corporate equivalent of probation for the Trump Organization. With the investigation appearing to gather momentum, the white-collar defense team, who had already met with the prosecutors twice, began to step up their campaign against the case. Paul Grand, Vance's former law partner, who represented one of the Trump SoHo brokers, called this the "internal appellate process." Particularly when well-heeled or high-profile defendants are involved, there can be a multimonth advocacy process that slowly makes its way up the hierarchy inside the Manhattan DA's office before any official charges are filed.

Grand and the white-collar defense team decided that it would be unwise to go over the heads of the staff prosecutors. Instead, on April 18, 2012, they sent a letter to Adam Kaufmann, then the chief of the investigative division, outlining their arguments. The next day, the defense lawyers met with Moser, Kaufmann, and others from the prosecution team. The defense team acknowledged that the Trumps made some exaggerated statements in order to sell the units. But they argued the statements were "puffery"—harmless exaggeration. Such language, they contended, didn't amount to criminal conduct. The Trumps weren't selling useless swampland in Florida. The condos existed. And the buyers' money was in escrow the entire time.

The defense lawyers argued that bringing such a case to trial would be wasteful and that resources would be better spent on more serious offenses. As Grand put in an interview with ProPublica's Jesse Eisinger: "I guess in a world that is completely pure and where there is no deviation between proprietary and the law, that kind of exaggeration and deliberately concentrated exaggeration can be pursued. But is that the kind of criminal-law enforcement the D.A. should be doing?"[15]

Moser's answer was Yes, and he found support among his supervisors, including Adam Kaufmann, who was in charge of all white-collar, money-laundering, and corruption investigations. At the meeting, Kaufmann peppered the defense team with questions, at one point raising his voice, according to a person who was there. "I believed in the case," Kaufmann said in an interview, though he declined to discuss the evidence. "But believing in the case doesn't mean we had reached the point when [I had] settled on what should happen with the case."

Moser, backed by his supervisors, persisted. "Peirce believed in his case," Grand said. "We did not succeed in talking him out of it and didn't succeed in talking one or two levels above him into dropping the case." This is the point at which Marc E. Kasowitz, Donald Trump's personal attorney, became involved.

—

By the spring of 2012, Kasowitz had been a Trump attorney for over a decade, suing Trump's partners in the Riverside yards development, suing journalist Tim O'Brien for defamation, representing Ivanka Trump in her prenuptial contract with Jared Kushner. Kasowitz could be ferocious in going after Trump opponents, issuing threats to legal counterparts he viewed as getting in his way. Or he could be charming, working his political connections to serve his clients' aims.

In the fall of 2011, two months before the Trump SoHo civil suit was settled, Kasowitz was introduced to the Manhattan district attorney, Cyrus Vance Jr., by an old friend of Trump's, Howard Lorber. Lorber is both the head of Douglas Elliman, one of the oldest and largest real estate brokerages in New York City, and the Vector Group, a holding company which owns the Liggett tobacco company. Lorber and Trump went back several decades; Lorber had traveled with Trump to Moscow on at least one occasion in the 1990s to explore the idea of a Trump Tower Moscow.

In September 2011, Lorber, Vance, and Kasowitz met for breakfast. Lorber and Vance raised the idea of Kasowitz holding a fundraiser for Vance's 2013 reelection campaign, and shortly thereafter, Vance traveled to Kasowitz's Times Square offices for a "thought-raiser" with Kasowitz and his partners, an opportunity to discuss legal strategies and policies with the DA.

In January 2012, two months after the Trump SoHo civil suit was settled, Kasowitz made a $25,000 contribution to Vance. Kasowitz had only ever made contributions that large in New York State to two other candidates: the Nassau County DA, and the governor, Andrew Cuomo. Kasowitz's contribution to Vance instantly made him one of Vance's largest donors.[16]

That was his status in April 2012, when Trump SoHo's white-collar defense team had their unsuccessful meeting with the DA's chief of investigations, Adam Kaufmann, to try and make the Trump SoHo case go away.

Kasowitz is not a criminal defense attorney, but he decided what he needed to do was leapfrog all the lawyers involved, and talk directly to the man on top: DA Cy Vance.

"It didn't have an air you'd like," Paul Grand said in the interview with ProPublica's Eisinger. "Kasowitz came from out of the blue," Grand said. "If you and I were District Attorney and you knew that a subject of an investigation was represented by two or three well-thought of lawyers in town and all of a sudden someone who was a contributor to your campaign showed up on your doorstep and the regular lawyers are nowhere to be seen, you'd think about how you'd want to proceed."

Vance had a policy of not accepting donations from lawyers actively arguing cases to him, so, on the recommendation of his chief assistant district attorney, Dan Alonso, whose job it was to vet these things, Vance returned the $25,000 donation. Right after that, Vance, Kaufmann, Alonso, and Kasowitz met in Vance's office, without the regular defense team, and without Peirce Moser or any of the lawyers from the Major Economic Crimes Unit.

In an interview, Vance said Kasowitz's pitch was no different from what the other defense lawyers were saying: it wasn't really a crime, the victims hadn't really lost anything. It would be a tough case. Vance said there was no talk of campaign donations, no implicit threat that he really didn't want to go up against the Trumps. "Marc never said that and I don't think he ever would say that," Vance said. Was it on his mind? "No," Vance said. "I was not, I'm not—as D.A. it's not uncommon for us to deal with individuals who are subjects of investigations that are financially prominent."[17]

After the meeting, there were more discussions inside the DA's office, weighing the pros and cons of the case. On the one hand, there was the air-tight email chain with emails from Don Jr. and Ivanka, but on the other hand there was the problem with the reluctant victims, and there was that letter, the one that said the victims didn't believe a crime had been committed. There was a debate, but ultimately, Vance's subordinates came down on the side of bringing the case to a grand jury, the path to indictment of Donald Trump Jr. and Ivanka Trump.

On August 1, Kasowitz offered a settlement. He said the Trumps would admit no wrongdoing, but would agree to market the Trump SoHo truthfully. He offered to have an independent monitor inside the Trump Organization to make sure they did so. Overruling his prosecuting attorneys, Vance decided the matter was one for the civil courts, not the DA. He chose not to prosecute Donald Trump Jr. and Ivanka Trump for felony fraud. On Friday, August 3, 2012, Vance closed the case.

"At the end of the day I have to look at all the evidence and weigh all the factors as the lead of the office—and my name's on the indictment—as to whether or not I feel this should be prosecuted as a crime," Vance said. "By the way, not every lie is a crime."

Just a month after the case was dropped—in September 2012—Kasowitz sent an email to Vance's reelection campaign, telling them he wanted to get back on schedule for a fundraising event. Over the next thirteen months, Kasowitz gave another $32,000 to Vance, and held two fundraisers for him, raising a total of $50,000, including his own donation, which was the largest donation Kasowitz had ever made in New York State, before or since.

"I donated to Cy Vance's campaign because I was and remain extremely impressed by him as a person of impeccable integrity," Kasowitz said in a statement. He said he viewed Vance, "as a brilliant lawyer and as a public servant with creative ideas and tremendous ability."

"Marc Kasowitz had no influence and his contributions had no influence whatsoever on my decision making in the case. And contributions by any lawyer have never in my time as District Attorney influenced my decision making on the merits," Vance said. But five years after the contribution was made, shortly before our story on the Trump SoHo case appeared in the *New Yorker*, ProPublica, and on WNYC, Vance said he would return the donation. He no longer accepts any donations from attorneys who have cases pending before his office.[18]

Years after the case was dropped, as Trump was taking off in the Republican primaries, Kasowitz was heard boasting that he'd gotten a criminal case against Don Jr. and Ivanka killed, a case that would have been "very dangerous" to the Trump family and the business. (Kasowitz has denied saying this.)

In December 2017, the Trump SoHo was still struggling, and the Trumps decided it was time to walk away. Only a third of the 391 units had been sold.

ACT IV

14

"TO SPEND WITHOUT LIMIT"

In October 2010, in the run-up to the midterm elections, I paid a visit to Canton, Ohio, the seat of Stark County, about an hour's drive south of Cleveland. Stark County is the kind of place that attracts reporters in election years: a place that had voted for Barack Obama in 2008, and George W. Bush before that, and Bill Clinton before that. Canton itself had become a recognizable archetype: a once-proud midwestern manufacturing town, with tall buildings and ornate movie palaces constructed on the premise that Canton would be Someplace for as long as those impressive edifices would stand.

By 2010, much of Canton's downtown was boarded up. Unemployment in Stark County had topped 13 percent earlier that year,[1] and desperation was palpable in the strip malls and Walmart parking lots, the only places with enough passersby for a reporter to gauge the mood of the electorate. There was widespread confusion and discontent about President Bush's Troubled Asset Relief Program, known as TARP, the $700 billion bank bailout, which was almost always mixed up with the Obama economic stimulus package, an $800 billion relief package containing funds for infrastructure investment, but also for tax cuts for the working class. Stimulus opponents—Republicans, mostly—

lambasted Obama's package for being too large, but it was, in fact, too small for most voters to notice. No one could understand why, if the federal government could give $700 billion to the banks, it couldn't give them enough money to save their homes.

In my hotel room in Canton, the campaign ads were nonstop. They were on every channel. Uniformly negative, they featured prison bars, bags of cash, and ominous music. Washington was doing nothing but stealing and stealing, committing every crime short of murdering your wife and kidnapping your children. Twenty-four hours a day, seven days a week, voters were told that government officials were untrustworthy, destructive figures, that government itself had undermined towns like Canton. Similar ads ran in Jackson County, Michigan, and in Hillsborough County, Florida, and in swing counties across the country. This was *not* just normal election-year television advertising. This was the television landscape in the year the US Supreme Court ruled in the case *Citizens United v. Federal Election Commission*, which gave corporations the First Amendment right to free speech in elections.

Campaign spending in 2010 topped three and a half billion dollars, shattering the previous record of under three billion dollars in a nonpresidential year.[2] After the *Citizens United* decision, expenditures by groups with hidden donors, which a few years earlier had been almost undetectable, approached one hundred and forty million dollars—and favored conservative groups at a rate of two-to-one.[3] "Democratic strategists began to feel a strange undertow, as if an offshore tsunami were gathering force," Jane Mayer wrote in her book *Dark Money*.[4]

As Mayer documented, *Citizens United* was the fruit of a decades-long plan to unshackle the campaign finance system from the controls that had been enacted in the wake of Watergate. Key to that effort was the DeVos family of Michigan, who had presided over the Amway direct-selling empire. "The government alleged that the company was little more than a pyramid scheme built upon misleading promises of riches," Mayer wrote of a Federal Trade Commission probe into Amway.[5] Family patriarch Richard DeVos became a top backer of "independent" political spending campaigns, and of efforts to undo campaign-finance laws. Ultimately, the FTC did not find Amway to be a pyramid scheme, but, in a 121-page decision, ordered the company to "cease and desist" from some of its business practices.

Richard's son Dick married Betsy Prince, the scion of another Michigan dynasty. Betsy DeVos became a founding board member of a nonprofit whose sole purpose was to dismantle all restrictions on money in politics, the James Madison Center for Free Speech. This group was funded by a variety of right-wing sources, including the National Rifle Association and the Christian Coalition. It shared a general counsel, James Bopp Jr., with the National Right to Life Committee.[6] "We had a 10-year plan to take all this down," Bopp told the *New York Times*. "And if we do it right, I think we can pretty well dismantle the entire regulatory regime that is called campaign finance law."[7]

To do this, Bopp took on as a client Citizens United, a right-wing agitprop group led by David Bossie, a former GOP congressional staffer and anti-Clinton researcher whose film *Hillary: The Movie*, scheduled for release in 2008, became the basis for the lawsuit. At issue was whether the film, an on-demand video distributed close to an election and advertised on television, should be banned as corporate-sponsored political advertising. Delivering the majority opinion for the US Supreme Court, Justice Anthony Kennedy wrote that while some people might find the movie *Hillary* instructive and others might see it as unfair, "those choices and assessments, however, are not for the Government to make." For purposes of campaign finance laws, Kennedy concluded, "political speech does not lose First Amendment protection 'simply because its source is a corporation.'" Citizens United had won. The decision was delivered January 21, 2010.[8]

Six days later, President Obama addressed both houses of Congress in his annual State of the Union address. "With all due deference to separation of powers," President Obama said, "last week the Supreme Court reversed a century of law that I believe will open the floodgates for special interests—including foreign corporations—to spend without limit in our elections." As Democrats rose to applaud the remarks, Supreme Court Justice Samuel Alito, in full robes, sitting right in front of the president, grimaced and shook his head as he mouthed the words "not true."

Obama continued with his speech. "I don't think American elections should be bankrolled by America's most powerful interests, or worse, by foreign entities. They should be decided by the American people."[9]

Alito and the rest of the court sat stone faced after that, looking straight ahead. Alito's silent utterance—"not true"—would prove to be wrong. Obama was also wrong, sort of. The effect of money and foreign influence on campaigns would be worse than he ever imagined.

In July 2011, as the Trump family prepared to cut the ribbon of the Trump Ocean Club Resort in Panama City, Panama—in an area newly crowded with developments—downpours swamped the city's infrastructure, turning the cramped roads near the tower into sewers.[10] This was the Trumps' first project in Central or South America, and the Trumps' first international hotel.[11] It was the tallest building in Panama, described by Ivanka Trump as resembling as a "gorgeous sail—some people say it resembles a giant D, as well."[12] (Locally it's known as *la mota, la micha, la cocada, el tontón,* or *la chucha,* all of them slang for "vagina.")

Donald Trump had put Ivanka forward as the point person on the project involved, as she said, in "every aspect," from scouting and pre-development planning through construction, sales, and marketing.[13] She had picked out the finishes and overseen the design of the fifteenth-floor sky lobby, touted the palette as "reminiscent of indigenous flowers." But in July 2011, days away from giving birth to her and Jared Kushner's first child, Arabella, she did not fly to Panama City to cut the ribbon for the Trump Ocean Club Resort.

Instead, Eric Trump and Don Jr. attended along with their father, and the Panamanian president, Ricardo Martinelli. There were other VIPs, and hotel workers, and dancers in vivid red-and-white traditional garments, performing for an approving row of men in dark suits. Martinelli told Donald Trump, "everything you touch turns to gold." Trump, in turn, had kind words for Martinelli. "They really love your president and I just want to thank you very much for being here today and you're my friend, great honor," before lining up with the men in suits to cut a giant ribbon with a pair of giant scissors.[14] Afterwards, Trump and Martinelli left, driven out through the flooded streets of Panama City in separate SUVs.

Just five months later, in November 2011, the Trump Ocean Club Resort's developer defaulted on its bond payments.

Though troubled from the start, the Panama tower established a Trump family template for accumulating foreign capital, in many different forms: as sales to foreign buyers, as collateral for construction loans, as financing for its US investments, and as a source of branding and licensing fees abroad. Much of this money came from the satellite countries of the former Soviet Union, the Middle East, and countries like Brazil, India, Turkey, the Philippines, and Uruguay, almost all of them places with few regulatory or financial controls, if not an outright business of corruption. It was not unusual for real estate companies in this period to rely on foreign capital. What was unusual was the Trumps' exceptional indifference to vetting their sources of income and taking steps to ensure their customers and investors would come out whole.

The developer Trump chose to work with in Panama had most of his prior experience not in construction or building, but in the garment import-export business; still, the licensor and licensee dreamed up a deal to build the tallest tower in Panama, a world capital known for its secrecy, and, in other contexts, for being a haven for laundering drug money. In 2005 and 2006, despite his initial success as the host of the *The Apprentice*, Trump still couldn't get a regular bank loan. To overcome this hurdle, Trump and the Panama developer signed a licensing deal predicated on Trump's obtaining construction financing for the project through a bond sale, essentially a deal that would farm out the financial risk of the loan to a potentially worldwide group of bond buyers.

According to the licensing deal uncovered by my *Trump, Inc.* colleagues Heather Vogell and Meg Cramer in files maintained at the Panama Securities and Exchange Commission, Trump agreed to arrange the financing (for which he would receive a two-million-dollar fee). But in order to unlock the construction bond, the sales team had to presell over 60 percent of the units; that is, enter into sales contracts before the building was fully constructed. These sales contracts were the collateral on which the entire deal was based; the buyers' deposits, with the promise of more money to come at closing, would in theory give bond buyers the financial assurances they needed to invest in the deal.

Despite a softening of the real estate market by 2006, early sales at the Trump Panama (at least on paper) appeared to be swift; in the first year of presales, the developers reported that there were 585 presales contracts. Many of those contracts may have been illusive; buyers later claimed that Trump and his associates had promised to help them "flip" the units before they closed, (wrongly) suggesting a no-lose situation for buyers. There were also built-in incentives for the brokers to sign deals that might never close, including an unusual provision that paid the brokers most of their commission after signing the deal, not at the usual time—when a deal finally closes.

It wasn't just that these unit sales were questionable; they may also have been vehicles for money laundering or attempted money laundering. Before the Trumps started developing in Panama, there wasn't much of a tourist market there. However, high-rises flourished in Panama City, their construction fueled by international drug cartels, wanting to turn their dirty cash into real estate, which could then be sold for clean cash.[15]

Panamanian laws make it easy to obscure financial transactions. For the Trump Ocean Club most purchases were made through anonymous shell companies. In Panama, buyers could change the ownership of a unit in secret. Often this was done using "bearer shares," which meant the transfer could be accomplished by passing a piece of paper to the buyer, without recording the transfer anywhere.

Bond documents show 60 percent of the early buyers in the Trump Ocean Club Panama came from outside the United States. Though buyers in Panama were not tracked by nationality, Trump's Panama developer said in an interview with ProPublica's Heather Vogell that buyers from Moscow and from Sunny Isles, a city in Florida known as "Little Moscow," did buy in.

But even with special incentives for buyers and brokers and structural incentives luring flight capital to Panama, it was still hard for the Trumps and their associates to find enough buyers to reach the "presold" threshold to obtain a $220 million bond from Bear Stearns.[16] To put false information in a bond prospectus would run afoul of securities laws. And yet the bond documents claimed 64 percent of units had been presold.

The bond sale went through in November 2007, barely. Not only had the real estate market begun to collapse, but so had the global financial markets. At the last minute, Bear Stearns postponed the offering only to reverse course a few days later. Trump had been a Bear Stearns client since the 1980s. (*The Art of the Deal* opens with a phone call with the then–Bear Stearns chief, and in the 1990s Trump was fined $750,000 for obscuring stock transactions with Bear Stearns.) The Panama development was the only bond issue to move forward among eight Bear Stearns was considering at that moment.

One of the lead real estate brokers on the project, Jack Studnicky, told ProPublica's Vogell, "I remember walking up Fifth Avenue and I put my arm around" the Panama project's developer, Roger Khafif. "And I said, 'You are the luckiest SOB I ever met.'"[17]

The bonds were a hard sell. They had been rated as "speculative"—or junk—for the perceived risk of the investment, and global investors weren't buying. Within months, Bear Stearns collapsed, disappearing into the maw of J.P. Morgan Chase. But the Trump Ocean Club had its construction loan. It could build.

Aggressive presales tactics; promises of flipping; front-loaded brokerage fees; anonymous purchases; all had created a rotten foundation. Only half the sales contracts ever closed. Buyers walked away from some $50 million in deposits, a volume that far exceeded ratings agencies' worst expectations for performance of the bond. And when the project defaulted, and ultimately went into bankruptcy, up to $120 million of the $220-million bond deal was never paid back.

The Trump Ocean Club Resort had been a bad investment for many involved—but not the Trumps. They still made money—on everything from obtaining the financing to their portion of minibar and terrycloth robe sales—between $30 million and $55 million, ProPublica's Heather Vogell calculated.[18] The Trumps also learned an important lesson about new ways foreign capital could keep them in the black, even when the world was falling apart.

Far north of Panama City, the Trumps were involved in another hotel condo licensing project. The Trump International Hotel and Tower in Toronto, also assigned to Ivanka Trump,[19] similarly relied on pumped-up presales. One judge found the sales team deployed "deceptive documents" that were "replete with misrepresentations of commission, of omission, and of half truth." An Ontario Court of Appeals judge found the developers engaged in "negligent misrepresentation," leading one buyer to lose nearly a million Canadian dollars. Another, who worked in a warehouse and had only recently come out of bankruptcy, lost $248,064.58.[20]

Like the Panama project, the Toronto project was beset with problems. Trump's original partner had fled the United States after pleading guilty to fraud and embezzlement, and the remaining partners had questionable experience in real estate development, construction, and hotel operations. One of them, Val Levitan, who ran a slot-machine company, was tasked with managing the construction and selling the condo units. The sales were made on the basis of fictitious financial estimates, the Ontario judge noted, that were "dreamed up" by

Levitan, "who, it will be recalled, had no previous experience in the hotel business."[21]

There was a new wrinkle in the Trump Toronto deal, something that set it apart from Panama. After Trump's initial Toronto partner was extradited to the United States, a man named Alex Shnaider stepped up to be the project's main financial investor. As the *Financial Times* described it, with the arrival of Shnaider, Trump Tower Toronto connected Donald Trump "with a shadowy post-Soviet world where politics and personal enrichment merge."[22]

Born in St. Petersburg, Alex Shnaider emigrated from the Soviet Union to Israel at age four, and to Canada when he was thirteen. In Canada, teenaged Shnaider stocked shelves at his parents' delicatessen in an immigrant neighborhood of Toronto.[23] In his twenties, Shnaider went to work at the international conglomerate Seabeco for Boris Birshtein, who was born in Soviet-occupied Lithuania and became rich during the disintegration of the Soviet Union. Shnaider married Birshtein's daughter.

Birshstein, the *Financial Times* reported, was by then a rare western businessman who could work on both sides of the Iron Curtain. Among other industries, he had interests in the Ukrainian metals market, the same lawless arena where Paul Manafort's patron Rinat Akhmetov had also jousted.[24] It was in that market that Birshtein's son-in-law, Shnaider, made a fortune after purchasing a Ukrainian steel mill with a partner for a vastly reduced price in 2001. Media reports put that price at $70 million.[25]

In separate investigations, the *Financial Times*, the *Globe and Mail*, and the *Toronto Star* with *Columbia Journalism Investigations*[26] marshalled evidence that Birshtein had, at best, rubbed up against the KGB and the Russian mob, if he didn't have more serious entanglements, ties that Birshtein denied. (He and Shnaider have said they have since had a falling out.)

In 2010, Shnaider and a business partner, Ukrainian metals trader Eduard Shyfrin, entered into negotiations to sell their steel mill.[27] According to Shnaider's statement to British arbitration court, unearthed by the *Financial Times*, buyers acting "on behalf of the Russian government" wanted to buy their stake in the mill. The documents say Shyfrin was told that Moscow regarded buying the mill as "politically strategic," that owning the mill was a way for the Russian government to maintain influence in Ukraine. Further, "a top Russian official told Shyfrin 'in very clear terms' to proceed with the deal, hinting that, if he did not, his Russian assets would be in jeopardy."

This is when things got weird. According to the *Financial Times*, Shnaider and Shyfrin's company, the Midland Group, was offered $850 million for the mill. This was $160 million more than they had been offered by another bidder, Rinat Akhmetov. But there was a catch: Shnaider and Shyfrin had to make some payments out of their proceeds from the sale. First they would have to pay a $50-million "termination penalty," as the *Financial Times* described it, to Akhmetov. Shnaider and Shyfrin would have to pay another $100 million to what Shnaider called "introducers." By the time of their British court case, Shnaider and Shyfrin were at odds. And yet, the *Financial Times* wrote, there appeared to be "no dispute in the documents that Shnaider signed off on the $100m payment on the understanding that it was heading for representatives of the Kremlin's interests." In the court papers, Shyfrin called the payment of these types of commissions "common practice" in Russia and Ukraine. Shnaider denies the "introducer" fee was ever paid. However, the entire $850-million deal was financed by Vnesheconombank, whose chairman at the time was Vladimir Putin. "In effect," the *Financial Times* stated, "Shnaider and Shyfrin's deal was with the Russian state itself."[28]

If the ultimate destination of the $100 million in commissions was unclear, one thing was not: months after his company was enriched by the sale of the steel mill, Shnaider set aside another $40 million for the Trump Toronto.[29] Trump, according to his own financial disclosures, subsequently made at least $3 million in fees from the deal.[30]

In April 2012, just months after the Panama default, the Trumps gathered to cut the ribbon in Toronto. Donald, this time with all three of his adult children, Ivanka included, stepped out of a black Cadillac

Escalade, and greeted white-hatted chefs and uniformed hotel workers brought together for the occasion, along with VIPs like the mayor of Toronto (the later-disgraced Rob Ford). In a room packed with cameras, the Trumps and the VIPs again formed a line of dark suits broken only by Ivanka's blue-flowered dress. Instead of traditional Panamanian music, there was Aaron Copland's "Fanfare for the Common Man." Instead of dancers in vivid white and red costumes, there were four women, all similarly coiffed, all with dresses V-necked in the back, carrying trays at precisely waist height bearing sets of gold-plated scissors. There were two Toronto police officers in dress uniform, saluting Donald Trump with white-gloved hands, before unfurling, as if they held a flag, a long red ribbon, cut to pieces on Donald Trump's count of three.[31] The building, Shnaider proclaimed, was a "great success."[32]

It was not a success. Buyers started suing for misrepresentation almost right away. Sales were much slower than predicted, and so were hotel occupancy rates. Alone among hundreds of tall condominium towers that had been built that decade in Toronto, the *Toronto Star* and *Columbia Journalism Investigations* reported, there was "only one that went bankrupt after completion: the Trump International Hotel and Tower Toronto."[33]

As with Panama, the Trumps made millions anyway.

After the *Citizens United*–fueled midterms of 2010, after the Democrats' crushing loss of control of the House of Representatives, Obama's economic initiatives largely came to a halt. In his first two years in office, he'd passed the Affordable Care Act and the Dodd-Frank Act, but when he proposed eliminating the carried-interest loophole, a tax provision that allowed private equity and hedge fund partners to halve the rates on certain of their taxes, the bill's very existence enraged Steve Schwarzman, CEO of the Blackstone Group. "It's a war," Schwarzman said at a private board meeting of a nonprofit organization in 2010. "It's like when Hitler invaded Poland in 1939."[34] Schwarzman soon apologized, but he showed up at the Koch donor conference that year, as Jane Mayer reported, with others, "checkbooks in hand, determined to prevent" Obama's reelection.[35]

The Federal Reserve kept the economy afloat using a move called quantitative easing, buying tens of billions of dollars of bonds every month in an effort to flood money into the economy, weakening the dollar. As Ilya Marritz wrote of this period for WNYC News, there was a side effect of the weak dollar: "a growing appetite for expensive New York real estate. Residential skyscrapers intruded on the skyline south of Central Park." He added: "Even in outer borough neighborhoods that were once synonymous with crime, elegant condominiums began to appear."[36]

By 2012, foreign money was flooding into New York real estate. Throughout the United States, money was flooding into campaigns. The total cost of the election reached $6.3 billion, a billion dollars more than the previous record.[37] Super PACs, now able to raise unlimited sums, spent $800 million. Another $312 million came in as undisclosed "dark money," 86 percent of that to conservatives, the Center for Responsive Politics found.[38]

Donald Trump poured money into the 2012 election, as did Ivanka. That February, she gave an interview to Piers Morgan. When asked if she was looking forward to another four years of Barack Obama, she replied, "Hmm. Let's hope not," adding she was "vehemently against most of Obama's policies. . . . I really wanted him to do a great job and I think that he hasn't."[39] Donald Trump gave $201,000 to Republicans running in federal races that cycle. Ivanka Trump gave $132,900, all but $2,500 to Republicans.[40]

Their money funded television buys in places like Canton, Ohio, where the ads kept running and running. Almost all of them about the harms of government, coming at voters in an endless stream.

15

LICENSE

In March 2011, Donald and Ivanka Trump descended the golden escalator in the Trump Tower atrium, joining with Trump Organization executive vice president and special counsel Michael Cohen, to a crowd of waiting reporters. The press release for the event had touted the announcement of a new corporate licensing deal in the country of Georgia, but the throng of journalists was there for another reason: days earlier, Cohen had returned from the state of Iowa, where he'd flown on Trump's jet, to meet with Republican officials, including the chairman of the Iowa Republican Party, whom Cohen treated to a meeting aboard Trump's gilded aircraft.[1]

A website called ShouldTrumpRun.com had appeared in the late fall of 2010. It was organized by Cohen, whose trip to Iowa was funded with a $125,000 contribution by Stewart Rahr, a billionaire friend of Trump's with an office on the floor below the Trump Organization in Trump Tower.[2] Yet ShouldTrumpRun.com billed itself as "independent" of Trump.

Few people outside of his own or Trump's circle had heard of Michael Cohen before that Iowa trip, but there he was, in early March 2011, being interviewed by Jonathan Karl and Amy Walter of ABC News, speaking via satellite, telling them about what he described as a hoped-for presidential bid by Donald Trump. "I met with eighteen G.O.P. operatives, grassroots organizers, finance people," a pink-tied, brown-haired Michael Cohen told the anchors that morning. "Every one of them expressed not just an interest but a fervent desire to see somebody like Donald Trump join the race in hopes that we can turn this country around."[3]

At Trump Tower, Cohen stood before a thrumming crowd of reporters, lured there by the whiff of a presidential campaign. "Okay, Michael," Donald Trump prompted Cohen.

"Good afternoon everybody. My name is Michael Cohen. I'm an executive at the Trump organization," Cohen said, his Long Island accent dominant. "Seven months ago at the request of a dear friend of mine from Georgia, Giorgi Rtskhiladze, I traveled to the Republic of Georgia to explore several real estate opportunities on behalf of Mr. Trump." Cohen had gone to look into the idea of a development on the Black Sea, a resort, possibly a casino. Mikheil Saakashvili, then the president of Georgia, joined Trump and Cohen at the press conference, posing before giant mock-ups of the proposed tower and flags from the United States and the country of Georgia.[4]

Prior to working at Trump Tower, Cohen, with his long face, prominent jowls, and downturned mouth, had an office inside a taxi dispatcher's garage in an industrial neighborhood of Long Island City, Queens, practically under the highway, handling auto insurance claims. He helped set up medical offices and represented more than a hundred car-crash victims in Brighton Beach, Brooklyn—also known as "Little Odessa" for its Russian émigré population—at a time when local prosecutors were investigating a criminal network in what they called "Operation BORIS," which stands for Big Organized Russian Insurance Scam. Cohen was never implicated; indeed, until 2018 he had never been arrested or charged with any crimes, even though almost all of his business partners had been arrested, investigated, convicted, or lost their professional licenses as a result of various infractions, criminal and otherwise.[5]

With help from his father-in-law, Fima Shusterman, a Ukrainian émigré and taxi entrepreneur who himself had once been convicted of conspiracy to defraud the IRS, Cohen began investing in New York City taxi medallions, then a coveted permit that allowed a limited number of drivers to pick up riders on the streets of New York City. Because the medallions were believed to be the entrée to a guaranteed pool of income, and because the number of them was limited, they were valuable. Cohen started investing in them in the 1990s, as New York's population and property values were rising in lockstep. Soon, Cohen drove a Bentley, and worked, he told associates, as general counsel for the Harry Winston diamond company, of "Diamonds are a Girl's Best Friend" fame. (The company said Cohen was never employed there.) Cohen was wealthy enough to join the finance committee for Dennis Vacco, the New York attorney general in the mid-1990s, to whom Trump was a donor. Cohen met Donald Trump at his apartment during a Vacco fundraiser.[6]

Cohen grew his operations until he declared, at the apex, that he possessed a net worth of almost eighty million dollars.[7] On his way up, he and his family members began to buy Trump properties: Trump World Tower, Trump Grande, Trump Palace, Trump Park Avenue, Trump Place, and Trump Plaza Jersey City. It was an attention-getting series of purchases in the buildings of a man who appreciated financial tithes. And then Cohen did something that cemented his relationship with Donald Trump: he took Trump's side in a property dispute.[8]

Early in the millennium, Cohen had started purchasing apartments in Trump World Tower, the building near the United Nations that was at the time particularly popular among Russians. Soon Cohen, his in-laws, and his taxi company partner (who had been convicted of assault), all bought units in the building, "for investment," as Cohen described it in congressional testimony many years later. Cohen and his associates bought a big block of units from a brokerage company, eventually taking over the condominium board, where a faction had come into conflict with the Trumps. Cohen's side won, and Donald Trump noticed.

He gave Cohen another task: helping Donald Trump Jr. in a business license dispute. And then, as if in a fairy tale, Michael Cohen was given the third test: reading through the bankruptcy statements for Trump's Atlantic City casino company. Sitting in Trump's office, Trump, Cohen said, "asked me if I was happy at the sleepy old firm that I was with. I said 'Yes.' He said 'Would you rather work for me?'"[9]

After that day, Cohen said, he never returned to his own office. He came to view Donald Trump as a second father, and Ivanka, and especially Don Jr., as siblings.[10] As the years went on, Cohen was subjected to a kind of Trump Organization hazing. Trump would ask him to cross a line. If Cohen would do it, Trump would push him to cross another one. And the more willing he was to break rules on Trump's behalf, the more trust Trump placed in him. "It's like Ramses from the Ten Commandments: so it has been said, so it shall be done," Cohen said. "That is how The Trump Organization works." He said this included telling outright lies.

"Michael, go take him into another room and make a good deal," Trump would say of business associates. Cohen said he knew "exactly what he was talking about. It wasn't about making a good deal; it was really lowballing it, and he wanted to almost technically get it for free." When Trump stiffed vendors, it was Cohen's job to "basically tell them that we just weren't paying at all, or make them offers of, say, 20 cents on the dollar." Cohen added, "Many of these folks, you know, lost everything."[11]

By 2011, four years into his stint at the Trump Organization, Michael Cohen had banked a lot of trust with Trump. He was Trump's fixer. He became the behind-the-scenes agitator of Trump's toe-in-the-water presidential bid as well as its public face. He was running international deals. He was describing businessmen from the country of Georgia as his "dear friends."

"In front of you . . . you have President Saakashvili and George Ramishvili of the Silk Road Group," Michael Cohen told the press that day in March 2011, the zenith of his career. "And, of course, Mr. Donald J. Trump. They will be signing an unprecedented license agreement today for the development of a Trump Tower in Batumi and soon in Tbilisi."

Batumi, as described at the press conference, would soon have a luxury hotel and marina, with a casino and a convention center to follow. It was to be a beacon of transparency and the auspicious advent of capitalism in a corner of the world beset by corruption and economic decline. "I think the world will see that Georgia is a great place to invest," Cohen said, already sounding like Donald Trump, "as more Western companies will follow Mr. Trump—as they usually do—to this amazing spectacular destination location."[12]

The project was a disaster; as the *New Yorker*'s Adam Davidson reported, "virtually none of the things that Saakashvili and Trump said about the deal were true." The planned development site, Batumi, was a run-down Georgian port with no discernable market for luxury housing. The project's budget was announced at $250 million, but, even in the planning stages, it was only $110 million. The developer, the Silk Road Group, was not a real estate development firm, but a company that shipped oil products by rail from the notoriously corrupt state of Kazakhstan. And BTA, the bank that was financing the developer, was at the very time of the Trump deal enmeshed in a sprawling and well-publicized international money-laundering scandal.

The Trump Organization was ignorant of all this, Cohen said, when he was still toeing the party line. "Remember, this was a licensing deal," he told the *New Yorker*. "The financing of the project was the responsibility of the licensee." Experts on international money-laundering laws disagreed, telling the *New Yorker* that the Trump Organization, even if only selling its name, should nevertheless have vetted its corporate associates.

But for Donald Trump, the project was a success. To earn his licensing fee, he had few requirements beyond making a trip to Georgia and appearing at the press conference at the Trump Tower atrium with Michael Cohen and President Mikheil Saakhasvilli.[13] "Ivanka is over here someplace and I just want to thank her for showing up," Donald

Trump said early in his remarks. "She's going to be spending a lot of time—she's now seven months pregnant. But as soon as she has the baby she's going to be going over to the Republic of Georgia."

Then he took questions. The first question, naturally, was about Trump's plans to run for president. He would decide, he promised, by June. The ensuing softball: Do deals like these count as experience? "Oh, I think so," Trump said. "I have a lot of relationships with many of the leaders of the world. We're doing a lot of projects all over the world. This is one that's very exciting to us but we are doing other projects and I understand how the world works. I deal with the world."

So, was he criticizing President Obama's leadership?

"We're being very very badly decimated by other countries, taking advantage of us," came the response, "and we're like a whipping post. And we could be great and we could be great again. But right now this country is doing very, very poorly."

Did he have anything to say about Michael Cohen's Iowa trip?

"No. You could ask Mr. Cohen," Trump said. But, he couldn't help himself. "Well I certainly was—I mean the response has been amazing actually."[14]

Immediately after Michael Cohen's Iowa trip and the attendant news conferences, Donald Trump began to promote claims nurtured by Roger Stone and a conspiracy theorist, Jerome Corsi, that Barack Obama was not born in the United States. Trump was everywhere on television in the latter half of March 2011, fueling the racist belief that Obama was an illegitimate president. "Why doesn't he show his birth certificate?" he asked on ABC's *The View*. "All of a sudden a lot of facts are emerging and I'm starting to wonder myself whether or not he was born in this country," he said to *Fox News*, a few days later. Two days after that, he appeared on the *Laura Ingraham Show*: "He doesn't have a birth certificate, or if he does, there's something on that certificate that is very bad for him. Now, somebody told me—and I have no idea whether this is bad for him or not, but perhaps it would be—that where it says 'religion,' it might have 'Muslim.' And if you're a Muslim, you don't change your religion, by the way." And on MSNBC's *Morning Joe* in early April: "His grandmother in Kenya said, 'Oh, no, he was born in Kenya and I was there and I witnessed the birth.' Now she's on tape and I think that tape's going to be produced fairly soon."[15]

When Obama finally, at the end of April, released his Hawaiian birth certificate, Trump claimed credit: "I'm very proud of myself, because I've accomplished something that nobody has been able to accomplish," he told a bank of television cameras at a news conference at the Portsmouth, New Hampshire, airport.[16]

At the White House Correspondents Association gala dinner days later, Obama skewered a simmering Trump, who sat with a tight smile pulled across his face as the crowd laughed and applauded Obama's jokes. "You fired Gary Busey!" Obama mocked, referring to an episode of *Celebrity Apprentice*. "These are the kinds of decisions that would keep me up at night." As the laughing and cheering became more uproarious, Trump's smile pulled tighter and tighter and he began to rock in his seat. Obama added, "Say what you will about Mr. Trump, he certainly would bring some change to the White House," before flashing an image of the executive mansion, hastily photoshopped with two women in bikinis plastered in the foreground and "Hotel-Casino-Golf Course" above the columns.[17]

The day of the press conference announcing the Georgia deal, a supporter of a potential rival candidate signed a complaint addressed to the Federal Election Commission, charging that Trump, in violation of election laws, had used his corporate resources, including his jet and Michael Cohen, an executive vice president of his company, to "test the waters" for a potential campaign. The complaint also charged that Trump's friend Stewart Rahr had breached campaign contribution limits by paying for the flight, and that Cohen had done the same by working for a potential campaign as Trump's employee.

After FEC lawyers reviewed the evidence, they found "reason to believe that the flight to Iowa may have resulted in an in-kind disbursement accepted by Trump." Michael Cohen, the lawyers argued, had worked with Rahr, the outside businessman, to pay for the use of Trump's jet to fly to Iowa. Trump, Cohen, and Rahr argued that the complaint should be dismissed because there was no candidate involved. "We disagree," the commission lawyers wrote, "because the available information suggests that Trump was involved in the activity." If you're testing the waters, the commission lawyers were saying, you have to file papers saying so. You can't simply ignore the rules. The contribution of $125,000 by Rahr was $122,500 over the legal limit.

The FEC attorneys also suspected that Cohen's trip was "at the direction of Trump," adding, "If Cohen was conducting these activities as Trump's employee, the Trump Organization would have made an in-kind disbursement to Trump using federally impermissible funds." In other words, if Trump had directed the ShouldTrumpRun efforts, the Trump Organization had illegally donated to the candidate, himself.

"Therefore, we recommend that the Commission find reason to believe that Rahr, Trump LLC, Cohen, and ShouldTrumpRun violated 11 C.F.R. §100.131(a), and that Donald J. Trump violated 11 C.F.R. §100.72(a)," the FEC staff report concluded.[18]

For the first thirty years of the FEC's existence, this ruling would have been enough to trigger subpoenas, further investigation, and perhaps produced a finding of wrongdoing and a fine, of the kind Charles Kushner once received. But in 2008, at the behest of Mitch McConnell, Donald McGahn, a conservative lawyer with roots in the Federalist Society (an organization funded by ultra-conservative foundations[19]) had been named the chairman of the FEC. McGahn, a lawyer who played in a 1980s cover band and wore his hair a bit long for Washington, grew up in Atlantic City, the nephew of Paddy McGahn, the local power broker who had, in the early eighties helped Donald Trump hide some of his more unsavory business associates.[20]

As a lawyer, Don McGahn hired himself out to fight the enforcement of election laws. As a commissioner of the FEC, he was determined to permanently block them. Under commission rules, there are six commissioners, of whom at most three can be from any one political party. In practice, this means that to have any enforcement action stick, Republicans and Democrats have to work together. McGahn sought to overturn almost every staff recommendation. According to an analysis by the *Boston Globe*, in 2007, the year before McGahn took over, there were 612 cases pursued and very few dismissals. By 2012, after McGahn's takeover, the number of cases had dropped to 135, and a fifth of those were thrown out.[21] As one of McGahn's fellow commissioners, Ellen Weintraub, wrote in an op-ed in the *Washington Post*, "appointed to be an arbiter of campaign-finance complaints, McGahn instead assumed the mantle of defense counsel, making an art form of devising byzantine arguments against investigating alleged wrongdoing."[22] McGahn, almost single handedly, was dismantling the FEC's ability to enforce the law.

When the matter of Cohen's 2011 plane trip to Iowa came before them, by a vote of 3–2, the commission overruled its own lawyers and tossed Donald Trump's case. One Republican commissioner refused to sign on to McGahn's decision; years later, before Trump nominated him to be a federal judge, this same commissioner wrote a four-years-after-the-fact opinion agreeing with McGahn,[23] who by then, as White House counsel, was in charge of selecting judges.

Barely a week after Trump's March 2011 press conference with Michael Cohen, Donald took a plane ride of his own, to Barcelona, Spain—this trip, too, would result in legal action. The trip wasn't to discuss a development or a hotel-casino-golf course. It was to discuss a bulky video phone, and Donald Trump was urging people to pay money to a company named ACN for the opportunity to sell it.

By March 2011, the demand for videophones was questionable. Skype was available on almost any desktop computer or smartphone—indeed, it had 150 million monthly users—and Apple had already launched its FaceTime service. ACN's videophones were bulky, by comparison, and only worked if users on both ends had a full complement of ACN equipment, making it impractical for travel and mobile use. By 2011 ACN's supplier had already slashed production, laid off 70 percent of its staff, and would later file to liquidate in federal bankruptcy court.[24] But none of this was apparent as Donald Trump entered the Palau Sant Jordi arena in Barcelona, Spain, green spotlights pulsing over a cheering crowd, the O'Jay's singing "Money, money, money, money" as "multi-billionaire, Mr. Donald J. Trump" took the stage against an enormous photograph of tall towers shining in a night sky.[25]

Trump was there to hawk a scheme: attendees could choose to become independent business owners: that is, sellers of the video phones. To do so, they were required to pay $499, plus a $149 yearly renewal fee. But to really make money, they not only had to sell phones, but recruit new sellers, new entrants at the bottom of the sales pyramid who would send their money upwards to the executives of ACN. Eventually, some of it would go to Donald Trump. It's not clear exactly how much Trump made in total from ACN, but disclosure forms filed when he ran for president put it at $450,000 per speech.[26] "It is a substantial amount of money, even if you're rich," he told the *Wall Street Journal*.[27]

After the raucous welcome in Barcelona, Donald Trump sat in a chair on the stage and heartily endorsed the project. "A lot of the people that I've met had their job for two or three years, and all of a sudden they started leaving out of their job and going full-time at ACN because they're making more money with ACN," Donald Trump said. By this time, according to a lawsuit filed in federal court in New York, ACN's internal numbers showed the chances of making money were "miniscule."[28]

Trump also praised ACN's executives (who by then, in addition to whatever fees they paid Trump, had purchased multiple properties near Trump's North Carolina golf course, and held charitable events there[29]). "I really like the guys," Trump told the crowd, adding they'd "really become friends of mine. . . . I give lots of money to charity, and they contribute to my charities. They really have been very generous."

The next week, Trump went even further, when *The Celebrity Apprentice* aired a ninety-minute prime-time Sunday night episode featuring ACN. On the show, standing in the elevator lobby of Trump Tower, next to Ivanka and Don Jr., Donald Trump introduced the theme of the show, and his "two friends." Everyone nodded and smiled. "They run a company called ACN, which I know very well." Donald Trump did not disclose to the show's contestants, or to its viewers, that he had a financial relationship with the company. "Your task," one ACN executive explained to the contestants, "is to create a thirty-second commercial showcasing ACN and our revolutionary new video phone." At which point the making of the thirty-second commercials became the subject of 180 times that amount of television time.[30]

"One of the hallmarks of my father's television show, has been the brand-backed tasks or projects the contestants are assigned," Ivanka Trump wrote in *The Trump Card*. "These invariably involve a corporate sponsor, which naturally looks to integrate its product or service into our story line so that there's a clear carryover benefit to its business. Think of it as a transparent form of product placement, but you can be sure that NBC and the show's producers (including my father, naturally) are being compensated handsomely for the 'free' airtime."[31]

The publicity had its intended effect: thousands of people signed up to sell videophones. Many lost money. Among them: a hospice worker, a food delivery driver, and a formerly homeless man. They paid hundreds or thousands of dollars to ACN, sometimes borrowing it from family members. Four people who said they were victims of the scheme filed a class-action suit, *Jane Doe et al. v. Trump*. The Trump Organization argued that Donald, Don Jr., Eric, and Ivanka were merely celebrity endorsers, not in any way involved in ACN's corporate structure, and that, from context, it was clear they were being paid by ACN. Nor, the defendants argued in a legal brief, was there any intent to commit fraud or any conspiracy to do so. "The alleged associates must share a common purpose to engage in a particular fraudulent course of conduct and work together to achieve such purposes," the Trumps' lawyers argued, calling the legal claim that they had done exactly this "plainly inadequate."[32]

In the summer of 2019, a federal judge dismissed the part of the case that alleged the Trumps had engaged in racketeering, because, she said, it hadn't been shown that the Trumps' inducements to sign up with ACN had directly caused specific losses by the plaintiffs. But, she ruled, the defendants "deliberately misled consumers regarding the nature of ACN's business." Consequently, the class-action fraud lawsuit against Donald Trump, Don Jr., Ivanka, and Eric could proceed.[33]

At the end of the ACN *Celebrity Apprentice* episode, after tangling with Donald Trump, Dionne Warwick was fired. Three weeks later, it was Gary Busey.

In May 2011, Trump announced he would not run for the Republican nomination for president in 2012. But, with Cohen at his side, he continued to act like a presidential run was in the offing. As the *New York Times* reported, Trump had by this time struck up a friendship with Citizens United's David Bossie and would use "forums hosted by Mr. Bossie's group to road test a potential campaign."[34]

Trump even held rallies, like one on the boardwalk at Jones Beach on New York's Long Island on a gorgeous late summer day in 2011 whose stated purpose was to prompt state officials to make concessions to Trump for a catering hall he wanted to build in the middle of Jones Beach State Park. The project would be called "Trump on the Ocean." Standing next to Cohen, surrounded by burly construction worker types—some of whom later said they were paid to be there[35]—chanting "Let Trump Build! Let Trump Build!" Trump excoriated state officials for what he saw as unnecessary delays in the permitting process for a project he claimed would create a thousand construction jobs and five hundred permanent ones. "We Need Jobs!" read one of the preprinted placards onlookers held aloft. Trump himself seemed confused about the rally's purpose; one person who was there said in an interview that Trump thanked her for showing up to support his presidential campaign. (Though she was there to protest Trump on the Ocean, she later supported his 2016 presidential campaign.)

Trump was taking on few domestic construction projects at this point, and this one, for a catering hall on the beach, appeared to be of outsized importance to him. There are some clues as to why. Not only would it be a visible construction project that could serve as the backdrop of a future campaign, but Trump, with Cohen as his representative, had wrangled a highly unusual concession from New York State officials: at a time when Trump desperately needed cash, the state parks department permitted him to use the entire value of his forty-year lease to collateralize borrowing, for any project he wanted.

Trump personally called four governors and a state comptroller to get the approvals he needed, the officials or their representatives said in interviews. He'd given each of the officials tens of thousands of dollars: well over $100,000 to committees controlled by Governor George Pataki; $48,000 to the state comptroller, Alan Hevesi; $41,000 to Governor Eliot Spitzer; $5,000 to Governor David Paterson.[36] A decade later, people familiar with the thinking of all of these state officials said Trump had reached out, personally, about Trump on the Ocean. "Oh I know exactly why Donald Trump gave that contribution," said a person familiar with the Comptroller's Office. "Donald was yelling and talking about his permit and the investment he had made." After a call from Trump, Spitzer asked his staff if there wasn't a way to give Trump a variance he wanted. (Spitzer said he didn't recall this.)

In the end, Trump got most of what he wanted. But in the fall of 2012, the site of Trump on the Ocean flooded during Superstorm Sandy. After all he'd put into it, Trump walked away.

In June 2011, a month after her father doused his nascent presidential bid, Ivanka Trump held a meeting in Trump Tower with Igor Krutoy, a Ukrainian-born Russian musician. According to the *Guardian,*

Krutoy and two other businessmen were there to discuss a possible Trump project in Riga, Latvia: a building to permanently house the New Wave music festival, which Krutoy had founded. A senior Trump Organization official had already discreetly scouted possible venues, and on that day in June 2011, as Krutoy and one of the other businessmen in attendance later told the paper, they met with Ivanka not just for their allotted forty minutes, but for four hours, and were walked into Donald Trump's office for a meet and greet. "We had an extraordinarily good meeting with Ivanka," one of them, Viesturs Koziols, told the *Guardian*, adding that he and Donald Trump "shook hands as possible partners."

The next month Krutoy held a press conference in Riga with Ainārs Šlesers, another businessman and a former Latvian deputy prime minister, who separately said that he too had met with Donald Trump in New York and discussed the collaboration "several times" with Ivanka.

But the project soon stalled. Šlesers's and Krutoy's talks with the Trumps came as Latvian anti-corruption authorities were carrying out an investigation that became known as "The Oligarchs Case." Voters responded by ousting the three eponymous oligarchs, including Šlesers, in September 2011. One recording of Šlesers had caught him bragging about working with Donald Trump, according to transcripts published by a Latvian newspaper. The Trumps were not implicated in the case and did not pursue business in Latvia.[37] "We went back and forth for a little while. Nothing went forward, but it's an area that we are interested in," Donald Trump Jr. told a pair of Latvian interviewers the following spring, in May 2012.

Don Jr. was in Riga that May for a conference, sponsored by the Baltic International Bank, where he spoke on the theme, "Inheriting a Family Business and Raising the New Generation."[38] The day after his speech, sitting at an ornate wooden table, in a dark suit and a pale blue tie, across from the two interviewers, Don Jr. explained, "They wanted to talk about generational wealth, family businesses. And, you know, I think it's something that I can actually talk very, you know, intelligibly about, something that is obviously very important to myself and my family, but not really a topic that is often spoken about."

In the same interview, he was asked about whether the Trumps would pursue a project in Russia. Yes, he told his interlocutors: "I've been there many times and I've spent quite a bit of time in Moscow looking at deals." When he traveled to places like Moscow, it was for the same reason he was in Riga to talk about intergenerational wealth: "A big part of my job is just forming the friendships that often lead to partnerships."[39]

Though the partnership with Igor Krutoy had failed to produce a project in Latvia, Krutoy had a connection to someone who would play a big role in the lives of all the Trumps: another pop star with ties to oligarchs, Emin Agalarov.[40]

After the Riga deal died, the Trumps soon made another deal in another former Soviet satellite, in Baku, Azerbaijan. This deal would go a lot farther and be far more problematic than Riga; Adam Davidson of the *New Yorker* called the Baku tower "Donald Trump's Worst Deal."[41] In April 2012, as the Manhattan district attorney's criminal fraud investigation of Ivanka, Don Jr., and the Trump SoHo was reaching a particularly sensitive phase, Ivanka Trump and Donald Trump filed paperwork to set up limited liability companies as the basis for a licensing deal for the Trump Tower Baku. According to the Transparency International Corruption Perceptions Index, Azerbaijan was among the most corrupt countries in the world in 2012, on par with Nigeria, and worse than Iran.[42]

The Trumps' partner in Azerbaijan was Anar Mammadov, the son of the transportation minister, Ziya Mammadov. Ziya Mammadov had become a billionaire while making a government salary of twelve thousand dollars a year. During the time he was transportation minister, his son Anar bought a seven-bedroom home in London and regularly rode a forty-one-million-dollar Gulfstream G450 jet.

The Mammadovs, Davidson found, were closely tied to a company linked to Iran's Revolutionary Guard Corps, the wing of the Iranian military that protects Iran's Islamic political system. Over the years, the US government has accused the Revolutionary Guard of drug trafficking and money laundering. (Later, the Trump Administration officially designated it as a terrorist organization.) Ziya's brother Elton, a member of parliament, signed much of the Trump paperwork.

Davidson spoke with a series of contractors who described accepting fees in cash. One of them, an Englishman named Frank McDonald, said he himself once collected one hundred and eighty thousand dollars in a laptop bag, and that on another occasion a colleague had to stuff two million dollars into a large duffel bag.

The Trump Organization maintained that it had done "extensive due diligence" and come away satisfied, that it was not responsible for others' behavior, and that it was "merely a licensor." Moreover, its chief legal officer Alan Garten told Davidson that the "flow of funds is in the wrong direction" for the Trumps to have any legal liability; the Trump Organization had no equity in the Baku tower and was not responsible for its financing.

"No, that's just wrong," Jessica Tillipman, an assistant dean at George Washington University Law School, told Davidson. She added, "Nor can you escape liability by looking the other way. The entire Baku deal is a giant red flag—the direct involvement of foreign government officials and their relatives in Azerbaijan with ties to the Iranian Revolutionary Guard. Corruption warning signs are rarely more obvious."[43]

In October 2014, Ivanka Trump posted a video on Instagram. Wearing a white hotel bathrobe, looking like she had just stepped out of a spa, she said "A very long flight but I'm here in Baku, Azerbaijan, check it out," before panning her cell phone to capture the city's "flame towers."[44] Her website proclaimed: "Ivanka has overseen the development of Trump International Hotel & Tower Baku since its inception, and she recently returned from a trip to the fascinating city in Azerbaijan to check in on the project's progress."

The hotel, located in a run-down area of Baku near a tangle of highway ramps, was very near completed. As late as 2015, Ivanka Trump told *Baku* magazine she couldn't wait to try out the "huge spa" there, and that it was slated to open in June. Instead, her father announced his campaign for president.

While Ivanka was working on Baku, Donald Trump had his eyes on another city, the biggest market in all of the former Soviet Union: Moscow. He wanted to bring the Miss Universe pageant, which he owned, to Russia. This was, he made clear, a springboard to a real estate development project there.

In early 2013, a portly British music publicist named Rob Goldstone was working with a client named Emin Agalarov. The brown-haired, doe-eyed Russian-Azerbaijani singer was a pop star in Russia and desperate to break into the US market. He and Goldstone had a plan: Emin would perform in the Miss Universe pageant.

According to an account in Michael Isikoff and David Corn's book *Russian Roulette*, Goldstone and Agalarov first pitched holding the Miss Universe pageant in Azerbaijan. When that didn't work, they suggested Russia.[45] Emin's father, Aras Agalarov, is known as "Putin's Builder" because he is often tapped by Putin's government to build large infrastructure projects for events where Russia needs to impress the world, such as sports facilities for the 2018 World Cup. One of Agalarov's residential developments, outside Moscow, according to the Luke Harding book *Collusion*, was modeled on homes in Alpine, New Jersey, where Emin had gone to high school.[46]

Aras Agalarov had built Crocus City Hall, a large theater complex where the Miss Universe pageant could be held, and where, in exchange for housing the event, Emin would get two slots at the Miss Universe contest and a cameo by the reigning Miss Universe in the music video for his song "Amor," shot on a Los Angeles backlot.[47]

In June 2013, the Agalarovs—Emin and Aras—the publicist Goldstone, and Donald Trump and his entourage all convened in Las Vegas, for the Miss USA contest, which is owned by Miss Universe. "These are the most powerful people in Russia, the richest men in Russia," Donald Trump said during one photo opportunity. (They were not actually the richest men in all of Russia.) This dinner party was captured on a video, obtained by CNN, that shows Trump and Michael Cohen chatting with the Agalarovs, Goldstone, and another man, Irakly "Ike" Kaveladze, the US-based vice president of Agalarov's company.[48]

Kaveladze had been scrutinized in 2000 by US Senator Carl Levin for establishing over two thousand Delaware shell companies to move $1.4 billion from foreign countries. Levin later called Kaveladze the "poster boy" for facilitating the movement of foreign wealth through the US financial system. Levin said that though the practice was not illegal under existing US law, it "allows individuals to set up shell companies—companies through which they can anonymously pass money, and which can readily be used to launder ill-gotten gains."[49] (Kaveladze called the report, back in 2000, a "witch hunt."[50])

The day after the dinner, Trump posed for photos at Miss USA, and touted the upcoming Miss Universe contest in Russia. "And honestly," he said "they really wanted it in Russia very badly, politically they wanted it. It really is a great country, it's a very powerful country. It's a country we have a relationship with but I would say not a great relationship and I think that this can certainly help that relationship." Miss Universe, and Trump, were going to Moscow.

"We all knew that the event was approved by Putin," a Miss Universe official told the authors of *Russian Roulette*. "You can't pull off something like this in Russia unless Putin says it's okay." As Corn and Isikoff put it: "Trump would only be making money in Russia because Putin was permitting him to do so."

In Moscow, in an interview with the Russian press preceding the pageant, Trump returned the favor, saying, of Putin, "Look, he's done a very brilliant job in terms of what he represents and who he's representing." (These Trump comments came just after a brutal anti-LGBT law passed in Russia, accompanied by a sharp rise in anti-LGBT violence there.) Trump kept gushing about Putin: "He's put himself at the forefront of the world as a leader in a short period of time."

In the days leading up to the pageant, Trump had been hoping and hinting that Putin might drop by the pageant. Instead, Goldstone later said, Trump had to settle for a call from Putin's spokesman, Dmitry Peskov, who told him Putin would be unable to stop by because he was waiting for a visit from the king and queen of the Netherlands who were stuck in Moscow traffic. (Later, Putin, standing next to Trump in Helsinki in 2018 as Peskov looked on, would deny he even knew Trump was in Moscow then.)

On the red carpet before the pageant, Trump kept up the puffery: "Russia's just been an amazing place. You see what's happening here, it's incredible." He was positioned in front of the logos of the Trump Organization, Miss Universe, the Russian state-owned Sberbank (the event's financial sponsor), and an NBC peacock logo faded to black and white so as not to appear to be promoting homosexuality under the new Russian law.

Trump left Moscow having spent just one night in the presidential suite of the Ritz-Carlton Hotel. Soon after, Sberbank said it had struck a "strategic cooperation agreement" with the Crocus Group to finance 70 percent of a Trump Tower Moscow.[51] Had that deal gone through, Trump would have been doing business with the government of Russia.

Just days after Trump's return from Moscow, the New York–based *Real Estate Weekly* reported that members of the Sapir family had also traveled to Moscow, to start talking about a Trump Tower there. The article quoted Trump saying "the Russian market is attracted to me," adding, "I have a great relationship with many Russians." Then he noted, of the festivities surrounding the Miss Universe contest, "almost all of the oligarchs were in the room."[52]

Donald Trump also tweeted at Aras Agalarov: "I had a great weekend with you and your family. You have done a FANTASTIC job. TRUMP TOWER-MOSCOW is next. EMIN was WOW!"[53]

Over the following month, Donald Trump Jr. started to draw up an agreement for a Trump Tower Moscow with Aras Agalarov's right-hand man, Ike Kaveladze. Emin soon traveled to the Trump National Golf Club at Doral, outside of Miami, for a golf tournament, singing at a concert and posing for photos with Donald Trump and Ivanka Trump. Over the next year, Don Jr. and Kaveladze corresponded frequently. They discussed fees. There was a project proposal for an 800-unit tower, design discussions, questions from Don Jr. about the demographics of prospective buyers and the specs of a competing project by Marriott. When Kaveladze wasn't available, Rob Goldstone acted as a stand-in.[54]

The next time anyone heard of the Agalarovs was when Donald Trump Jr. released an email chain he'd been sent from Rob Goldstone, offering dirt on Hillary Clinton. "This is obviously very high level and sensitive information but is part of Russia and its government's support for Mr Trump—helped along by Aras and Emin," Goldstone wrote to Don Jr.

"Thanks Rob I appreciate that," Don Jr. replied. "I am on the road at the moment but perhaps I just speak to Emin first. Seems we have some time and if it's what you say I love it especially later in the summer. Could we do a call first thing next week when I am back?"[55]

This was early June 2016, after Trump, shocking the US political world, wrapped up the Republican nomination for president.

16

OTHER PEOPLE'S MONEY

Former New York City councilmember David Yassky had an image in his head: Jared Kushner's socks. "They had a pink argyle pattern," Yassky said in an interview, remembering the day he had made his way from his district in Brooklyn Heights to the midtown headquarters of the *New York Observer*.[1] Unlike the offices of Jared Kushner's wife and father-in-law—where framed magazine covers leaned against the walls and covered their desks—Jared's office was dominated by an imposing dark wood table, a vast slab untroubled by papers.

Yassky, who was then preparing a run for city comptroller, went to see the twenty-seven-year-old CEO of the Kushner Companies, and owner of one of the most expensive buildings in Manhattan, at the offices of the tiny weekly newspaper Jared published. Though the *Observer*, still salmon-colored in those days, had a small total circulation, it was a well-connected readership. Editors and opinion writers read it, as did politicians and their consultants, real estate titans, people in advertising and media, and financiers. All the important power sectors in New York.

Yassky remembers little of the conversation, only that it skittered along the general concerns of politicians and real estate magnates in New York—the financial crisis, national politics—and that it was interrupted when Jared took a call from Ivanka, in Turkey at the time. "Sweetheart!" was how Jared answered the phone.

Visiting Jared at his office had become an obligatory stop for ambitious office seekers and government officials in New York City: for his newspaper's editorial endorsement, for the hope that attention from Jared could translate into favorable coverage, or at least coverage that took one's candidacy seriously (a limited and highly coveted commodity in New York, like a parking space), and for the possibility that Jared would not only make major contributions, but would unlock his social network to do the same. "You had to kiss the ring," Yassky said.

This was new. When Eliot Spitzer, himself the Harvard-educated scion of a New York real estate family, had run for governor of New York in 2006, the Kushners had not been on his radar, despite their having given millions of dollars to Democrats. "They were New Jersey," Spitzer said in an interview.[2] It wasn't until the Kushners bought 666 Fifth Avenue for $1.8 billion, and Jared took over the *New York Observer*, that Jared Kushner became a stop on New York's political circuit.

Not long before he was married, in October 2009, Jared's relationship with *Observer* editor in chief Peter Kaplan was becoming increasingly frayed. Years before "clicks" and "search engine optimization" became buzzwords of the industry, Jared demanded spreadsheets showing internet traffic. "We really crashed the staff and we went from producing 30 items a week to almost 50 items a week in the paper," Jared Kushner said in a later interview. "The metabolism of the newsroom changed dramatically. From there on out it was a mandate to close the paper on time—on budget, which is something that they were never very good at before I got there."

In this interview, for a commemorative book about the *Observer, The Kingdom of New York*, Jared tacitly acknowledged that Kaplan did not embrace his changes. "My father had extra tickets to the Yankees playoff game against the Tigers, and the banker who was going to use them cancelled," Jared said. "So I called Peter Kaplan and said, 'What are you doing tonight?' He told me he had to be home with his family, and when I told him I had two front-row seats for the Yankees, he said he would call me back in five minutes, as Lisa would understand. So we went to the game and we were sitting there, eating hot dogs and drinking beers, and it was drizzling and we start talking and it was just *pouring.*" That evening, in Jared's version, the water-logged outing at Yankee Stadium unlocked a sense of common purpose. "We got on the same page that night," Jared said.[3]

But for Kaplan the changes Jared was insisting on were a burning misery. He fought with Jared daily on the side of deeply reported, long-form stories; fought for a standard of journalistic ethics; fought for his writers. "Peter loved that paper like a woman," his wife, Lisa Chase, also an editor, said in an interview. "We were fighting every night, because I wanted him to quit." And then one night, Peter Kaplan came home and said, "Get off my case, I quit tonight."[4]

Kaplan joined Condé Nast, but when he died of cancer four years later at age fifty-nine, it was his work at the *Observer* that defined him. His funeral was packed. The *New York Times*'s David Carr wrote, "Manhattan publishing took a very sad holiday on Tuesday." The grief was for Kaplan, but also, for his "ideology," as Carr called it, "bringing truth to the pageant of power in Manhattan. Dozens of his acolytes and colleagues came to work at the magazines, newspapers and eventually, the websites in Manhattan, all bringing with them a belief that journalism was both a caper and a calling."[5]

After Kaplan left the *Observer,* Jared used his perch to consolidate his relationships with the area elite. He'd started an offshoot, the *Commercial Observer,* with a "Power 100" list of the top people in New York real estate. His business partners would get top rungs of the ladder. His father-in-law regularly got bumped up the list. It was understood in the industry that Jared was playing favorites, but real estate titans cared about their place on the list all the same.

To replace Peter Kaplan, Jared recruited Kyle Pope, who had worked for a decade at the *Wall Street Journal* and who had been an editor at Condé Nast's *Portfolio*, the business glossy. Pope had got wind of the tensions between Kaplan and his publisher but Jared seduced him anyway. It seemed like the job of a lifetime; but Pope, too, soon became appalled. Jared had ordered up a "hit piece on an official at Bank of America, and was now in my office to check on how the story was coming together" as Pope described it years later in the *Columbia Journalism Review*, where Pope is now publisher and editor in chief. "I had spent the previous weeks trying to avoid the subject with him, knowing full well that the *Observer* was never going to pursue a story about an anonymous banker whose only sin was running afoul of the Kushner family." Pope finally told Kushner that the piece "was not going to happen, that talk of a 'hit job' was a textbook definition of malice, and that I considered the issue closed." As Pope described it, Jared "pursed his lips, paused a beat, and ended the conversation." Some time later, Pope, who as part of his job attended weekly meetings at the Fifth Avenue offices of the Kushner family business, came face to face with Charlie Kushner, who asked him what happened to the "hit job." Now Pope understood why Jared had been so singularly obsessed with this particular, non-journalistic story. It was important to his father. The story never ran. Pope was soon pushed out.[6]

"There's always going to be conflicts," Jared later told a forum at the 92nd Street Y in Manhattan, when asked about being a publisher and a developer. "If you don't want conflicts" he said, smiling, "just go in your apartment and stay there and lock the door. Don't go to work, don't do anything. As it comes up, you trust people to do the right thing, and we've found that we really haven't had any issues."[7]

During the tenure of Kyle Pope as editor in chief, the Kushner Companies were performing a series of fraught financial maneuvers to keep 666 Fifth Avenue afloat. The Kushners had purchased the building in 2007 for just $50 million in equity: that is, they spent just $50 million of their own money, and took out $1.75 billion in debt. The purchase was made near the top of a bubble. "With very little development opportunities available, a sense of near panic set in among the institutional investors to place long-term capital in NYC real estate," one Columbia University study said. Trophy buildings had become "a whole new asset class." When it came to office buildings, 666 Fifth Avenue was the most expensive trophy of them all, the biggest deal of its kind in the United States at the time. It was purchased for more than three times what its previous owners had paid, $518 million, just seven years earlier.[8]

In their hunger to purchase the building, Charles and Jared Kushner had taken on far riskier debt than other borrowers would have, including $535 million in short-term debt at a strikingly high interest rate. Friends were stunned by the level of risk Charlie could tolerate. "I buy it, you make it work," Charlie told his accountants, according to *Bloomberg News*. The deal was put together during a series of all-nighters over Thanksgiving weekend.[9]

Officially, Charles wasn't part of it. The loan documents noted, "Charles Kushner, the former sole chairman of the Kushner Companies, has an interest in the related borrower." They added: "Charles Kushner has been released from jail," and warned that as a convicted felon he was "not permitted directly or indirectly to control the borrower." There was a "springing full recourse to the sponsors and Charles Kushner in the event Charles Kushner has any involvement in the management of the property."[10]

Part of the justification for the enormous loan had been the value of its location, and an optimism that prices would keep rising, that the building could become more profitable. "The in-place rents are significantly below market," one analysis said, "providing the potential for increased revenue."[11] But by 2008, it was clear the rental market was softening, the real estate market was teetering, and banks were coming under pressure. The building was 94 percent rented when the Kushners purchased it. The next year, it slipped to 89 percent.[12] That year, the Kushners created a condominium that comprised the retail portion of 666 Fifth Avenue, and sold off a 49 percent stake in this portion for $525 million, staving off the high-interest loan due dates.[13] But the family still had $1.2 billion of debt remaining, all of which their diminished portion of the building had to sustain.

Their financiers were under pressure, too. The summer after the Kushners bought the property, their bankers sold the right to collect the debt from Kushner Companies for seventy-five cents on the dollar, some of it to financier Richard Mack, then at Apollo Real Estate Advisors. Like Jared, Mack was the scion of a New Jersey real estate family; his father, William Mack, was chairman of the board of Mack-Cali Realty, one of the nation's largest publicly traded real estate investment trusts. Dick Mack had attended Jared and Ivanka's wedding. Now, he held $95 million of Kushner Companies debt in 666 Fifth Avenue.

Real estate prices were sinking. The building's net operating income was dropping further and further below the debt payments.[14] Its occupancy rate slid to 78 percent.[15] One of the building's largest tenants, the law firm Orrick Herrington & Sutcliffe, had a lease up for renewal. Orrick was paying $45 a square foot under their old lease. Mack counseled Jared to take $90 a square foot. Jared insisted on $120 a square foot. In a law firm, such an increase is particularly onerous; the way such firms are structured, the increased rent would have come directly from each partner's compensation. The partners rejected Jared's offer and moved to a building on the same block. Dick Mack expressed his displeasure. Jared yelled at him: "Who do you think you're talking to?" according to a person familiar with the conversation. "I'm working my ass off!" Mack was taken aback. It's unusual to yell at people who lend you money. But Mack moved on. Jared, apparently, did not.

Not long after, Jared spoke to Elizabeth Spiers, then his third editor in chief at the *Observer*, and told her at their weekly meeting that he had a really good lead on purported financial chicanery by Dick Mack. Jared said the story was "very important" to him. This, Spiers later wrote in a blog post, was unusual in itself, since "Jared actually didn't pitch specific stories on a regular basis, just made broad generalities about what and who should be covered." Spiers said she knew Jared had an agenda, but people with agendas pitch actual stories all the time.

"So I agreed to put a reporter on the story with the caveat that it had to 100% check out," Spiers wrote, "because if Jared was willing to tell me about it, he'd probably told other people and if there was even one tiny inaccuracy, no matter how small, the guy would probably have a case for defamation. Jared was sure it would check out. 'Just talk to anybody in the industry,' he said."

The story did not check out. Spiers assigned a reporter who "called everyone within a 100 mile radius of the subject and came back after a few days and told me he couldn't find anything." So she went back to Jared, and he insisted she assign it to someone else. Spiers did this, but said that "if it didn't check out this time, the story had to be dead. Permanently." And this second reporter came back and said "point blank that the story was bullshit." Jared still wasn't done. He insisted that all of them—him, Spiers, and the two reporters—meet with his source, at which point Jared concluded the reporters were questioning the source too aggressively. "And that's finally what killed the Big Dick Mack story," Spiers wrote.

But not entirely. Several months after she herself was fired (while traveling in China), her future husband, who was then the editor in chief of the *Commercial Observer*, "came home and said, laughing, 'You'll never believe the conversation I had with [the new editor] Ken today: he came over and said he had a really great story for me . . . About a guy named Richard Mack.' "[16]

(Years later, when Sarah Ellison of *Vanity Fair* published a story with some of these details, "a person close to Kushner" maintained that Kushner had never done business with Mack and that it was a former business partner of Mack's who presented the tip to Kushner.[17])

By 2011, the New York economy was coming back to life and commercial real estate rents were once again on the rise. But Orrick had moved out and the lease for the Kushner Companies' largest tenant at 666, Citibank, was coming due. The building's offices were now only 77 percent occupied.[18] The net operating income was little more than half the debt payments.[19] Kushner's lenders were facing default, or huge losses. A special servicer, LNR Partners, a Florida firm that handles distressed real estate debt, stepped in to staunch the potential losses to the lenders. (The co-CEO of LNR was Justin Kennedy, the son of US Supreme Court justice Anthony Kennedy. Justin Kennedy had previously worked at Deutsche Bank's real estate capital markets division, which had loaned hundreds of millions of dollars to Donald Trump.)

Facing the possibility of not being able to make their debt payments, the Kushners, father and son, had to make another deal under pressure.[20] This one involved selling 49.5 percent of the office portion to LNR's part owner, Vornado Realty Trust, run by Steven Roth, a real estate magnate who had started off in New Jersey. Vornado negotiated a deal in which, in exchange for up to $80 million in investment and the obligation of taking on half the debt, it would gain ownership of almost half the office portion of the building.

The deal was so favorable to Vornado that it didn't actually require the company to spend $80 million, just to promise it could spend up to that amount. Eying Kushner warily in the refinancing, lenders now insisted the deed to the building be placed in an escrow account, where they could seize it in the event of default.[21] Kushner Companies now owned just a hair over 50 percent of the office portion of the building, and just a hair over 50 percent of the remaining retail portion of the building. The building still carried a debt of more than $1.1 billion.

Joe Kushner, like Fred Trump, hadn't much liked debt. They both borrowed, but settled their obligations quickly. Charlie and Jared and Donald Trump had a different business model, one that relied on a willingness to take out massive debt and not necessarily pay it back. As long as they could find partners who were willing to take the risk with them, it worked. The lesson Jared learned from the refinancing of

666 Fifth Avenue, according to someone familiar with the deal, "was not 'holy shit I almost lost everything,' it was 'I should take on as much risk as I can.'"

To get to the Kushner Companies offices on the fifteenth floor of 666 Fifth Avenue, a visitor had to walk by a framed picture of the words beginning Charles Dickens's *A Tale of Two Cities*, which famously opens: "It was the best of times, it was the worst of times, it was the age of wisdom, it was the age of foolishness, it was the epoch of belief, it was the epoch of incredulity. . . ." Also in the reception area was a prominently displayed copy of *The Miracle of Life*, the story of Joe and Rae's escape from the Nazis.

Past the reception area, a large portrait of Joe and Rae dominated the conference room. The Kushner family worked closely here: Charlie, Seryl, Jared, and, sometimes, Nicole, greeting each other warmly, kissing each other as if they were newly reuniting, even though they worked together and spoke to each other multiple times daily. This was—apparent to dozens of employees and associates and partners who worked with the Kushners—a tightly-knit family business, where no one with the last name "Kushner" could be at fault for anything, and no one else was safe. Jared sometimes boasted about upcoming "hit jobs" at the *Observer*. Or he'd hold up the newspaper containing them, as if to suggest: This could be you. Charlie once conspicuously gave an *Observer* scoop to a reporter at the *New York Post*. Jared and Charlie could be warm and caring and attentive. When relatives were sick or dying they could be generous to a fault. But the constant threat of their mercurial tempers created a deep level of unease. "He was lovely until he was not," said a person who knew Jared through real estate. "Until you had a falling out and were dead to him and he was out to get you."

And always, the Kushners presented an outsized picture of their assets: one Kushner promotional booklet included glossy photos of buildings in which the company owned only a few percentage points in equity.[22] It was a business model not unlike Donald Trump's: suggesting a much larger financial base than the company had, which in turn helped enable it get financing for further projects.

While Kushner Companies was grappling with the giant debt on its trophy building, the family quietly moved back into their old business, the Kushners' cash cow since the days of Joe and Rae: multifamily housing complexes. In June 2011, while they were renegotiating the terms of their 666 Fifth Avenue financing, the company and its partners bought 4,681 "distress-ridden Class B apartments" in cities including Pittsburgh, Toledo, and Cincinnati, some so underwater that the previous owner couldn't afford to keep the lights turned on, as ProPublica's Alec MacGillis reported in the *New York Times Magazine*. Jared Kushner had to settle some two hundred liens before he purchased the properties, for which he paid just half the face value of the mortgages. The Kushner Companies bought another 1,700 units in the Midwest. The next year, they doubled their portfolio with an acquisition of 5,500 units, these past a tangle of highway ramps in the exurbs of Baltimore.[23]

By the summer of 2012, months after it restructured its debt on 666 Fifth Avenue, the company had acquired nearly 12,000 apartments, more than two-thirds of what it had owned in New Jersey before the big sell-off in 2007. "Kushner Comes Back" was the headline in the trade publication *Multifamily Executive*. The subhead was "Jared Kushner has been busy re-amassing his namesake company's multifamily portfolio in leaps and bounds." According to Jared, the occupancy rate of these properties had risen under their management to the mid-90s, up from 75 percent at the time of sale. (This was almost exactly the opposite of the numbers at 666 Fifth Avenue, which had slid from 98 percent to 77 percent.) "It was a lot of construction and a lot of evictions," Kushner told the magazine. "But the communities now look great, and the outcome has been phenomenal."[24]

"A lot of construction and a lot of evictions" appeared to be the Kushner family business model in New York City, too. That same year, 2012, the Kushners were the biggest buyer in Manhattan of buildings with fewer than 100 units, most of them in Lower Manhattan: in the East and West Village, and in SoHo.[25] These were old-world apartment buildings with rent-stabilized tenants, with red brick fronts and fire escapes, some of them without elevators, a sharp contrast to the gleaming tower of Jared's wife's branded building nearby, the Trump SoHo.

The Kushners and their partners purchased their East Village portfolio from a group led by a man named Ben Shaoul, who himself had snapped up seventeen buildings in 2007, making so many repairs and renovations that he was nicknamed "the Sledgehammer," after he was photographed with a worker holding one outside one of his buildings. But to do this work so quickly, Shaoul had hidden from New York City's buildings department that there were rent-regulated tenants in his buildings, which would have drawn an extra level of oversight to the renovations. The disclosure requirement had been instituted to prevent landlords from driving tenants out through unpleasant, untenable repairs, but according to an exposé in the *New York Times*, during the course of the aggressive renovations in these seventeen buildings, two-thirds of the rent-regulated tenants moved out. This made the buildings that much more valuable, because the incoming landlord—the Kushner Companies—could then charge more rent.[26] *Bloomberg News* reported Jared's purchases that year: " 'Walk-ups are really a phenomenal asset class' because they're a hedge against inflation, Kushner said. 'They are like gold, only they cash flow.' "[27]

The Kushner family financed the $190 million it spent on downtown properties with other people's money. As Jesse Drucker reported in the *New York Times*, "for much of the roughly $50 million in down payments, Mr. Kushner turned to an undisclosed overseas partner. Public records and shell companies shield the investor's identity. But, it turns out, the money came from a member of Israel's Steinmetz family, which built a fortune as one of the world's leading diamond traders." The Steinmetz who quietly backed the Kushners was Raz Steinmetz. His uncle, Beny, has been at various points under scrutiny by law enforcement authorities in four countries, including for bribery. Representatives of the Steinmetzes told the *Times* that Raz and his uncle were separate business entities, but Drucker reviewed records showing, he wrote, that the two "have shared offshore investment vehicles, employed the same company director and were once connected to the same Swiss bank accounts."[28]

The Kushner Companies' lower Manhattan acquisitions were emblematic of a shift in financing sources for the Kushner family, an arc that had started with friends and family in New Jersey, grew to the major US banks, and eventually led to Israel. Beginning in 2010, Israelis were becoming significant players in New York real estate, investing $500 million that year alone,[29] despite Israel having a population at the time smaller than New York City.[30] Jared traveled repeatedly to Israel during this period: according to the *New York Times*, his company took out at least four loans from one of Israel's largest banks, Bank Hapoalim, and partnered with Harel, an Israeli insurance company, on another deal.[31]

In Baltimore, at this time, a Kushner family company, JK2 Westminster LLC, engaged in an aggressive series of lawsuits against tenants in its Baltimore complexes. JK2 was named for Jared's initials, and for Westminster Avenue, the road in Elizabeth, New Jersey, that ran by the house Joe built and Charlie and his siblings grew up in. The limited liability company and its affiliates began filing hundreds of lawsuits against tenants who they said, often wrongly, hadn't followed proper procedures to terminate their leases, who had been late on their rent, or who otherwise had possibly violated their rental agreements. These tenants were often barely eking out a living, with sick parents, young children whose health was sometimes threatened by poor maintenance, or other mitigating circumstances, yet the Kushner Companies' lawyers pursued them with relentless zeal, adding charge after charge so the amounts due would pile up, often sanctioned by unsympathetic judges, as painstakingly documented by MacGillis. Most galling to some of these tenants was that building management would post their late notices out in public, for everyone to see. The Kushner Companies didn't deny that it was doing these things; rather, it claimed a "fiduciary obligation" to its partners to maximize the revenue from these modest apartments.[32]

Charlie had certain moral rules, according to associates. He never drove a Mercedes. None of his apartments could contain German appliances, even if that would save money. But at the same time the Kushner Companies were holding their poorer tenants to the letter of their agreements, they were flouting their own obligations. After their foray into Manhattan, the Kushners began buying more multifamily units, in Brooklyn and Queens. Beginning in 2013, the advocacy group Housing Rights Initiative found, Kushner Companies routinely failed to pay fines for everything from "loose rubbish" to not getting permits for electrical work. They amassed $350,000 in fines before they were caught. And, according to an Associated Press investigation based on Housing Rights Initiative research, the Kushners had adapted "the Sledgehammer's" business playbook; the company filed paperwork as a matter of course saying it had no rent regulated tenants, when it in fact had hundreds, thus evading the extra level of scrutiny that was supposed to be triggered.[33] (The Kushner Companies said a contractor had filled out the forms incorrectly. The company was fined an additional $210,000.) Operating without that scrutiny, the AP found, the Kushners emptied some buildings of three-quarters of their rent-regulated tenants, bringing in revenue of $155 million in just a few years.

"There's probably not a lot I can tell you about Brooklyn," Jared Kushner said at a real estate conference at the Brooklyn Academy of Music in May 2014.[34] His company had just acquired a portfolio of town houses in Brooklyn Heights from the Brooklyn Law School. It was about to invest in property in trendy Williamsburg, and on Third Street, on the Gowanus Canal. Its biggest deal, however, was to participate in the purchase of the former Jehovah's Witness headquarters, including the Watchtower building. This had been an imposing landmark for decades, its iconic red sign and digital display providing the time and temperature for tourists walking the Brooklyn Bridge. The complex dominated the neighborhood of DUMBO, an acronym for Down Under the Manhattan Bridge Overpass, what Jared's father-in-law might have called "a chic artist's enclave."

"The last place I thought I would be, would be spending a lot of time in is Brooklyn," Jared Kushner told the audience.

Jared, had begun to hear from his employees at the *New York Observer* and what he called "our venture business." "A lot of kids in the companies were really living and wanting to work here and it led us to start really exploring so we crossed that river that is such a moat for a lot of Manhattan people."

Jared had been influenced by his brother Josh, who worked in the tech sphere. "I saw that in all the different technology businesses that my brother was investing in, all of our best creative people were all living in Brooklyn and loving it," Jared said at another forum.[35] He saw a way to monetize this interest, to use the burgeoning creative community as a way to lure a big, important tenant to one of his Brooklyn properties: a tenant like Facebook, or Google, that would be willing to pay top dollar.

"It always struck me the Kushner Companies were late on the Brooklyn arc but thought they were early," a former city official said in an interview. By the time Jared bought the Watchtower complex, Brooklyn had been rapidly gentrifying for over a decade: Mayor Bloomberg's rezonings had had their predictable effect and high-rises were now dotting the Brooklyn skyline, the Nets had been playing NBA basketball for two seasons at Barclays Center, and oligarchic wealth from Ukraine had already been used to buy Paul Manafort's town house in Carroll Gardens.

"He understood good real estate, not necessarily good investments," another major builder said of Jared, in an interview. "You could look at a building, great location, if you're paying too much and the capital structure is wrong it's not going to be a good investment." When Jared entered Brooklyn, he seemed unaware of the existing development ecosystem, a racially diverse group who were either born in the borough or who arrived before it was fashionable. "It was awful," one business associate said of an interaction with Jared. "He didn't know any facts, but was so righteous. I had a million times more information than him."

In June 2014, a group including the Kushner Companies entered into contract to purchase a plot of land at 175–225 Third Street in the Gowanus neighborhood.[36] Soon after, Ivanka Trump was quoted in *Vogue* saying that Jared had taken her to a "great restaurant" in Brooklyn, and then to the roof of the newly built Gowanus Whole Foods in the pouring rain to view the Kushner development site across the street.[37] (Though the Kushner name was on the deal, most of the equity was owned by another partner, SL Green.)

As Jared's business increasingly bought into Brooklyn, Jared and Ivanka tried to repeat their success with Manhattan society, showing up at events like a gala dinner for St. Ann's Warehouse, a cultural venue beside Brooklyn Bridge Park beloved of Brooklyn's elite, a circle led by wealthy creatives and heads of large nonprofit institutions as well as bankers and real estate developers. This group had in many ways crafted its identity in opposition to Manhattan society. "It's not exactly like bringing Ivanka to Brooklyn is going to help him in Brooklyn," one member of that elite said in an interview. Ivanka could sell a lot of things: jewelry, handbags, hi-end condos, her father's presidency. She could not sell Brooklyn to Brooklynites.

As Jared and Ivanka embarked on this new social campaign in Brooklyn, Jared began to show a new edge. After Public Advocate Bill de Blasio became the upset winner of the Democratic primary in the 2013 mayoral campaign—running in part on promise to rein in the real estate industry—a major developer hosted an off-the-record meet and greet to make peace with the all-but-certain next mayor. This was the kind of event where pleasantries are usually exchanged, because the real estate community knows how badly it needs the mayor. Jared did not make nice. He told de Blasio, "what a disaster he was going to be, how crime was going to go up," according to a person in the room.

"Jared was very vocally critical," another attendee said. "He was blunt and aggressive about his views. I was taken a little aback because of my prior experiences with him." Jared had always been considered exceedingly polite—"well groomed" or "well spoken." Now, a new Jared was emerging, far more political—and politically conservative. For many, this was a surprise, given his family history of supporting Democrats.

At the *Observer*, Jared kept talking about his weekends with Rupert Murdoch. "There were several conversations on Monday mornings that started 'Wendi, Rupert, Ivanka and I were out sailing,'" said a former colleague. "He would talk about how Ivanka was the trustee for the Murdoch children, their guardian, that's how close they were." The ideas that Jared had brought to the *Observer* at age twenty-five—vaguely liberal, Democrat—were tilting towards Rupert Murdoch's conservatism. Now in his thirties, Jared talked about cutting the national debt, cutting the deficit, pulling back government spending, and reducing taxes on the wealthy. In 2013, the New York City Council considered a bill that would grant five paid sick days to employees of large companies. Supporters saw it as a modest but essential measure to help the city's working class, now largely un-unionized, many undocumented, who would lose their jobs if they or someone in their families became sick. Under Jared's direction, the *Observer* opposed it. "Paid sick leave sounds fine in the abstract, but those who understand the realities of running a small business know that it would be an intolerable burden," the editorial read. "Such a mandate inevitably would result in more job losses—just what the city doesn't need at a time when the unemployment rate is 8.8 percent, significantly higher than the national figure of 7.8 percent. The bill should stay on the shelf." The byline was "The Editors."[38] The idea was pure Jared.

Not long after, President Obama proposed a small increase in the federal minimum wage, a major plank of progressive Democrats in 2013. The *Observer*'s editorial page came out against that, too. "The best way to create jobs that pay a living wage is not by mandating pay increases from Washington—a one-size-fits-all policy that does little to recognize regional economic issues and challenges," the editorial said. "The best way to achieve the president's goal is by creating economic policy that inspires the nation's job creators to do what they do best: create jobs. Prosperity will follow."[39]

"I thought even Jared would be for a higher minimum wage," a former *Observer* staffer said in an interview. "When he wasn't—that's when I saw the evolution as complete. Now he was Rupert Murdoch's understudy."

17

THE MERGER

Not long after Eric Schneiderman was elected New York attorney general, his office began investigating a scam. Its targets were lured by the promise of "Trump University," from which they were told they could learn from Donald Trump's "handpicked experts" the "Trump process for investing in today's once-in-a-lifetime real estate market." Some seven hundred New Yorkers had fallen prey to this sales pitch, as had thousands of others nationwide.

When the victims got a call from the Attorney General's Office about the case, some of them cried, they were so relieved. They had felt ashamed, and powerless, and many were quietly taking their lumps, pushing back the knowledge they'd spent up to $35,000 on real estate tips that they could have found with an internet search.

Like almost all New York politicians at the time, prior to the lawsuit, Schneiderman had made his own pilgrimage to Trump Tower. He'd traveled to Fifth Avenue and Fifty-Sixth Street, ridden the elevator to the twenty-sixth floor, sat before Donald Trump and his framed magazine covers, and asked for money. And he received a check: for $12,500 signed in Donald's sharpie-wielding hand. After that Trump may or may not have introduced Schneiderman to other people who gave him money. Trump claimed he did.[1]

By the next spring, the Trump University investigation was under way. Records were pulled. Witnesses were interviewed. On May 17, 2011, the New York Attorney General's Office issued a subpoena to the Trump Entrepreneur Initiative, the name Trump had chosen after New York education regulators finally convinced him he could not call the operation a "university."[2] The subpoena asked for a wide range of documents: emails, marketing materials, and information about the corporate structure of Trump University; set up, like all Trump companies, in a series of interrelated and nesting entities.

Most often, the details of a politician's courtship of potential donors is hidden from the public. But we know some of what happened next because of a complaint the Trumps later filed against Schneiderman with the New York State Joint Commission on Public Ethics. Though the complaint was ultimately dismissed, Ivanka Trump's accompanying sworn affidavit offers a rare view into a world where contributions and credit for soliciting contributions are the combined currency of power.

In May 2011, "the very same month Mr. Schneiderman launched his investigation into TEI," Ivanka wrote, "Mr. Schneiderman had his former transition committee leader reach out to my husband, Jared Kushner, and I, requesting that we introduce Mr. Schneiderman to some of our young, wealthy and accomplished friends and colleagues. Mr. Schneiderman's representative told us that Mr. Schneiderman was interested in establishing relationships with the 'next generation of influential New Yorkers' in the hopes of gaining their respect, thereby assuring their financial support of his future political aspirations." By this time, records showed that Jared and Ivanka had given over $170,000 in political contributions.[3]

In these early years of their marriage—2010, 2011, 2012—Ivanka and Jared were indeed seen as the next generation of influential New Yorkers. They attended the Met Gala and fundraisers for Freedom to Marry. Ivanka was on the board of the New York City Police Foundation. People who know them say the couple strategized carefully. They had a playbook: "Who they would have to dinner, who they would get to know, where they would go on the weekend."

Shortly after Schneiderman's office issued the subpoena, Ivanka and Jared organized a breakfast for Schneiderman. "I agreed to oblige Mr. Schneiderman's request," Ivanka wrote, "and, on June 20, 2011, my husband and I hosted a meet-and-greet breakfast for Mr. Schneiderman at Jean Georges in the Trump International Hotel & Tower. At the breakfast, Mr. Schneiderman was introduced to and had the opportunity to speak with approximately 15–20 of our most accomplished friends and colleagues." Ivanka was eight months pregnant at the time.

After the breakfast, Schneiderman sent a note on official State of New York, Office of the Attorney General, letterhead, handwritten in kind of a scratchy, teenage boy scrawl: "Jared and Ivanka," it read. "Many thanks for the great breakfast. I love meeting people, and that was a great group. Good luck with your next big adventure. It is much more important than any of the rest of the stuff we deal with!" Ivanka wrote that she took this to be "a reference to the OAG's investigation into TEI," though she did not say whether Schneiderman raised the investigation at this breakfast.

In September, there was more outreach, Ivanka said, from a Schneiderman advisor, who "said that Mr. Schneiderman would 'greatly appreciate' if I attended a fundraising event for newly elected California Attorney General Kamala D. Harris as Mr. Schneiderman's guest. He also asked that we make a substantial contribution to Ms. Harris's re-election campaign." Ivanka's father, Donald Trump, wrote a five-thousand-dollar check to Harris's campaign, but Ivanka attended the fundraiser, "an intimate gathering of New York business people. I was one of only a small handful of Mr. Schneiderman's personal guests." There was more courting, more outreach, and "on January 12, 2012, my husband and I met Mr. Schneiderman for dinner at Lure Fishbar in Manhattan. Marc Lasry, billionaire and co-founder of Avenue Capital Group, and his wife, also joined us for dinner that evening." Lure Fishbar is a short walk down Prince Street from the Trump SoHo, a restaurant at the time popular with people from the financial sector.

There was another encounter, this one unplanned, on June 30, 2012, at "a wedding we were both attending at Cipriani Wall Street."[4] The wedding was of Sean Eldridge and Chris Hughes, the Facebook cofounder; other guests included Mark Zuckerberg and his wife Priscilla Chan, then–Newark mayor Cory Booker, and Senators Chuck Schumer and Kirsten Gillibrand.[5] There was a big jazz band, and four hundred guests. "This time," Ivanka wrote, "Mr. Schneiderman was far more outspoken than he had ever been before, volunteering that the OAG's investigation was 'very weak' and stating that it was a 'non-event' which was 'going nowhere'. Without me even inquiring, he assured me that he had 'no intention of moving forward' with a lawsuit and that TEI should just 'be patient' and 'let things play out'. Mr. Schneiderman went on to volunteer that his office was 'highly bureaucratic,' and that one of the 'most difficult' aspects of being Attorney General was managing the 'hundreds of attorneys' on his staff. He asked that we give him time to 'go through the motions,' to satisfy the long-time staff members of his office."

Not long after the wedding at Cipriani, Schneiderman's team invited Ivanka to a fundraising dinner for the American Friends of the Yitzhak Rabin Center at the Plaza Hotel, where Schneiderman was going to be honored. "Not wanting to disappoint Mr. Schneiderman, I purchased a ticket and attended this event," Ivanka wrote. Nor, she alleged, did he let up. His staff "repeatedly called my assistant" to set up a dinner date with her and Jared; "after many failed attempts" they met for drinks at the bar at the Four Seasons Hotel. At that meeting, two hours long, Ivanka said, Schneiderman "talked openly with me about his aspirations for higher office and his frustration with what he thought was a lack of leadership from government leaders. Mr. Schneiderman also talked extensively about what he believed to be the importance of friendship and loyalty, qualities that he commented were 'so rare in politics.'"[6]

Finally, Ivanka Trump wrote Eric Schneiderman a check for five hundred dollars.

In August 2013, the State of New York sued Trump University for swindling thousands of Americans out of millions of dollars.[7] Donald Trump soon filed his ethics complaint against Eric Schneiderman, along with Ivanka's affidavit, claiming that Schneiderman "aggressively targeted" the Trump Organization, using the threat of a lawsuit as a way to ply funds from the Trumps. (Schneiderman denied the allegations, and the case was ultimately dismissed.) To help advance the complaint, Trump turned to a man who understood New York's ethics laws better than anyone: David Grandeau. The former executive director of the New York Temporary State Commission on Lobbying, had, in the year 2000, caught Trump and Roger Stone running a fake grassroots campaign against legalized gambling in New York and levied the largest lobbying fine in New York history against Donald Trump. For his work on the case against Schneiderman, Grandeau charged Trump double his normal rate, so he could be sure he had covered his fee when Trump inevitably refused to pay the second half.[8]

The Trumps' complaint was filed on December 3, 2013. On the same day, a story appeared in *Vanity Fair* called "Big Hair on Campus," outlining the Trump University scam and profiling its victims.[9] "Too bad about New York Magazine," Donald Trump tweeted, misidentifying the magazine that had run the story, "but there's a much bigger one out there, currently doing a story on me to get even, that I'll soon discuss!"[10]

Two months later, the *New York Observer* ran a seven-thousand-word story titled "Clockwork Eric." It was accompanied by a picture of Schneiderman, in a bowler hat, staring through a triangle, wielding a pen, in the style of the dystopian Stanley Kubrick crime file "Clockwork Orange." The story argued that Schneiderman's modus operandi was to threaten potential targets with investigation while simultaneously raising money from them. There was also a lengthy defense of the Trump Organization's actions in Trump University, saying "it strains credulity to think an intelligent person would believe a three-day real estate seminar was an actual university."[11]

(It should be stipulated that Schneiderman had behaved awfully, though not for the reasons the *Observer* wrote about. Years later, Jane

Mayer and Ronan Farrow wrote a *New Yorker* exposé of Schneiderman that documented a series of violent relationships with women.[12] Schneiderman resigned soon after.)

The "Clockwork Eric" article was accompanied by an unusual editors' note: "The day before this story went to press, someone from Mr. Schneiderman's press operation apparently told another publication, 'Donald Trump ordered up a hit piece in his son-in-law's newspaper to retaliate against Schneiderman for bringing a lawsuit against him.' Bullshit. The notion that Mr. Trump can 'order' the *Observer* to publish or not publish a story is ludicrous."

By this time, Jared had a new editor in chief, his fourth. Ken Kurson had known the Kushners since before Charlie went to jail. A former speechwriter for Rudy Giuliani, he had been working for the political consulting firm Jamestown Associates when Jared hired him to edit the paper. He had an indie rock band, called the Lilacs.

The Schneiderman assignment caught the attention of the *New York Times* and *BuzzFeed News*. According to the *Times*, Kurson had made various attempts to recruit a writer for the Schneiderman story, beginning just around the time Schneiderman brought his suit. One writer he approached said of Kurson: "He didn't say 'hit piece' in so many words, he said Eric Schneiderman is going after Jared's father-in-law and he's a bad guy and we're going to do something about that." But the first writer passed, and as with the Dick Mack story, another writer was sought: this time, a Rutgers poli-sci graduate who was managing an ice cream store in Maplewood, New Jersey, named Bill Gifford. After several weeks, Gifford concluded that he was supposed to write a "smear piece" and decided against it. "He does come to my shop," Gifford told the *Times*, referring to Kurson. "He did want to give me this opportunity, but I do feel like he might have been using me. To even call me a journalist is a reach, and to write such an important piece on an important person . . ." he said, tailing off.[13] The person who ultimately wrote the story, Michael Craig, told *BuzzFeed News* that he was "not discouraged or encouraged" to have a particular angle. Kurson said he wasn't trying to assign a story "to suit a particular agenda," and said he did not recall saying anything negative about Schneiderman.[14]

In early 2014, the idea of using of Jared Kushner's newspaper as a way to "get even"—in Donald Trump's words—caused a stir in media circles. But in an environment where Jared Kushner and Ivanka Trump were seen as red-carpet Democratic Party donors, the ice-cream-store-manager, Trump-influenced-hit-job story came and went. Few noticed.

The Trump and Kushner families were joining their worlds, molding facts to augment their power over law enforcement, over the truth itself. It was a small canary, signaling the world to come.

In 2011, facing default on his family's 666 Fifth Avenue debts, Jared needed to convince his lenders—including billionaire Tom Barrack—to extend the repayment period. Tall and polo-playing, Barrack is an Angeleno of Lebanese Christian descent who grew up speaking Arabic. He is a friend of Middle East royalty and also of Donald Trump. The two had met in the 1980s when Barrack was working for the seller of the Plaza Hotel when Trump was buying, and Barrack played a role when Trump was negotiating a position in the Riverside yards project in the 1990s. In 2011, the *Washington Post* reported, Trump called Barrack, asking him to meet with his son-in-law. "Donald called and said: 'Look, I have no idea what's going on,'" as Barrack later told the *Post*. "'Jared has some deal you have an interest in.'"[15]

Jared flew to California, alone, and met with Barrack without lawyers, asking, as Barrack told the story, that he accept the new payment plan, even though Barrack stood to lose out on millions of dollars. Jared argued that it was better than losing everything. "After 75 minutes," the *Post* wrote, "Barrack agreed to help, concluding that 'it seems like it is in everyone's interest to restructure this.' He said he called Trump and told him: 'You should get down on your knees that your daughter found this kid. He is out of central casting. He was respectful, he was totally up to date on the facts and the numbers and had a very persuasive demeanor.'"[16]

Around this time, the Trumps also needed money, and Jared, in turn, helped them find it. Donald Trump was on the hook, personally, for part of a loan he had guaranteed to build the Trump Tower Chicago. Before the financial crisis, Trump had borrowed $640 million from Deutsche Bank, a large German bank willing to take on risky loans from high-profile clients as a way to establish itself in the United States. A German institution, Deutsche Bank's history was entwined with the history of the country. It was founded in the nineteenth century to buttress German companies overseas. It financed the chemical company that supplied the gas for the Auschwitz death camp, and later provided loans for rebuilding the German economy after the war.[17]

By the turn of the twenty-first century, Deutsche Bank was pressing its way into the US market. And Donald Trump needed a banker: he was a decade past his Atlantic City crash and still unable to borrow from mainstream American banks. To demonstrate his family's commitment to the building, Donald Trump promised that Ivanka, then just a year out of college, would be put in charge of the project.[18] He courted Deutsche Bank's leadership, personally guaranteeing $40 million of the total. Trump got his $640-million loan, a feat that, he boasted at the Chicago tower ribbon cutting in September 2008, was "virtually impossible." He added: "The banks are shut down, but we got this one built."[19]

Two months later, Trump was on the brink of default. So he sued Deutsche Bank. "This action arises out of defendant Deutsche Bank's attempt to derail the successful completion of one of the most acclaimed construction projects to be built in the United States in recent times," the lawsuit began. It went on to accuse the bank of acting in "bad faith, breach of fiduciary duty, fraudulent inducement and self-dealing."[20] Trump claimed that he couldn't pay back the loan because the financial crisis was a force majeure, an act of God, and that Deutsche Bank was partially responsible for the crisis, anyway. He asked for billions of dollars in damages. Deutsche Bank countersued.

Eventually, the cases were settled, but Trump still had to pay, out of his own pocket, the $40 million he had personally guaranteed. To get it, Trump turned to a surprsing source: another division of Deutsche Bank. Around the time Trump was introducing Jared Kushner to Tom Barrack, Jared Kushner was introducing the Trump family to his private banker. Rosemary Vrablic, who wore her greying hair short and whose attire tended to conservative blazers and slacks, managed the great wealth of her Deutsche Bank clients, structuring investments to avoid tax authorities and acting as a sort of a financial concierge. Her unit—Private Wealth—dealt with clients with "many homes, ex-wives, and many children" as Vrablic described it in a 1999 interview with the *American Banker.*[21]

Vrablic was an old Kushner family friend. She'd known the Kushners prior to her career at Deutsche Bank, when she'd worked at the Bank of America. When Vrablic moved to Deutsche, Jared and Seryl moved their business there. (The family prohibition on doing business with German entities didn't extend to Deutsche Bank.) Deutsche Bank had a large real estate division to handle commercial real estate, but Trump had just defaulted and sued that division. So Deutsche Bank allowed him to take out loans for commercial real estate—through Vrablic's Private Wealth division.

In early 2012, with the Chicago loan still unsettled, the Trump family business got the go-ahead for two major projects: a lease for the Old Post Office building in Washington for a planned Trump hotel, and the acquisition of the Doral golf resort, a fabled set of golf courses on the outskirts of Miami that had fallen into bankruptcy.

There's an origin story about the Doral golf resort, as chronicled in *Forbes*. The headline read, "How Ivanka Trump Got The Doral Resort (And The Blue Monster) For A Bargain Basement Price And Had A Baby At The Same Time." The story reported that when the resort went underwater following the real estate crash, "Ivanka Trump swooped in and got the deal of a lifetime." One hundred and fifty million dollars was the price cited, for a property including "land alone that could be worth close to $1 billion." As she told the story to *Forbes,* just before she gave birth, she got a call saying that the sellers had chosen another bidder. Days later, she got another call, saying that the deal was back on again. Ivanka flew to Doral to view the property when Arabella was just a week old. The Trumps told *Forbes* they would spend $200 million on renovations.[22] (In a later press release, that amount swelled to $250 million.) But as with most things Trump, especially having to do with origin stories, the account elided the truth.

Even before the financial crisis, the golf industry had been under pressure as millennials shied away from the game.[23] By 2011, the Doral Golf course was in distress; the industry considered it past its prime. Its owners had filed for bankruptcy after the financial crash, and a committee of debtors needed to evaluate the sale, which then had to be approved by a bankruptcy judge. The Trumps seduced the debtors with a bid that came with a promise: they would buy the course outright, without any financing, for $170 million. Their offer carried "the greatest economic value, including the ability to quickly consummate a transaction without financing or other contingencies," according to a document filed in bankruptcy court.[24] But the Trumps did not pay $170 million in the end, they paid $150 million, for both the property and the business. And they did get financing, from a banker who'd flown down to Miami to walk the course: Rosemary Vrablic.

According to Miami-Dade County land records, the Trumps paid $105 million for the property portion of the business, but borrowed more than that—$106 million—against it, promising to give the bank the course and the resort buildings if they defaulted. The Trumps then borrowed another $19 million, also through Rosemary Vrablic, also collateralized by Doral. The Trumps now held $125 million in loans secured by property for which they'd paid $105 million. Documents in the public record do not explain the discrepancy.

In August 2012, two months after closing on the Doral, the Trumps got yet another loan from Deutsche Bank: for $48 million, to pay off the commercial real estate division of Deutsche Bank for Trump's personal guarantee on the Chicago tower. One division of the bank was paying off another division of the bank. "No one has ever seen anything like this," *New York Times* finance editor David Enrich said in an interview for the *Trump, Inc.* podcast. "In fact, a lot of the people I've talked to at the bank, and previously at the bank, had initially insisted this just hadn't even happened. It's not the way it worked at all. And it is the way it worked and it's just so extraordinary and unusual that no one believed it to be possible."[25] To protect themselves from future losses, banks are usually loath to do business with companies that have defaulted on their loans and then sued them. Deutsche Bank was an exception.

After his wife's family business closed on the Doral and Chicago loans with his own personal banker, Jared Kushner took a signature step. He asked the editor of another *New York Observer* offshoot, the *Commercial Mortgage Observer*, to write a profile of Rosemary Vrablic. The editor, Carl Gaines, was aware that Kushner was a Vrablic client, and balked.

"Just go meet with her," Kushner said. "You'll figure something out." The resulting profile included the following line: "the mere mention of her name yielded descriptors you'd probably want in someone handling your money." It also quoted people who touted Vrablic as "one of the top private bankers to the U.S. ultra-high-net-worth community" and "a really good client advocate, but also someone who can balance the interests of the institution." She was also described as someone who "combines that with a very strong and deep skill set—across products."

The article ended with a disclaimer that "Ms. Vrablic's past clients include Observer Media Group publisher Jared Kushner."[26] It did not mention her work for Jared's wife on Doral, or Chicago.

On a foggy Wednesday around the time the article landed, in February 2013, Vrablic took the elevator to the twenty-sixth floor of Trump Tower. Her rapport with Donald Trump was clear, an executive with knowledge of the meeting told the *New York Times*, which wrote that "Mr. Trump's assistant greeted her as an old friend, and she seemed relaxed with Mr. Trump and his daughter." Around the same time, Deutsche Bank produced a promotional video, featuring Ivanka Trump, touting the bank's work.[27]

The Doral golf course deal marked another turning point for the Trump Organization: around this time, it began spending large amounts of its own cash on deals. Trump had proudly called himself the "King of Debt," but in this period he changed course and began to park cash around the country: a $7-million mansion in Beverly Hills, a $16-million winery in Virginia. Even with aggressive borrowing, Trump still put $25 million of his own money into the Doral deal. "He had incredible cash flow and built incredible wealth," Eric Trump told the *Washington Post* when reporters David Fahrenthold, John O'Connell, and Jack Gillum first reported on the cash outlays, which grew to total over $400 million. "He didn't need to think about borrowing for every transaction. We invested in ourselves."[28] The available evidence suggested Donald Trump did not have limitless cash.

In 2011, a court dismissed a case Trump had brought against Tim O'Brien, a financial journalist for the *New York Times* (and later for *Bloomberg Opinion*) who researched Trump's net worth for his book *TrumpNation*. Contrary to Trump's repeated claims that he was a billionaire, O'Brien's sources and documents put Trump's wealth at the time the book was published, in 2005, as more like $150 to $250 million. "Comfortably wealthy," as O'Brien put it, but not "remotely close to being a billionaire." Deutsche Bank, according to documents released in the lawsuit, valued Trump's assets at $788 million.[29]

There was a clue about where all the cash was coming from. A golf writer, James Dodson, had been previewing a course with Eric Trump at the Trumps' newly acquired North Carolina golf course. "So when I got in the cart with Eric, as we were setting off," Dodson said later in an interview with WBUR public radio, "I said 'Eric, who's funding? I know no banks—because of the recession, the great recession—have touched a golf course. You know, no one's funding any kind of golf construction. It's dead in the water the last four or five years.'"

"And this is what he said. He said: 'Well, we don't rely on American banks. We have all the funding we need out of Russia.' I said: 'Really?' And he said: 'Oh, yeah. We've got some guys that really, really love golf, and they're really invested in our programs. We just go there all the time.' "[30] (Eric Trump later said in a tweet, "This story is completely fabricated.")

In 2012, with his business increasingly in foreign licensing deals, hotel management, and golf course acquisition, there was a particular building project that Donald Trump very badly wanted: the redevelopment lease for the Old Post Office building in Washington, DC. The Old Post Office is a striking building on the stretch of Pennsylvania Avenue between the Capitol and the White House. With a 315-foot-tall bell tower, the 1899 Romanesque revival structure is listed on the National Register of Historic Places. For years, the General Services Administration, the branch of the federal government in charge of buildings, had struggled to make something of this prized property, which had been reduced to renting portions for a low-end food court. But the agency was slow and lumbering, and beset by scandal. It finally put the building out to bid.

In February 2012, not long after Donald Trump's pursuit of his birtherism crusade, the federal government selected the Trump Organization as its preferred bidder. According to a February 2012 press release, "GSA determined the Trump Organization proposal represented the strongest development team, best long term potential for the local community, and most consistent stream of revenue for the Federal Government."[31] There was an outcry, and one protest from a rival who called the GSA decision "unlawful and unwise." The protest went on: "either GSA failed to properly assess the hundreds of publicly accessible records regarding Trump entity bankruptcy and loan defaults related to real estate development projects that Trump had a duty to disclose; or alternatively Trump's proposal failed to fully disclose these bankruptcies and loan defaults." The rival bidder wrote, correctly: "Trump is an unreliable business partner. Trump has a distinctly different posture at bid and award press conferences and unfavorable history revealed in bankruptcy and court proceedings that emerge as the project fails. The record reveals that Trump projects often fail, and fail publicly. In those instances of failure, Trump has often walked away arguing that: (1) the Trump organization only lent its name through licensing and/or (2) the Trump organization disparages or sues the business partner in GSA's position; while (3) suggesting the failure is anyone else's fault other than Trump's."[32]

Four former GSA officials said in interviews the GSA had no choice: Trump had the highest bid, which under the law, the GSA was required to select. And the White House instructed them not to play politics. This was Obama acting apolitically, as he thought a president should, and Trump using Obama's uprightness to gain advantage.

In public, GSA officials noted Trump's bid contained a guarantee of financing from Colony Capital, Tom Barrack's firm, which, GSA thought, had a good reputation. They also privately pointed out that Donald Trump wasn't really involved in the negotiations with the federal government: Ivanka was. Here was a glamourous, statuesque businesswoman with a degree from Wharton, a television star, negotiating with government bureaucrats. One GSA official, no friend of the Trumps, described Ivanka Trump's business in an interview as "completely separate" from her father. Donald Trump's daughter said she was so committed to running the hotel for the long haul that she hoped her infant daughter, Arabella, would grow up to run it.[33]

Lease negotiations continued for a year and a half. Colony Capital dropped out. Trump was willing to put up around $40 million, but still needed financing. And so, he turned again to Rosemary Vrablic, to obtain his largest loan yet from the private banking division: $170 million, putting up as collateral the lease itself. That meant that if he defaulted, the lease would belong to the bank, rather than revert to the federal government. According to one academic analysis, the loan to value ratio was unusually high.[34] More than that, Trump succeeded in something else through a financial sleight of hand: he set up an LLC that would create a 7.45 percent equity share in the Old Post Office project for each of his three oldest children, thereby using the value the deal created to divert tens of millions of dollars of future earnings from himself to his children, tax-free.[35]

In 2015, Jared Kushner entered into a business deal of his own that would lead to an outsized loan with Deutsche Bank: his company bought six retail floors of the former New York Times Building from the Israeli-Uzbek billionaire Lev Leviev for $296 million. Then, just over a year later, the Kushners went to Deutsche Bank to refinance their investment. They got a generous appraisal that said the property was worth $170 million more than they had just paid for it. The Kushner Companies argued the increased value flowed from the more lucrative tenants they would bring in to "better position" the retail floors. When the refinancing went through, the Kushners still owned the building, and now had an extra $74 million in cash.

The prestige location of the former New York Times building, as it turned out, was not able to create that much new value. There were a string of legal disputes with the tenants, and some moved out, or never moved in. Kushner Companies defaulted on a piece of its debt.[36] As of the spring of 2019, a large, prime, first-floor property was available, with a sign in the window directing interested parties to contact raeleasing.com.

During this period of remarkable transactions with the Trumps and the Kushners, Deutsche Bank had a systemic, serious problem: from 2011 to 2015, New York regulators found, it was laundering money for wealthy Russians. A consent order signed by the bank, which means the bank accepts the facts as laid out, showed in devastating detail the internal workings of Deutsche Bank.[37] There was pressure to bring up profits post-financial crisis, insufficient compliance staff, and an overall go-along, get-along culture that allowed billions of dollars to be laundered from Moscow to London and New York. Moreover,

Deutsche Bank was already on notice for rate rigging, lax oversight and failing to comply with US economic sanctions. It would end up paying billions of dollars in fines.

For the Moscow scheme, the New York regulators fined the bank $425 million, finding it had displayed "compliance deficiencies" that "spanned Deutsche Bank's global enterprise. These flaws allowed a corrupt group of bank traders and offshore entities to improperly and covertly transfer more than $10 billion out of Russia." Deutsche Bank's failure to comply with banking laws "could have facilitated capital flight, tax evasion, or other potentially illegal objectives," the consent decree said.[38]

The scheme involved "mirror trades," whereby a Deutsche Bank trader in Moscow, acting on behalf of a client, would make a purchase, for, say, a billion rubles of stock in a Russian company like Gazprom or Sberbank. Then, in London, another Deutsche Bank trader would make a sale of the same amount of Gazprom or Sberbank stocks, collecting the sales price in pounds, or euros, or US dollars. What the bank didn't ferret out—and should have, under the law, was that the buyer and the seller were secretly related. Their connection was hidden by nesting shell companies.

There were plenty of signals that Deutsche Bank could have seen, had it been looking. One Deutsche Bank trader was told, "I have a billion rouble today. . . . Will you be able to find a security for this size?" This is not the way most people buy securities—by saying how much they want to spend: rather, a legitimate investor would select the company first. At one point, a single attorney without training in compliance with anti-money-laundering laws served as Deutsche Bank Moscow's head of compliance, head of legal, and its anti-money-laundering officer, "all at the same time."

When they announced the consent order, New York regulators did not make any connection to the Trumps or the Kushners. But the coincidence caught the attention of David Enrich, the *New York Times* finance editor, who has written the book *Dark Towers: Deutsche Bank, Donald Trump and an Epic Tale of Destruction*. "They were laundering money for wealthy Russians and people connected to Putin and the Kremlin in a variety of ways for almost the exact time period that they were doing business with Donald Trump," Enrich said in an interview for the podcast *Trump, Inc.*[39]

Trump was not done with Deutsche Bank after the Old Post Office deal. In 2014, he bought another golf course—this time from a United Arab Emirates group, with another $63 million in cash—in Turnberry, Scotland, the kind of course that won Trump status in his beloved golf world. After purchasing this property, the *New York Times* reported, he went to Deutsche Bank in early 2016, asking it to expand his Doral loan so he could put that money into Turnberry. Vrablic's division recommended the loan. Her superiors rejected it. She appealed to Frankfurt, where the bank is headquartered, but this time, according to the *New York Times'* reporting, her superiors refused, saying that Donald Trump had become too controversial, and the reputational risk was too great.[40]

In the summer of 2016, Enrich reported, an anti-money-laundering specialist from Deutsche Bank named Tammy McFadden, based in Jacksonville, Florida, got a computer readout alerting her to a financial transaction between the Kushner Companies and "Russian individuals." It was McFadden's job to investigate, and determine whether the transaction was suspicious enough to alert the US Treasury, as banking laws required. McFadden decided the financial transfer needed to be reported, and told her superiors. Usually, such a recommendation would go to the next level of anti-money-laundering specialists. In this case, after input from Rosemary Vrablic's private banking unit, in New York, the transaction was not reported.[41]

When asked about this, years later, by Axios HBO's Jonathan Swan, Jared Kushner brushed it off. "That's probably the 20th story between the *Washington Post* and the *New York Times* where they've accused companies or me of something that's been very salacious. Nothing that they've accused us of has panned out in any way."[42]

In early February 2014, during the period of all of the Deutsche Bank loans and just three months after Donald Trump had flown to Moscow for the Miss Universe contest, Jared Kushner and Ivanka Trump took their own trip to Russia with Arabella, then a toddler. Among other reasons, the Kushner family made the trip to attend a gala for Moscow's Jewish Museum and Tolerance Center, and for four days of Russian travel, including a visit to the ballet in St. Petersburg with Arabella.[43] While in Russia, with the possibility of a Trump Tower Moscow still very much alive, Ivanka toured Crocus City, the Moscow commercial complex, with Emin Agalarov, the pop-star son of the oligarch Aras Agalarov.[44]

The Kushner family trip was hosted by Dasha Zhukova,[45] then the wife of Putin friend Roman Abramovych, a Russian-Israeli billionaire victor of the aluminum wars and owner of the British Chelsea Football Club. By the time of the gala at the Jewish Museum in Moscow, Zhukova had a financial tie to the Kushners as well as one of friendship; Thrive Capital, a firm that Jared's brother Josh had started and in which Jared owned a stake, had invested in her online art-selling platform, Artsy.

Ivanka posted a photo on Instagram of the Jewish Museum gala with Zhukova and Wendi Murdoch. Also at the gala, as reported by *Bloomberg News*: Leonard Blavatnik, a Ukrainian-born British-American businessman, who was about to be a major donor to Republican political causes,[46] and Viktor Vekselberg, owner of the Renova group and the fourth-richest person in Russia. The dinner, which included an exhibition of Andy Warhol portraits of twentieth-century Jewish luminaries, raised $4.5 million.[47]

The trip was a display of the Kushners' increasingly transnational view of the world and their ever-strengthening cross-border ties with the international oligarchy, the jet-setting class of people who controlled resources, money, and real estate around the globe. A world of possibilities opened up that night.

Before the month was out, however, Viktor Yanukovych fled Ukraine, and Putin sent tanks and troops to invade Crimea. President Obama imposed severe economic sanctions. The European Union followed suit. Everything about the business relationship between Russians and Americans—and between the Trumps and the Kushners and their Russian counterparts—was drastically altered.

Early in 2015, Miriam Elder, then the world editor for *BuzzFeed News*, began to notice something she saw as odd: the *New York Observer* was publishing regular columns by a writer with "a slavishly pro-Kremlin bent." Elder, who had previously covered Russia for the *Guardian*, started counting: "the reporter, Mikhail Klikushin, has written 15 articles for the outlet since November 2014. He has no online presence—in English or Russian—beyond the stories he has written for the *Observer*, which have also been picked up by other outlets."

Ken Kurson defended the hire. "Of all of the strange, unfair, preposterous attacks made on the Observer or me personally," he said in an email, "the Klikushin one was the craziest." "He's a writer," he told Elder. "He lives in the tristate area. He's a Russian national who has been in America for at least 10 years or so." Elder was skeptical. The "articles are remarkable in how directly they line up with pro-Russian propaganda points," she wrote. "The Kremlin regularly issues talking points, either via official statements or, more often, by reports in state-run or Kremlin-friendly media."[48] The *Observer* kept running Klikushin's articles, but it began labelling them as "opinion."

This was now just months before Trump announced his campaign for president.

ACT V

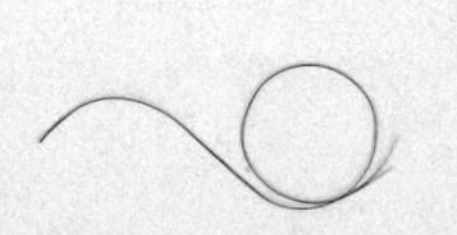

18

THE INFOMERCIAL

On a cloud-flecked winter afternoon in Council Bluffs, Iowa, the day before the first contest of the 2016 election campaign, I attended a campaign rally for Donald J. Trump. The candidate was still a curiosity in those days, a television celebrity running for president, drawing a snaking line of Iowans hours before his scheduled appearance. This was before Trump began to roll up victories, before his rallies were marred by violence, often egged on by the candidate himself. Before he began selectively banning media outlets from campaign events, before neo-Nazis began threatening his opponents, before evidence of Russian influence began to seep into the presidential race, before allegations emerged that he'd been a sexual predator.

Wearing a hot pink tie and a goofy flat-mouthed smile, Trump took the stage at the Gerald W. Kirn middle school gym and bantered in a pseudo-talk-show style with Jerry Falwell Jr., the son of the conservative televangelist and founder of the Moral Majority. Seated in matching leather chairs, one red, one blue, the two chatted about Middle East policy, the economy, the polls. Trump vowed that if any refugees came to the United States, he would send them back. The crowd hooted. Trump sat up straighter. He invited the families up on to the platform.

Then he paused, stood on the low stage in front of a bank of flags.

"I have somebody that nobody knows," Trump said, pausing for dramatic effect. "Ivanka!" There was high-pitched, sustained yelling and applause. If the crowd was tickled at being in the presence of the host of *The Apprentice*, it was awed by his tall daughter. Ivanka, seven months pregnant with her third child, rewarded the crowd with a relaxed wave and smile, right hand fleetingly cradling her belly. That very month, Ivanka had graced the cover of *Town & Country* magazine next to the cover-line "VOTE IVANKA! The Trump In Charge of a Growing American Dynasty."[1] Her belly, photographed months earlier, had been enhanced to appear larger. Trump talked about what a political benefit it would be to have a grandchild born in Iowa.

"And her husband, Jared, come on up Jared!" Jared Kushner, even taller than Ivanka, thirty-five, but looking a decade younger, stepped on stage, dimples flashing across his cheeks. Trump went on, "Jared is a great young man, went to Harvard, very smart, great, doing a fantastic job in business. He's in the real estate business, done an amazing job, in his own right, just incredible."

Standing at the back in the media pen, I looked up from my digital recorder. It caught my attention that the publisher of the *New York Observer*—a known person in New York society, but by no means a famous person—was stepping forward into the national arena.

In the coming years, he would hold this same pose: planted firmly at center stage, largely silent, beside the favorite daughter of the American president—unexpectedly one of the most powerful people in the world.

The crowds in Iowa, the gathering polls, the crash of inevitability surrounding the Trump campaign; all of it had started years earlier, in plain sight. He showed up in Iowa and New Hampshire and at the obligatory events for Republican candidates, like the Conservative Political Action Conference. Speaking at that conference in 2014, shortly after the invasion of Crimea, Trump praised Putin, who, he said, "even sent me a present, a beautiful present."[2] Audiences loved Trump, loved that he said he wasn't "politically correct." On the air, he was derided. "Nobody's going to mistake Donald Trump for a presidential candidate, I don't think, other than Donald Trump," NBC News *Meet the Press* host Chuck Todd said during this period.[3]

What no one knew then was that while Trump was preparing a public run, a secret shadow campaign was also forming, seven time zones away. The "Internet Research Agency" was putting together an operation to inject Russian propaganda and disinformation into US social media platforms. It was funded by an oligarch named Yevgeny Viktorovych Prigozhin—who ran a private army of soldiers for hire, as well as a high-end restaurant group and catering company. This latter affiliation won him the nickname "Putin's Chef."

In June 2014, three months after the invasion of Crimea and the ensuing US and EU sanctions, two Russian women, carrying cameras, drop phones, and SIM cards, traveled through Nevada, Colorado, California, New Mexico, Illinois, Louisiana, New York, Texas, and Michigan, pretending to be tourists. They would later be charged with being Russian spies, reporting back to the Internet Research Agency. Their goal, prosecutors said, was "to defraud the United States by impairing, obstructing, and defeating the lawful functions of the government . . . for the purpose of interfering with the U.S. political and electoral processes, including the presidential election of 2016."[4]

—

In early March 2015, the US Treasury Department imposed a $10-million civil money penalty against Trump Taj Mahal Casino Resort, "for willful and repeated violations of the Bank Secrecy Act."[5] It was, at that point, the highest fine in US history against a casino for failing to enforce anti-money-laundering measures, the second time the Trump Taj Mahal had received the highest fine in US history. Trump was no longer the casino's majority owner by this point, though he was still making money from the Taj Mahal by selling the right to use his name. That same month, Trump signaled that he was filing paperwork for an exploratory committee for his presidential campaign.

—

In June, Ivanka Trump stood at a podium in the atrium of Trump Tower, and said of her father, "His legend has been built and his accomplishments are too many to name. . . . My father is the opposite of politically correct," Ivanka said to cheers. "Throughout his career, my father has been repeatedly called upon by local and federal government to step in and save long-stalled, grossly over-budget public projects." Then, Ivanka looked up, to watch Donald and Melania Trump descend a marble-sided escalator as loudspeakers played Neil Young's "Rockin' in the Free World."

Minutes after Ivanka's warm introduction, Trump indeed veered from the "politically correct," saying of Mexicans crossing the border: "They're bringing drugs. They're bringing crime. They're rapists. And some, I assume, are good people." The speech was three-quarters of an hour of deeply nursed grievances, how the United States "has become a dumping ground for everybody else's problems." He put his total net worth at "well over $10 billion." He promised to build a "great wall," before signing off "we will make America great again." The strains of Neil Young rose as Ivanka, Jared, and their children Arabella and Joseph; Don Jr. and Eric and their wives; Melania, Barron, and Tiffany joined Trump on stage, stamping the nativist, anti-immigrant speech with the family seal of approval.[6]

That day, Donald Trump was polling at 3.6 percent, according to the Real Clear Politics polling average.[7] He was ninth in the field. By mid-July 2015, he was leading in the Republican primary polls, and his lead grew and grew, until he was the winner. For many Americans, especially those on the coasts, a Trump victory was an inconceivable outcome. Their imaginations failed them. But if one looked at the numbers from a distance—for example, from Moscow—it was easy to see that Trump was running away with the Republican primary.

The crowds, the excitement, the glitz, the winning poll numbers, the near-constant television coverage: all of this offered untold opportunity for leveraging the Trump name. He'd spent millions on political contributions in the past to help his business, and was now willing to spend many tens of millions more of his own money on his bid; it would ultimately redound to his business's benefit. That was in fact the plan, according to Donald Trump's executive vice president and special counsel, Michael Cohen. "Donald Trump is a man who ran for office to make his brand great, not to make our country great," Cohen said in come-clean sworn public testimony years later. "He had no desire or intention to lead this nation—only to market himself and to build his wealth and power. Mr. Trump would often say, this campaign was going to be the 'greatest infomercial in political history.'" Cohen added: "He never expected to win the primary. He never expected to win the general election. The campaign—for him—was always a marketing opportunity."[8]

Almost everyone around him saw business opportunities for themselves, too: Jared Kushner and Ivanka Trump; Trump's money man Tom Barrack; strategist and lobbyist Paul Manafort and his deputy, Rick Gates; Trump's secret political advisor Roger Stone; Trump's secret business partner Felix Sater; and Michael Cohen. It was equally an opportunity for Vladimir Putin and his oligarchs to make money, by persuading Hillary Clinton's opponent to lift the economic sanctions.

The attempts to use the campaign to unleash a cash bonanza started immediately, across the globe.

By September 2015, Trump was leading his nearest competitor by more than ten points. Felix Sater, Trump's on-again, off-again business associate, was reading the polls and thinking about business in Moscow. He began communicating with an old buddy from his high school days in Brighton Beach, Brooklyn, an area known as "Little Odessa."[9]

Cohen and Sater met there when they were about seventeen. Sater was living in Brighton Beach and attending yeshiva and Cohen was a high-school kid from just across the city's border in the Five Towns, Long Island.[10] After high school, the two fell out of touch while Cohen was working in the taxi industry and Sater was involved in illicit stock-selling schemes and informing to the government on the Russian and Italian mob.

They met again twenty years later at the Trump SoHo: Sater had put together Bayrock, Trump's partners on the SoHo project, and Cohen had gone to work as Trump's fixer and special counsel. After the SoHo project, despite Sater's past, Donald Trump made Sater a "senior advisor" at the Trump Organization. Sater took an office, rent-free, on the twenty-sixth floor of Trump Tower, near Donald Trump, and one floor above Ivanka, Eric, and Donald Trump Jr.[11] There was tension. "The kids weren't too happy with him," Cohen later testified, about Sater. Negative publicity around him "ended up having them decide that he needs to leave the 26th floor, to leave the building altogether." When Sater left, Cohen took over this office.[12]

Over the years, Trump minimized his connection to Sater. In 2013, Trump walked out on a BBC interviewer who pressed him over their partnership in a failed Florida deal. "Why didn't you go to Felix Sater and say, 'you're connected with the mafia, you're fired?'" Trump was asked. "You're telling me things that I don't even know about," Trump said of Sater. After being pressed further, Trump stood and walked out, saying he had people to meet, the reporter and camera following him to the door.[13]

Despite his public discomfort, Trump was privately pleased with Sater's scouting a licensing deal in Moscow, and signed off when Sater and Cohen developed a plan: they would use the publicity around Trump's campaign to launch an audacious new Trump Tower Moscow, which they envisioned as the tallest building in Europe. The Agalarov deal hadn't gone anywhere—it died, Don Jr. said, "of deal fatigue."[14] This was a new chance to brand a building in the capital of the old Soviet empire.

By the fall of 2015 both Sater and Cohen were seeking financial success and redemption, of a sort. Within the Trump Organization, Cohen hadn't presided over a splashy announcement of a foreign deal since the press conference for the Batumi, Georgia, project in 2012. He had not flown to Moscow for the Miss Universe pageant. And he was personally coming under financial stress, as ride-hailing services like Uber and Lyft drove down the value of his taxi medallions. His net worth was slipping precipitously from its 2014 peak of almost $80 million down into negative territory.[15]

By late September 2015, Sater had a well-developed vision for a Trump Tower Moscow. He had already commissioned renderings, which he sent to Cohen: a faceted glass tower that would thrust above the Moscow skyline with a top shaped like a kite, emblazoned with the word "TRUMP."[16] And Sater had found a developer: Andrey Rozov. Rozov sent Cohen a letter, pointing to his experience with real estate in Moscow, Manhattan, and North Dakota.

Rozov's Manhattan building was a nondescript twelve-story structure in the garment district that he and Sater had bought and flipped in a little over a year. The North Dakota project was a $500-million mall, hotel, and indoor water park in a town of less than 30,000 that got zoning approval but was never built. The Russia project—a suburban housing complex—was beset with delays.[17]

But neither Donald Trump nor anyone else at the Trump Organization seemed to care that their development partner in Moscow had limited and troubled experience. By early October, Sater and Cohen were putting the final touches on a letter of intent—a term sheet, essentially, containing the outlines of what could have been Donald Trump's most profitable licensing deal ever. He'd get a million dollars for signing it, another million dollars once he approved the building site, and two million dollars more within two years, whether or not the project was finished.[18] More than that: with Trump's cut of the sales, leases, and hotel revenue, he could make over a hundred million dollars if the project were completed.

While Cohen was negotiating the letter of intent, Trump tweeted a link to a *Washington Examiner* story with the headline "Putin Loves Donald Trump."[19] Then, on October 28, 2015, the letter of intent arrived at the Trump Organization. When Donald Trump took out a sharpie and scrawled his familiar signature at the end of the letter of intent, he made it official: he planned to go ahead with a business deal in Moscow while also running for president of the United States of America.

October 28, 2015, was the same date as the third Republican primary debate, one where Trump was asked, by moderator John Harwood, "Is this a comic book version of a presidential campaign?"

"No," Trump replied. "It's not a comic book, and it's not a very nicely asked question the way you say that." Trump was also asked, for the first time in a debate, about the ways his own wealth derived from depriving other people of theirs: about his failed casinos and all the bondholders and creditors and vendors and employees and residents of Atlantic City who'd been hurt when they had to pay for his failures. Trump had used the bankruptcy laws, he said "to my advantage as a businessman, for my family, for myself," adding, "I used the laws of the country to my benefit, I'm sorry."[20] Voters accepted this.

While this was playing out publicly, Felix Sater quietly took the next step on Trump Tower Moscow: he sought financing. Sater emailed Cohen that Andrey Kostin of VTB Bank "is Putins top finance guy and CEO of the 2nd largest bank in Russia"—which at the time, was under US Treasury financial sanctions as a result of the Crimea invasion. (In his book *Collusion*, *Guardian* journalist Luke Harding wrote that intelligence sources believed Kostin to have been a KGB spy.[21])

Kostin, Sater asserted, "is on board and has indicated he would finance Trump Moscow. This is major for us, not only the financing aspect but Kostin's position in Russia, extremely powerful and respected. Now all we need is Putin on board and we are golden . . . buddy I can not only get Ivanka to spin in Putins Kremlin office chair on 30 minutes notice, I can also get a full meeting."

After Trump signed the letter of intent, Sater enthused: "Buddy our boy can become president of the USA and we can engineer it," he wrote to Cohen. "I will get all of Putins team to buy in on this, I will manage this process. There is no one on this planet who wants Donald elected more than I do a) for selfish reasons, pretty cool to get a USA President elected and b) because he will be a great president. C) after that I can tell all that negative nasty gangster bullshit press to kiss my ass." Sater laid out his vision: "Putin gets on stage with Donald for a ribbon cutting for Trump Moscow, and Donald owns the republican nomination."[22]

Over the months that followed, Cohen kept Donald Trump apprised of their progress. "Michael, come walk with me," Trump would say, as he was heading to a rally or to his car. And as Cohen would walk him to the elevator, Donald Trump would ask Cohen questions about the Moscow deal.[23]

On at least ten occasions, Michael Cohen said, he also briefed Don Jr. and Ivanka Trump on the Trump Tower Moscow.[24] "The Moscow Project was discussed multiple times within the Company," the Special Counsel's Office wrote in its charging documents in Cohen's case, a few years later. The approvals that were needed from local politicians and the Kremlin, the necessity of a financing package: these were tasks Donald Trump and his family understood well. They'd been using the same strategies to put together deals for forty years.

In mid-November 2015, just over two-and-a-half months before the first primary contests, Ivanka received an email from a woman named Lana Erchova. In the email, Erchova offered the assistance of her husband Dmitry Klokov to the Trump campaign. Ivanka then forwarded to Cohen this offer of assistance, which was about politics, not a business deal.

In subsequent communications with Cohen, Klokov expanded on this theme. He described himself to Cohen as a "trusted person" who could offer the campaign "political synergy" and "synergy on a government level." He invited Cohen to Russia, offering to facilitate an "informal" meeting between Trump and "our person of interest"—Vladimir Putin. Cohen pushed for an official Trump-Putin meeting that could be used to advance the Trump Tower Moscow. The politics would be used in service of the business. Klokov said sure. A meeting with Putin could have "phenomenal 'impact' in a business dimension."[25]

But Cohen did not pursue the relationship with Klokov. He already had a conduit to the Kremlin: Felix Sater.

Ivanka Trump sent a second email to Cohen, suggesting an architect for the Moscow tower project. The letter of intent also specifically mentioned Ivanka: she would have ultimate authority over design decisions for the fitness facilities and the spa for the tower in Moscow; it would be called "Spa by Ivanka Trump," as it was at other Trump properties. (Later, Ivanka Trump's lawyer issued a statement: "Ms. Trump did not know and never spoke to Dmitry Klokov. She received an unsolicited email from his wife (who she also did not know) and passed it on to Michael Cohen who she understood was working on any possible projects in Russia.")

Another businessman approached Michael Cohen in this period: his "dear friend" from the Georgia deal back in 2011, Giorgi Rtskhiladze, who had yet another proposal for a meeting "in New York at the highest level of the Russian Government and Mr. Trump." In an email to Cohen, Rtskhiladze noted that the "Mayor of Moscow (second guy in Russia)" would pledge his support. Cohen did not pursue Rtskhiladze's suggestions; he was committed to the Sater proposal. This was the third vector through which Russians had approached Cohen, suggesting a meeting between Trump and Putin.[26] All of them linked, seamlessly, as if it weren't even a question, Trump's business with his political campaign.

In mid-December, Trump was polling two times higher than his nearest competitor. That month, Putin praised Trump, calling him "talented." Cohen took this as a signal, emailing Sater: "Now is the time." Sater seemed to think so, too. He texted Cohen, asking for scans of his and "Donald's" passports. They were planning a meeting with Putin in Moscow, and, according to Cohen, the Trumps all knew about it.[27]

The same month, the Associated Press ran a story about Felix Sater's criminal past and his longtime connection to Donald Trump. And so, while Sater was negotiating what was, potentially, Trump's most profitable licensing deal ever, Trump told the AP: "Felix Sater, boy, I have to even think about it. I'm not that familiar with him."[28]

At the moment the story ran, Sater was trying to set up a trip to Moscow for Cohen. But in order to do so, Cohen needed an invitation from a bank. Though he had initially promised VTB, Sater started talking about another bank: Genbank. This bank had set up shop in Crimea after the invasion, was operating under US sanctions, and was owned in part by a man named Yevgeny Dvoskin who, like Sater, had spent his childhood in the 1970s and 1980s in Brighton Beach. Dvoskin had served time in US prison for his role in a massive Mafia-led gasoline-tax-evasion scheme—the same hustle that allowed David Bogatin to buy five apartments in Trump Tower—after which Dvoskin had been deported to Russia. In Russia, the Organized Crime and Corruption Reporting Project found, Dvoskin once again became linked to criminal networks.[29]

Dvoskin's bank, GenBank, issued an invitation for Cohen to travel to Moscow, but the trip was postponed. Cohen had never heard of this bank. "Not you or anyone you know will embarrass me in front of Mr. T when he asks me what is happening," Cohen texted Sater.[30]

In January—right around the time Jared joined Ivanka on stage in Council Bluffs—Michael Cohen called the Kremlin and asked for help on Trump Tower Moscow. Such requests had been part of the Trump business model since the days of the Commodore Hotel. Cohen spoke with an assistant to Dmitry Peskov, Putin's spokesman, for twenty minutes. Cohen outlined the project, including the Russian development partner. Then he asked for help in moving the project forward, both in securing land to build the proposed tower and financing the construction.[31] Peskov's assistant asked detailed questions, and said she'd look into it.[32] The next day, Sater wrote to Cohen, telling him to call. He wrote, "It's about Putin they called today."[33]

Not long after Trump, via Cohen and Sater, asked for help from a hostile foreign power, Russia's military intelligence, known as the GRU, opened a new front in Russia's attack on the 2016 elections, far more tangible than the Internet Research Agency's trolling efforts. Vladimir Putin's top military intelligence officers were authorizing a massive theft of emails and documents from Democrats and Hillary Clinton.[34]

—

In November 2015, Jared Kushner accompanied his father-in-law to Springfield, Illinois. "People really saw hope in his message," Jared later told *Forbes*, of a speech where Trump mused about sending Hillary Clinton to jail. "We don't have any victories any more," Trump said in this speech, adding, "we're stupid, we have stupid people leading us." The crowd roared its approval. That night in Illinois, Kushner realized, "They wanted the things that wouldn't have been obvious to a lot of people I would meet in the New York media world, the Upper East Side or at Robin Hood [Foundation] dinners."[35]

The next month, speaking from a podium in front of a "Make America Great Again" sign in Mount Pleasant, South Carolina, Trump read aloud, using the third person: "Donald J. Trump is calling for a total and complete shutdown of Muslims entering the United States until our country's representatives can figure out what is going on." Some Jewish leaders reacted with revulsion: Rabbi Jack Moline, executive director of Interfaith Alliance, issued a statement saying, "Rooting our nation's immigration policy in religious bigotry and discrimination will not make America great again."[36]

Jared Kushner did not react with revulsion. Instead, he spent more and more time a few blocks up Fifth Avenue from the Kushner Companies headquarters—at Trump Tower, where there was a vacuum waiting to be filled. To call the Trump campaign staff "lean" was like calling Trump Tower "gaudy." For much of the time, the campaign was on the unfinished fifth floor of Trump Tower, with concrete walls and electric wires and plumbing pipes draping down from the ceiling. In early January, the only staff with any kind of authority were campaign manager Corey Lewandowski and spokesperson Hope Hicks, who had done brand PR for Ivanka Trump and Trump resorts. Lewandowski had been recommended by Citizens United's David Bossie.[37]

For Jared, the campaign was a beckoning invitation, a place where his power and control could settle and grow. Through the turbulent terms of three campaign chiefs, Jared was the constant. "As the campaign progressed," Jared later wrote in a statement to Congress, "I was called on to assist with various tasks and aspects of the campaign, and took on more and more responsibility. Over the course of the primaries and general election campaign, my role continued to evolve. I ultimately worked with the finance, scheduling, communications, speechwriting, polling, data and digital teams, as well as becoming a point of contact for foreign government officials."[38]

On March 12, Trump held a rally at a large hangar-like hall, the I-X Center, off the interstate near the airport in Cleveland. It was packed, maybe not with as many people as Trump said were there ("thirty thousand"), but it was crowded. This Trump rally was set up differently from other political rallies; usually, the media riser, situated somewhere in the middle of the hall, is more or less at the level of the candidate's riser. But Trump's platform had been elevated; only he had a view of the whole crowd. He punctuated his speech about "us" and "them," with, periodically, a shout of "Get-em-out!" referring to protesters whom only he could see. And when he did that, the crowd turned on that person: yelling, threatening, shaking fists. Watching these rallies on television, it appeared these interruptions were random, but up close, it was clear that Trump strategically drew attention to the protesters to punctuate his speech; they underlined his message of us and them, in a visceral way. I had covered hundreds of campaign rallies before this. I had seen candidates whip up sentiment against an opponent, against bogeymen real and imagined—George W. Bush, Hillary Clinton, the ultra-rich, "welfare queens." But until Cleveland,

I had never attended a political rally where people turned on their fellow rally-goers, the very real threat of violence hanging in the air.

The next Tuesday, Trump continued to sweep up primary victories. By mid-March he had more than half the delegates he needed to secure the nomination, and only two opponents left.

—

As Trump's lead grew, Jared Kushner expanded his role in Trump's foreign policy. There was, first, a speech on a subject Jared cared deeply about: Israel. Jared oversaw Trump's address to the American Israel Political Action Committee, AIPAC. The talk got mixed reviews; Trump read from a teleprompter and therefore sounded mostly cogent, though he slashed away at Barack Obama for his peace deal with Iran. This was considered outré for this crowd, though many in attendance agreed with Trump. There was another reason this speech drew negative attention: Ken Kurson, editor in chief of the *New York Observer*, acknowledged he'd played a role in crafting the address. Inside the *Observer* newsroom, this was seen as a breach. Kurson said he wouldn't do it again.

Jared also took an interest in Russia-US relations. In mid-March, he attended a luncheon at the Time Warner Center in Manhattan, given by the Center for the National Interest, an organization that, among other things, promotes "strategic realism in U.S. foreign policy." After the luncheon, Jared introduced himself to Henry Kissinger and the center's president, the Soviet-born Dimitri Simes. Kushner and Simes began planning a major foreign policy address for Trump the next month, to be held at the Mayflower Hotel in Washington, DC.[39]

—

As the primary season thrummed along, a pressing deadline occupied Jared Kushner's mind: the February 2019 due date for more than a billion dollars in debt on his family's trophy skyscraper, 666 Fifth Avenue. In the spring of 2016, when Jared met Henry Kissinger at the CNI luncheon, the Kushners were promoting an audacious plan: to rip down the 1957 aluminum-clad skyscraper built for the era of *Mad Men* and replace it with an eighty-story tower designed by Zaha Hadid, complete with luxe retail shops, condos, and a hotel, all topped with a skydeck that looked like a high-end airport lounge. The company prepared a shimmering vision book, renaming the property "660 Fifth Avenue" and revealing a design that looked like an enormous rocket thrusting out of an opera house. An image of the building's exterior displayed the proposed tower in yellow, sunset light; there was a nighttime view of its interior, looking *down* on the Empire State Building. The drawings were seductive. There were no financials attached. This was a plan for people who sought status and influence—people like the Kushners.[40]

Jared began making calls to finance this reconstruction plan. "Jared reached out," one financier said, who remembered Jared calling shortly after architect Zaha Hadid had died. "He thought we'd be a good partner who could bring in international capital." Another banker observed that Jared, who at the time still thought there was little chance of winning the general election, was "utilizing his position." Trump's momentum gave Jared new opportunities to seek capital. With each Trump victory, this person said, "Jared felt more power."

At his first major foreign policy address at the Mayflower Hotel in Washington that April, Donald Trump put forward an idea—"America First"—that had been championed in the 1940s by pilot turned politician Charles Lindbergh, who opposed the United States fighting the Nazis. "America First will be the major and overriding theme of my administration," Trump said in his Mayflower speech, while also signaling a willingness to work with Russia, still an unusual stance for a Republican candidate. "Russia, for instance," Trump said, "has also seen the horror of Islamic terrorism. I believe an easing of tensions, and improved relations with Russia from a position of strength only is possible, absolutely possible."[41]

At this speech, the Russian ambassador, Sergey Kislyak, sat near the front. Afterwards, Jared was introduced, shook Kislyak's hand, met some other ambassadors. They then "exchanged brief pleasantries," Jared later said, "and I thanked them for attending the event and said I hoped they would like candidate Trump's speech and his ideas for a fresh approach to America's foreign policy. The ambassadors also expressed interest in creating a positive relationship should we win the election."[42]

By the day of this speech, Russian military intelligence had already hacked the computer networks of the Democratic Congressional Campaign Committee, the Democratic National Committee, accounts belonging to the Hillary Clinton campaign, and the personal emails of Clinton's campaign chairman, John Podesta, according to the Special Counsel's Office. Russian agents had spied on the computers of dozens of Democratic campaign workers, implanted malware, stolen thousands of emails, and begun to plan how to release them.[43] One member of Trump's campaign advisory team, George Papadopoulos, had been tipped off that the Russians had "dirt" on Hillary Clinton, in the form of "thousands of emails." The Russians kept asking him, too, about a meeting with Putin. He kept conveying what he knew to campaign officials.[44]

Right around this time, another American with Russian ties was assuming power in the campaign: Paul Manafort.

19

BIG CAVIAR

By 2016, Paul Manafort was in financial distress. Over the previous decade he had made at least $75 million working for Viktor Yanukovych. But that ended in 2014, when Yanukovych was chased out of Ukraine and into Russia, just a few weeks before Putin's forces invaded Crimea and the United States and the European Union imposed sanctions. Manafort was also having an affair, paying for rehab, and fighting a lawsuit from Oleg Deripaska, the Russian oligarch for whom Manafort used to work, about a $18.9-million investment in a Ukrainian telecommunications company they had purchased together.

To raise money, Manafort began mortgaging his New York City homes. He borrowed more than double the $3-million purchase price of his four-story Brooklyn town house in "construction" loans. (All told, that year Manafort took out more than $16 million in loans on homes in Brooklyn, SoHo, and the Hamptons.) He hid money from the IRS and rented his SoHo apartment out on AirBnb, then lied to a bank, telling them it was a primary residence, so he could get a more favorable loan.

Despite all that financial pressure, Manafort wrote "I am not looking for a paid job" at the top of a two-page memo pitching himself for work in the Trump campaign.[1] Offering to do a high-level strategy job for free is virtually unheard of in campaigns, and while it may be technically true that Manafort did not wish to collect a salary from the Trump campaign, he still had plans to profit from it. "Manafort intended, if Trump won the Presidency, to remain outside the Administration and monetize his relationship with the Administration," Manafort's business partner, Rick Gates, later told investigators.[2]

In his pitch memo, called "TPs for Trump Conversation," Manafort noted, accurately, that he was the owner of Trump Tower apartment 43-G, that he'd worked on Republican political campaigns since 1976, and that his "blood enemy in politics, going back to college in the 1960s, is Karl Rove."

The rest of the memo was full of outright lies, including: "I have not been a part of the Washington establishment since I de-registered as a lobbyist in 1998" and "I have no client relationships dealing with Washington since around 2005."[3] In fact, Manafort had been working through much of the intervening period for his Ukrainian clients as a lobbyist in Washington, a stint that included at least one client meeting he arranged inside the White House, multiple communications with congressional leaders, and a US public relations campaign that obscured his own client's interest in the messages being disseminated, in much the same way that Donald Trump and Roger Stone had hidden Trump's interest in the New York "anti-gambling" campaign back in 2000. Revealing the source of the money would have undermined the argument.

Though Roger Stone had been a Trump political advisor going back to the last century, early in the 2016 campaign, Trump and Stone put out that Stone would have no formal role. Yet Trump and Stone continued to speak, Stone acting like an invisible devil on Trump's shoulder. Stone pitched Trump on Manafort,[4] with whom he'd worked for fifteen years as a lobbyist in the 1980s and 1990s. Also making a pitch for Manafort: Trump's old friend, Colony Capital's Tom Barrack, who had met Manafort in Lebanon in the 1970s, when they were both working there.

As a spokesman for Manafort later told the *New York Times*, Barrack and Manafort had chatted over "coffee and snacks" at the Montage hotel in Beverly Hills. Barrack "wanted his old friend to help the struggling campaign deal with potential challenges at the convention." To move this plan forward, Barrack emailed Manafort's "TPs for Trump Conversation" memo to Jared and Ivanka, and Ivanka printed it out for her father, along with a cover letter by Barrack, that described Manafort as "the most experienced and lethal of managers" and "a killer."[5]

At the end of March, as Trump's delegate lead became all but insurmountable, some Trump campaign news appeared in the *New York Times*. "Donald J. Trump, girding for a long battle over presidential delegates and a potential floor fight at the Cleveland convention, has enlisted the veteran Republican strategist Paul J. Manafort to lead his delegate-corralling efforts."[6] Manafort reveled in the press that described him as the adult in the room in the Trump campaign. His business partner, Rick Gates, joined the campaign, too.

Right after the announcement, Manafort asked Gates to send the news to a Russian-Ukrainian business partner, Konstantin Kilimnik, who would later be identified by US authorities as having "ties to Russian intelligence," but who, at this point, was understood to be "Manafort's Manafort," the guy in Ukraine who made everything work. Kilimnik had another important role. He was in touch with Victor Boyarkin, a deputy to Oleg Deripaska (known to associates as "OVD")—a man to whom Manafort owed a great deal of money.

Two weeks after the splashy announcement of his new role in the Trump campaign, Manafort wrote directly to Kilimnik: "I assume you have shown our friends my media coverage, right?" The "friends" Manafort was referring to were Deripaska and his aide.

"Absolutely," Kilimnik responded. "Every article."

"How do we use to get whole," Manafort asked. "Has Ovd operation seen?"

"Yes, I have been sending everything to Victor"—the aide to Deripaska—"who has been forwarding the coverage directly to OVD," Kilimnik responded. "Frankly, the coverage has been much better than

Trump's. In any case it will hugely enhance your reputation no matter what happens."[7] (Deripaska's "official spokesperson" said, "Mr. Deripaska doesn't know Kilimnik and has never spoken to him." Deripaska denied receiving reports from Manafort.)

Manafort's debt to Deripaska stemmed from the $18.9 million that Deripaska had transferred to a private equity fund to purchase a telecom company called Black Sea. In 2007, Manafort, having done business with so many oligarchs, wanted to emulate their financial strategies. He set up the private equity fund, Pericles, to acquire resources, with funding from Deripaska. But the deal went sour. In a lawsuit filed in the Cayman Islands, Deripaska alleged that Manafort and Gates, "had simply disappeared."[8] When asked about the lawsuit by the *Atlantic*, Manafort's spokesman called the dispute "dormant."[9]

Crossing an oligarch was dangerous. Deripaska's lawsuit was a lingering threat, a sword of Damocles hanging over Manafort. This is the posture in which he began work for the 2016 campaign.

On May 3, Trump won the Indiana primary, and Ted Cruz, the last hope of the never-Trumpers, dropped out. Trump was going to be the GOP's nominee.

The day after this primary victory, Sater texted Cohen: "I had a chat with Moscow. ASSUMING the trip does happen the question is before or after the convention. . . . Obviously, the pre-meeting trip (you only) can happen anytime you want but the 2 big guys"—Putin and Trump—were "the question."[10] Cohen responded: "My trip before Cleveland"—the site of the Republican National Convention in July—"Trump once he becomes the nominee after the convention." Cohen later said he had raised the matter with Trump, and that Trump had told him to discuss possible dates with Corey Lewandowski, which he did.[11] Sater texted Cohen: "I know this is going to turn into 1. A major win for Trump, makes you the hero who bagged the elephant and 2. Sets up a stream of business opportunities that will be mind blowing."[12]

Two days after the Indiana primary, New Jersey Governor Chris Christie got a call from Lewandowski. Christie's own presidential campaign had ended in New Hampshire, where he failed to win a single delegate. After that he became one of the first "serious" politicians to endorse Trump. He was offered the job of transition chief. (For national security reasons, campaigns are required to establish transition teams five months before the general election.) According to Christie's book *Let Me Finish*, Lewandowski told him: "We're ready to do it. We'll launch the transition with an announcement next week. Can you come in tomorrow morning, see Donald yourself, and sign off on the press release?"[13]

The next day, May 6, Christie was in Trump's office in Trump Tower, Trump calling out for his assistant Rhona Graff to put through calls, sipping Diet Coke, with his desk, his couch, and "almost every other flat surface—except for the executive chair" strewn with magazine covers featuring Donald Trump.

As Christie tells it, he was sitting in Trump's office when Lewandowski walked in with the press release. "I'm really happy you are doing this for me," Christie said Donald Trump told him. And then, as Christie was preparing to stand and leave, he heard a "soft voice coming from just inside the open office door." The "soft voice" was Jared Kushner. "I don't think we need to rush on this," Jared said, per Christie. "Why do I have to wait on this?" Trump asked. To which Jared replied. "Because I don't trust him to have this, and you know why I don't trust him to have it."

Christie's criminal case against Jared's father had been a vendetta, Jared said, stoked by his disgruntled uncle, working in league with Christie. "It wasn't fair," Jared said, in Christie's telling of the meeting with Trump. "This was a family matter, a matter to be handled by the family or the rabbis."

Donald Trump pushed back. "Chris was just doing his job," he said. "And your other problem was you didn't know me at the time. Maybe if you would have known me, maybe I could have helped." Christie bristled with the implication that Donald Trump could have made the prosecution go away, but he held his peace. Donald Trump was overruling Jared. For now.

Then Christie turned to Jared. "You and I are both burdened with things that are difficult for the other person to understand. You're burdened with a love for your father that I can't possibly understand because he's not my father. And I'm burdened with facts about your father that even you don't know, that I can never tell you, because if I did I would break the law."[14]

Charlie Kushner's 2004 plea deal had limited the opportunity for facts about his life to enter the public domain. Christie was telling Jared he knew them still. Both Christie and Jared Kushner were from Livingston, New Jersey, and they both understood the code. "I have this on you, don't cross me," Christie was signaling to Jared. But Jared had something Christie didn't have: to Trump, Jared was family. Very soon, he would wield that weapon.

On May 26, 2016, Trump won his 1,237th delegate, officially clinching the nomination for president.[15] That's when the real frenzy began, when foreign states, including Russia and the United Arab Emirates, stepped up their efforts to connect with Trump and his campaign. In messages later released by the House Oversight Committee, Trump's old friend Tom Barrack was shown to have corresponded around this time with an Emirati businessman named Rashid al-Malik, with the aim of introducing pro-Gulf messaging into a Trump energy speech. Barrack asked al-Malik "to reblew for me quickly"—that is, to review the language of the speech. "I need a few Middle East aspects," Barrack wrote. After Barrack received al-Malik's comments, Trump did, indeed, include pro-Gulf messaging in his speech.[16]

In a second series of emails, Yousef al Otaiba—the UAE ambassador to the United States—and Barrack rekindled a business relationship from years earlier with the aim of forging a connection between Mohammed bin Zayed Al Nahyan (known as "M.B.Z."), the crown prince of Abu Dhabi, and Trump. The day Trump crossed the delegate threshold, Barrack emailed Otaiba: "Could you meet with Jared Kushner (DJT son in law and closest advisor) in DC on June 8th! You will love him and he agrees with our agenda." Otaiba responded that he "would be delighted."[17] Otaiba was arguing for a new axis of power in the Middle East, from the Emirates to Saudi Arabia—where a rising prince named Mohammad bin Salman, M.B.S., was positioning himself to inherit the Kingdom.

On June 3, 2016, Donald Trump Jr., the candidate's son, received an email of his own, this one from Rob Goldstone, who worked for the Russian oligarch Aras Agalarov and his son Emin, the pop star—and with whom Don Jr. had negotiated a Trump Tower deal almost up until the campaign started. The email was titled "Russia - Clinton - private and confidential."

"Emin just called and asked me to contact you with something very interesting," Goldstone wrote. "The Crown prosecutor of Russia met with his father Aras this morning and in their meeting offered to provide the Trump campaign with some official documents and information that would incriminate Hillary and her dealings with Russia and would be very useful to your father. This is obviously very high level and sensitive information but is part of Russia and its government's support for Mr. Trump—helped along by Aras and Emin." Goldstone offered to send this information directly to Trump, via his assistant Rhona Graff, but said "it is ultra sensitive so wanted to send to you first."

Seventeen minutes later, Don Jr. responded: "Thanks Rob I appreciate that. I am on the road at the moment but perhaps I just speak to Emin first. Seems we have some time and if it's what you say I love it especially later in the summer. Could we do a call first thing next week when I am back?"

Goldstone did indeed arrange a call, on June 6. Two days later, Don Jr. forwarded the email chain from Goldstone to Jared and Paul

Manafort. It said: "Subject: FW: Russia - Clinton - private and confidential. Meeting got moved to 4 tomorrow at my offices. Best, Don."[18]

The meeting that took place on June 9, 2016, at Trump Tower in New York, has been subjected to tens of thousands of news stories and dozens of hours of congressional testimony, amounting to thousands of pages in transcripts, much of it contradictory. Manafort and Kushner attended, and Goldstone brought the Russian lawyer Natalia Veselnitskaya, who was closely tied to the Russian government. Goldstone also brought Ike Kaveladze, Aras Agalarov's point person in the United States, who had, years earlier, gotten in trouble with the US Senate for setting up thousands of Delaware corporations to move $1.4 billion of Russian money into the United States.[19]

Donald Trump Jr. knew Kaveladze and Goldstone well. Before the campaign, the three of them had been working on a deal to build a Trump Tower Moscow.[20] No one seemed to question the seamless pivot from business to politics to discussing "Russia and its government's support" for the Trump campaign, and dirt on Hillary Clinton, which by this time, the Russian government did indeed have.

Veselnitskaya made a presentation about how some Clinton donors had allegedly profiteered by buying shares of Russian companies at a price only allowed to Russians. She spoke about the Magnitsky Act, which had imposed economic sanctions on prominent Russians after the murder of a lawyer for an American-born investment fund owner. But Don Jr. wasn't interested in sanctions; nor could he follow Veselnitskaya's presentation about the Hillary Clinton donors. He characterized it as "inane nonsense." Kushner emailed his assistants asking them to call him, so he'd have an excuse to leave the meeting.

But this meeting was a highly significant moment, an inflection point, an indicator of a broad breakdown of restraints on corruption, foreign influence in elections, and the power of big money in politics. Whatever strictures were left in the wake of *Citizens United* were arguably breached in this meeting. Campaigns are not allowed to coordinate with independent actors. They are not allowed to use business resources, their own or others', without declaring in-kind contributions. They are especially not allowed to accept money, or any "thing of value," from foreign actors or governments. They're not even allowed to accept offers of help: the law specifically bans not just actually receiving aid, but accepting from a "foreign national" any "express or implied promise to make a contribution."[21] This was, previously, a bedrock of campaign finance laws, to ensure that campaigns didn't become tools of a foreign government's geopolitical aims.

In this case, the Russians offered dirt, that is, opposition research, to the Trump campaign. Campaigns are usually willing to pay a great deal of money, millions of dollars, for such research. Of the people in that room from the campaign, at least one person certainly knew the value of what was on offer: the veteran of four decades of US political campaigns, Paul Manafort.

The day this Trump Tower New York meeting took place, Felix Sater, still pursuing his Trump Tower Moscow deal, wrote to Michael Cohen that he was filling out the badges for the St. Petersburg forum. "Putin is there on the 17th very strong chance you will meet him as well." Then Sater sent a visa application form and the official invitation.[22]

On June 14, the *Washington Post* reported that "Russian government hackers penetrated the computer network of the Democratic National Committee and gained access to the entire database of opposition research on GOP presidential candidate Donald Trump, according to committee officials and security experts who responded to the breach."[23] The day of the *Post* story, Sater and Cohen met in person at the snack bar in the atrium of Trump Tower. Cohen told Sater the Moscow deal was off.

The next month, Manafort was asked by CBS *This Morning* anchor Norah O'Donnell, "So to be clear, Mr. Trump has no financial relationships with any Russian oligarchs?" Manafort replied "That's what he said, uh, I uh, that's what I said, that's obviously what the, our position is."[24]

By the Fourth of July weekend, it was time for Trump to pick a running mate. His top choices were Christie, whom he'd known for a long time; former House Speaker Newt Gingrich; and Indiana Governor Mike Pence. Trump flew to Indiana to meet Pence, who looked the part—a very important consideration for Trump. Manafort, Ivanka Trump, and Jared Kushner were pushing the candidate towards Pence. They wanted Trump to stay in Indiana. Trump intended to fly home, but there were technical problems on his plane, and he stayed overnight after all. But he still hadn't decided.

Two days later, a story appeared in the *New York Observer* about David Samson, the disgraced chairman of the Port Authority of New York and New Jersey, and a key figure in the Bridgegate scandal. Samson had been caught demanding a special flight route from United Airlines for his personal use at a time the airline was seeking tens of millions of dollars in fee reductions. Jared's newspaper had not been leading coverage of Samson's conflicts of interest, but under the byline of Ken Kurson, editor in chief, the article read: "The Observer has exclusively learned that David Samson, a mentor to Chris Christie . . . will plead guilty to a single felony charge as early as the end of this week."[25] (In an email, Kurson said, "Jared had no knowledge of that story and the first he learned of it was when he read it in the Observer like everybody else.") But the fact remained that the *Observer* was resurfacing Christie's greatest political failure just as Trump was selecting a vice president. Samson's guilty plea was set for July 14. The next day, Trump tweeted he'd chosen Pence.

These machinations were obscured by another set of machinations, far more comprehensible. Dana Schwartz, an entertainment writer for the *Observer*, published an article on Observer.com responding to a Trump retweet of an image of Hillary Clinton and a six-sided star, both superimposed on piles of cash. Schwartz wrote the article in the form of an open letter to her boss, Jared Kushner.

"Forgive me if I condescend in any way or explain what you already know, but I'm sure you've been busy lately so just a quick refresher: America First was a movement led primarily by white supremacist Charles Lindbergh advocating against American intervention during World War II," Schwartz wrote, noting that the Anti-Defamation League had asked after Trump's Mayflower Hotel foreign policy speech that the slogan be avoided "due to its overt anti-Semitic associations."[26]

"You went to Harvard, and hold two graduate degrees," Schwartz continued. "Please do not condescend to me and pretend you don't understand the imagery of a six-sided star when juxtaposed with money and accusations of financial dishonesty. I'm asking you, not as a 'gotcha' journalist or as a liberal but as a human being: how do you allow this? Because, Mr. Kushner, you are allowing this. Your father-in-law's repeated accidental winks to the white supremacist community is perhaps a savvy political strategy if the neo-Nazis are considered a sizable voting block—I confess, I haven't done my research on that front. But when you stand silent and smiling in the background, his Jewish son-in-law, you're giving his most hateful supporters tacit approval. Because maybe Donald Trump isn't anti-Semitic. To be perfectly honest, I don't think he is. But I know many of his supporters are, and they believe for whatever reason that Trump is the candidate for them."[27]

It was an argument that was to be repeated in many quarters as the anti-Semitic images and sentiment metastasized: the targeting of Jewish reporters, the use of anti-Semitic memes, a new, open embrace of Nazi symbolism and ideology.

Jared had a response. "This is not idle philosophy to me. I am the grandson of Holocaust survivors," he wrote in his own post. "On December 7, 1941—Pearl Harbor Day—the Nazis surrounded the ghetto of Novogrudok, and sorted the residents into two lines: those selected to die were put on the right; those who would live were put on the left." He went on to describe the multiple horrors of his grandmother Rae's early life, the mass murders of thousands, the death of her sister, mother, and brother, the horrors she'd witnessed before she made it to the forest, where "she met my grandfather, who had escaped from a labor camp called Voritz. He had lived in a hole in the woods—a literal hole that he had dug—for three years, foraging for food, staying out of sight and sleeping in that hole for the duration of the brutal Russian winter."

Jared continued, "I go into these details, which I have never discussed, because it's important to me that people understand where I'm coming from when I report that I know the difference between actual, dangerous intolerance versus these labels that get tossed around in an effort to score political points."[28]

In the wake of these comments, Jared's cousins for the first time joined the public fray. Marc Kushner, Murray's son, a New York City–based architect whose gay marriage was profiled in the *New York Times*, posted on Facebook: "I have a different takeaway from my Grandparents' experience in the war. It is our responsibility as the next generation to speak up against hate. Antisemitism or otherwise."

Someone else spoke up: Jacob Schulder, the cousin who was one week younger than Jared, who had grown up almost like a twin brother. For the first time since his uncle Charlie, Jared's father, entrapped his father with a prostitute and then sent a tape of the event to his mother just before his engagement party, Jacob Schulder also made a statement. He added a comment to Marc Kushner's post: "The very first thing a responsible campaign manager should do, I'd think, and I mean the very first thing, would be to take away his father-in-law's Twitter account. Even Joseph Kushner would've had the street smarts to figure that one out while living on boiled potatoes in the forest." Jacob continued, "That my grandparents have been dragged into this is a shame. Thank you Jared for using something sacred and special to the descendants of Joe and Rae Kushner to validate the sloppy manner in which you've handled this campaign."[29]

Jared had been prepared for such critiques. "I know the difference between actual, dangerous intolerance versus these labels that get tossed around in an effort to score political points," he wrote. "The difference between me and the journalists and Twitter throngs who find it so convenient to dismiss my father in law is simple. I know him and they don't."

It was a line that he and Ivanka would repeat over and over. He didn't use the words yet—their coinage was yet to come—but the sentiment was firmly in place by July of 2016. It was "fake news. "

In the run-up to the Republican National Convention in Cleveland, Paul Manafort had been getting questions from the *Kyiv Post* on the Black Sea cable deal. He wrote to Konstantin Kilimnik. "Is there any movement on this issue with our friend?" Manafort asked, referring to Deripaska. "I would ignore him," Kilimnik wrote back, speaking of the reporter. "I am carefully optimistic on the question of our biggest interest." He then added of the Deripaska aide: "Our friend V said there is lately significantly more attention to the campaign in his boss's mind, and he will be most likely looking for ways to reach out to you pretty soon, understanding all the time sensitivity. I am more than sure that it will be resolved and we will get back to the original relationship with V.'s boss." Eight minutes later, Manafort wrote back. "Tell V boss that if he needs private briefings we can accommodate."[30]

Two weeks later, on the fourth night of the convention, Trump was introduced by Tom Barrack, burnishing Trump's business credentials, and Ivanka, burnishing Trump's pro-women credentials. Then Trump spoke: "I have joined the political arena," he said, "so that the powerful can no longer beat up on people who cannot defend themselves. Nobody knows the system better than me," he said, pausing and smiling, "which is why I alone can fix it. I have seen firsthand how the system is rigged against our citizens, just like it was rigged against Bernie Sanders—he never had a chance."[31]

The next day, Wikileaks released nearly twenty thousand emails the Russians had hacked. The leak was designed to highlight the ways the Democratic Party had thwarted the campaign of Bernie Sanders, "rigging" the system against him.

The leaked DNC emails—and the unflattering story they told—muddied the Democrats' intended message of unity at their convention. The Clinton campaign blamed Russia for the release. Trump deflected, saying at a press conference "this whole thing with Russia" is "far fetched." He repeated, five times: "I have nothing to do with Russia." Then he added—this was startling, at the time—"Russia, if you're listening. I hope you're able to find the 30,000 emails that are missing. I think you will probably be rewarded mightily by our press." Russia may indeed have been listening. That day, "for the first time," as Special Counsel Robert Mueller later noted, GRU officers tried to hack into Hillary Clinton's private server.[32]

Two days after Trump's public remarks, Manafort received another email from Kilimnik, this one with the subject line "Black Caviar," deliberately written to conceal the message's contents. "I met today with the guy who gave you your biggest black caviar jar several years ago," Kilimnik wrote. "We spent about 5 hours talking about his story, and I have several important messages from him to you. He asked me to go and brief you on our conversation. I said I have to run it by you first, but in principle I am prepared to do it, provided that he buys me a ticket. It has to do about the future of his country, and is quite interesting. So, if you are not absolutely against the concept, please let me know which dates/places will work, even next week, and I could come and see you."

"The guy who gave you your biggest black caviar jar," was code for Paul Manafort's former client, the former Ukrainian President Viktor Yanukovych, who, after he won election in 2010, gave Manafort a present of a large jar of black caviar worth $30,000 to $40,000.[33] By 2016, Yanukovych, driven from his own country, where prosecutors had accused his government of draining $100 billion from the Ukranian treasury—for, among other things, a lavish compound with an artificial lake[34]—was living in Moscow. There, Yanukovych met with Kilimnik to discuss a plan to take over part of eastern Ukraine. Then Kilimnik asked if Manafort would meet with him in New York.

Manafort agreed to have dinner at the Grand Havana Room, along with his deputy, Rick Gates, the following Tuesday, August 2. "I need about 2 hours," Kilimnik wrote to Manafort on July 31, "because it is a long caviar story to tell." The members-only Grand Havana Room, with a menu tending to steak and martinis, is located at the top of a skyscraper at Fifty-Third Street and Fifth Avenue, where it hosts the one of the largest cigar bars in the Western Hemisphere, with sweeping views of midtown.

At their dinner on August 2, Manafort and Gates and Kilimnik discussed a supposed "peace plan," which Manafort later acknowledged was a "backdoor" way for Russia to control Eastern Ukraine. Manafort was passing something along to Kilimnik—highly sensitive internal polling data and a briefing on four states: Michigan, Wisconsin, Pennsylvania, and Minnesota. "Months before that meeting," the Special Counsel's report said, "Manafort had caused internal polling data to be shared with Kilimnik, and the sharing continued for some period of time after their August meeting."[35] This kind of data, which is expensive to procure, would typically be used to micro-target voters with social media and other messaging. Prosecutors were ultimately unable to determine what Kilimnik did with the data, but they made their suspicions known. "This goes to the larger view of what we think is going on, and what we think the motive here is," prosecutor Andrew Weissmann said at a later court hearing. "This goes, I think, very much to the heart of what the Special Counsel's office is investigating."

Weissman added that this "in-person meeting [came] at an unusual time for somebody who is the campaign chairman."[36] Especially suspicious, the prosecutor noted, was that Manafort, Kilimnik and Manafort's deputy, Rick Gates, all "took the precaution" of slipping out separately. As the Mueller report put it, this was "because they knew the media was tracking Manafort and wanted to avoid media reporting on his connections to Kilimnik."[37]

After leaving the penthouse-level Grand Havana cigar bar, the Republican campaign manager, his deputy, and the Russian asset separately took the elevator down forty floors and exited the aluminum-clad skyscraper. On the way out to the street, each of them passed a small placard on the side of the building that identified its owner: Kushner Companies. Then they disappeared, melting into the crowds of Fifth Avenue.

20

DIRT

In mid-August, the *New York Times* published a story saying Paul Manafort had been paid $12.7 million off the books by the political party of Viktor Yanukovych.[1] Manafort quit the campaign and went sailing on a yacht with Barrack. He remained in touch with Trump, and with the campaign. Ivanka and Jared took their own trip to Europe, with Wendi Murdoch. When they returned, the campaign went into warp drive.

From the sidelines Roger Stone had continued the work he'd long performed for Trump: deception and dirty tricks. In a series of emails, Stone attempted to communicate via intermediaries with Wikileaks founder Julian Assange, in order to gather information about the timing of Wikileaks releases. Stone was later charged with lying about this to Congress, to which he pleaded not guilty.[2] Gates said the campaign was already planning a press strategy around the releases. On a drive to LaGuardia airport around this time, following a phone call, Trump told Gates that "more releases of damaging information would be coming."[3] Around this time, Stone sent out a tweet. It said: "Trust me, it will soon the [*sic*] Podesta's time in the barrel."

On October 7, at around 3:30 p.m., the Obama administration put out an anodyne statement saying that "The U.S. Intelligence Community (USIC) is confident that the Russian Government directed the recent compromises of e-mails from US persons and institutions, including from US political organizations."

Just after 4:00 p.m., David Fahrenthold of the *Washington Post*, who had been covering Trump's charitable contributions, and lack thereof, published a story about a 2005 videotape of Donald Trump joking with *Access Hollywood* host Billy Bush. The tape was made a few months after Donald married Melania. In the audio, Trump said: "I moved on her, actually. You know, she was down in Palm Beach. I moved on her. . . . I did try and fuck her. She was married. . . . I moved on her like a bitch. But I couldn't get there. And she was married. Then all of a sudden I see her, she's now got the big phony tits and everything. . . . You know, I'm automatically attracted to beautiful—I just start kissing them. It's like a magnet. Just kiss. I don't even wait. And when you're a star, they let you do it. You can do anything. Grab 'em by the pussy."[4]

After the tape was released, the servers that measured traffic to the *Washington Post*'s website were so overwhelmed, they broke. Half an hour later, at 4:30 p.m., Wikileaks began releasing emails by John Podesta, Hillary Clinton's campaign chairman. An associate of a "high-ranking Trump campaign official," as court papers described it, texted Stone the message: "well done."[5]

Throughout the campaign season, when Trump was attacked for his record on women, Ivanka stepped forward. Prior to the campaign, she had adopted a hashtag, #womenwhowork. It peppered an Instagram account filled with photographs of her family—now including three beautiful children, Arabella, Joseph, and Theodore—and their neatly arranged outfits and toys, interspersed with photos of Ivanka at her desk, photos of Ivanka in hard hats, at construction sites, photos of Trump real estate and Ivanka Trump–branded jewelry, handbags, shoes, and clothing. Her personal and public brand was an embodiment of a certain view of confident modern womanhood. At crucial moments, she deployed this brand to blunt her father's sharper edges.

In May, the *New York Times* had published a cover story: "Crossing the Line: Donald Trump's Private Conduct With Women." It documented a long history of "unwelcome romantic advances, unending commentary on the female form, a shrewd reliance on ambitious women, and unsettling workplace conduct."[6] The accounts were detailed, on the record, and disturbing. Trump's lawyer, Marc Kasowitz, threatened to sue the *Times*. (He did not sue.)

Ivanka appeared on *CBS This Morning*. "Based on the facts as I know them, and obviously I very much know them, both in the capacity as a daughter and in the capacity as an executive," she said, playing off her #womenwhowork brand, the *New York Times* story had "largely been discredited." This was false. "Look he's not a groper," Ivanka Trump said of her father. "It's not who he is and I've known my father obviously my whole life and he has total respect for women."[7]

In her convention speech introducing her father, Ivanka said: "At my father's company, there are more female than male executives," an assertion without backup. "Women are paid equally for the work that we do and when a woman becomes a mother, she is supported, not shut out." The crowd stopped her to chant "Trump! Trump! Trump!" This was her biggest applause line of the night. After the speech, @IvankaTrump tweeted out "Shop Ivanka's look from her #RNC speech," along with a link to the "Ivanka Trump Studded Sheath Dress," a look-alike of the one Ivanka wore during her address.[8] The dress sold out at both Macy's and Nordstrom within two days.[9]

But Ivanka's biggest moment to be a validator came at the debate between Donald Trump and Hillary Clinton, on October 9, 2016, hardly more than forty-eight hours after the release of the "pussy tape," on a weekend when even Mike Pence seemed to doubt his own running mate. For the debate, Ivanka and her siblings, Don Jr., Eric, and Tiffany Trump, showed up, as did Melania, Vanessa, Lara, and Jared. Donald Trump, egged on by Stone, brought with him three women who had accused Bill Clinton of sexual assault (which he had denied).

During the broadcast, Trump stalked around the debate stage glowering, lurking behind Hillary Clinton as she answered questions. He threatened at one point to send her to jail, if elected. He dismissed the *Access Hollywood* tape as "locker-room talk." But still, Hillary Clinton, when asked to come up with a nice thing to say about Trump, said this: "His children are incredibly able and devoted, and I think that says a lot about Donald."[10] She didn't add, but might have: especially Ivanka.

For the next weeks, Ivanka kept granting interviews. "He's embarrassed by it," she said of the *Access Hollywood* tape. "It was crude language, he was embarrassed that he had said those things, and he apologized," adding, "I have the good fortune of knowing my father so well, not only as a parent, and he's been an amazing parent to me, and I'm now the mother of three kids."[11]

At the end of October 2016, in the wake of the battering it had taken after the *Access Hollywood* tape, the Trump campaign was facing what Michael Cohen thought was an existential threat. A woman named Stephanie Clifford, also known as the porn star Stormy Daniels, had been warning she'd go public about an affair she said she'd had with Donald Trump shortly after his son Barron was born. Through the final months of the campaign, one of Cohen's jobs had been to managing incoming fire. He'd worked closely with David Pecker, the chairman and CEO of American Media, Inc. (AMI), which published the *National Enquirer*, to keep stories of affairs out of the public eye. Pecker would alert Trump and Cohen that a story was circulating and then the *Enquirer* would "catch" the story and "kill" it, by first buying the life rights from the woman and then not running the story. In August 2016 Pecker had caught and killed the story of Karen McDougal, a model and former *Playboy* bunny who also said she began an affair with Trump in 2006.[12]

Pecker had maintained this arrangement with Trump for years. He had a safe full of stories on Trump, while at the same time the tabloid routinely ran brutal coverage of Hillary Clinton. In September 2016, after McDougal had signed her agreement with AMI, Cohen and Trump discussed whether this safe full of stories, what Cohen called, "all the stuff," could eventually come out. "Maybe he gets hit by a truck," Trump said, of Pecker, in a conversation Cohen secretly recorded.

"Correct," Cohen replied. "So, I'm all over that. And, I spoke to Allen Weisselberg"—Trump's chief financial officer—"about it, when it comes time for the financing, which will be—"

"Wait a sec," Trump interjected, "what financing?"

"We'll have to pay him something," Cohen replied, speaking of Pecker.

What Trump said next was unintelligible, though you can clearly hear him say the words "pay with cash," to which Cohen replied, emphatically. "No, no, no, no, no. I got it."

In this conversation, Cohen and Trump also discussed the payment to Stormy Daniels. "What do we got to pay for this, one fifty?" Trump asked.[13]

Sometime after his conversation with Trump, Cohen went to Allen Weisselberg and told him he'd do something he knew very well how to do: set up a shell company to obscure the origins of the money. But he still needed to figure out where the money would come from. "I had asked Allen to use his money," Cohen later told the House Oversight Committee, about this conversation. "Didn't want to use mine, and he said he couldn't. And we then decided how else we can do it. And he asked me whether or not I know anybody who wants to have a party at one of his clubs that could pay me, instead, or somebody who may have wanted to become a member of one of the golf clubs."[14]

But Cohen couldn't find a straw man, so he set up the shell company, "Essential Consultants LLC," funded it through a fraudulently obtained home equity line of credit, and wired money to keep Stormy Daniels quiet, all with the agreement that the Trump Organization would eventually reimburse him with a retainer of $420,000, which included "grossing up" the Stormy payment so Cohen wouldn't suffer tax consequences, $50,000 for a doctored poll Cohen had commissioned early in the election, and a $60,000 "bonus."[15]

"I don't think anybody would dispute this belief that after the wildfire that encompassed the Billy Bush tape that a second follow up to it would have been unpleasant," Cohen later testified, adding that Trump "was concerned with the effect that it had had on the campaign, on how women were seeing him and ultimately whether or not he would have a shot."[16] So, Trump directed Cohen to carry out the secret payments, which violated campaign finance laws, just as Federal Election Commission lawyers suspected they had done with ShouldTrumpRun.com. Thanks to Don McGahn, neither Trump nor Cohen was ever investigated in that case.

Ten days later, Trump lost the popular vote by 2.1 percentage points—almost three million votes—but won the electoral college, carrying Wisconsin, Michigan, and Pennsylvania with a combined margin of 78,000 votes. A majority of white women, 52 percent, voted for Donald Trump over Hillary Clinton.

The election was called at 2:40 in the morning. Shortly after that, Kirill Dmitriev, the head of Russia's sovereign wealth fund and a close Putin advisor, received a text message from an associate traveling to the 2016 World Chess Championship in New York.

It said, "Putin has won."[17]

Three days after the election, Jared Kushner had Chris Christie fired as transition chief. For five months, Christie and his team had been vetting candidates for different positions, researching policies, learning about how the federal government worked, and compiling all their findings into large black binders. Trump barely paid attention, except, according to author Michael Lewis, to occasionally scream at Christie that he was "stealing my fucking money," thinking, wrongly, that transition money could be spent on the campaign.[18] (Christie said in an email that Trump had never berated him, and that Trump had merely "called to get clarification.") But after the election: "the kid's been taking an ax to your head" is what Christie said Trump's campaign CEO Steve Bannon told him when he was fired.[19] Under the new leadership of Bannon, Pence, and Kushner, Christie wrote, the transition team threw the thirty binders of material Christie had compiled into the Trump Tower dumpsters.

As Christie wrote: "Jared Kushner, still apparently seething over events that had occurred a decade ago, was exacting plot of revenge against me, a hit job that made no sense."[20]

In Moscow, Putin was having his own reorganization. He called together a group of stupendously wealthy Russians who understood their continuing success depended on carrying out Putin's political agenda. One of these men, Petr Aven, a Russian national who heads Alfa-Bank, Russia's largest commercial bank, explained, as the Mueller report put it, that "he is one of approximately 50 wealthy Russian businessmen who regularly meet with Putin in the Kremlin; these 50 men are often referred to as 'oligarchs'." Their meetings, as Aven described them, were quarterly: Aven's fourth-quarter meetings with Putin took place after the US elections.

At their meeting, Putin conveyed to Aven that he wanted to develop a channel of communications into the incoming administration. As with Trump, Putin's directives were sometimes indirect, coded. But Aven caught their meaning. He "understood that any suggestions or critiques that Putin made during these meetings were implicit directives, and that there would be consequences for Aven if he did not follow through." Aven added that Putin "did not expressly direct him to reach out to the Trump Transition Team," but that he "expected him to try."

A few weeks after his Q4 one-on-one meeting, in December 2016, Aven "attended what he described as a separate 'all-hands' oligarch meeting between Putin and Russia's most prominent businessmen." The "main topic of discussion" was the prospect of additional US economic sanctions, which Putin feared would be imposed for his election interference.

With Putin's wishes in mind, Aven tried to set up a back channel to Jared Kushner via Dimitri Simes, the think tank president who helped organize the 2016 Trump foreign policy speech at the Mayflower Hotel. Aven told an intermediary that "he had spoken to someone high in the Russian government" (that is, Putin) who was interested in "establishing a communications channel between the Kremlin and the Trump Transition Team." Simes told investigators that he rebuffed the approach, saying that it "was not a good idea in light of the media attention surrounding Russian influence in the U.S. presidential election."[21]

Then Putin opened another channel of communication, through Kirill Dmitriev, the head of the Russia Direct Investment Fund, or RDIF. The Russian super-rich understood that they could amass wealth, but only if they kicked some of it back to the Kremlin. Their assumption was that wealthy Americans close to the incoming president, like Jared Kushner, would understand how this system worked.

Through an associate of Prince Mohammed bin Zayed of the United Arab Emirates, Dmitriev was introduced to Rick Gerson, who ran a hedge fund in New York, Falcon Edge Capital. Gerson, who during this period was informally advising the Trump transition team, was described in the Mueller report as "a friend of Jared Kushner."

Even though, at the time, RDIF was operating under US sanctions, Gerson and Dmitriev met in New York, where "they principally discussed potential joint ventures between Gerson's hedge fund and RDIF," according to Gerson's later testimony and communications reviewed by the Special Counsel's Office. Dmitriev told Gerson he was "interested in improved economic cooperation between the United States and Russia and asked Gerson who he should meet with in the incoming Administration who would be helpful towards this goal." Gerson said he would ask Kushner. But, Gerson cautioned, "confidentiality would be required because of the sensitivity of holding such meetings before the new Administration took power."

Dmitriev prepared a two-page memo on Russia-US relations, and gave it to Gerson, who gave it to Kushner, who shared it with Steve Bannon and the incoming secretary of state, Rex Tillerson. Following up with Gerson, Dmitriev said his "boss"—Putin—"was asking if there had been any feedback on the proposal." He told Gerson that Putin and

Trump would be speaking by phone that Saturday. This latter piece of information was "very confidential."[22]

At this time, it wasn't even clear to many Americans that Jared Kushner would be joining the administration, but the Russians had figured out that Jared had rare influence over his father-in-law. Putin kept opening fronts in his maneuvers to reach Jared: in addition to Aven and Dmitriev, he sent his ambassador, Sergey Kislyak, to create a third channel. Kushner agreed to meet, even though after the election, he said he couldn't remember Kislyak's name. Kushner has offered this as evidence he couldn't have colluded with Russia during the campaign.

On November 30, Kislyak, Kushner, and Michael Flynn, the incoming national security advisor, met at Trump Tower.[23] (Flynn, it later emerged, had secretly accepted $600,000 from a firm linked to the Turkish government for lobbying work that coincided with the campaign.) "I asked Ambassador Kislyak if he would identify the best person (whether the Ambassador or someone else) with whom to have direct discussions and who had contact with his President," Kushner later said.[24]

Kislyak did have someone he wanted to speak with Kushner: "his 'generals.'" He asked Kushner if there was a secure communications line they could use.[25] Kushner came up with a suggestion: how about if they used the communications equipment at the Russian embassy? This was a shocking suggestion to Kislyak: that the incoming American administration, albeit a friendly one, could get access to Russia's most secret methods of communications, its inner sanctum. Alarmed, Kislyak said no. He transmitted his alarm to Moscow. These communications were monitored and recorded by US intelligence agencies. That's how they found out about the president-elect's son-in-law's talks with the Russian ambassador.

Kislyak pushed Jared for yet another meeting. Jared was by now impatient; he'd decided that Kislyak didn't really have enough juice with Moscow. But Kislyak was persistent, and set up a meeting with Jared's assistant. At that meeting, Kislyak asked for yet another appointment with Jared: this time, as Kushner put it, with "a person named Sergey Gorkov who he said was a banker"—the head of Vnesheconombank, or VEB, the Russian state-owned development bank. Gorkov, Kushner was told, had a "direct line to the Russian President who could give insight into how Putin was viewing the new administration and best ways to work together."

So they met. "I agreed to meet Mr. Gorkov," Jared later wrote, "because the Ambassador has been so insistent, said he had a direct relationship with the President, and because Mr. Gorkov was only in New York for a couple days. I made room on my schedule for the meeting that occurred the next day, on December 13."[26] Kushner saw no conflict for the son-in-law of the incoming American president, a real estate developer with a billion-dollar debt coming due, to meet with a banker for the Russian State to talk about foreign policy.

The meeting took place not in Trump Tower, but at Tom Barrack's Colony Capital building in Manhattan.[27] At the time of the meeting VEB was (and remained) the subject of US sanctions imposed in the wake of the Crimea invasion.

Gorkov told Kushner a little about his bank and the Russian economy. "He said that he was friendly with President Putin," Kushner said, and "expressed disappointment with U.S.-Russia relations under President Obama and hopes for a better relationship in the future." There were no discussions about sanctions, Kushner said, or "about my companies, business transactions, real estate projects, loans, banking arrangements or any private business of any kind."[28]

VEB disputed this characterization, telling the *Washington Post* that "the session was held as part of a new business strategy and was conducted with Kushner in his role as the head of his family's real estate business."[29]

When questioned by Mueller's investigators, Jared Kushner wanted to make sure they understood how little he thought of this meeting, to advance his argument that he couldn't have been conspiring with Russian state actors. He said that he "did not engage in any preparation for the meeting and that no one on the Transition Team even did a Google search for Gorkov's name."[30]

But Gorkov, another of Putin's wealthy and powerful emissaries, *had* done his research. Gorkov carried with him two gifts, gifts that showed a careful and deliberate investigation into the person he was meeting with. "One was a piece of art from Nvgorod, the village where my grandparents were from in Belarus, and the other was a bag of dirt from that same village," as Jared Kushner later explained.[31]

During the campaign, "dirt" on Hillary Clinton had been the currency Russians had tried to trade. Now, the Russians were giving Jared Kushner a literal bag of dirt, reminiscent of the bags of dirt that Rae Kushner and her family had dug from the earth and hidden in the walls of the Novogrudok ghetto so the Nazis wouldn't know they had dug a tunnel to safety.

Had it not been for those bags of dirt, Rae would never have made it out of the ghetto, to the forest, to the refugee camp, or to New York, where she had four children, including one named after her brother who had died during the escape.

And whose own son, Jared Corey Kushner, was now one of the most powerful people in a new and uncertain world, slinking again towards darkness.

21

TRUMP, INC.

On January 11, 2017, Donald Trump strode to a podium in Trump Tower wearing a black suit, white shirt, red tie, and American flag pin. Next to the podium, there was a table with stacks of manila folders, filled with reams of white paper, fastened by butterfly clips. It looked serious, official. The press conference had been billed as an explanation of how Donald Trump would handle his business affairs while president. At the time, there was a good deal of suspense about this.

The sobriety of the press conference was preempted by what had happened in the days prior. In his first major intelligence briefing, Trump had learned about the existence of a "dossier": a collection of raw intelligence memos, gathered by the former British intelligence officer, Christopher Steele, on behalf a firm working for the Hillary Clinton campaign.[1] Steele made a startling assessment: that the "Russian Regime has been cultivating, supporting and assisting TRUMP for at least 5 years. Aim, endorsed by PUTIN, has been to encourage splits and divisions in western alliance."[2]

The memos collected by Steele, beginning in June 2016 and extending through the conclusion of the campaign, running thirty-five pages in all, contained what was at the time a mind-blowing set of assertions:

That Russian intelligence assets had made a series of runs at Trump and his operation. That, in effect, the Russians were working through Trump to disrupt American democracy and to defeat Hillary Clinton. The dossier named names: among others, Paul Manafort, Michael Cohen, Michael Flynn, Viktor Yanukovych, Dmitry Peskov, Sergey Kislyak, and Vladimir Putin. The most salacious claim was that Russia had collected compromising information ("kompromat") on Trump, in this case an alleged video tape of Trump at a Moscow hotel with prostitutes he'd hired to pee on a bed that President Barack Obama and his wife Michelle had slept on.

The dossier had been circulating around Washington for weeks. James Comey, then director of the FBI, privately reviewed the dossier with Trump, who at first thought Comey was trying to shake him down in some way.[3] Days later, *BuzzFeed News* decided to post the entire dossier on the internet; as it happened, this was the night before the news conference on Trump's business arrangements.

This made for a raucous hour-long exchange. Already that morning, Trump had tweeted out that "intelligence agencies" were behind the "leak," adding, "Are we living in Nazi Germany?" He said at the news conference, of the release of the dossier: "That's something that Nazi Germany would have done and did do. I think it's a disgrace."

The idea that Russia had attacked the United States seemed of little import to the incoming president. "If Putin likes Donald Trump, guess what, folks? That's called an asset, not a liability."

"Does Russia have any leverage over you, financial or otherwise? And if not, will you release your tax returns to prove it?" he was asked.

And he responded, "So I tweeted out that I have no dealings with Russia. I have no deals that could happen in Russia, because we've stayed away." This was not true. "And I have no loans with Russia. As a real estate developer, I have very, very little debt," he said. "So I have no loans, no dealings, and no current pending deals."

A month before this press conference, the Russian American journalist Masha Gessen, author of the Putin biography *The Man Without a Face* and the magnificent chronicle of the death of democracy in Russia *The Future Is History*, had written a piece published by the *New York Review of Books* comparing Trump's lies with those of the Russian president. "Putin insisted on lying in the face of clear and convincing evidence to the contrary, and in each case his subsequent shift to truthful statements were not admissions given under duress: they were proud, even boastful affirmatives made at his convenience," she wrote. "Putin's power lies in being able to say what he wants, when he wants, regardless of the facts. He is president of his country and king of reality. . . . Both Trump and Putin use language primarily to communicate not facts or opinions but power: it's not what the words mean that matters but who says them and when."[4] These words were prescient.

Before this press conference, "fake news" had meant actual fake news stories dressed up as real ones. But on January 11, 2017, Trump gave the words "fake news" a new meaning: a news story or organization he didn't like, in this case, CNN and *BuzzFeed News*, which he called a "failing pile of garbage." Trump's allies had invented stories, or used "hit jobs" to tarnish their foes. Now Trump was suggesting any story could be made up, that all journalism had an agenda. He was undermining the notion of objective truth.

When Jim Acosta of CNN tried to ask Trump a question, Trump raised his voice, threateningly. "I'm not going to give you a question," Trump said. Acosta tried, gamely, to interject. "Can you state—" he began.

"You are fake news," Trump said, the rumble of threat in his voice growing louder, as his staff started to applaud. "Sir, can you state categorically that nobody—" Acosta tried once more, as the applause of the Trump supporters gained strength. Acosta, still playing by the old rules of White House decorum, did not get to ask his question. Trump was rewriting the rules; he would lie and the world would know he was lying, and the press and the public would be powerless to stop him.

There was, still, the question of how Donald Trump was going to handle his tangled, privately held, international family business while also being president of the country. Walter Shaub, watching from Washington, was particularly concerned. Shaub was director of the US Office of Government Ethics. Except for two years when he worked in private practice, Shaub had spent his whole adult life as a federal employee. He worked for the Office of Government Ethics under President George W. Bush and Barack Obama; on the day of the press conference, he was working for president-elect Trump. In a later interview for the podcast *Trump, Inc.*, Shaub described himself as the guy who is so squeaky clean, so persnickety, no one really wants him around. "You know, nobody likes when the Ethics Guy shows up at a party," he said.[5]

The director of the OGE has a sworn duty to ensure that the president and his top advisors and cabinet appointees don't have financial and business conflicts that would get in the way of their public service. For the five months before the election, Shaub had maintained constant contact with both the Clinton and Trump transition teams. When Trump won, Shaub sent an email congratulating the Trump team. He expected to get to work right away.

"But after that," Shaub said, "they disappear, and we lost contact with the transition team for roughly three weeks. It was a very unnerving experience." This was the period when Jared Kushner fired Chris Christie, and the new team threw thirty binders of vetted personnel information that Christie's team had prepared into the dumpsters at Trump Tower. Transitions are seen as particularly vulnerable times, when foreign actors can take advantage of the hand-off of government. Part of Shaub's job was ensuring this didn't happen.

By January 11, 2017, despite everything he'd seen with the shake-up in the transition, Shaub still hoped that the president-elect might honorably acquit himself and fully divest, give up ownership of his company, and set up a blind trust. This would have meant Trump wouldn't know where his assets were invested, so he could make presidential decisions without thinking how it would affect his personal bottom line.

Then Shaub saw the stack of folders at the press conference and his heart sank. "I think it was immediately obvious to anybody who's ever had a folder in their life that the lack of labels or the lack of dog ears or weather-beaten quality of the papers means that this was not a stack of files that had been in use," he said in the interview, adding. "I just remember watching with dismay as the worst of my fears were coming to pass."

Trump announced that "my two sons, who are right here, Don and Eric, are going to be running the company." He pointed to the stack of file folders next to him, which, the Associated Press later reported, appeared to contain blank pages and unlabeled folders. (The campaign refused to allow journalists to examine them.[6]) "These papers are just some of the many documents that I've signed turning over complete and total control to my sons," Trump said.

"As a president," he also said, "I could run the Trump Organization, great, great company, and I could run the company—the country," he said, confusing the words "company" and "country." "I'd do a very good job, but I don't want to do that."

For Shaub, these words were meaningless. Because, as Trump's lawyer Sheri Dillon was about to make clear, Trump wouldn't do what every modern president had done: he wouldn't divest from his company, or set up a blind trust. Instead, she said, Trump would give up the day-to-day management. But that management would not go to an independent party. It would go to a loyal forty-year employee of both Fred and Donald Trump, Allen Weisselberg, as well as to two people as close to Trump as anyone, his sons.

Dillon made a series of promises: that there would be no new foreign deals, that there would be a "wall" between the presidency and the business, and that there would be no cross promotion between the White House and the Trump Organization. "All of these actions," Dillon said, "complete relinquishment of management, no foreign deals, ethics adviser approval of deals, sharply limited information rights—will sever President-elect Trump's presidency from the Trump Organization"

Even as Dillon was saying these things, Trump muddied the waters. "We could make deals in Russia very easily if we wanted to. I just don't want to because I think that would be a conflict," he proclaimed. Then, right away, he talked about a $2-billion deal with Dubai that he said he had just turned down. "I didn't have to turn it down, because as you know, I have a no-conflict situation because I'm president."

Ethics rules assume that because the president is the head of government, involved in every decision, the president should not have any conflicts. President Obama had gone so far as to check with the Department of Justice to see if receiving his Nobel Prize would violate the Emoluments Clause of the Constitution. Trump had turned the no-conflict rule on its head. He was saying, I might have conflicts, but because I am president they are no longer conflicts. *La loi, c'est moi.*

Watching from her office at Fordham University School of Law, Zephyr Teachout noticed that Trump appeared to be laying the foundation for an argument that a president cannot break the law. A constitutional scholar who has also been a Democratic candidate for various offices in New York State, Teachout had written extensively on this little-known clause of the Constitution, the Emoluments Clause.

But it was only when a journalist asked her about emoluments that Teachout said she experienced a "moment of real shock, because . . . he was headed on this pretty straight collision course with what I had previously argued was a central and sacred part of the Constitution," Teachout said in a later interview.[7]

The Emoluments Clause states: "No Person holding any Office of Profit or Trust under them, shall, without the Consent of the Congress, accept of any present, Emolument, Office, or Title, of any kind whatever, from any King, Prince, or foreign State." This was a profoundly American idea, Teachout had written. "It showed a real split from the old European corrupt ways. The new Americans were insistent on this clause even though it caused some problems with diplomacy because there had been a lot of financial interchange between diplomats before. I had used it as an example of the American commitment to anti-corruption. I had never expected there would be a president who would blatantly violate it." Corrupt governments and oligarchs had plenty of experience with Trump's new corporate structure: you turn over a company to your children to wink at the world that you're really still in charge. Teachout called this "Corruption 101."

She added, "In some ways you can see that press conference as an announcement of an auction of American foreign policy. I imagine a lot of foreign governments saw it that way."

Sheri Dillon disagreed. She said, "Some people want to define emoluments to cover routine business transactions like paying for hotel rooms. They suggest that the Constitution prohibits the businesses from even arm's-length transactions that the president-elect has absolutely nothing to do with and isn't even aware of. These people are wrong. This is not what the Constitution says. Paying for a hotel room is not a gift or a present and it has nothing to do with an office. It's not an emolument."

As the press conference wrapped up, Walt Shaub decided he had to take what was, for him, drastic action. "I just thought you know, for reasons I can explain, the entire ethics program was now in jeopardy and I had to do something," Shaub said. He was overcome with emotion. "This was the scariest thing I'd had to do in my career and I checked my conscience one more time to ask: Do I really have to do this? And I came to the conclusion that I do." He went over to the Brookings Institution, and made a speech. He wore a dark suit, a wide-striped tie. He frequently looked up from his notes, and at his audience.

"I think *Politico* called this a 'half-blind' trust, but it's not even halfway blind," Shaub said in his speech. "The only thing it has in common with a blind trust is the label, 'trust.' His sons are still running the business and of course he knows what he owns." Shaub expected to be fired for this. In the end, he stayed on till the summer, when he took a job with the Campaign Legal Center, before moving on to Citizens for Responsibility and Ethics in Washington, a watchdog group.

In that press conference at Trump Tower, nine days before he took the oath of office, Trump signaled that he would run the country as he had run his family company, with him at the center of the wheel, all channels of power pointing back to him, inside and outside of government. It would prize secrecy, loyalty, and family above all. The business structure would remind former FBI director Jim Comey, and his deputy, Andrew McCabe, of the way Mafia businesses were structured. Trump, Comey wrote in his book, *A Higher Loyalty*,[8] wanted to "ensure I was 'amica nostra.'"

This structure also meant there would be a myriad of routes of possible influence: not just through campaign donations, not just through the furrows of dark money that *Citizens United* had unleashed, but through Trump's hotels, his condos, his golf courses. There were tens of thousands of points of entry across the globe.

That stack of folders beckoned the world's corrupt leaders and oligarchs to do what developer Donald Trump would have tried to do in their position, to use money to influence government decision-making. And the public would never know if his decisions were made to benefit his country or his bottom line.

By the time of this press conference, there had been some discussion about what Russia "won" through its intervention in the 2016 election, in addition to general discord, which is not an inconsiderable feat. One thing became clear that January day with this Potemkin press conference: Russia was bending America's style of government towards its own.

In her *New York Review of Books* article comparing Trump and Putin, Masha Gessen described the Russian government: "The best available definition of the kind of state Putin has built is provided by the Hungarian sociologist Bálint Magyar, who calls it a mafia state: it's run like a family by a patriarch who distributes money, power, and favors. Magyar uses the word 'family' to mean a clan of people with longstanding associations; it is important that one cannot enter the family unless invited—'adopted,' in Balint's terminology—and one cannot leave the family voluntarily. In this model the family is built on loyalty, not blood relations, but Trump is bringing his literal family into the White House. By inviting a few hand-picked people into the areas that interest him personally, he may be creating a mafia state within a state. Like all mafias, this one is driven primarily by greed."

Gessen described mafia states as, previously, existing in the wake of totalitarian regimes, but suggested Trump might "introduce the world to the post-democratic mafia state. In this model, he will still be the patriarch who distributes money and power. The patriarch's immediate circle will comprise his actual family and a few favorites. . . . They will concern themselves with issues of interest to the president, and with enrichment of themselves and their allies. The outer circle will be handed issues in which Trump is less interested. In practical terms, this will mean that the establishment Republicans in the cabinet will be able to pursue a radically conservative program on many areas of policy, without regard to views Trump may or may not hold, and this will keep the Republican Party satisfied with a president it once didn't want."[9]

These words, published on December 13, 2016, exactly predicted the Trump presidency.

By the time of this press conference, Donald Trump, his daughter Ivanka, his son-in-law Jared, his former campaign aides Paul Manafort and Rick Gates, his attorney Michael Cohen, and his inaugural chairman, Tom Barrack, were already using the prestige of the presidency to boost their private business negotiations.

Eight days after the election, a dinner was held at the Waldorf Astoria Hotel. As Susanne Craig, Jo Becker, and Jesse Drucker later reported in the *New York Times*, "The table was laden with Chinese delicacies and $2,100 bottles of Château Lafite Rothschild. At one end sat Wu Xiaohui, the chairman of the Waldorf's owner, Anbang Insurance Group, a Chinese financial behemoth with estimated assets of $285 billion and an ownership structure shrouded in mystery. Close by sat Jared Kushner, a major New York real estate investor whose father-in-law, Donald J. Trump, had just been elected president of the United States. It was a mutually auspicious moment."[10]

Jared Kushner, still CEO of his company, took the November meeting even though Anbang had such close ties to the Chinese state that the Obama administration would no longer allow President Obama to stay in the presidential suite at the Anbang-owned Waldorf Astoria because of security concerns. Wu, the *New York Times* noted, expressed a desire to meet Donald Trump, who, he was sure, "would be good for global business." The topic under discussion was the proposed redevelopment of 666 Fifth Avenue. According to Kushner's spokeswoman, discussions with Anbang had been initiated six months prior. This was right around the time Jared, buoyed by Trump's primary victories, was shopping his newly envisioned eighty-story tower to investors.

The lines were blurring. In one of his earliest acts as president-elect, Trump had taken a call from Taiwanese leadership, a move that greatly displeased the mainland government. This was relayed back to Trump not through his national security team, but through Jared Kushner, who was at that moment negotiating a deal worth as much as four billion dollars with Anbang, a company closely linked to the Chinese government. "Mr. Kushner is committed to complying with federal ethics laws," his lawyer at the time, Jamie Gorelick, told the *New York Times*. "We have been consulting with the Office of Government Ethics regarding the steps he would take."

But there was no controlling how the Chinese might have viewed the transaction; Chinese business and political leaders are highly attuned to family connections. As *Washington Post* journalists Emily Rauhala and Will Wan have written, "There is even a name for second-generation sons and daughters of wealthy business executives and government officials—such as Ivanka Trump and Jared Kushner—who have access to power through family ties. They are called 'fuerdai.'"[11]

By the time he was named in early January to be a senior White House advisor, in charge of a broad portfolio including government operations, trade deals, and Mideast policy, Jared had already met with Russians, Chinese, and Emiratis, and intervened to block a UN resolution condemning Israeli settlements. Initially, Jared didn't disclose his interactions on his security forms. He said there was an error in making the filing. After a four-month delay, he submitted a hundred names of foreign contacts. His personal financial disclosure forms were revised thirty-nine times.[12]

With the template that his father-in-law had set, Jared did not fully divest from his holdings. Some he turned over to family members. His lawyer said he would recuse himself from any government matters his family business had an interest in.

But he couldn't unknow what he knew: that his prized family building had just two years to pay off more than a billion dollars in debt, that he, himself, had negotiated.

Colony Capital's Tom Barrack, Trump's old friend from the Plaza Hotel days, was put in charge of Trump's presidential inaugural committee, and the money soon came pouring in. It came from blue-chip industries who were caught off guard by Trump's win and wanted to get on his good side, but also from industries Trump might particularly favor: gaming, real estate, and extraction industries like coal, gas, and oil. At least one Ukranian oligarch, Serhiy Lyovochkin, donated as well; he laundered his contribution through a straw donor.[13]

Inaugural committee donations have traditionally been key levers for people who want to influence governmental decisions; it's an opportunity to give unfettered amounts of money and claim it's to support the peaceful transition of power. But when Barrack came calling for inaugural donations, donors had an added impetus to contribute. Coming into office was a president whose professional career had been steeped in transactional politics, who had already signaled that large donors would have especially key influence. Trump's presidential inaugural committee raised more than twice the amount of previous such committees, $107 million, for a series of parties and events smaller than Barack Obama's. In the filings that followed, $40 million of that $107 million was not accounted for.

Barrack set up a first-ever event for a presidential inaugural committee, "The Chairman's Global Dinner," an event meant to showcase his own new power role as the chairman of the inaugural committee. As my *Trump, Inc.* colleagues Ilya Marritz and Justin Elliott reported, "The dinner was billed as a celebration for Washington's diplomatic corps, and it took a week to configure the Washington venue to accommodate the featured entertainment, a Las Vegas revue known as Steve Wynn's Showstoppers." The stage alone cost $2.7 million to build. "In addition to ambassadors from around the world," Marritz and Elliott wrote, "over 100 guests from different walks of life are listed as being invited by Barrack. Among them: Mohamed Alabbar, an Emirati property developer, Yousef al Otaiba, the ambassador of the United Arab Emirates in Washington, and the ambassadors of Qatar and Saudi Arabia."

Barrack, one memo suggested, was planning to leverage these new connections to lure money to his private business, at that point called Colony NorthStar. "The key is to strategically cultivate domestic and international relations while avoiding any appearance of lobbying," an internal Colony memo obtained by Marritz and Elliot said. There were indeed meetings that highlighted Barrack's connections, including one in April at a private room at the Georgetown restaurant Fiola Mare with Treasury Secretary Steven Mnuchin and the ambassadors of Oman, Kuwait, Jordan, the United Arab Emirates, Bahrain, Qatar, and Saudi Arabia. Barrack was angling to profit off of a Trump infrastructure plan, never introduced. A Colony spokesman said that the memo was "never acted upon."[14]

Barrack sat atop the inaugural mechanism, but his key aide was Rick Gates, Paul Manafort's deputy, who had stayed on at the campaign beyond Manafort's ouster. Gates, often working out of Donald Trump Jr.'s office in Trump Tower,[15] asked some vendors to accept money from donors directly, in an apparent bid to get even more money into the system without disclosure.[16] He later admitted in court that it was "possible" he had used the inaugural fund to reimburse himself for personal expenses (a person close to Gates subsequently told the *New York Times* there was "no issue with his reimbursements").[17]

Manafort himself was lurking in the background, sending at least one missive to Gates about a banker who had helped him get $16 million in loans, including $6.5 million borrowed against the brownstone he had purchased for less than half that a few years earlier on Union Street in Brooklyn. The man was Stephen Calk, the CEO of the Chicago-based Federal Savings Bank. "We need to discuss Steve Calk for Sec of Army," Manafort emailed Gates during the transition period. Manafort also lobbied Jared directly, sending him Calk's résumé, later court filings revealed. "On it!" Jared replied. Calk got an interview for an army position, but did not get a job in the Trump administration.[18]

With all these machinations swirling, there was one person who was unequivocally making money off her father's presidency: Ivanka Trump. In mid-December, 2016, Ivanka Trump was alerted to a dispute between Rick Gates and the Trump International Hotel at the Old Post Office in Washington, in which she owned a 7.5 percent stake. The hotel was demanding top dollar for use of its Presidential ballroom for each of four days.

By contrast, other venues, like Union Station in Washington, were offering the use of their facilities for the incoming president for free. After some negotiating, the hotel brought its rate down to $175,000 a day, or $700,000 total. Stephanie Winston Wolkoff, a friend of Melania Trump and the lead planner for the inaugural events, emailed Ivanka: "I wanted to follow up on our conversation and express my concern. These events are in PE's [the president-elect's] honor at his hotel and one of them is for family and close friends. Please take into consideration that when this is audited it will become public knowledge." Wolkoff added, "I understand that compared to the original pricing this is great but we should look at the whole context," suggesting a day rate of $85,000, less than half of the Trump Hotel offer. That did not happen. The inaugural committee paid the Trump hotel $700,000. An

Ivanka Trump spokesman said she was defending "a fair market rate" at the hotel.[19]

By January 18, guests started arriving at the hotel. True VIPs had booked rooms there, according to people familiar with the arrangements: Charles and Seryl Kushner, Rudy Giuliani, Tom Barrack, incoming treasury secretary Steve Mnuchin, Wendi Murdoch, and Trump and Kushner's personal banker at Deutsche Bank, Rosemary Vrablic. The inaugural, more broadly, had attracted the interest of Russian oligarchs, some half dozen of whom were in town, the *Washington Post* found,[20] including Viktor Vekselberg, who, using an American company controlled by his cousin, had just begun to pay Michael Cohen $500,000 through Essential Consultants LLC, the same shell company that Cohen had used to pay off Stormy Daniels. This payment was not even for lobbying or any particular services. It was pure shakedown from someone who by now was allowed to sign his emails, "Michael Cohen, Personal Attorney to President Donald J. Trump."

There's one person who would have kept a keen eye on these comings and goings, these transactions: journalist and author Wayne Barrett. On the evening of January 19, 2017, Barrett, "the people's detective," died of interstitial lung disease at age seventy-one. In the weeks before he died, attached to an oxygen tank, he was still working sources on the incoming administration's tainted deals.

On January 20, 2017, Donald J. Trump stood on a platform outside the US Capitol for his swearing-in. In the relatively small group in the area right around Trump were billionaires, incoming cabinet officials, corporate leaders, members of Congress and the Supreme Court, and three former US presidents. At the center of it all was the Trump family, Ivanka in white and Melania in pillbox blue, watching as Donald Trump delivered his inaugural address.

"Mothers and children trapped in poverty in our inner cities; rusted-out factories scattered like tombstones across the landscape of our nation; an education system flush with cash, but which leaves our young and beautiful students deprived of knowledge; and the crime and gangs and drugs that have stolen too many lives and robbed our country of so much unrealized potential. This American carnage stops right here and stops right now."[21]

As with so much that Trump says, the reverse was true.

When Jared Kushner moved his operations to the White House, occupying a room adjacent to the Oval Office, his father gave him a wrapped present, and watched while Jared opened it. It was a photo of Joe and Rae Kushner. As Charlie told associates, he said: "No matter what you do here, keep that picture. Look at it every day to remember who you are and where you come from."

Many people had opposed Jared's move to DC. Charlie's friends and business partners told him that Jared needed to choose: either go to Washington, and fully cut himself off from the company, or stay home, and run it. Charlie, a convicted felon, couldn't sign documents, couldn't take out loans. Josh, Jared's younger brother, had his own venture capital firm, and did not want to run the real estate company. Nicole, Jared's younger sister, was drafted into the family business. She mourned Jared's exit from it.

But Charlie supported Jared's move to Washington. Jared still called his father twice a day. Both claimed they did not discuss business. But Jared's financial disclosures show he was still profiting from many aspects of the family portfolio, some of which he did not initially disclose to Walt Shaub's Office of Government Ethics.[22]

Charlie took a dim view of government employees like Shaub. In an interview with Will Parker and Konrad Putzier of the *Real Deal*, Charlie said: "You want to know what I think about ethics watchdogs? Do you really want to know what I think about those jerks?" A Kushner employee tried to stop him, but Charlie went on. "I think they're a waste of time. They're guys who can't get a real job. . . . All they want to do is assure that poor, not successful people go into government. That's all they want to do. Because if you're successful, you shouldn't be penalized by stupid ethics watchdogs raising things that are potential. You know when there's a conflict."[23]

White House spokeswoman Hope Hicks offered a more restrained message: "Like other government employees, Mr. Kushner will recuse from particular matters that would have a direct and predictable effect on his financial interests and will comply with financial disclosure requirements."[24]

In early 2017, Jared met with two bank officials in the White House. One was with Joshua Harris, a founder of Apollo Global Management. Among other things, Harris and Kushner discussed a White House job that never materialized. The other meeting was with Michael Corbat, the CEO of Citigroup, to discuss US trade policy and NAFTA, which Jared was tasked with renegotiating. Shortly after this meeting, as the *New York Times* first reported, Citigroup loaned Kushner Companies $325 million for its development in DUMBO, Brooklyn. Also that year, Apollo loaned $184 million to Kushner Companies to refinance its mortgage on a Chicago skyscraper. Both were among the largest loans Kushner Companies received that year. The Apollo loan, the *Times* reported, "was triple the size of the average property loan made by Apollo's real estate arm, securities filings show."[25]

Jared's spokesman said that Jared had "met with hundreds of business people." Citigroup said the meetings were "completely appropriate."[26] Apollo said they "went through the firm's standard approval process."[27]

But it was impossible to know if these companies' decision-making was somehow affected by the fact that the family business seeking the loan was that of the president's son-in-law, a man also responsible for international financial policy. The founding fathers had framed the Constitution in a way to limit the temptation to be corrupt. The way that Jared—and the Trumps—structured their financial relationships with their family businesses had the opposite effect.

On March 29, 2017, Ivanka Trump officially joined the White House as an "Assistant to the President." In addition to having been the executive vice president for development and acquisitions at the Trump Organization, and being married to a man with his own tangled real estate empire, Ivanka also had her eponymous brand. Like her father and her husband, Ivanka did not cease profiting from her companies, and did not place her assets in a blind trust, but in one controlled by Jared's younger siblings, Josh Kushner and Nicole Meyer. Prior to March 2017, any part of this would have been shocking, up to and including that both she and her husband were joining her father's White House. But by March 29, 2017, so many norms had been broken that this move by Ivanka was only passingly noted.

One week later, on April 6, 2017, Donald and Melania and Ivanka Trump ate dinner at Trump's private club in Palm Beach, Florida, Mar-a-Lago, with the Chinese president, Xi Jinping, and his wife, Peng Liyuan. There was Dover sole on the menu, and New York strip steak, and for dessert, chocolate cake with vanilla sauce.[28] Prior to the dinner, Jared and Ivanka had presented their two older children, Arabella and Joseph, to Xi and Peng, and Arabella sang for them, in Mandarin.[29] "Very proud of Arabella and Joseph for their performance in honor of President Xi Jinping and Madame Peng Liyuan's official visit to the US!" Ivanka wrote on her Twitter feed, posting the video on Instagram[30] as well. She was a *fuerdai*, presenting her own children to the leader of the most populous nation in the world.

On the same day as the dinner at Mar-a-Lago, the Associated Press reported, "Ivanka Trump's company won provisional approval from the Chinese government for three new trademarks, giving it monopoly rights to sell Ivanka brand jewelry, bags, and spa services in the world's second-largest economy." Since her father's inauguration, she had received four other approvals and had thirty-two pending. "Ivanka will not weigh in on business strategy, marketing issues or the commercial terms of agreements," her attorney, Jamie Gorelick, told the Associated Press when it first wrote of this confluence of dates. "She has retained authority to direct the trustees to terminate agreements that she determines create a conflict of interest or the appearance of one."[31]

In India, too, Trump's rise to the White House gave Trump-owned businesses a marketing boost. The Trump family had been working on establishing a business presence in India for a decade prior to Trump's presidency, according to reporting by Anjali Kamat for *Trump, Inc.* and the *New Republic*.[32] But India, as the family came to learn, is complicated. Transparency International has rated India far down its global corruption scale. Corruption is so endemic in the country that a bribery "rate card" even circulated in Mumbai and was published by the *Times of India*. At first, the Trumps' business partners had relatively little political juice. By the time of the 2016 campaign, they were working with, among others, a lawmaker in Prime Minister Narendra Modi's political party, a nativist party that, like Trump, traffics in anti-Muslim rhetoric. There were five Trump projects under way, all across India, when Trump became president.

These projects were still active in June 2017, when Trump hosted Modi himself at a joint appearance in the Rose Garden of the White House. There had been a point in Trump's business history when he and his partners had to hustle to get building permits from relatively low-level Indian officials. But now, images of him with the prime minister beamed across the globe while his family business prepared to market condos in India.

Trump noted, "I'm excited to report that the Prime Minister has invited my daughter Ivanka to lead the U.S. Delegation to the Global Entrepreneurship Summit this fall." And, indeed, she traveled to Hyderabad, where Modi threw a big party for his guest of honor. The streets were cleaned up, the beggars removed, roads repaired; Ivanka was treated to a five-course meal. Coverage of her official visit was nonstop, much of it positive. Her speech at the Global Entrepreneurship Summit seemed delivered to a parallel universe, one where black and brown people and women were actually being promoted by the Trump administration. After praising Modi for making India "a beacon of democracy and a symbol of hope," Ivanka Trump told the crowd, "As a former entrepreneur, employer, and executive in a male-dominated industry, I've seen first-hand that all too often women must do more than their male counterparts to prove themselves at work, while also disproportionately caring for their families at home." The crowd applauded.[33]

Three months after Ivanka's trip, her brother Donald Trump Jr. went to India to sell condos. He was greeted upon arrival with a full-page newspaper ad that read, "Trump has arrived. Have you?" Another one said: "Trump is here. Are you invited?" There was a television news segment on a CNBC affiliate in India that sounded almost indistinguishable from *The Apprentice*, right down to the musical cues: horns, cymbal clashes, and a frantic string section. The announcer said, breathlessly, "The fourth Trump Tower arrived in Delhi with a big bang, selling twenty apartments on the very first day out of two fifty plus an offer." She noted the building was "under the brand license from the Trump organization, led by Donald Jr. Trump, son of the U.S. president."

And then the cherry on top: "First hundred buyers of Trump Tower get to fly to New York to be hosted by Trump Junior himself." There is no indication that this trip happened. But Donald Trump Jr. did host dinners for anyone willing to put down a $40,000 deposit. "You're offering a dinner date with yourself to all your new buyers?" Don Jr. was asked by another Indian journalist.

"Well, but if I didn't," Don Jr. answered, "I'd be the first person in the history of real estate to not go meet with their buyers, right? But that's the problem: because my father happens to be the president, there's always a catch," he said, his voice dipping down as if to let the audience in on a secret. "It's like, wait a minute, I'm functioning as a real estate developer—that's what we do."

When the Trump Organization lawyer Alan Garten was asked if there was any communication or coordination between Trump's two eldest children about their respective India trips, the answer, he said, was No.

But the trip exposed the tangled web of conflicts Trump encouraged, and which other presidents had taken pains to avoid. The man whose name was licensed to appear on five new Indian developments met with the Indian prime minister, who then invited the president's daughter to lead an official government delegation to the country just months before the president's son went to market condos there. There was no way for the public to know who was buying those condos. Or if any of those buyers wanted to influence the US president. Or how much profit the president's company was making from these deals.[34]

Trump had promised "to fix" the "rigged system." Instead, he broke it almost beyond recognition.

When she got back from India, Ivanka Trump seemed to have one main job: to help her father pass the tax bill. Ivanka Trump's appearances on television during her father's first year in office had been carefully controlled: she preferred to communicate via social media feeds or visual imagery from White House events. But there were certain occasions where she did offer interviews, and the tax bill was one of them.

According to Ivanka Trump, the Tax Cuts and Jobs Act of 2017 was, first and foremost, a boon to women and children; it doubled the child care credit, as she pointed out in interview after interview. "The President said he wanted to deliver middle income tax relief, targeted middle income tax relief, and he also wanted to cut corporate rates to enable our businesses to be competitive," she told *Fox and Friends*.[35]

In another interview, she touted the tax bill as addressing the cost of child care, "as, until recently, wages have stagnated." She promised that the bill gave more money to regular people, while eliminating the "loopholes that benefited lobbyists and the special interests." Traveling across the country, she said, she had come to see "the sense of financial fragility most American families experience, even middle-income American families. The average American family can't come up with four hundred dollars in the event of an emergency." She continued, "My father is committed to changing that." The tax bill, she promised, coupled with deregulatory action, would be "an enormous vehicle to create the type of growth that will lend itself to prosperity for all Americans."[36] Senator Bob Corker had told Fox News that without Ivanka's intervention and personal assurances to wavering senators, the law would never had passed.

On page 130, subchapter Z of the law, which passed with no hearings and no formal debate, there was a description of an obscure provision: Opportunity Zones. By definition, these were to be poorer census tracts; investors were able to obtain steep tax discounts if they put their money in these zones. But the zones were so broadly defined that most real estate developers could benefit from this new tax loophole, including the Kushner Companies, who owned land in qualifying tracts in four states.

While the tax law was clearing Congress, the *New York Times*'s Jesse Drucker and Alan Rappeport wrote a story summarizing the bill's winners and losers.[37] Among the biggest winners: "President Trump and His Family." They wrote, "Numerous industries will benefit from the Republican tax overhaul, but perhaps none as dramatically as the industry where Mr. Trump earned his riches: commercial real estate. Mr. Trump, along with his son-in-law Jared Kushner, who is part owner of his own real estate firm, will benefit from lower taxes." Other winners were "Big Corporations," who were seeing rates cut from 35 to 21 percent; any income they'd stashed abroad could be repatriated at a rate as low as 8 percent. "Multimillionaires" were winners too, because there would be no estate tax on the first twenty-two million dollars of inheritance for married couples, up from the already stratospheric level of eleven million dollars. Other winners included "Private Equity Managers," and "Private Schools and the People Who Can Afford Them."

The losers, according to the *Times*: "People Buying Health Insurance," "Individual Taxpayers in the Future," "The Elderly," "Low-Income Families," and people in high-income, highly taxed states like

California and New York. "In the long run, most Americans will see no tax cut or a tax hike," the *Washington Post* wrote in its own analysis.[38] The final loser was the US Treasury, and government itself: by the end of the fiscal year in which the bill went into effect, the deficit had grown to $779 billion.[39]

When Ivanka Trump spoke of the feeling of economic precariousness among ordinary Americans, she was correctly describing a frightening phenomenon that had accelerated with the tax cuts enacted the year she was born, and those that followed in the decades after. But the new tax bill wasn't going to make economic inequality better; it was going to make it worse. Once, Friedrich Trump and Joseph and Rae Kushner had come to America and had been able to change their social class. But the tax law, passed with the urging of big business and all the American oligarchs, would now make such a move almost impossible.

22

"A TERRIBLE SITUATION"

After the 2016 election, a delegation from Saudi Arabia visited the United States on a reconnaissance mission, of sorts. After the visit, the Saudis produced a strikingly accurate assessment of Trump and Kushner as transactional businessmen with an anti-intellectual understanding of world affairs, according to David Fitzpatrick of the *New York Times*. "The inner circle is predominantly deal makers who lack familiarity with political customs and deep institutions, and they support Jared Kushner," the delegation wrote in a slide presentation obtained by the Lebanese newspaper *Al Akhbar* and cited in the *Times*'s story.[1]

The Saudis would soon put this intelligence to use.

During the Obama years, American diplomats had worked to keep both the Saudis and the Iranians from regional warfare, and had struck a deal with Iran to keep it from gaining nuclear weapons. The Iran deal, and the rapprochement it signaled, had infuriated the Saudis. A young Saudi prince, Mohammed bin Salman, M.B.S., saw in the Trump administration an opportunity to reorder the American government's priorities—and to leverage support from Kushner and Trump to elevate his own status at home.

While the Saudis were developing their assessment, the United Arab

Emirates were making their own inroads in the incoming administration. An Emirati prince, Mohammed bin Zayed, known as M.B.Z., made an overture to Jared Kushner through their mutual associate, Rick Gerson of Falcon Edge Capital, who had also been a conduit for Vladimir Putin's investment fund. "I am always here as your trusted family back channel any time you want to discreetly pass something," Gerson wrote in text message to M.B.Z., as reported by the *Times*'s Fitzpatrick. In December 2016, M.B.Z. had planned to meet President Barack Obama at the White House, but abruptly cancelled the meeting, going to see Kushner secretly, instead. Intelligence agencies detected his arrival in New York.[2] Obama's aides were shocked at the breach of protocol.

In the *New Yorker*, Dexter Filkins painted a vivid picture of this encounter. "M.B.Z. arrived at the meeting, in the Trump Tower penthouse, with an entourage of about thirty people," Filkins wrote. "He was dressed in combat boots and jeans, and some of his men were armed. For most of the first hour, he and the Trump aides engaged in a relatively conventional discussion of Middle East policy, but the talk grew more animated as the two sides realized that they shared a common fixation on Iran. The meeting evolved into a planning session on how the Trump White House would confront the Iranian regime in the Gulf."[3] For dealing with Jared Kushner, this was an especially effective approach: the prime minister of Israel, Bibi Netanyahu, viewed Iran as a particularly destructive threat; so did Jared.

"They were deeply impressed with you and already are convinced that you are their true friend and closest ally," Gerson wrote to M.B.Z. in a text message, after the meeting with Jared. "I promise you this will be the start of a special and historic relationship." In another text, Gerson wrote, "You have a true friend in the White House."[4]

Around this time, M.B.Z was working on opening up another channel with the new administration, this one through Erik Prince, who had founded the now-defunct private security company Blackwater and was the brother of the secretary of education, Betsy DeVos.[5] M.B.Z. made overtures through a man named George Nader, a Lebanese-American businessman who acted as a middleman between high-level

Emiratis and Saudis and Trump and his associates. Nader had previously served prison time for child molestation; he was later seized in 2019 at John F. Kennedy airport in possession of child pornography, arrested, and charged with the possession and with human trafficking.[6] Nader entered a plea of not guilty to the charges.

Before Nader's arrest, Prince reluctantly testified to members of Congress. He told them that he had flown to the Seychelles—an archipelago in the Indian Ocean, a resort destination for the ultra-rich—to meet with Emirati business contacts. Prince said that after an outdoor meeting with M.B.Z., a member of M.B.Z.'s entourage "mentioned a guy I should meet who was also in town."[7] This was the head of the Russian Direct Investment Fund, Kirill Dmitriev, the man who called Vladimir Putin "boss." In his report, Special Counsel Robert Mueller found Nader had prearranged the whole thing, with Prince's knowledge. Before leaving the Seychelles, Prince sent incoming White House senior advisor Steve Bannon two texts. The texts were not preserved.[8]

In Washington, Tom Barrack was advising emissaries from the Saudis and the Emiratis, trying to secure a diplomatic post from the White House, which he called "Middle East Marshall Plan Commissioner," and meeting with administration officials to lift a US prohibition on a potential Saudi nuclear power plant, from which Barrack was looking to profit, according to a House Oversight report. Barrack met with multiple administration officials about this, including Jared Kushner.[9] But it was Kushner who the Gulf States had their eyes on.

"Thanks to you, I am in constant contact with Jared and that has been extremely helpful," Emirati Ambassador Otaiba wrote in an email correspondence with Tom Barrack that was later reported by the *New York Times*.[10] According to the *Washington Post*, "Officials from the UAE identified Kushner as particularly manipulable because of his family's search for investors in their real estate company."[11]

Kushner and Saudi Prince Mohammed bin Salman struck up a set of communications, often by the encrypted messaging service

WhatsApp. They were already correspondents by the time they met face to face. This happened in Washington, in March 2017, during a snowstorm that had forced German chancellor Angela Merkel to cancel a visit to the White House. Jared took advantage of the change of plans:[12] M.B.S., then still the deputy crown prince of Saudi Arabia, was given the kind of treatment a visiting head of state would receive: lunch in the State Dining Room with the president, a media spray, a photo opportunity. These kinds of pictures had already become coin of the realm abroad: they conferred instant legitimacy on aspiring leaders, autocrats, and businessmen.

Jared and M.B.S. bonded. They were two men in their thirties who thought of themselves as tech-savvy, modern leaders for whom "disruption" was a central tenet of their style. They had both been raised in extreme wealth in a world of growing income inequality. Both had complicated and combative histories with members of their extended families. And both shared an abiding hatred for Iran. Jared became convinced M.B.S. could pressure the Palestinians to agree to a Middle East peace proposal. Their relationship was frequently referred to as a "bromance."

Under Jared's urging, President Trump's first foreign trip was to Saudi Arabia. The Saudis gave Trump, accompanied by Melania, Jared, and Ivanka, a royal welcome, featuring banquets, dancing, and music, including a memorable moment where the president, the Saudi king, and the president of Egypt laid their hands on a small glowing orb of the planet Earth. There was an announcement that the Saudis would invest tens of millions of dollars in a US infrastructure fund, and would purchase a billion dollars worth of equipment from US arms contractors. Jared helped broker these deals.

He was also quietly brokering other deals, which he kept secret from the US secretary of state at the time, Rex Tillerson. The night the US delegation arrived, according to testimony released by the House Foreign Affairs Committee, there was a private dinner with then–White House advisor Steve Bannon, Jared Kushner, and the rulers of Saudi Arabia and the Emirates. During the dinner, the Saudis and the UAE leaders laid out their plans for a blockade of Qatar, which hosts a US air base, and which Saudi Arabia and the UAE view as an enemy. Tillerson said that he did not learn of this dinner, or these plans, until his congressional testimony, two years later. Did he have a reaction? "It makes me angry," he said, "because I didn't have a say. The State Department's views were never expressed."[13] When the testimony was released, a White House spokesman maintained that "Jared consistently follows proper protocols," and insisted that "the alleged dinner to supposedly discuss the blockade never happened."

The second day of the Saudi trip, there was a very large banquet in Riyadh. Tillerson had expected to be seated with the Qatari foreign minister, but when Tillerson arrived, it turned out that the minister had been moved to a table near the kitchen, a sign of disrespect. "I began to get an inkling that something was going on involving the Qataris," Tillerson testified, "because of the way the session had been conducted and the way the Emir had been treated in the meeting. I didn't know exactly what was going on. I just realized, I was kind of looking around the table at people trying to figure out: What is this, what is going on around here?"

After this trip, as the *New Yorker*'s Filkins wrote, "a series of dramatic events suggested that the attendees had quietly made a number of major decisions. Trump declared that the U.S. would move its Embassy in Israel from Tel Aviv to Jerusalem, something that no American President had attempted since Israel occupied the West Bank, in 1967. M.B.S. leapfrogged over [his cousin] bin Nayef to become crown prince. And the Gulf monarchies, led by Saudi Arabia, entered an open confrontation with Qatar."[14] Tillerson learned of the blockade while he was traveling in Australia, from an aide.

At the same time Jared was holding quiet, high-level meetings with Saudi Arabia, his father was discussing business with the Qataris. In April 2017, the month before the Saudi summit, Qatar's finance minister, Ali Sharif al-Emadi, flew to New York, rented a suite at the St. Regis Hotel, and met with a series of Americans interested in obtaining financing, including Charlie and Jared's sister, Nicole. At that point, the Qataris did not commit to investing in 666 Fifth. Charlie said he simply attended to be polite.[15] But then Jared backed the blockade. Suddenly, his father's business talks raised a thicket of questions: Was Jared supporting the action against Qatar because Qatar had denied his family funding? Was this a retaliatory move, or a signal? Because Jared had not severed ties to his family business, these questions were impossible to answer.

Kushner continued his friendship with M.B.S. In October 2017, he made a trip to the Kingdom that went unpublicized until his return. The two stayed up late into the night, talking about how they could remake the Middle East. Just before Jared had arrived, his brother, Josh Kushner, had spent three days at a Saudi conference where M.B.S. discussed investing billions in a high-tech future for Saudi Arabia. The *New York Times* reported that "as others sat through speeches in a gilded conference hall, several participants said, the younger Mr. Kushner frequently ducked out for more exclusive conversations with Saudi officials."[16]

A spokesman for one of Josh's companies, Thrive Capital, told the *Times* that Thrive was not actively fundraising when Josh made his trip. But according to *Bloomberg*, the real estate investment platform Cadre, of which Josh and Jared were co-founders, discussed "an investment of at least $100 million from a private fund that receives much of its capital from the governments of Saudi Arabia and the United Arab Emirates."[17] Jared, too, had an investment in Cadre—a company that also benefited from the new US tax law—which he did not initially disclose to the federal government. His lawyer said that was because his stake in Cadre was nested inside another company, BFPS Ventures LLC. As late as 2019, Jared still owned as much as $50 million worth of Cadre.

Weeks after Jared's unannounced trip, M.B.S. had some two hundred Saudis, many of them blood relations, rounded up into a virtual prison at the Ritz-Carlton hotel. There were reports of extortion, torture, even a death. In the press, M.B.S. and his subordinates denied these reports, and described the moves as "anti-corruption."

These arrests, as the Saudi journalist and *Washington Post* columnist

Jamal Khashoggi told the *New Yorker*'s Filkins, put M.B.S.'s main opponents out of commission: giving him effective control over the army, the interior ministry, and the national guard. "He can do whatever he wants now," Khashoggi said. "All the checks and balances are gone."[18]

By the spring of 2018, Jared Kushner appeared to be in trouble. The *New Yorker* had reported that Kushner took frequent visits with the Chinese. "In the months after Trump was sworn in," Adam Entous and Evan Osnos wrote, Kushner and the Chinese ambassador to the United States "met more often than Kushner could recall."[19] On at least one occasion, they met alone, a practice that counterintelligence officials frowned upon, because it meant the Chinese could make any claim they wanted about what had been discussed. Officials told Entous and Osnos that Kushner was briefed on the dangers of foreign-influence operations within months of his arrival at the White House, and told that he was "among the top intelligence targets worldwide," not only for China, but also the Russians, the Israelis, and others. Kushner was given a very specific warning, as well, about Wendi Murdoch. The FBI official who briefed Kushner told him that they'd picked up hints Chinese intelligence "had influence over her," though the evidence was "inconclusive." (A spokesperson for Wendi Murdoch told the *New Yorker* that "The idea that she is involved in anything covert is so absurd, it could only have come from an unnamed source.")

Kushner brushed all of this off. He told associates that New York real estate was no "baby's business." On a trip to China, Kushner had a lunch at Wendi Murdoch's Beijing home that was not mentioned in briefings or in his public schedule.

"Why do I have more of a risk of telling her state secrets than anyone else?" Kushner said. "Either I'm qualified to handle state secrets or I'm not qualified to handle state secrets. I think I understand my responsibilities."

Officials remained alarmed. Osnos and Entous reported that in December 2017, US intelligence had concluded that " 'a member of the president's family' was being targeted by a Chinese influence operation."[20] In February, the *Washington Post* expanded on this reporting, noting, "Officials in at least four countries"—China, Mexico, Israel, and the United Arab Emirates—"have privately discussed ways they can manipulate Jared Kushner, the president's son-in-law and senior adviser, by taking advantage of his complex business arrangements, financial difficulties and lack of foreign policy experience."[21]

Kushner didn't work hard to hide the fact he was circumventing normal channels. "I happened to be having a business dinner at a restaurant in town," Tillerson said in his testimony to the House Foreign Affairs Committee. "And the owner of the restaurant, proprietor of the restaurant came around and said: 'Oh, Mr. Secretary, you might be interested to know the Foreign Secretary of Mexico is seated at a table near the back and in case you want to go by and say hello to him.' Very innocent on his part."

Tillerson continued. "And so I did. I walked back. And Mr. Kushner and I don't remember who else was at the table, and the Foreign Secretary were at the table having dinner. And I could see the color go out of the face of the Foreign Secretary of Mexico as I very—I smiled big, and I said: 'Welcome to Washington.' And I said: 'I don't want to interrupt what y'all are doing.' I said: 'Give me a call next time you're coming to town.' "

As Tillerson said he later found out, "the Foreign Secretary was operating on the assumption that everything he was talking to Mr. Kushner about had been run through the State Department and that I was fully on board with it. And he was rather shocked . . . [when] I told him, 'This is the first time I'm hearing of it.' "[22]

In January 2019, NBC News reported that Jared Kushner's application for a top-secret clearance had been rejected by career security officials because of his business entanglements, but that their supervisor, a Trump appointee, had overruled them.[23] Kushner's was one of at least twenty-five cases in which career security experts were overruled in the Trump administration, something that had happened only once in the three years prior.

That month, Ivanka Trump gave an interview to Abby Huntsman of ABC. Ivanka had agreed to the interview to talk about Women's Global Development and Prosperity, a Trump administration program that Ivanka said would focus resources to help women thrive around the world. "We know there's a correlation between gender inequality and conflict, there's tremendous amounts of research. There's a reason today, the president signed WGDP as a national security presidential memorandum," she said. "It is in our domestic security interests to empower women."

When Ivanka talked about this initiative, she smiled, her eyes brightened, she talked with her hands, exuding the warmth and friendliness that has engaged interviewers for decades. But when Huntsman raised a new subject, security clearances, Ivanka's face froze. Her hands dropped to her lap, and the warmth in her eyes drained as Huntsman said, "There were some issues early on. And there are a lot of people that question whether you were given special treatment by the President, overriding other officials—"

"Absolutely not," Ivanka interrupted. "There were anonymous leaks, about there being issues," she said, with a tight smile, "but the president had no involvement pertaining to my clearance or my husband's clearance. Zero."

"What were the problems early on?" Huntsman asked.

"There weren't any, other than a backlog that exists of close to a million clearances across government. This isn't new, this was happening under the Obama administration, the Clinton administration."

"So no special treatment?" Huntsman confirmed.

"No," Ivanka said.[24]

Ivanka was contradicted, not by an anonymous leak, but by a person inside the White House, Tricia Newbold, who had worked on security issues for eighteen years, under presidents Trump, Obama, George W. Bush, and Bill Clinton. "She handles security clearance determinations for some of the most senior officials in the White House and throughout the Executive Office of the President," the late US Representative Elijah Cummings wrote in a letter to the White House.[25]

Newbold told Cummings' House Oversight Committee that she had recommended against granting clearance to Jared Kushner—whom she called "Senior White House Official 1." Newbold wrote a denial "after the background investigation revealed significant disqualifying factors, including foreign influence, outside activities ('employment outside or businesses external to what your position at the EOP entails'), and personal conduct." Newbold testified—on the record—that she was overruled by her supervisor, Carl Kline, who merely noted in Jared's file that "the activities occurred prior to Federal service."

Newbold told the committee she'd begun to keep a list of officials whose denials were overturned, a tally that grew to include twenty-five people who "had a wide range of serious disqualifying issues involving foreign influence, conflicts of interest, concerning personal conduct, financial problems, drug use, and criminal conduct." One of the people on Newbold's list was senior White House advisor Ivanka Trump, Cummings said.

Newbold has a form of dwarfism, and after she raised her concerns, she said, Kline "repeatedly altered her office environment to cause impediments to her work, such as physically elevating personnel security files out of her reach."[26] (Kline said he had moved the files but denied that it was retaliation.[27])

The White House said it wouldn't comment on security clearances, but in an interview with the Fox News host Laura Ingraham, Jared, wearing a crisp white shirt and charcoal suit with a gray tie, laughed it off. "Over the last two years that I have been here I've been accused of all different types of things, and all of those things have turned out to be false," he said. "We've had a lot of crazy accusations like that we colluded with Russia. I complied with all the different investigations whether it be the Senate, the House, the Special Counsel—I sat for nearly 20 hours of interviews with them. When I came to Washington I had a very successful business career, I had extensive holdings. I disclosed all my holdings to the Office of Government Ethics and what I did with that is they told me what to divest, what to keep, what rules to follow."[28]

On October 2, 2018, Jamal Khashoggi, the *Washington Post* columnist and a US resident, entered the Saudi consulate in Istanbul to obtain paperwork he needed in order to marry his fiancée, Hatice Cengiz. Inside, according to transcripts of a Turkish government audio recording described to the *Washington Post*, Khashoggi was told, "You're coming back with us." After that, according to a note in the transcript, Khashoggi was given an injection, after which a bag was placed over his head and he screamed, "I can't breathe. I have asthma. Don't do this." He died soon after. Then, the *Post* reported, "the transcript describes a buzzing noise, perhaps from an electric saw as his body was cut into pieces." One of the assassins, Turkish authorities said, brought a bone saw for the task.[29]

After the killing, Trump defended the Saudis. Speaking to reporters, standing under an umbrella, he said: "The king firmly denied any knowledge of it. He didn't really know, maybe—I don't want to get into his mind but, it sounded to me like maybe these could have been rogue killers, who knows?" Ten days later, CIA director Gina Haspel flew to Ankara, where she was played the tapes.[30] The CIA had intercepts of communications attempting to lure Khashoggi back to Saudi Arabia; their intelligence analysts were all but certain the murder was not a rogue event, and concluded with a medium to high degree of confidence that it had been ordered by M.B.S. After Haspel briefed a group of senators, the US Senate voted unanimously to lay the blame on the crown prince. Trump still refused to accept this conclusion. "They have nothing definitive, and the fact is, maybe he did, maybe he didn't," he told reporters on the White House lawn.

On another occasion, the *Washington Post*'s Josh Dawsey pushed Trump to comment on the CIA's conclusion that M.B.S. ordered the killings.

"No, Josh, they didn't conclude," Trump said, erroneously. "They didn't come to a conclusion, they have feelings certain ways, but they didn't have the report."

While the CIA was at work, Kushner and M.B.S. were calling each other "Jared" and "Mohammed" on the phone and in WhatsApp messages, the *New York Times* reported.[31] Kushner became the prince's biggest defender inside the White House. Weeks after Khashoggi was murdered in the embassy, Jared was asked by CNN's Van Jones if he believed the Saudi version of Khashoggi's death, which was that a fist fight had broken out in the embassy, resulting in Khashoggi's death.

"Saudi Arabia's been—I think, a very strong ally in terms of pushing back against Iran's aggression," Kushner said, citing Iranian support for a faction in Yemen and actions by Hamas and Hezbollah. "We have a lot of terrorism and in the region, the Middle East is a rough place. It's been a rough place for a very long time and we have to be able to pursue our strategic objectives. But we also have to deal with obviously what seems to be a terrible situation."[32]

This was Jared Kushner's grim bargain. The transactional view of a real estate developer raised as a Zionist. The Saudis, by opposing Iran, could potentially help Israel. All else could be overlooked.

23

AMERICAN OLIGARCHY

On October 26, 2016—less than two weeks to election day—travel writer Zach Everson covered the ribbon cutting at the Trump International Hotel in the Old Post Office building in Washington, DC, just a few blocks from the White House. Everson frequently covered hotel openings, which often featured lavish food spreads and "the owners sipping champagne with a few travel writers." But this one was different. A horde of political reporters trailed Donald and Ivanka Trump as they toured the hotel. "The political reporters were amazed they had complimentary pastries," Everson said in an interview.[1]

A couple months later, Everson got an assignment from *Condé Nast Traveller* to cover the growing political and social scene at the hotel. In the course of researching that story, Everson booked a night at the hotel. One of his fellow guests told Everson he was about to leave for a restaurant outside the hotel, when he noticed workers polishing the banisters and the manager nervously pacing. The guest concluded, correctly, that the president was on his way, cancelled his outside reservation, and ate at the hotel instead.

To track presidential comings and goings for his story, Everson started monitoring social media feeds. And he noticed something: not even a year into Trump's presidency, the hotel had become a unique locale in Washington. "It became like Melville's white whale," Everson said. "If you want it to be your opportunity and a place for you to go and rub elbows with the President, it's that. If you're a lobbyist or a businessman or a foreign leader and want to portray you are close to the president, it's that too. It's everything you hate or love about Donald Trump." Everson quit travel writing to cover, full time, the Trump International Hotel. He began publishing a newsletter, *1100 Pennsylvania Avenue*. He had plenty of material.

It wasn't always clear that Trump, once elected, would get to keep his lease with the federal General Services Administration. The lease specifically stated that "no . . . elected official of the Government of the United States . . . shall be admitted to any share or part of this Lease, or to any benefit that may arise therefrom."[2] To get around that, Trump moved his ownership interest to an LLC company, DJT Holdings Managing Member LLC. And the federal agency that reported to him allowed this. In a 166-page letter, in which he cited "legal professionals" who were quoted in a *Politico* article, GSA contracting officer Kevin Terry concluded that because "President Trump is not an officer, director, manager, employee, or other official in any of the entities" with an interest in the hotel, the Trumps could continue to hold the lease.[3] Terry crucially ignored the fact that Donald Trump was still an owner and could financially benefit from everything from the $8 Budweisers sold at the bar to the $18,000 suites at the hotel.

"This is the best global example of a conflict of interest I can think of," George Washington University professor of government procurement law Steven Schooner said in an interview. When he instructs foreign governments on what not to do, Schooner said, he uses the Trump International Hotel as an example. Having the president's children—in this case Don Jr. and Eric Trump—negotiate with a federal agency is exactly the kind of tangled financial and government structure that the Department of Justice warns US companies to watch out for when they do business abroad, lest they run afoul of anti-corruption laws and the Foreign Corrupt Practices Act.[4]

In addition to ignoring the prohibition against having a lease with "an elected official," the GSA also decided to ignore that the president could be violating the Emoluments Clause of the Constitution by accepting payments, as the hotel would quite frequently, from foreign leaders and from state governments using his hotel. In a report, the GSA inspector general sharply criticized the GSA for its "unwillingness to address the constitutional issues," calling the omission "improper."[5] But the remedy was weak tea: the inspector general essentially told the GSA not to do it again, and the GSA said, essentially, okay.

By the time this report was issued, in 2019, the Trump International Hotel, just blocks from the White House, had become an open invitation to foreign leaders, political groups, lobbyists, and anyone who wanted things from Trump. Showing up at the hotel, and spending money there, was, for Donald Trump, akin to writing checks to a political fundraiser, but without disclosure laws. It was, as Robert Maguire of the Center for Responsive Politics and later Citizens for Ethics and Responsibility in Washington called it, "the new dark money."[6] Trump didn't need, as President Obama had mockingly suggested at the White House Correspondents Association Dinner years earlier, a black and pink neon-lettered sign over the White House that said "Trump: The White House: Hotel, Casino, Golf Course, Presidential Suite." He had opened its equivalent just down the block.

When they started their jobs in Washington, senior Trump officials Steve Mnuchin, Linda McMahon, and Gary Cohn moved into the hotel. Others took meetings there, or showed up for dinner. Vice President Pence was regularly driven five blocks to 1100 Pennsylvania in his motorcade from the White House. Lesser-known government appointees also patronized the hotel, in effect, kicking part of their government, taxpayer-funded salaries back to President Trump's business.

There was always the possibility that Donald Trump, Ivanka Trump, or Jared Kushner would show up. The uncertainty itself lured daily crowds. They arranged themselves on the seafoam couches in the lobby in a room that feels like a giant terrarium, to sip, at bottom, a $12 Grenache, and, at the top, Hungarian Tokay from a crystal spoon for $140.

Rudy Giuliani showed up regularly. So did Rick Gates, before he was indicted. The gambling magnate Sheldon Adelson, the Republican Party's largest donor, let himself be seen dining at the hotel. Lobbyists like Corey Lewandowski, fired from Trump's campaign, and people like Sebastian Gorka, forced out of Trump's administration, would always find a place at the Trump Hotel, and also a place in Trump's heart. Republican government officials, like the governor of Maine, stayed at the hotel, while in Washington, on the Maine taxpayers' dime. Political fundraising committees regularly held events at the Trump hotel; one diplomat told the *Washington Post* it would be "rude" to stay at a rival establishment. Republican members of Congress, keenly conscious of how their perceived power would be measured by proximity to Trump, frequented the space; one told Anita Kumar of *Politico* that events were held there because "donors want to come."[7] Industry groups, like the National Mining Association,[8] held events there, often inviting administration officials, which meant that these groups were paying Donald, Ivanka, Don Jr., and Eric Trump to host cabinet members at their hotel.

T-Mobile, while seeking a merger with Sprint, sent nine of its top executives to stay at the hotel, in bright-pink company-branded T-shirts, spending $195,000, while they were lobbying the Justice Department, a block away, for approval of the $26-billion merger. Lobbyists paid by Saudi Arabia made five hundred nights' worth of room bookings. And then there was a parade of foreign officials who had their own problems with corruption: Malaysia's prime minister at the time, Najib Razak, arrived during a period when the Justice Department was probing a wide-ranging Malaysian money-laundering scheme; a candidate for president of Nigeria, barred from visiting the United States for years because of allegations of corruption, showed up weeks before his election day, seeking to launder his own reputation by staying in a hotel owned by the president of the United States. The prime minister of Romania, Viorica Dăncilă, arrived in 2019, and dined near Rudy Giuliani, Trump's personal attorney, who while working for Trump had written a letter to the Romanian president urging the country to drop an anti-corruption probe. Giuliani, the erstwhile corruption buster, had been hired as a lobbyist to write the letter "to express my concerns about continuing damage to the rule of law in Romania being done under the guise of effective law enforcement."[9]

Trump's administration made sure there wouldn't be meaningful competition for his hotel, which had been a very real possibility. For a decade, for both cost-savings and security reasons, the GSA had sought to relocate the FBI headquarters, which is across the street from the Trump International Hotel, to the Washington suburbs. The old FBI building, like the Old Post Office, had been seen as the site of a possible new hotel. But GSA's Trump-appointed administrator, Emily Murphy, scrapped that plan. Questioned by Congress, Murphy was asked, "To your knowledge was the President or anyone at the White House involved in those discussions either with your predecessors or people you're working with now or yourself?"[10]

Murphy answered: "Sir, to my knowledge—the direction that we got came from the FBI." But Murphy concealed that she'd actually personally spoken to the president in the Oval Office about the decision. According to an inspector general report, "Murphy told us that she attended two meetings about the FBI project at the White House on January 24, 2018. The first meeting occurred in [then White House Chief of Staff John] Kelly's office, and immediately preceded the second meeting. The second meeting was in the Oval Office with the President."[11]

In public filings, Ivanka Trump disclosed what she'd earned in income from the Trump International Hotel: $3,890,775, part of at least $82,000,000 in income she and Jared had earned in the year they became White House advisors. In 2018, Ivanka earned nearly another $4 million from the hotel. During the first two years of his presidency, Donald Trump reported, he earned $80 million from a property that was owned by the taxpayers.[12]

The hotel was an example of a larger phenomenon in Washington, where businessmen and de facto foreign agents profited from their proximity to the president. There was, for example, the businessman Elliott Broidy, who had once pleaded guilty to illegally making gifts to New York State officials. (His lawyers eventually persuaded a judge to reduce the charge to a misdemeanor.) Broidy resurrected himself as the owner of a private security firm and Republican Party fundraiser in 2016. After Trump was elected, Broidy struck up a mutually beneficial relationship with George Nader, the convicted child molester, later arrested for possessing child pornography, who was a middleman for Emirati and Saudi rulers. As a deputy finance chairman of the RNC, Broidy was able to get an Oval Office meeting with Trump. Afterwards, Broidy sent Nader a detailed email, telling Nader he'd pitched his causes right to the president.[13] Broidy did one more thing: he helped pave the way for a photo of Nader and Trump at a Republican fundraiser in Dallas, over the objections of the Secret Service.[14] The month after the photo, Broidy made his biggest donation ever, $189,000, directly to the RNC.

Broidy got something, too, from his relationship with Nader, the Associated Press reported. Not long after his meeting in the Oval Office, Broidy sent via Nader a contract for his private security firm to work in the Emirates. Broidy soon started getting payments, through a company in Canada. The first installment was for $36 million, a down payment on Broidy's contract with the UAE, worth up to $600 million. (Broidy's lawyer told the *New York Times* that he had never taken money from a foreign country "for any interaction with the United States government.")

There were many other examples of this type of conduct. Trump personally lobbied the prime minister of Japan at Mar-a-Lago, according to ProPublica, to grant a casino license to major donor Sheldon Adelson.[15] A consultant developed a plan for Tom Barrack to profit from infrastructure investment.[16] Erik Prince urged the United States to leave Afghanistan and instead place the war in the hands of a private contractor: his. Chris Christie and Marc Kasowitz were hired as part of the legal team of Malaysian businessman Jho Low, under investigation for money laundering by the US Justice Department; another lawyer on the team was Bobby Burchfield, the outside attorney the Trump Organization hired to monitor its conflicts of interest.[17] (Jho Low denied the charges.) A trio of Mar-a-Lago club members, private businessmen, unelected and unconfirmed, ran Veterans Administration policy from afar.[18]

It wasn't new that rich business leaders were trying to monetize their connections to the president of the United States. What was new was that access was so easily given: that these leaders could cozy up to Trump at his hotel or his golf courses or at Mar-a-Lago, and, because so many protocols and norms were being tossed aside, the ensuing chaotic environment created fertile ground for people who wanted to influence the president. The door to the Oval Office was wide open.

There was, also, the bevy of cabinet officials who both participated in petty corruption and who beckoned in—or had been themselves—the lobbyists and industry leaders their agencies had once regulated. The Trump administration was bent on deeply cutting government, but this did not prevent its own appointees from helping themselves to the taxpayer dime.

Scott Pruitt, Trump's first head of the Environmental Protection Agency, resigned after undergoing seventeen separate investigations for, among other things: living at below-market rent in an apartment co-owned by the wife of an energy-industry lobbyist; spending an excessive amount of government money on first-class flights; using government resources in an attempt to get his wife a Chick-fil-A franchise; sending a staffer to hunt for a used mattress from the Trump International Hotel; and spending taxpayer money on "security" enhancements, including a $43,000 soundproof phone booth in his office. Prior to joining the EPA, Pruitt had sued the agency fourteen times; as EPA chief, he rolled back the Clean Power Plan, lifted controls on air pollution, stopped efforts to ban neurotoxin-containing pesticides, supported ending US participation in the Paris climate accord, lowered automobile efficiency standards, and packed scientific advisory board panels with cronies.[19] When Pruitt stepped down he was replaced by Andrew Wheeler, himself a former coal-industry lobbyist.

Other Trump cabinet appointees were similarly pushed out after embarrassing violations. Health and Human Services Secretary Tom Price overspent by at least $341,000 on flights, some on chartered planes—twenty of his twenty-one trips examined violated government spending rules.[20] The Department of Veterans Affairs chief David Shulkin charged taxpayers for a trip to Europe that included a riverboat cruise for him and his wife. Interior secretary Ryan Zinke chartered a plane to fly home from giving a twelve-minute speech to a Las Vegas hockey team, and while in office struck a land deal in his home state of Montana with the company Halliburton. After the latter incident was referred to the Justice Department, Zinke resigned.[21] His replacement, David Bernhardt, a former oil and agribusiness lobbyist, apparently never stopped lobbying; he came under investigation for having used his previous position as deputy secretary to block the release of a scientific report showing the harmful effects of certain pesticides. (Bernhardt said that he had not committed ethical violations.)[22]

Some cabinet officials lasted. Notable in that category: Treasury Secretary Steve Mnuchin, whose own government-funded travel included a trip that brought him to a prime viewing area for the 2017 solar eclipse. Wilbur Ross, the commerce secretary and billionaire financier, reached an agreement with the Office of Government Ethics to divest from his many businesses, but as the *New York Times* reported, he "retained investments in a shipping firm he once controlled that has significant business ties to a Russian oligarch subject to American sanctions and President Vladimir V. Putin's son-in-law, according to newly disclosed documents."[23] Five days before this story was published, *Forbes* reported, Ross shorted his stock, meaning that when the price dropped as a result of the story, he had positioned himself to make money. Ross also continued to secretly hold stakes in a Cypriot bank and companies co-owned by the Chinese government.

Instead of divesting, Ross was availing himself of a template used by the Trump family. He put some of his holdings into a trust for his family members, which meant, as commerce secretary, he "continued to deal with China, Russia and others while evidently knowing that his family's interests were tied to those countries," Dan Alexander wrote in *Forbes*. The ethics laws of the United States lacked the tools to track these many holdings; disclosure forms don't require the listing of business partners, investors, or members of a limited liability company. "Maintaining all those conflicts of interest appears to be entirely legal," *Forbes* wrote, "a reflection of ethics laws woefully unprepared for governing tycoons like Donald Trump and Wilbur Ross."[24]

In her book, *Thieves of State*, Sarah Chayes, who had lived and worked in Afghanistan as both an NPR journalist and head of a nongovernmental organization, examined Afghani corruption as a template for corruption around the world.[25] Officials subordinate to then–Afghan president Hamid Karzai maintained their own power by "paying off Karzai or his apparatus. What the top of the system provided in return was, first, unfettered permission to extract resources for personal gain, and second, protection from repercussions."

In an interview years after her book was published, for the *Trump, Inc.* podcast, Chayes added: "What's going on currently in the United States as far as I'm concerned is an American version of a phenomenon that I've been seeing all over the world. Which is to say networks made up of top government officials, captains of industry, and out and out criminals, woven together, are hijacking government and economic function and bending it to serve the purposes of their personal enrichment and not the public interest." This network, Chayes said, is a key feature of corruption: "an operating system" in which "governing is kind of at best a front operation and at worst is one of the ways in which members of the network achieve their objective of enriching themselves."[26]

In the past, Chayes said, the US government had made an effort to set itself apart. Under Trump, with little compunction, it was becoming more and more like governments of the countries she had studied, the ones that had devolved into kleptocracy.

24

JUSTICE

When Attorney General Jeff Sessions told President Donald Trump that his deputy Rod Rosenstein had appointed Robert S. Mueller III to be special counsel to investigate the Russian government's efforts to interfere in the 2016 election campaign, Trump slumped back in his chair and said, "Oh my God. This is terrible. This is the end of my presidency. I'm fucked." More upset than he'd been since the release of the *Access Hollywood* tape, Trump berated Sessions, who had recused himself from the Russia investigation because of his own work as a campaign surrogate and his own contacts with the Russians. "How could you let this happen, Jeff?" the president said angrily. "You were supposed to protect me." Sessions offered to resign.[1]

Trump had already excoriated Sessions for recusing himself, and brought up his lawyer from a long time ago, Roy Cohn, saying he wished Cohn was his attorney. "I don't have a lawyer," Trump said, to Sessions. He told other White House staffers that Cohn would win cases for him when they didn't have a chance, and that Cohn had done incredible things. Cohn, Trump said at the White House, had been "a winner and a fixer, someone who got things done."[2]

After Mueller's appointment, Sessions handed Trump a resignation letter, which he took. When other presidential staffers learned this, they were alarmed, and tried to retrieve the letter, fearing that Trump could use it as a "shock collar" to hold "DOJ by the throat." The next day, Trump left for the Middle East, where, on the flight from Saudi Arabia to Tel Aviv, he took the letter from his pocket and showed it to a group of senior advisors. Two weeks after he'd received the letter, he finally returned it to Sessions, with a notation that said, "not accepted."

His anger did not let up.

Two weeks later, the *Washington Post* published a story saying that Mueller's office was investigating whether the president had tried to obstruct justice. This was stunning news at the time—the first public report that Trump, himself, was under investigation. Trump called Don McGahn, the White House Counsel, at 10:31 the night the story broke.

McGahn had been one of Trump's earlier appointments after he was elected, a loyal Republican who was raised by Democrats, including his uncle, Paddy McGahn, the Atlantic City fixer who Trump had hired thirty-five years prior to navigate a thicket of political and mob relations in Atlantic City. Paddy McGahn and Donald Trump had a falling out after about a decade, when Trump stopped paying his bills. Paddy's nephew Don joined the Federalist Society, an organization set up in the Reagan era to groom and elevate conservative justices, and had a series of jobs in Republican Washington, including FEC chairman, where he buried the campaign finance complaint against Trump and Cohen.

On a June weekend in 2017, three days after the *Post* story, Trump asked McGahn to bury another investigation. McGahn refused. Trump, at Camp David, called McGahn, at home. "You gotta do this. You gotta call Rod," Trump said, fixating, as, McGahn described to investigators, on "silly" conflicts, including a dispute Mueller had had about membership fees at one of Trump's golf courses. McGahn said he did not want to interfere, that he had grown up admiring conservative judge Robert Bork and did not want to be "Saturday Night Massacre Bork," who, as acting attorney general, had fired the special prosecutor investigating Richard Nixon after the Watergate investigation heated up.

Later, Trump called again, and said, "Call Rod, tell Rod that Mueller has conflicts and can't be the Special Counsel," adding "Mueller has to go," and "Call me back when you do it." McGahn left Trump with the impression he would do it, "to get off the phone," he said. He did not do it. He felt trapped. He did not know what he would say the next time Trump called. So he drove to his office to pack his belongings and submit his resignation letter. He called the then–chief of staff, Reince Priebus, and then–senior advisor Steve Bannon, who talked him out of it.

It was Chris Christie, apparently, who talked Trump down from his tree. Christie, still the New Jersey governor, told Trump that there was no substantive basis for firing Mueller, and that if he did so, he would lose the support of Republicans in Congress.[3] Trump did not continue to press the issue, and McGahn acted like it hadn't happened.

Until January 2018, when the *New York Times* published a story about the incident that said, "after receiving the president's order to fire Mr. Mueller, the White House counsel . . . refused to ask the Justice Department to dismiss the special counsel, saying he would quit, instead." Trump called the story, "Fake news, folks. Fake news. A typical New York Times fake story." The next day, according to the Mueller report, "the President's personal counsel called McGahn's attorney and said that the President wanted McGahn to put out a statement denying that he had been asked to fire the Special Counsel and that he had threatened to quit in protest." McGahn refused, saying the report was mostly accurate.

This did not sit well with President Trump. He told another White House staffer, Rob Porter, that McGahn had leaked to the media to make himself look good. Then he told Porter to tell McGahn to create a record—a false one—saying that the president had never directed McGahn to fire the Special Counsel. This was going to be a letter "for our records." McGahn, Trump told Porter, was a "lying bastard." There is usually only one reason to create such a record, and that is to deflect investigators—that is, to obstruct justice.

McGahn wouldn't do it. He told Porter that it was true Trump had wanted him to get Mueller fired. Porter said that McGahn might now be fired, if he didn't write the fake memo. McGahn said the optics would be terrible if Trump followed through. Then Trump summoned McGahn, telling him he needed to correct the story. "I never said to fire Mueller," Trump said. "I never said 'fire.' This story doesn't look good. You need to correct this. You're the White House counsel." McGahn replied: "What you said is, 'Call Rod, tell Rod that Mueller has conflicts and can't be the Special Counsel.'" Trump denied this. He asked McGahn if he would "do a correction." McGahn said no.

Trump asked: "What about these notes? Why do you take notes? Lawyers don't take notes. I never had a lawyer who took notes." McGahn responded he took notes because he was a "real lawyer," and that notes create a record.

To which Trump responded, "I've had a lot of great lawyers, like Roy Cohn. He did not take notes."[4] In the White House, Trump asked, "Where's my Roy Cohn?"[5]

In April 2018, an FBI agent filed a sheaf of paperwork under seal with federal magistrate judge Henry Pitman, 269 pages in all, outlining a years-long scheme by Trump's attorney Michael Cohen to defraud banks, violate campaign finance laws, and lie repeatedly about his cash flows and net worth to various financial institutions, his accountant, and business partners.[6] Cohen, the papers noted, had been promoting himself "as the personal attorney for President Donald Trump" and had "previously served for over a decade as an executive in the Trump Organization." In early 2017, the papers said, he began accepting millions of dollars in payments from a company controlled by the Ukrainian-Russian oligarch Viktor Vekselberg, a South Korean aerospace company, the Swiss drug company Novartis, AT&T, and BTA bank, the Kazakh bank embroiled in a massive money-laundering scandal that had once been behind the potential funding for Cohen's Trump project in Georgia. In total, the search warrant showed Cohen receiving over three million dollars in the account of the shell company he'd set up, Essential Consultants LLC, which was not a consulting company at all, but merely a way to take in funds from individuals and companies who believed Cohen could give them access to President Trump.

Cohen had hidden the Essential Consulting assets from a bank he owed money to, Sterling National Bank, while at the same time claiming he'd lost so much money on his taxi medallion investments he needed Sterling to write off some of his debt. Cohen also hid sixty thousand dollars a month he was receiving from a private loan he'd issued and several million dollars held in some dozen bank accounts. The search warrant request revealed that the FBI had scoured Cohen's emails on three prior occasions, beginning in July 2017; but law-enforcement agents concluded destruction of evidence was a very real possibility, and asked for judicial permission to search Cohen's office on the twenty-third floor of 30 Rockefeller Plaza; his apartment, then undergoing renovations, at 502 Park Avenue (the same Trump building where Jared and Ivanka maintained an address); room 1728 at the Loews Regency hotel, where Cohen was temporarily staying; his safety deposit box; a MacBook Pro, an iPad Mini, and various phones, which they were allowed to unlock, if necessary, using Cohen's fingers or face.

The raid was executed on April 9, 2018.

In the White House, seated between Vice President Mike Pence and his third national security advisor, John Bolton, at a meeting with military leaders, Trump's anger ran hot. "So I just heard that they broke into the office of one of my personal attorneys. Good man. And it's a disgraceful situation. It's a total witch hunt, I've been saying it for a long time." The law for Trump was a subjective thing—righteous when wielded against his enemies, but a conspiracy when wielded against his friends and associates.

There was, also, the fact that the evidence the FBI found was extremely dangerous to Trump. For a decade, Cohen had kept Trump's financial secrets. At first, Trump's lawyers fought alongside Cohen's to keep the US attorney from reviewing the documents. Trump's lawyers claimed attorney-client privilege. They promised to "take care of" Cohen, and to pay his legal fees. Trump kept urging Cohen to "hang in there," and to "stay strong."[7] A friend of Trump's reached out to say he was with "the Boss," in Mar-a-Lago, and to convey that the president had said "he loves you," not to worry. A lawyer who was close with President Trump's attorney Rudy Giuliani emailed Cohen, "You are 'loved.'" He added: "Sleep well tonight, you have friends in high places."[8]

Trump retained Giuliani, by now almost bald, rounder in face, and heftier in girth, to represent him in negotiations with Mueller, but his main job, as Giuliani saw it, was to win in the court of public opinion. He did this by sewing confusion, attacking prosecutors' motives, and dangling the idea of pardons to key witnesses.

Cohen also spoke to the president's personal counsel, who told him to stay on message, that everything was going to be fine, which, Cohen understood, meant Trump would either shut down the investigation, or Cohen would be pardoned. The message came from inside the Trump Organization, too. "The boss loves you," one intermediary told him. Another: "Everyone knows the boss has your back."[9]

The boss did not have his back. The president's team stopped paying the bills for Cohen's legal team. Trump began to talk about Cohen in the past tense, telling reporters he'd "liked" Michael Cohen.

At the end of June, Cohen, who had once said he'd take a bullet for Donald Trump, who had once embraced the nickname "Tom," after Tom Hagen, Don Corleone's attorney in *The Godfather*, told ABC, "My wife, my daughter, and my son have my first loyalty and always will. I put family and country first."[10] The president started attacking Cohen, accusing him of making up "stories in order to get a 'deal.'"

That July, Ivanka Trump said she'd shut down her clothing and accessory business. The next month, the Kushner Companies, unable to find bank financing, gave up control of 666 Fifth Avenue to Brookfield Asset Management, which said it would renovate the building. Though the Kushners kept their offices, and retained ownership of the land underneath the building, they leased it to Brookfield for ninety-nine years. "Kushner Companies remains a very strong real estate business," Charles Kushner said in an emailed statement. "The future of Kushner Companies is indeed very bright."

On July, 13, 2018, the US Department of Justice issued a press release. It "announced that a grand jury in the District of Columbia returned an indictment presented by the Special Counsel's Office. The indictment charges twelve Russian nationals for committing federal crimes that were intended to interfere with the 2016 U.S. presidential election. All twelve defendants are members of the GRU, a Russian Federation intelligence agency within the Main Intelligence Directorate of the Russian military."[11] Though US intelligence agencies had fingered Russian military intelligence two years earlier, Robert Mueller's indictment laid out a highly specific criminal plot, directed by the Kremlin.[12]

The indictment was stunning in its detail. The more so, because President Trump was about to board a plane to hold his first official summit with Vladimir Putin, who, Mueller said, had directed the attack.

Three days later, Presidents Donald Trump and Vladimir Putin stood together, casually tossing a soccer ball (it was the day after the final of the Men's World Cup, in Moscow) at twin podiums at the press conference following their summit meeting in Helsinki, Finland.

"Just now," Jonathan Lemire of the Associated Press asked of Trump, "President Putin denied having anything to do with the election interference in 2016. Every U.S. intelligence agency has concluded that Russia did. What—who—my first question for you, sir, is, who do you believe? My second question is, would you now, with the whole world watching, tell President Putin—would you denounce what happened in 2016? And would you warn him to never do it again?"

Trump did not immediately answer the questions; instead, he slipped into an old trope, discussing Hillary Clinton's email server. As for Russian interference, his answer verged in incoherence. "My people came to me—[Director of National Intelligence] Dan Coats came to me and some others—they said they think it's Russia. I have President

Putin; he just said it's not Russia. I will say this: I don't see any reason why it would be, but I really do want to see the server. But I have—I have confidence in both parties. I really believe that this will probably go on for a while, but I don't think it can go on without finding out what happened to the server. What happened to the servers of the Pakistani gentleman that worked on the DNC? Where are those servers? They're missing. Where are they? What happened to Hillary Clinton's emails? Thirty-three thousand emails gone—just gone. I think, in Russia, they wouldn't be gone so easily. I think it's a disgrace that we can't get Hillary Clinton's 33,000 emails."

"So I have great confidence in my intelligence people," Trump continued. "But I will tell you that President Putin was extremely strong and powerful in his denial today."

Putin, for his part, brought up Bill Browder, the American-born financier whose former lawyer, Sergey Magnitsky, had died in a Russian prison while investigating the theft of corporate seals belonging to Browder's companies. Putin was making the same argument Natalia Veselnitskaya had made two years prior to Donald Trump Jr. in Trump Tower. "Business associates of Mr. Browder have earned over one and a half billion dollars in Russia," Putin said. "They never paid any taxes, neither in Russia nor in the United States, and yet the money escaped the country. They were transferred to the United States. They sent a huge amount of money—four hundred million—as a contribution to the campaign of Hillary Clinton."

"President Putin, did you want President Trump to win the election?" Jeff Mason of Reuters asked, "And did you direct any of your officials to help him do that?"

"Yes, I did. Yes, I did. Because he talked about bringing the U.S.-Russia relationship back to normal."

This entire exchange was left out of the Kremlin transcript of the event. So was, initially, the first part of Mason's question, about wanting Trump to win, left out of the official White House transcript. After an outcry, that part was restored.[13]

The event showed the two presidents on remarkably parallel tracks:

both bending the truth, fanning the flames of conspiracy theories, assaulting the rule of law, betraying a twin shared obsession with Hillary Clinton. And showing the world that their power lay in being able to get away with all of this.

—

Two weeks after Trump returned from Helsinki, his former campaign chairman, Paul Manafort, went on trial for bank fraud and tax fraud in a courtroom in Alexandria, Virginia. Manafort, along with his deputy, Rick Gates, had been indicted in Washington, DC, in the fall for money laundering and conspiracy against the United States; new charges were later added in the Eastern District of Virginia for bank fraud and tax fraud. Rick Gates pleaded guilty to conspiracy against the United States. Manafort held firm.

Manafort initially had been out on bail, monitored by two electronic bracelets, but he had violated a gag order by ghostwriting an English-language op-ed in a Ukrainian newspaper. (Manafort denied he'd really had input, but Mueller's team was monitoring his email traffic and produced Manafort's extensive track changes as part of the record.)

And then, in the District of Columbia, where he faced the charges for money laundering and conspiracy against the United States, Manafort committed another crime: witness tampering. Working with Konstantin Kilimnik, the former colleague with "ties to Russian intelligence" whom he'd met at the Grand Havana Room in August 2016 to discuss Manafort's "biggest black caviar jar," Manafort had reached out to witnesses, trying to shape their testimony. This latter infraction was too much for Judge Amy Berman Jackson, the federal judge in Washington; she revoked Manafort's bail and sent him to jail.

Manafort arrived in the courtroom in Alexandria for jury selection on a steamy July day, changing from his green prison jumpsuit with a white undershirt underneath to a black suit with a white shirt. His reddish-brown hair was showing some white, but Manafort still had a fashion statement; from the front row of the courtroom I could see his nice loafers, worn with no socks.

The trial was memorable for the verbal ejaculations of Judge TS Ellis, a seventy-eight-year-old Virginian known for setting his own rules in the courtroom. Ellis repeatedly excoriated prosecutors and rushed them through their case, infuriated that they were presenting evidence of Manafort's ill-gotten wealth, which included a $15,000 ostrich-leather jacket, the brownstone in Brooklyn and the apartment in SoHo, a Land Rover, stereo systems, high-end rugs, an outdoor kitchen for his daughter, and landscaping. "It isn't a crime to have a lot of money," Ellis said.

But the case was notable for another reason: Manafort's political work in Ukraine was a glimpse over the political horizon, of a system where the rules of democracy were so bent by the transactional desires of the wealthy that democracy itself became unrecognizable.

"Beginning in 2005," Assistant United States Attorney Uzo Asonye explained in his opening statement, "Paul Manafort worked for politicians in Ukraine. He represented the government of Ukraine; Viktor Yanukovych, who would become the president of Ukraine, and two Ukrainian political parties."

"For that work for these foreign officials," Asonye said, "Paul Manafort was paid handsomely. During this trial, you will learn that for his political work in Ukraine, Manafort was paid by Ukrainian oligarchs, some of the country's most powerful and wealthy men. Men who, as oligarchs, controlled entire industries with the aid and comfort of the Ukraine government."[14]

Worse, the entire payment scheme was hidden. "In order for Paul Manafort to receive his consulting fees," Osonye told the Virginia jury, "he set up his own shell companies," so the money went "from the oligarchs' foreign shell companies to Manafort's foreign shell companies." Then, hidden from the IRS, Manafort moved tens of millions of dollars from the oligarchs into real estate in Brooklyn and Manhattan and the Hamptons and Virginia, into cars and clothes and rugs and a myriad of physical manifestations of the proceeds of a scheme to subvert democracy.

—

The second day of the trial, Judge Ellis shut down any further talk of oligarchs. "An oligarchy," Ellis said from the bench, "is just despotic power exercised by a privileged few, autocratic control of any government. And so people involved in that are commonly referred to as oligarchs."[15] Ellis wanted to avoid the use of "the term 'oligarch' to mean that [Manafort] was consorting and being paid by people who are criminals." Ellis asserted, "There will be no evidence about those people, about their activities. The only thing we really will know about them is if they had a lot of money."

The prosecutor, Greg Andres, pushed back: "Ukraine businessmen are referred to as oligarchs by the witnesses. Those are the facts of this case, and that's how they refer to them because—"

"No, they're not the facts of this case," Ellis interjected. "That's an opinion by a witness, and I don't expect witnesses to offer opinions about that. Find another term to use."[16]

While the Manafort jury was deliberating, the president of the United States spoke about the trial to reporters. "I think the whole Manafort trial is very sad, when you look at what's going on there. I think it's a very sad day for our country," Trump said. "He worked for me for a very short period of time. But you know what? He happens to be a very good person. And I think it's very sad what they've done to Paul Manafort."[17]

Manafort was found guilty on eight counts, and the jury deadlocked on ten others, with eleven of the twelve voting to convict.[18] Juror Paula Duncan, a self-described Trump supporter, told Fox News, "I did not want Paul Manafort to be guilty, he was, and no one's above the law."

—

I wasn't in the courtroom when the jury read eight counts of "guilty" against Paul Manafort. I was in another courtroom, 200 miles northeast, when Michael Cohen, his hair graying, his tie yellow, walked through a side door. He nodded with a short, New York bob of the head, to some of the reporters in the room. Thomas McKay, a tall and lanky assistant US attorney from the public corruption bureau of the Southern District, in his early thirties, walked over to Cohen and had him sign legal papers, there in the courtroom. Cohen's own copy of the paperwork looked crumpled. The whole thing had a hasty air.

"You can change your mind right now," Judge William Pauley told Cohen, as he stood before him. Just four days shy of his fifty-second birthday, Cohen faltered. "Yes, your honor," he said. Then the judge listed the charges: tax fraud, making false statements to a bank, campaign finance violations. Eight in all.

Did Cohen understand, Pauley asked, that he faced a maximum sixty-five years of imprisonment? Cohen inhaled, his voice catching a bit as he said, "Yes, sir." And then he admitted his crimes: filling out false tax returns, hiding information from his accountant, knowingly falsifying his financial condition. But all of that was the prologue. "I jotted down some notes so that I can keep my focus," Cohen told the courtroom.

"As to count number seven: on or about the summer of 2016, in coordination with, and at the direction of, a candidate for federal office, I and the CEO of a media company at the request of the candidate worked together to keep an individual with information that would be harmful to the candidate and to the campaign from publicly disclosing this information."

Count eight was similar: "In coordination with, and at the direction of, the same candidate, I arranged to make a payment to a second individual with information that would be harmful to the candidate and to the campaign to keep the individual from disclosing the information. . . . I participated in this conduct, which on my part took place in Manhattan, for the principal purpose of influencing the election."

On that afternoon, Michael Cohen was not only admitting guilt, he was, under oath and penalty of perjury and an even longer sentence, implicating President Donald Trump, "a candidate for federal office," in the crimes. For years, it had been Cohen's job to make sure trouble never found its way to Trump. Now Michael Cohen said: I committed a crime, because the man who is now the president of the United States told me to do it.[19]

That fall, legal developments moved rapidly. In Washington, DC, Manafort, broke, already facing years in jail, pleaded guilty to conspiracy against the United States—including conspiring to launder money—and conspiracy to tamper with a witness. He agreed to cooperate with the Special Counsel. But then—he didn't cooperate. He continued to communicate with the White House. He intentionally lied to prosecutors at least three times. He continued, apparently, to audition for a presidential pardon. And because he stopped talking to prosecutors, they were never able to get him to say, truthfully, what exactly had happened in the black caviar meeting, and to what purpose Konstantin Kilimnik, the man with "ties to Russian intelligence," had put the polling data Manafort had passed him on Michigan, Wisconsin, and Pennsylvania, three states Trump won by the thinnest of margins. Manafort was ultimately sentenced to seven and a half years in prison.

Roger Stone, Manfort's long-ago business partner, a proud dirty trickster since the days of Richard Nixon, was also indicted, for lying to Congress. He'd told a congressional committee plainly that he hadn't retained his communications about WikiLeaks; his emails and phone records plainly showed that he had.[20] The day of his indictment, Stone held his arms out in a wide "V," his fingers also in V for "peace" or "victory," the same gesture Richard Nixon gave when he boarded a military helicopter, departing the White House after resigning.

Stone denied all the charges.

Unexpectedly, Michael Cohen pleaded guilty in November to yet another crime: lying to Congress about Trump Tower Moscow, saying the deal died before the Iowa caucuses (it did not); saying that he had never spoken with the Kremlin (he had); and saying that he barely briefed Trump and his family, when he was in frequent touch with Donald Trump and briefed Don Jr. and Ivanka on at least ten occasions.

At his sentencing hearing, Cohen's lawyer pleaded with the judge. "He came forward to offer evidence against the most powerful person in our country," Guy Petrillo said. "It is important that others in Mr. Cohen's position who provide assistance to this historic inquiry take renewed courage." Cohen, Petrillo said, had fallen victim to Donald Trump's persuasive charm. "Mr. Cohen had a client whose extraordinary power of persuasion got him elected to the highest office in the land," Petrillo read, from a letter written on Cohen's behalf.

In the courtroom that day, I had unexpectedly been placed by the bailiffs in a seat in front of the low wooden barrier that normally separates the parties—the prosecution and the defense, judge and jury—from everyone else. Cohen's daughter Samantha, hobbling in on a sheepskin-lined crutch, chastised the bailiff for the seating arrangements, until he placed her in front of the partition, behind the defense table, about three feet from where I was sitting. As she sat, her father turned and gave her a wide and warm, loving smile, a glimpse into the Michael Cohen that his family saw: not the huckster on the make, the liar, and the bully protector of Donald Trump, just the adoring father of a daughter who had recently finished college.

As Cohen took the podium, tears started to slip down Samantha's cheeks. "I take full responsibility for each act," Cohen said of his crimes. "The personal ones to me and those involving the President of the United States." He continued: "It was my own weakness, and a blind loyalty to this man that led me to choose a path of darkness over light.

"Recently, the President tweeted a statement calling me weak, and he was correct, but for a much different reason than he was implying. It was because time and time again I felt it was my duty to cover up his dirty deeds rather than to listen to my own inner voice and my moral compass." When Cohen said, "there is no sentence that could supersede the suffering that I live with on a daily basis, knowing my actions have brought undeserved pain and shame upon my family," Samantha started to quietly sob.

"I'm sorry," Cohen said, pausing, hearing Samantha's sobs, his own voice choking. Tears were now pouring in rivulets down Samantha's face, sitting alone as her father confessed his crimes. I looked at her, about the age of my own daughter, and reached into my purse for a scuffed-up pack of tissues, leaning across the few feet that separated us to hand them to her. She looked at the crumpled package, took it, wiped her eyes, and looked back at her father.

"I am committed to proving my integrity and ensuring that history will not remember me as the villain of his story,"[21] Cohen said, his voice recovering a little.

After he was sentenced to three years in prison, he turned and walked to the defense table, handing Samantha a brand-new package of fluffy white tissues.

In a tweet, Trump called Cohen "a 'Rat'."

The Cohen and Manafort legal actions were an accounting: an edifying look at what happens when the rule of law is finally brought to bear on individuals who have worked the system as if the laws did not apply. But under Trump, the rule of law itself was under assault: the Special Counsel found ten instances where his office could not exonerate the president of obstruction of justice. "If we had had confidence that the president clearly did not commit a crime, we would have said so," Special Counsel Robert Mueller said in his report, a redacted version of which was released to the public on April 18, 2018.[22] But Mueller determined Justice Department rules did not allow him to indict a sitting president, citing an opinion from 2000 from the department's Office of Legal Counsel. Donald Trump escaped this time, as he had for five decades, with no legal consequences.

"TOTAL EXONERATION," the president said on Twitter.

As with so much else, the reverse was true.

After the release of the Mueller report, the new attorney general, William Barr, pushed a line of argument that seemed positively Putinesque: it was the investigation that was corrupt, not the deeds. Weeks after the Mueller report, Barr named the US Attorney for Connecticut, John H. Durham, to investigate the origins of the Mueller probe. Barr had already signaled his own thinking. "I think spying did occur," he said before a US Senate committee, about the FBI's 2016 counterintelligence investigation into Trump associates. Over the months that followed, Barr personally travelled to Italy and Britain to secure help from those countries' governments in his counter investigation.

On July 24, Special Counsel Mueller testified before Congress. The testimony was a letdown to proponents of the rule of law. Mueller refused to answer basic questions more than two hundred times, and instead repeatedly told lawmakers—and the television-watching public—to read the report. The last chance for Trump to be held accountable for his actions related to Russian interference in the 2016 campaign seemed to be slipping away.

On Twitter, Giuliani said, "Let's now find out how many are guilty of real conspiracy to bring false charges and illegally unseat the President." He was, actually, already working on this. According to a whistleblower report later turned over to Congress,[23] Giuliani was, in late 2018 and early 2019, talking and meeting in Warsaw, New York, and Paris with a series of corrupt current and former Ukrainian prosecutors. While Mueller was wrapping up his investigation, Giuliani, the erstwhile corruption buster, was engaged in a two-pronged effort. His first aim was to gather evidence for a counter-narrative to the Mueller report: that it wasn't Russia that had interfered in the 2016 election to benefit Trump, but rather Russia's enemy Ukraine that had colluded with the Hillary Clinton campaign. This had happened, this line of thinking went, when Trump opponents cooked up a secret "black ledger"—the document showing that Paul Manafort had accepted $12.7 million in off-the-books payments from the political party of Victor

Yanukovych. Bringing this document to light—the work of Ukrainian anti-corruption activists—had precipitated Manafort's departure from the Trump campaign and stimulated the FBI's investigation into Russian interference in the 2016 election that summer.

To promulgate his counter-narrative, Giuliani had gone so far as to contact Manafort in prison, via his lawyer, to gain support for this theory. There was no evidence to support the idea that the black ledger was a fake, and the information it contained had been widely corroborated. But Giuliani plowed forward, pushing for an investigation into whether Ukraine, rather than Russia, had interfered in the 2016 election. Besides exculpating Trump and his campaign, this narrative would allow Russia's leader to argue that there had been no Russian interference—that it was all a hoax. It would allow Russia to argue that its invasion of Ukraine, its years-long war, was legitimate, and that economic sanctions should be lifted.

There was a second promise Giuliani sought from the Ukrainians: an investigation into a potential Trump 2020 rival, the former vice president, Joe Biden. Biden's son, Hunter, had served on the board of a Ukrainian energy company, Burisma, being paid at least fifty thousand dollars a month, while his father was in the White House. According to a theory Giuliani was advancing, Ukrainian prosecutors had dropped a valid investigation of Burisma and Hunter Biden because of untoward interference by the then–vice president.

Giuliani was fed information on both these alleged plots by three widely discredited, high-level Ukrainian prosecutors, all of whom had been accused by anti-corruption activists of abuses including slow-walking authentic corruption investigations and targeting opponents of Ukraine's moneyed class on trumped-up corruption charges. The officials dispute this. But Ukrainian prosecutors in general are notoriously corrupt. As British journalist Oliver Bullough wrote in his book *Moneyland*, "Ukraine had 18,500 prosecutors, who operated like foot soldiers for a mafia don. If they decided to take you to court, the judge did what they asked. With the entire legal system on their side, the insiders' opportunities to make money were limited only by their imagination."[24]

"To say that he was an anti-corruption fighter," Organized Crime and Corruption Reporting Project journalist Aubrey Belford said of one of the prosecutors who fed information to Giuliani, "is kind of like saying that Danny DeVito won the silver medal for rhythmic gymnastics. It's absurd on its face. This guy was fired for being massively corrupt and for protecting corrupt people." The second man Giuliani spoke with had become prosecutor general despite having no legal education.[25] The third had been taped slipping advice to witnesses and tipping off suspects in anti-corruption cases, for which he was roundly criticized by Marie Yovanovitch, then the US ambassador to Ukraine. "Nobody who has been recorded coaching suspects on how to avoid corruption charges can be trusted to prosecute those very same cases," Yovanovitch said. Yovanovitch, a state department employee officially criticizing Ukrainian corruption, became the target of a smear campaign by the President, Giuliani, his associates, and the Ukrainians she'd called out.

The corrupt prosecutors were the men from whom Giuliani kept gathering information, widely discredited though it was, that he passed along to Trump. In April, Ukraine elected a new president, Volodymyr Zelensky, a television actor with a hit show, *Servant of the People*, in which he played a history professor who accidentally becomes president after his rant about corruption goes viral. "Good morning, Mr. President!" a civil servant tells Zelensky's stunned character in the first episode, which aired in 2015. Three years later Zelensky ran for president and won, as leader of a party named after his television show, Servant of the People.

In May 2019, Kurt Volker, then the US special representative for Ukraine negotiations, became concerned about Giuliani's back-channel efforts in Ukraine. He warned Giuliani that one of his sources, the prosecutor Yuriy Lutsenko, was not credible. Giuliani continued his conversations with the Ukrainians. Toward the end of the month—this was now five weeks after the Mueller report had been released—Volker and a group of diplomats met with President Trump. As Volker later testified to Congress, Trump told them that Ukraine was "a corrupt country, full of 'terrible people.' He said they 'tried to take me down.' In the course of that conversation, Trump referenced conversations with Mayor Giuliani," Volker said.[26]

Two months later, on July 18, Volker learned of an unexplained hold on hundreds of millions of dollars in military aid to Ukraine. This aid was intended to support the US ally, still in a hot war with Russian separatists that had begun after the 2014 Russian invasion of Crimea. A day after he learned of the hold, Volker sat down to breakfast with Giuliani and a man named Lev Parnas, a Soviet émigré with a history of US business disputes who, along with an associate, Igor Fruman, had abruptly became major donors to US political causes, coinciding with Trump's presidency. (The two were arrested in October of 2019, one-way tickets to Europe in hand, for allegedly funneling hundreds of thousands of dollars into the US campaign finance system, through a shell company, in order to gain influence for a Ukrainian government official who wanted Yovanovitch fired. They pleaded not guilty.)

During the breakfast with Parnas and Volker, Giuliani raised the topic of the Bidens. The same day, Volker initiated a text message exchange connecting Giuliani with Andrey Yermak, an aide to Zelensky. Giuliani and Yermak soon agreed to meet in Madrid, in early August.

At the White House, a call between the American president and his Ukrainian counterpart was set for July 25. Early that morning, US time, Volker arrived in Kyiv for a long-planned series of diplomatic meetings. Shortly before Trump's call, Volker texted Yermak: "Heard from White House-assuming President Z convinces trump he will investigate/'get to the bottom of what happened' in 2016, we will nail down date for visit to Washington."[27]

Then Trump got on the phone with Zelensky. "I will say that we do a lot for Ukraine. We spend a lot of effort and a lot of time," Trump said during the call, according to a rough transcript later released by the White House. "I wouldn't say that it's reciprocal necessarily."

"Yes, you are absolutely right. Not only 100%, but actually 1000%," Zelensky said, correctly deducing that flattery was the way to Trump's heart. "I would also like to thank you for your great support in the area of defense. We are ready to continue to cooperate for the next steps. specifically we are almost ready to buy more Javelins from the United States for defense purposes."

To this, Trump responded, "I would like you to do us a favor, though."[28]

Trump was saying, I will give you something you want, but you must do something for me. This was the Trump that people close to him knew, the man who repeatedly demanded that those around him compromise themselves for some benefit to him. He had something they badly needed or wanted. To get it, they had to agree to do Trump a favor, corrupt as it might be.

As he had done during his summit with Putin in Helsinki a year earlier, Trump abruptly raised Hillary Clinton's email server in his call with Zelensky. "The server, they say Ukraine has it," Trump said. "I would like to have the Attorney General call you or your people, and I would like you to get to the bottom of it." Trump asked Zelensky to cooperate with Giuliani. Then he added, "There's a lot of talk about Biden's son, that Biden stopped the prosecution and a lot of people want to find out about that so whatever you can do with the Attorney General would be great. Biden went around bragging that he stopped the prosecution so if you can look into it . . . It sounds horrible to me."

At the end of the call, Trump returned to his earlier theme. "I will tell Rudy and Attorney General Barr to call." He added of the former ambassador, Yovanovitch, "She's going to go through some things." A week later, Giuliani, who had previously said he was undertaking his foreign trips as "a private citizen," quietly met in Madrid with Yermak, the Zelensky aide. As described in the whistle-blower report, this rendezvous was "a 'direct follow-up' to the President's call with Mr Zelenskyy about the 'cases' they had discussed."[29] Volker got involved, too, as did two other US diplomats. All three officials were representing the State Department of the United States of America while working with the president's unpaid private attorney. One of them was William "Bill" B. Taylor, who became the acting US ambassador to Ukraine when the White House recalled Yovanovitch. The other diplomat was Gordon Sondland, the US ambassador to the European Union, who had donated more than a million dollars through various LLCs to Trump's inaugural committee and who had become involved in the Ukraine matter, though Ukraine is not part of the European Union. The diplomats began messaging each other, not through official State Department emails or accounts, but on WhatsApp. On August 9, Sondland texted Volker that there was an effort to set up a meeting with Trump and Zelensky, something the Ukrainian president had coveted. "Excellent!!" Volker responded. "How did you sway him? :)"

"Not sure i did," Sondland responded. "I think potus really wants the deliverable." The deliverable, the messages suggest, was an announcement of the investigations. For the month of August, the texts continued, outlining a series of negotiations about a statement Zelensky could make to the press about proceeding with the probes, with the implied understanding among the diplomats that this would unfreeze the military aid and pave the way for a White House meeting. Earlier on August 9, Volker had texted Giuliani and Sondland asking, "Can we all get on the phone to make sure I advise Z correctly as to what he should be saying?" Giuliani said he could take the call, but it would have to be before he left for a fundraiser that afternoon.[30] This fundraiser was in the Hamptons, on Long Island, New York, hosted by Donald Trump Jr. and attended by his father, the president.

The next day, Yermak and Volker texted back and forth. Though Volker later denied he understood that an investigation into the Bidens was being discussed, Yermak told him, specifically, that a press briefing would include "among other things Burisma"—the firm on whose board Hunter Biden had served—"and election meddling." On August 13, Volker texted Sondland a proposed statement that was even more specific: "We intend to initiate and complete a transparent and unbiased investigation of all available facts and episodes," the American diplomat's proposed statement for the Ukrainian president read, "including those involving Burisma and the 2016 elections, which in turn will prevent the recurrence of this problem in the future."[31]

The day before this exchange, unbeknownst to Volker, Sondland, or Taylor, a whistle-blower—an intelligence officer temporarily posted at the White House—filed a complaint with the intelligence community inspector general. The complaint laid out the untoward interference of the president's personal attorney in foreign affairs and his attempts to damage the political chances of the person Giuliani and Trump thought was their most formidable foe: Joe Biden. The complaint centered on the Trump-Zelensky "do me a favor" phone call, and its subsequent cover-up: according to the report, people with knowledge of the call had told the whistle-blower that "senior White House officials had intervened to 'lock down' all records of the phone call, especially the word-for-word transcript of the call that was produced—as is customary—by the White House situation room," and that they had been, "'directed' by White House lawyers to remove the electronic transcript from the computer system in which such transcripts are typically stored."

Volker, Sondland, and Taylor kept communicating. Yermak shared a new draft of Zelensky's anticipated statement, a more general one about corruption fighting that did not make specific reference to Burisma or the 2016 elections. Giuliani rejected this. The Ukrainians wouldn't budge. Volker said in his testimony that he had agreed with the Ukrainians' position, and "further said that I believe it is essential that Ukraine do nothing that could be seen as interfering in 2020 elections. It is bad enough that accusations have been made about 2016—it is essential that Ukraine not be involved in anything relating to 2020." After this, "the idea of putting out a statement was shelved."[32]

At the end of August, *Politico* ran a story about the delayed military aid.[33] "Need to talk with you," Yermak texted Volker, with a link to the story. The day after the story came out, Trump canceled a trip to Poland, where he was to meet with Zelensky. Vice President Mike Pence went instead. There was still no White House visit set up for the newly elected Ukrainian president, the leader of a country long allied with the United States. "Are we now saying that security assistance and WH meeting are conditioned on investigations?" Taylor texted to Sondland. "Call me," Sondland replied. As late as September 8, the diplomats were still trying to arrange what they now called "an interview." Taylor texted Volker and Sondland, "The nightmare is they give the interview and don't get the security assistance. The Russians love it. (And I quit.)" Twelve hours later, past midnight Washington, DC, time, Taylor texted Sondland again. "As I said on the phone, I think it's crazy to withhold security assistance for help with a political campaign," he wrote. After this message, Sondland spoke to Trump. Early the next morning, Sondland texted Taylor in a far more formal tone. "Bill, I believe you are incorrect about President Trump's intentions." Taylor had it wrong, Sondland said: "The president has been crystal clear no quid pro quo's of any kind."[34]

The prosecution of Paul Manafort, stemming from Manafort's long association with Russian and Ukrainian oligarchs and the corrupt politicians they supported, had been tested in federal courts in two jurisdictions. Manafort had been tried and convicted by a jury that included Trump supporters. But Giuliani and Trump were making an all-out effort to discredit the prosecution, by, among other things, declaring the black ledger records a fake. Along the way they deployed the full force of the US government—the White House, the State Department, the US diplomatic corps, the Office of Management and Budget, the Defense Department, and the Justice Department—to achieve a political aim: legitimize Trump's 2016 election and tarnish a 2020 opponent. Up until Trump became president, it had been longstanding US policy, along with that of the European Union, to work to bend Ukraine's political system toward the West's—to end corrupt prosecutions and install the rule of law. Instead, Trump and Giuliani led the effort to bend the United States' system of government toward Ukraine's: toward an oligarchy where prosecutions—especially corruption prosecutions—are used as cudgels to dominate opponents and consolidate one's own power.

In early September, word of the whistle-blower report reached Congress. Representative Adam Schiff, the chair of the House Intelligence Committee, subpoenaed it. The *Washington Post* began to circle, publishing reports saying the whistle-blower report involved an invitation from Trump to a foreign country to involve itself in the 2020 presidential election campaign; then that the country was Ukraine; and then that Trump had pushed Zelensky to investigate the Bidens. The White House initially refused to turn over the rough transcript of the call or allow the whistle-blower report to be released. Democrats in swing districts, the representatives who'd won by the narrowest of margins in 2018, began to come out in favor of an impeachment inquiry. Then, on September 24, 2019, House Speaker Nancy Pelosi did, too. At five in the afternoon, she made a televised announcement: "The actions of the Trump presidency revealed the dishonorable fact of the president's betrayal of his oath of office," Pelosi said in front of a backdrop of American flags. "Therefore, today I am announcing the House of Representatives is moving forward with an official impeachment inquiry." That week, the White House released the rough transcript of the call, and the whistle-blower report itself.

It was still unclear if there would be a consequence for the president. But after five decades, there would be, finally, a public reckoning for Donald J. Trump.

He had more cards to play.

Trump's second year in office, unlike the first, contained few legislative battles. There had been no massive bill like the tax cut bill that served to reshape the social order. But there had been another, less remarked upon but equally far-reaching change. By December 2018, according to a Brookings Institution study, Trump had appointed twenty-nine new appellate judges to the courts just one level down from the US Supreme Court, "the highest number of any president at this point in his tenure."[35] The entire judicial selection process was overseen by the White House Counsel Don McGahn, a member of the Federalist Society, who favored more members of the society on the bench.

Trump inherited one Supreme Court opening after Antonin Scalia died and Senate Majority Leader Mitch McConnell defied the Constitution to keep Scalia's seat empty for the final year of Obama's term. That seat went to Neil Gorsuch. The second opening was created when Anthony Kennedy resigned, after what the *New York Times* called a "quiet campaign to create a Supreme Court opening" by Donald and Ivanka Trump.[36]

Kennedy had been the swing vote who had helped keep *Roe v. Wade* alive. He had written, just days after Trump rode down the escalator to announce his campaign for president, a decision granting same-sex couples the constitutional right to marry. Kennedy was, on many social issues, the opposite of what Don McGahn and the Federalist Society wanted, yet almost immediately upon taking office, Trump showered positive attention on the justice.

As Trump made his way out of the House of Representatives chamber after his first address to Congress, in February 2017, he shook hands with Elena Kagan, then Sonia Sotomayor, then paused to focus his charm and personality on Kennedy, who praised him for his speech.[37] "That's very nice, thank you, coming from you," Trump said, adding "Say hello to your boy."

Kennedy's "boy"—Justin Kennedy—had been a banker on Trump's early Deutsche Bank loan for his Chicago Tower and had been on the team that restructured the debt on the Kushners' 666 Fifth Avenue in 2011.

"Your kids have been very nice to him," Kennedy told the president. "Well," Trump said, "they love him, and they love him in New York. Great guy."

A week before Trump's address to Congress, Ivanka Trump had paid a call on Justice Kennedy at the Supreme Court with her daughter Arabella. As the *New York Times* reported, the President "used the first opening to help create the second one," showering praise on Kennedy at Neil Gorsuch's swearing in. White House officials had already started mentioning two judges as candidates for a possible next opening: both, like Gorsuch, were former Kennedy clerks. One was Brett Kavanaugh, Trump's eventual nominee.

Before the infamous congressional hearings, there was a long and sustained fight against Kavanaugh, who would be in a position not only to rule on laws, but to define the rule of law itself.

A year and a half into the Mueller investigation, a point when the entire effort of bringing the law to bear on Trump and his associates felt as delicate as a glass thread, Kavanaugh came before the Republican-controlled Senate Judiciary Committee, where the Democrats tried, futilely, to get traction on Kavanaugh's views on *Roe v. Wade*, same-sex marriage, affirmative action, voter suppression, voting rights, gerrymandering, and all the threats to democracy that had recently reasserted themselves.

In the middle of all of this, California US Senator Kamala Harris, her face stern, her eyebrows arched in what looked like disgust but was more likely a permanent expression of skepticism, grilled Kavanaugh on something else, a seemingly small thing.

"Judge," she asked, "have you ever discussed Special Counsel Mueller or his investigation with anyone?"

"Well, um," Kavanaugh replied, "It's in the news every day."

"Have you discussed Mueller or his investigation with anyone at the law firm Kasowitz, Benson, and Torres, founded by Marc Kasowitz, President Trump's personal lawyer?"

"I'm not remembering," Kavanaugh said.

"Are you certain you've not had a conversation with anyone at that law firm?"

"Kasowitz, Benson?" he said quizzically. "I'm just trying to think do I know anyone who works at that firm," Kavanaugh said.

This went on for five minutes, and produced no answers.[38]

Within a day, it emerged that Kavanaugh was a friend of Ed McNally, a Kasowitz, Benson partner, from when they had both worked in the George W. Bush administration. Both said they had not discussed the Mueller investigation into Russian interference in the 2016 elections. But Kavanaugh had created a small but indelible tear in the fabric of truth that was perceived to surround Supreme Court justices: the sense that whatever their ideological predilection, they were committed, first and foremost, to a finding of fact. Kavanaugh, in this moment of questioning, displayed the opposite tendency: to ask not, What's the truth? but instead, What's the angle?

After all of this came the part of the Kavanaugh hearings that was watched live by twenty million viewers, at least:[39] when Dr. Christine Blasey Ford came forward to testify, in gripping and credible detail, about the day she said Kavanaugh sexually assaulted her in the upstairs bedroom of a friend's house, holding his hand over her mouth so she couldn't scream, laughing afterwards. Even Fox News thought it was over for Kavanaugh. Then, he came out, in a rage. "This whole two-week effort has been a calculated and orchestrated political hit, fueled with apparent pent-up anger about President Trump and the 2016 election. Fear that has been unfairly stoked about my judicial record. Revenge on behalf of the Clintons, and millions of dollars in money from outside left-wing opposition groups," Kavanagh said, his face contorting in anger, his cheeks pinkening, his mouth pulling down in a sneer.[40]

His world view was Trump's world view: if you weren't for him, you were an enemy; if you disagreed with him, your sole motive was to get power through any means necessary, because that is what Trump or Kavanaugh would have done if they were in their opponent's shoes.

Trump undermined the press by calling it "the enemy of the people" in a way that caused many Americans to doubt that any journalist represented truths, and to believe that all are merely out to pursue a political agenda. He viciously attacked and undermined prosecutors and investigators, and extended the opprobrium to anyone who disagreed with him. He refused to respond to oversight in Congress, as outlined by the Constitution; simply not budging. He arguably violated the Constitution every day he was in office, by taking payments from foreign countries to a company he still profited from.

And now, here was a US Supreme Court justice who would tip the balance of power, with a world view shared with Trump.

After Kavanaugh said the thing about a "political hit," and "revenge," he said something that was arguably true, for everyone. "The consequences will extend long past my nomination. The consequences will be with us for decades."

EPILOGUE

As I write this, in the fall of 2019, the headlines come rolling in, wave after wave on a gray, insistent sea. Thousands of children separated from their parents at the border, 680 migrant meat-packing workers swept up in one of the largest US raids ever on migrant workers, dozens of their children left alone and bereft on the first day of school. Fifty-eight thousand asylum seekers stranded in Mexico in camps vulnerable to violent gangs, the number growing every day. The number of refugees allowed into the US slashed drastically, to 18,000, the lowest number in forty years. Even as Trump presided over these actions, for two decades his company employed undocumented workers to build the specialty fountains at his golf courses; many more worked in his resorts, personally serving him Diet Cokes with the paper on his straw folded just so. The White House announced it would be hosting the 2020 G7 summit at Trump's golf resort in Doral, Florida. His acting chief of staff said: "It's almost like they built this facility to host this type of event." The president's lawyers went to court against the Manhattan DA to argue a sitting president cannot even be investigated. Neither can his business associates, nor his company, for anything the president has ever done, even prior to his presidency. The Justice Department weighed in on the side of

Trump's lawyers. A federal judge ruled that Trump's arguments were "repugnant to the nation's governmental structure and constitutional values." Trump appealed. *La loi, c'est lui.*

In July 2019, Vice President Mike Pence was accompanied by a small group of reporters to a border detention facility in McAllen, Texas. As the *Washington Post*'s Josh Dawsey wrote it up: "almost 400 men were in caged fences with no cots. The stench was horrendous. The cages were so crowded that it would have been impossible for all of the men to lie on the concrete. There were 384 single men in the portal who allegedly crossed the border illegally. There were no mats or pillows—some of the men were sleeping on concrete. When the men saw the press arrive, they began shouting and wanted to tell us they'd been in there 40 days or longer. The men said they were hungry and wanted to brush their teeth. It was sweltering hot. Agents were guarding the cages wearing face masks."[1] Afterwards, Pence said families in border detention centers told him they were "well cared for," and that reports to the contrary were "harsh rhetoric."

At the end of the nineteenth century, the Jewish writer and activist Emma Lazarus wrote the poem "The New Colossus" to raise funds for the construction of the pedestal for the Statue of Liberty in New York Harbor. The poem begins: "Not like the brazen giant of Greek fame, / With conquering limbs astride from land to land; / Here at our sea-washed, sunset gates shall stand / A mighty woman with a torch, whose flame / Is the imprisoned lightning, and her name / Mother of Exiles." Lazarus's ideas about exiles and immigration were contested before she wrote the poem, and after. Yet the United States of America still likes to think of itself as a nation of immigrants, though for some this means immigrants are welcomed so long as they arrive in ways that are in accordance with an ever-varying set of laws. Even so, in late summer of 2019, the Trump administration announced it would penalize *legal* immigrants who availed themselves of government services. Ken Cuccinelli, the acting head of Citizenship and Immigration Services, proclaimed that this policy was entirely consistent with "a hundred and forty-year old tradition in this country, legally."

"Would you also agree," Cuccinelli was asked by NPR's Rachel Martin, "that Emma Lazarus's words etched on the Statue of Liberty—'give me your tired, your poor'—are also part of the American ethos?" Cuccinelli responded: "They certainly are: give me your tired and your poor who can stand on their own two feet and who will not become a public charge."[2] He later said Emma Lazarus was thinking about immigrants from Europe, only.

In El Paso, Texas, the same month Cuccinelli was saying these things, a man killed twenty-two people in a Walmart, after posting a manifesto that referred to an "Hispanic invasion of Texas," and that articulated a fear of "replacement," referring to a white supremacist theory of "great replacement." In a speech, President Trump claimed he condemned acts of racism. Then his campaign said it would continue to speak of "an invasion" in its Facebook ads, a locution it had employed two thousand times in 2019 alone, according to an analysis by the *New York Times*.[3] El Paso's shooting recalled one in Pittsburgh, in the fall of 2018, where, the murderer said he "wanted all Jews to die," killing eleven in a spray of gunfire during Saturday morning Shabbat services at the Tree of Life synagogue, the deadliest attack ever against Jews on US soil. This in turn came after the rally in the summer of 2017, in Charlottesville, Virginia, where neo-Nazis marched to the chant, "Jews will not replace us"; where a white supremacist man deliberately rammed his car into the crowd, murdering a woman; after which President Trump said at a press conference that there were "very fine people on both sides."

In 1982, Rae Kushner had begun to tell her story. "Certain things should not be like in this country," she said, her English inflected with Yiddish cadences. "Nazis are going with the swastikas in front of the White House, and they're going around free; and this scares us, this is very painful."[4] Telling her story was an obligation, as she saw it, but it was also prophylactic: by recording the history, by making sure the world did not forget, Rae and other Holocaust survivors could erect the protective shield of truth; they could press modern human beings to bear in mind their terrible history as they built a more enlightened future.

In the summer of 2019, Rae's grandson Jared Kushner was asked to discuss his grandparents' legacy by journalist Jonathan Swan, for Axios on HBO. "My grandparents came here as refugees and they were able to build a great life for themselves. You know my father worked hard and was able to be successful," Jared Kushner said.

"How has that experience changed the way you think about things?" Swan asked. "Have they shared what it was like being a refugee?"

"It was more they would share what it was like being persecuted," Kushner responded. "I mean my grandparents survived the Nazis." He added, "Seventy years later their grandson's working in the White House."

"It's true," Swan said, before pressing. "The flip side is, that picture is also a reminder of, you know, you guys have dramatically reduced the number of refugees intake into this country. I think the lowest level in forty years."

Jared Kushner deflected: "I think right now you've got sixty-five million refugees in the world. You can't have all of them come into your country—"

"I know," Swan interjected, "but what's the rationale for cutting so dramatically?"

"It doesn't make a difference one way or the other," Kushner answered.

Swan disagreed. "Well, it does. It means people are either living here or they're not."

"Yeah," Kushner said. "But in the scheme of the magnitude of the problem we have, I think that we're doing our best to try to make as much impact to allow refugees to be able go back to their places and conflicts in places like Syria and find ways to make sure that you're funding these situations so that the people who are immediately becoming refugees can have as much care as possible. But we have a lot of tragedies all over the world and that, again is one of the reasons why as Americans we're very lucky to be where we are."[5]

Jared Kushner's wife, Ivanka Trump, daughter, granddaughter, and great-granddaughter of immigrants, has faced her own questions on US immigration policy. What was her low point in the White House, she was asked by journalist Mike Allen at a Washington, DC, forum in the summer of 2018. Was family separation a low point? Yes, she acknowledged, it was. "I am very vehemently against family separation and the separation of parents and children." But she added. "I think immigration is incredibly complex as a topic, illegal immigration is incredibly complicated. I am a daughter of an immigrant, my mother grew up in Communist Czech Republic, but we are a country of laws. So, you know, she came to this country legally and we have to be very careful about incentivizing behavior that puts children at risk of being trafficked, at risk of entering this country with coyotes or making an incredibly dangerous journey alone. So, it is—these are not easy issues, these are incredibly difficult issues and like the rest of the country, I experienced them in a very emotional way."[6]

Ivanka Trump invoked a frequent trope used by those who defend President Trump on immigration: her own mother "came to this country legally"—had played by the rules. But Ivanka Trump's husband's grandparents, the great grandparents of her own three children, had not played by the rules. "We went from border to border, from border to border, from Austria, to Hungary—" Rae said in 1996. "Nobody wanted to open the doors for us."

"How did you get across the border into Italy?" she was asked by an interviewer from the USC Shoah Foundation.

"From—the Israelis helped us to cross the borders. They organized that," Rae said.

"Did you have to sneak across?" she was asked.

"Sneak across, they showed us the way, they had people—they knew what to do. They took us around the border." That's how she and her husband and father and sister got to the displaced persons' camp in Italy. "Oy yoy yoy we were three and a half years in Italy," Rae said. They were stuck in the limbo so many refugees face; no place to go back to, no place to move on to. They were told: "we cannot take you to Israel, we cannot go to Palestine, you must sit here until you gonna get the visas." Twenty people to a room, some with young babies, waiting. "Nobody wanted to open the borders for us," Rae said.

But, in 1996, Rae was still keeping a secret about her immigration to the United States of America.

"What is your name?" her interlocutor asked her, at the outset of her interview.

"My name is Rae Kushner," Rae answered.

"And what was your maiden name?"

"My maiden name was Kushner."

"Your maiden name and your married name are the same names?" her interviewer asked, sounding baffled.

"Yeah," Rae answered. "We were relatives."[7]

This was a misdirection. Rae's husband's name was Yossel Berkowitz, a name erased before her family crossed the border into the United States, where the immigration law in 1949 pushed Rae to identify herself as her own father's daughter-in-law, and for her husband to be her own father's son. This breaking of the rules is referred to in the self-written family history, *The Miracle of Life*. "Because sons and fathers were given priority to get visas, Yossel assumed his wife's maiden name being that he traveled with his father-in-law."[8] The Berkowitz family became the Kushner family: Joe was not Joe Berkowitz, Charlie was not Charlie Berkowitz, Jared was not Jared Berkowitz. In 1949, right before sailing to the United States, the matrimonial name became the patrimonial name.

The family's ruse continued when they docked in New York, where aid workers discovered that the Kushners' named sponsor disavowed any knowledge of them. Joe told the aid workers Rae's father was his father, her sister was his sister. The aid workers recorded "Germany" as their country of origin, at a time when immigrants from Poland were subject to stricter rules. The Kushners, with two dollars to their name, were given shelter and food, helped to find jobs and housing by the Hebrew Immigrant Aid Society, HIAS. They were, in Emma Lazarus's words, "Your tired, your poor, / Your huddled masses yearning to breathe free, / The wretched refuse of your teeming shore." In New York Harbor, the Statue of Liberty spoke directly to them: "Send these, the homeless, tempest-tost to me, / I lift my lamp beside the golden door!"

The Kushners uttered untruths to enter America's golden door. These were deemed necessary for survival, necessary to confront a bureaucratic immigration system in a still hostile-to-Jews-and-foreigners nation. The Kushners did what they needed to do so their family could live, and thrive and grow, like millions of refugees, before and after, so their grandson would have every opportunity, including to work as a senior White House advisor for President Donald J. Trump, who erected barriers and policies so that what Jared Kushner's grandparents could do, others could not.

It is no coincidence that Donald J. Trump, the head of a family business who brought that business model to the White House and the executive branch of the government of the United States of America, is undoing decades of refugee and asylum and immigration laws at the same time he is tilting the country towards oligarchy. These are two heads of a Hydra, not discrete, unrelated phenomena. Oligarchy means government by the few, and privileging a few necessarily means viewing concentric rings of people outside this circle of privilege as "superfluous," a term coined by the political scientist Hannah Arendt.

Tilting the country towards oligarchy requires confusing—as Trump did in his first formal press conference as president-elect—"company" and "country," making no distinction between the national interest and what he sees as his broader "family" interest. Trump's family is, necessarily, his own family: his wife and children and their spouses and their children. "Family" also includes those officials and employees from whom he demands obsequious loyalty, though unlike his actual family, these people can move in and out of favor at Trump's whim. This broader group also includes the very rich, who can prove their own loyalty through incessant financial favors: campaign donations, club memberships, hotel stays, condo purchases. His own attorney general booked a ballroom at a Trump hotel for a holiday party, for the price of thirty thousand dollars.

The entire apparatus of government, the president argues almost every day, should serve his interests: intelligence and national security officials must see the world his way, the military's generals are his generals, the treasury secretary's job is to protect him from having his personal tax forms revealed. As he sees it, the attorney general should be his lawyer, his Roy Cohn; the Justice Department should target businesses he doesn't like and favor those he does like. The judges Trump appoints are to rule in his favor. The officials he names are to serve the needs of rich and influential Americans who see the entire apparatus of state as an impediment to making money as rapidly as they'd like to, an impediment to be lifted, no matter who might be poisoned, killed, or stolen from along the way. The Federal Bureau of Investigation and other law enforcement agencies' most important function should be to investigate and indict and otherwise thwart his enemies, and his family's enemies, because for him there is no distinction between his family business and the government itself.

When officials block him, he fires them; when they stand up to him, he goes around them; when those outside his sphere of influence oppose him, he discredits, or sues them, or threatens to sue them, or deploys his enormous social media audience against them. And because the Justice Department has determined it cannot indict a sitting president, there are no consequences for Trump; he can do all this with relative impunity. Trump is constantly promoting the strands of oligarchy in his current government, a government where the rules that apply are those that Trump decides will apply; a government racing towards a world where it's impossible to play by the rules, because the rules exist only according to Trump's whim.

The flip side of such a system, where the president's family and his wealthy or influential friends who can keep him in power set rules only for themselves, is that some human beings are seen as "superfluous." This group begins with those who are black and brown, or Muslim, or women, or queer, but expands daily under Trump to encompass political enemies, journalists, Puerto Ricans, Jews who he believes are insufficiently loyal to Israel, even some members of Congress. For "superfluous" people, the right to belong to a system of laws to which they can appeal—what Hannah Arendt called "the right to have rights"—is diminishing. Asylum seekers and refugees are given narrower and narrower access to judges who can hear their cases, and the Justice Department has seen to it those judges almost always rule against immigrants. "Send them back," has become a new chant at Trump rallies, referring to members of Congress who are black, or brown. Gerrymandering, restricting access to polling sites, scrubbing voter rolls, and outright denial of suffrage is increasingly common.

Many critics have rightly pointed out that American representative democracy never extended to everyone: it was, dating back to the Declaration of Independence, something that was reserved for the privileged, for men, and above all, for whites. Expanding that privilege has been the work of more than two centuries, but, as President Barack Obama said after the election of Donald Trump, "the path that this country has taken has never been a straight line. We zig and zag and sometimes we move in ways that some people think is forward and others think is moving back." American government has always been imperfect; it has committed acts of brutality and segregation and outright theft from black, brown, and indigenous people and marginalized large portions of its population. But the fact that it has been ever thus does not excuse the Trump administration for molding government so that more and more people experience this marginalization, this loss of the right to have rights.

In 1951, when she published *The Origins of Totalitarianism*, Hannah Arendt identified the problem of statelessness, "the newest mass phenomenon in contemporary history, and the existence of an ever-growing new people comprised of stateless persons, the most symptomatic group in contemporary politics."[9] The problem has set and grown in the nearly sixty years that have passed since 1951; Trump's response is to deploy the language of "invasion." This not only inflames his supporters, it displaces blame for Trump's not actually alleviating the problems of the working class, of his not making health insurance or education more affordable, of his not protecting against abuse or theft by banks or credit card agencies, of his not ameliorating inequality. The constant stream of news about refugees, new policies on migration, tweets about raids on migrants without proper paperwork, even the negative reaction itself to Trump's policies and announcements serves to build anti-immigrant fervor, deflecting attention from the unraveling of democratic institutions and norms.

The language of invasion serves a similar function as the repeated surfacing of conspiracy theories, the incessant battle cries of "fake news" and "alternative facts," the systematic dismantling of government systems that record history and facts and scientific observations themselves. Because Trump interprets all negative press through the lens of "hit jobs," his view is that all critiques are subjective, not fact-based. Trump's lies, delivered blatantly, don't just cover up the truth, they undermine the notion that truth can exist, suggesting that all scholarship, history, and journalism is merely opinion.

In 1967, Arendt wrote an essay for the *New Yorker* called "Truth and Politics" that articulated where such mendacity could lead. "The result of a consistent and total substitution of lies for factual truth is not that the lies will now be accepted as truth, and the truth be defamed as lies, but that the sense by which we take our bearings in the real world—and the category of truth vs. falsehood is among the mental means to this end—is being destroyed."[10]

"People should know what happened to us," Rae Kushner said in 1996. "If we are not going to tell now, in twenty years, I don't know who's going be to tell. And now we have still the strength and the power to do this, and to warn the rest of the world to be careful: who is coming up on top of your government?" Rae pushed for remembering, for the past as a caution for the future, for building an edifice of fact and truth that would stand as a levee against the rising tide of relativism that was for her the vanguard of a murderous regime. Jared Kushner has interpreted Rae's testimonies to buttress an ideology that suggests the way to beat enemies is to bar them, suppress them, kill them, and build walls to keep them out. Above all, it means propping up his father-in-law, whose very presidency draws strength from the forces Rae warned against.

"I have a different takeaway from my Grandparents' experience in the war," Jared's first cousin, Marc Kushner, wrote on Facebook during the 2016 campaign, after Jared had defended his father-in-law against charges of racism and anti-semitism by invoking their grandparents' experiences during the Holocaust. Marc Kushner wrote: "It is our responsibility as the next generation to speak up against hate. Antisemitism or otherwise." Marc's sister Melissa founded an organization, Yamba Malawi, that endeavors to break the cycle of poverty for children in Malawi. "I will not allow hate to beget hate, but rather use hate to embolden kindness and love," Melissa posted on Facebook the day of the Tree of Life massacre, which coincided with Marc's daughter's birth.

Marc Kushner is an architect and a proselytizer for architecture; he has given a TED talk and written a book, where he articulates architecture as a collective imagining of a common future, where beautiful and functional buildings are a physical manifestation of what binds humans together. Marc Kushner talks about a building his firm designed in The Pines, a gay community on Fire Island, replacing a beloved dance hall that had burnt to the ground. The replacement couldn't be just a reconstruction, which would have been a reminder of the loss. Instead, he argued, the new building had to be a more beautiful structure than the one that had been reduced to ashes, and to build such an edifice required community re-imagining of the new space that would in itself serve as foundation for new collective memories.[11] It was a small example of a community coming together to create a public space, but it represented a broader lesson. The lesson that Marc and Melissa Kushner took from their grandparents is that public shared spaces and a sense of community are not only possible; they are a necessary precondition for a human, and humane, future.

Rae Kushner's own life was a testimony to resilience and resistance, playing out against what Arendt called "a background of both reckless optimism and reckless despair."[12] Rae would not succumb, or fade, or give up, even in some of the worst conditions imaginable to a human being. Escape is a sign of hope, a signal that all is not lost, a belief made real that there is a promised land, on earth, that is reachable through human action.

The Origins of Totalitarianism did not merely document, in excruciating detail, a terrifying low point of human history. In the writing, there's a query—where were the moments people could have acted differently? *Origins,* as my father, the philosopher Richard J. Bernstein, wrote, is "Not History, but Politics." Arendt "refused to become a prophet of doom."[13] Her book itself stands as a testament to the ever-present possibility of better outcomes.

Over the years, I have interviewed another Kushner, not related in any way that I know to the descendants of Rae and Joe: the author and playwright Tony Kushner, most famous for his play *Angels in America.* I've spoken to him at points in history when the tides of disenfranchisement and destruction of community have seemed particularly high. "You have to have hope," he told me the first time we spoke, in 1995. Over the next decades, as we spoke periodically, I would ask him: Do you still have hope?

"Well," he told me in 2011, "I think I may have said it first to you, that I think that hope is a moral obligation and I've been saying that for a long time now. I don't think that hope is just a feeling state. I think that hope is a choice that you make. It's not a choice to deny reality, but it's a choice to use your intelligence to examine the world in front of you and the obstacles to progress and to try to identify places from whence progress can reasonably be anticipated and to try to put your efforts into making those—I mean that, to me, is what hope is, it's an activity, it's an action in the world. Just as I think despair is, I think that both take effort. And I remain optimistic, I think there is still work to do."[14]

I'm often asked, What drives you to do what you do, to document the crashing of norms and laws and the mixing of family and business in the Trump administration? What difference will it make? I'm often asked. For a long time, this was a difficult question to answer.

But then I realized something: the act of telling the story is itself an action, a chance, a tilt toward the future. I still believe in truth, and facts. I still believe that the telling reinforces those things. I believe that in the telling, there is hope.

ACKNOWLEDGMENTS

For their patience and love, I thank, first, my wife, Liz Schalet, and my children Maya, and Jonah, who fuel my sense of adventure and curiosity, and keep me laughing, and hoping.

My parents, Carol L. and Richard J. Bernstein, who taught me to love books and writing and the joy of learning new things every day.

My editor, Tom Mayer, who came to me months after Trump was elected to ask me to think about writing this book, and who told me "You know this world. You can do this." And who then helped me to think this book through at every single step, in ways that made it much more sweeping and far better than it otherwise would have been.

My agent, Alia Hanna Habib, who unfailingly has my back, while also being as lovely as can be and as tough as nails, two qualities I especially prize.

All of the more than two hundred people who spoke to me for this book, who gave generously of their time, who answered questions, often despite personal risk.

Friends of mine, busy with their own work, who never failed to take the time to meet and discuss ideas and book-writing itself: Adam Davidson, Margaret Hempel, Masha Gessen, Ellen Lippmann, Matt Katz, Ilya Marritz, Ed Pilkington, Lisa B. Segal, Linda Villarosa, and Jacqueline

Woodson, you helped me over many, many hurdles. I especially thank David Rohde, in so many ways the guardian angel of this book.

My colleagues at WNYC and ProPublica on the *Trump, Inc.* project who have dug with me and thought things through with me and whose collaboration has made us all better and more knowledgeable: along with my brilliant cohost Ilya Marritz, I am deeply indebted to Meg Cramer and Eric Umansky, Jesse Eisinger, Peter Elkind, Justin Elliot, Stephen Engelberg, Robin Fields, Charlie Herman, Anjali Kamat, Derek Kravitz, Ian MacDougal, Alex MacGillis, Bill Moss, Jake Pearson, Daniela Porat, Jim Schachter, Katherine Sullivan, Anjali Tsui, Nick Varchavar, Heather Vogell, Alice Wilder, Katie Zavakski, Emily Botein, Jared Paul, and Marilyn Thompson. And to Hannis Brown, whose music makes it all make sense.

I am blessed to have so many beloved and talented colleagues at WNYC, and I thank all of you for your amazing work. I especially thank my editors: Karen Frillmann, John Keefe, Nancy Solomon, Charlie Herman, David Lewis, and Jim Schachter, as well as WNYC's extraordinary archivist, Andy Lanset and the talented data news journalist Jenny Ye. And the colleagues who inspired me from the moment I first sat in front of a WNYC microphone: Amy Eddings, Beth Fertig, Marianne McCune, Kaari Pitkin, Patricia Willens, Soterios Johnson, Richard Hake, Brian Lehrer, and Brooke Gladstone. And those I have had the privilege of editing, sometimes often, sometimes just once, I have learned so much from you: Kat Aaron, Bridget Bergin, Collin Campbell, Ailsa Chang, Lisa Chow, Alex Goldmark, Sarah Gonzalez, Jessica Gould, Kathleen Horan, Kate Hinds, Yasmeen Khan, Jim O'Grady, Fred Mogul, Elaine Rivera, Cindy Rodriguez, Anna Sale, Matthew Schuerman, Arun Venugopal, and Manoush Zamorodi.

I offer many, many thanks to the broader group of journalists who have helped us on the *Trump, Inc.* reporting project: Daniel Alarcon and the team at Radio Ambulante, Dan Alexander, Ailsa Chang, Susanne Craig, Adam Davidson, David Enrich, David Fahrenthold, Ronan Farrow, Michael Finnegan, Franklin Foer, Nick Fountain, Alex Goldmark, Esther Kaplan, John Kelly, David Kocieniewski, Anita

Kumar, Caleb Melby, Michael Rothfield, Zoe Tillman, Jeffrey Toobin, and Brian Urstadt.

There were a host of journalists, writers, historians, and scholars who helped me think through what became this book, but I can't overstate the assistance given to me by long-time *New York Times* real estate journalist Charles V. Bagli, who generously shared his time, his papers, and his ideas.

Thank you as well to Bill Bastone, Gwenda Blair, Nina Burleigh, Lisa Chase, Sarah Chayes, Kathleen Clarke, Joe Conason, Anthony Cormier, Joe Donohue, Jesse Drucker, Sarah Ellison, Zach Everson, Emily Jane Fox, Luke Harding, James Hughes, Dawn Garcia and the staff of the JSK Fellowship at Stanford, Mary Ann Giordano, Dan Golden, Terry Golway, Justine Gubar, Jason Leopold, Peter Kaplan, Lisa Kron, Tony Kushner, Joshua Margolin, Robert Maguire, Tom McGevern, Tom Moran, Tim Nostrand, Tim O'Brien, Azi Paybarah, Jeff Pillets, Michael Powell, Andrew Rice, Tom Robbins, William Rashbaum, Richard Rothstein, Dominic Rushe, Mark Schoofs, Tony Schwartz, Gabriel Sherman, Ted Sherman, Deborah Solomon, Zephyr Teachout, and Rebecca Traister.

I am grateful to Benjamin Wright and the entire staff of the Wayne Barrett Papers at the Dolph Briscoe Center for American History at the University of Texas, Austin; the staff of Holocaust Research Center at Kean University; the USC Shoah Foundation; the Hedi Steinberg Library at Yeshiva University; the New York University Furman Center; the Municipal Archives of the City of New York; and the Center for Responsive Politics.

I am deeply indebted to the journalists and researchers who helped me work on this book: to Decca Muldowney for unearthing New Jersey land records from their original microfilm, and to Alice Wilder for locating tape no one else could find. I especially want to thank Fergus McIntosh, sine qua non, whose natural investigative instincts, extraordinary journalism skills, and inexhaustible patience guided the checking of every fact in this book. Needless to say, any errors that remain are my own.

I would also like to thank Robert Caro and Jane Mayer for inspiring me to read every page of everything and run down every source I possibly could. Both were a constant yardstick against which to measure my own work.

And A. M. Homes, who said to me, some summers ago, why don't you write a book? Before telling me: *I mean it,* thereby setting off a chain of events that led to the book in your hands.

And Wayne Barrett, the first biographer of Trump, who set the standard. He died on January 19, 2017, leaving much unfinished work for me to do. I miss you, Wayne.

Brooklyn, New York, Autumn 2019

NOTE ON SOURCES

Twenty-five years ago, after a six-year stint working in New York government where I learned up-close how politics works, I began writing about politics and political corruption for the *New York Observer.* This book is rooted in the reporting that I embarked on in 1994 for the *Observer* and for WNYC; many of the same New York and New Jersey campaign contributors, real estate owners, financiers, lobbyists, and politicians that I covered are still working today, on a much larger stage. The thousands of people I've interviewed and countless records I've combed through in a quarter century's coverage of money, power, and influence have served as an invaluable guide for this book.

In the past three years, I have read over one hundred thousand pages of documents—court cases, regulatory filings, land records, mortgage documents, government leases, email chains, campaign filings, tax filings, bank records, personal testimonies—more than a hundred books, and thousands and thousands of news articles. I have listened to weeks of hearings and testimony, mined audio archives, reviewed years' worth of social media accounts, and watched scores of hours of videotapes, movies, and documentaries—including dozens of episodes of *The Apprentice.* I have consulted with top journalists, scholars, and historians who have shared documents, ideas, and frameworks of understanding, all of which have made my own reporting more complete.

One challenge of writing a story about individuals hailing from Eastern Europe, Russia, and the former Soviet Union is the transliteration of proper names. Wherever possible I have followed the style of papers of record, official reports, Yad Vashem, and the United States Holocaust Memorial Museum. For reasons of simplicity and consistency I have chosen to use the Russian spelling of the town where Rae Kushner was born: Novogrudok. I have also chosen the most common spelling of the town where Yossel Berkowitz was raised: Korelitz.

Since November of 2016, writing and reporting about the Trump and Kushner families and their family businesses has presented a unique set of challenges. Their companies are private and closely held, with financial deals that stretch back decades and around the globe. Many of their holdings are in limited liability companies, or LLCs, whose secrecy US law protects. Both family businesses have demonstrated an aversion to disclosure of any kind, and both families have taken extraordinary steps to keep secrets and thwart perceived opponents.

Some of the ways they have done this have been obvious: President Trump uttered over twelve thousand lies and misrepresentations in his first thirty-two months in office, as documented by the *Washington Post*, the number accelerating from about five a day at the outset of his administration to roughly twenty a day by the summer of 2019. Lying and shading the truth have long gone hand in hand with American politics; what's different now is that President Trump and his administration have no shame about lying when everyone knows they are lying; sometimes, even their denials or responses to questions can be so blatantly untrue that printing them without comment does a disservice to the truth.

President Donald J. Trump has issued near-daily attacks on foes, real and perceived, on Twitter. He has a decades-long history of pursuing opponents through the courts that extends through his presidency. He's displayed an obvious propensity to use all tools available to him, including the use of his own Justice Department, to go after his perceived enemies. He plays favorites, and everyone knows it and almost everyone is afraid to speak on the record. They rightly fear for their reputations, their livelihoods, their jobs, their ability to freely navigate the world. Most of the more than two hundred people I interviewed for this book, scores of whom had firsthand knowledge of the events described in these pages, including many who consider themselves on good terms with the families, did not wish to be identified in any way.

For this reason, though my endnotes are copious, not everything in this book is annotated or attributed, and not all quotes identify the speaker. In those cases, I have vetted firsthand accounts with multiple sources, and have, wherever possible, relied on documents to corroborate these accounts.

None of the main subjects of this book—neither Donald nor Ivanka Trump, nor Charles nor Jared Kushner—agreed to be interviewed. I sent each of them scores of questions. Donald Trump and Ivanka Trump did not respond. Through his attorney, Charles Kushner answered some of the questions; his answers are reflected in these pages. Jared Kushner, through a White House spokesman, addressed some factual queries but otherwise did not answer my questions.

Some of the people who have associated with the Trumps or Kushners over the years have their own criminal or legal histories; some of them have been convicted of lying. I have taken extra care in those cases to vet their accounts, but have not shied away from relying on their statements when they are corroborated. No account of the history of the Trumps and the Kushners could be comprehensive without them.

My task has been made more difficult by the Trumps' and Kushners' extensive use of broad nondisclosure agreements that prohibit almost everyone who has worked with them from saying anything about their experiences: among those required to sign them were people who worked for the Trump Organization, for *The Apprentice*, for Ivanka Trump's business, for the Kushner family business, for Donald Trump's campaign, and even for the White House. Ex–White House employees have been given lucrative jobs in the Trump campaign, which extend the obligation to keep silent. Nondisclosure agreements have made writing this history all the more challenging.

Donald Trump had other, well-documented ways of trying to keep people silent; those included hush money payments and using the *National Enquirer* to "catch and kill" stories about alleged improprieties. As shown in these pages, he has tried to compromise and threatened to sue or actually sued journalists; his suit against journalist Tim O'Brien lasted five years.

The Trump White House has been an especially secretive White House: breaking with decades of tradition, Trump refused to release his tax returns. The administration has repulsed congressional subpoenas, it has asserted executive privilege to keep witnesses from testifying; the Trumps have sued bankers and accountants to hinder them from releasing information to congressional investigators. He has sued the Manhattan DA to prevenet a grand jury from reviewing his taxes. Trump has gone to court trying to prevent litigants from learning about payments from foreign governments; he has gone so far as to order the creation of false memos that would preserve an untrue historical record.

Dark money accounts support the Trump campaign; his inaugural committee has not explained how it spent more than a third of its funds; its deputy chairman, Rick Gates, tried to keep money off the books altogether by having donors pay vendors directly. Trump's former campaign chairman, Paul Manafort, is in prison for fraud and conspiracy against the United States; Trump's personal attorney, Michael Cohen, is in prison for fraud, violating campaign finance laws, and lying to Congress; a campaign advisor, George Papadopoulos, served a sentence for lying to the FBI; Trump's deputy campaign manager, Gates, and national security advisor, Michael Flynn, pleaded guilty to the same crime.

The White House no longer releases visitor logs; it doesn't maintain records for visitors at the private clubs like Mar-a-Lago and the Trump National Golf Club at Bedminster that have operated as weekend

White Houses. The Trump administration has decimated the ranks of government scientists and gutted databases.

The president's disclosure forms list more than two hundred assets, most of them LLCs, but don't require that he file information about partners, investors, or debtors. Jared Kushner amended his initial disclosure form thirty-nine times; his filings and Ivanka Trump's filings list hundreds of limited liability companies but do not require information about partners or investors. In a court dispute in 2017, Kushner Companies went to court to keep the members of just one of its limited liability companies secret.

There has been one more challenge: writing a history as it unfolds before me. New news keeps breaking, new facts come to life that explain old ones, and new information emerges that expands and fills out our body of knowledge. I have done my best to account for all of this and to present this volume in a timely fashion. Given the nature of the times, I did not allow the perfect to be the enemy of the good. For this, I beg the reader's indulgence.

Brooklyn, New York, Autumn 2019

NOTES

EPIGRAPH

1. Interview with Charles V. Bagli, long-time *New York Times* real estate reporter, 2017.

PROLOGUE: THE WEDDING

1. For descriptions of the wedding I have relied on interviews with dozens of attendees, cross-checked against a score of contemporaneous and subsequent press reports and accounts in Emily Jane Fox, *Born Trump: Inside America's First Family* (New York: HarperCollins, 2018) and Nina Burleigh, *Golden Handcuffs: The Secret History of Trump's Women* (New York: Gallery Books, 2018).
2. Daniel Golden, *The Price of Admission: How America's Ruling Class Buys Its Way into Elite Colleges—and Who Gets Left Outside the Gates* (New York: Three Rivers Press, 2007).
3. Peter W. Kaplan, introduction to *The Kingdom of New York: Knights, Knaves, Billionaires, and Beauties in the City of Big Shots*, by *The New York Observer* (New York: HarperCollins, 2009), 5.
4. "Republican Candidates Debate in Cleveland, Ohio (August 6, 2015)," *The American Presidency Project*, https://www.presidency.ucsb.edu/documents/republican-candidates-debate-cleveland-ohio.

INTRODUCTION

1. Ilya Marritz and Andrea Bernstein, "Paul Manafort's Puzzling New York Real Estate Purchases," WNYC News, March 28, 2017, https://www.wnyc.org/story/paul-manaforts-puzzling-new-york-real-estate-purchases/.
2. US Bureau of the Census, "Chapter A. Wealth and Income (Series A 1–207)," in *Historical Statistics of the United States, 1789–1945* (Washington, DC: US Government Printing Office, 1949), https://www2.census.gov/library/publications/1949/compendia/hist_stats_1789-1945/hist_stats_1789–1945-chA.pdf.
3. Rick Ewig, "The Railroad and the Frontier West," *Organization of American His-*

torians Magazine of History 3, no. 2 (Spring 1998): 9–10, https://academic.oup.com/maghis/article-abstract/3/2/9/1029757?redirectedFrom=fulltext.

4. *American Experience*, season 30, episode 3, "The Gilded Age," directed by Sarah Colt, aired February 6, 2018, on PBS, https://www.pbs.org/wgbh/americanexperience/films/gilded-age/.
5. Esther Crain, *The Gilded Age in New York, 1870–1910* (New York: Black Dog & Leventhal Publishers, 2016), 69.
6. Jacob Riis, *How the Other Half Lives: Studies Among the Tenements of New York* (New York: Scribner, 1890); History.com Editors, "Tenements," *History.com*, April 22, 2010, https://www.history.com/topics/immigration/tenements.
7. Thomas Piketty, *Capital in the Twenty-First Century* (Cambridge, MA: The Belknap Press of Harvard University Press, 2014), 441.
8. Piketty, *Capital*, 300.
9. Piketty, *Capital*, 188.
10. Gwenda Blair, *The Trumps: Three Generations That Built an Empire* (New York: Touchstone Books, 2001), 86.
11. Blair, *The Trumps*, 97.
12. Blair, *The Trumps*, 146.
13. Piketty, *Capital*, 344.
14. The Kushner family with Ellen Robinson Epstein, *The Miracle of Life: The Story of Rae and Joseph Kushner* (Chevy Chase, MD: E. Epstein, 1998), 95.
15. David Barstow, Susanne Craig, and Russ Buettner, "Trump Engaged in Suspect Tax Schemes as He Reaped Riches from His Father," *New York Times*, October 2, 2018, https://www.nytimes.com/interactive/2018/10/02/us/politics/donald-trump-tax-schemes-fred-trump.html.
16. Wayne Barrett, *Trump: The Deals and the Downfall* (New York: HarperCollins, 1992), 142–43; Donald J. Trump with Tony Schwartz, *The Art of the Deal* (New York: Ballantine Books, 2015), 134.
17. Emmanuel Saez, Thomas Piketty, and Gabriel Zucman, "Economic Growth in the United States: A Tale of Two Countries," *Washington Center for Equitable Growth*, December 6, 2016, https://equitablegrowth.org/economic-growth-in-the-united-states-a-tale-of-two-countries/.
18. Financial Crimes Enforcement Network, "FinCEN Takes Aim at Real Estate Secrecy in Manhattan and Miami," news release, January 13, 2016, https://www.fincen.gov/news/news-releases/fincen-takes-aim-real-estate-secrecy-manhattan-and-miami; and Financial Crimes Enforcement Network, "FinCEN Targets Shell Companies Purchasing Luxury Properties in Seven Major Metropolitan Areas," news release, August 22, 2017, https://www.fincen.gov/news/news-releases/fincen-targets-shell-companies-purchasing-luxury-properties-seven-major.
19. Matthew Stewart, "The 9.9 Percent Is the New American Aristocracy," *The Atlantic*, June 2018, https://www.theatlantic.com/magazine/archive/2018/06/the-birth-of-a-new-american-aristocracy/559130/.
20. Miles Corak, "Income Inequality, Equality of Opportunity, and Intergenerational Mobility," *Journal of Economic Perspectives* 27, no. 3 (Summer 2013): 79–102, https://www.aeaweb.org/articles?id=10.1257/jep.27.3.79.
21. Jared Kushner, "Executive Branch Personnel, Public Financial Disclosure Report," OGE Form 278e, (Washington, DC, Office of Government Ethics, 2018 [filed May 15, 2018] and 2019 [filed May 15, 2019]; Ivanka Trump, "Executive Branch Personnel, Public Financial Disclosure Report," OGE Form 278e (Washington, DC, Office of Government Ethics, 2018 [filed May 15, 2018] and 2019 [filed May 14, 2019].
22. Jim Tankersley, "How the Trump Tax Cut Is Helping to Push the Federal Deficit to

$1 Trillion," *New York Times*, July 25, 2018, https://www.nytimes.com/2018/07/25/business/trump-corporate-tax-cut-deficit.html.

23. Michelle Ye Hee Lee and Anu Narayanswamy, "Trump Enters the 2020 Election Cycle with a Massive Fundraising Lead Over Democrats," *Washington Post*, January 31, 2019, https://www.washingtonpost.com/politics/trump-reelection-effort-raised-21-million-in-the-fourth-quarter-campaign-says/2019/01/31/6e2a736a-2588-11e9-ad53-824486280311_story.html.
24. Zephyr Teachout, *Corruption in America: From Benjamin Franklin's Snuff Box to Citizens United* (Cambridge, MA: Harvard University Press, 2014), 49.
25. Teachout, *Corruption in America*, 37.
26. Carl Bernstein and Bob Woodward, "FBI Finds Nixon Aides Sabotaged Democrats," *Washington Post*, October 10, 1972, https://www.washingtonpost.com/politics/fbi-finds-nixon-aides-sabotaged-democrats/2012/06/06/gJQAoHIJJV_story.html.
27. Buckley v. Valeo, 424 U.S. 1 (1976), https://supreme.justia.com/cases/federal/us/424/1/#tab-opinion-1951589.
28. Jane Mayer, "Preface to the Anchor Books Edition (2017)," in *Dark Money: The Hidden History of the Billionaires Behind the Rise of the Radical Right* (New York: Anchor Books, 2017), xix.
29. Jesse Eisinger, *The Chickenshit Club: Why the Justice Department Fails to Prosecute Executives* (New York: Simon & Schuster, 2017).
30. Transactional Records Access Clearinghouse, "White Collar Prosecutions Fall to Lowest in 20 Years," *TRAC Reports*, Syracuse University, May 24, 2018, http://trac.syr.edu/tracreports/crim/514/.
31. Transactional Records Access Clearinghouse, "White-Collar Prosecutions Half Level of 8 Years Ago," *TRAC Reports*, Syracuse University, September 25, 2019, https://trac.syr.edu/tracreports/crim/577/.
32. Robert F. McDonnell v. United States, 136 S. Ct. 2355 (2016), https://casetext.com/case/mcdonnell-v-united-states-9.
33. Barrett, *Trump*, 455.
34. Barstow, Craig, and Buettner, "Trump Engaged in Suspect Tax Schemes."
35. Paul Krugman, "Why We're in a New Gilded Age," *New York Review of Books*, May 8, 2014, https://www.nybooks.com/articles/2014/05/08/thomas-piketty-new-gilded-age/.

1. THE ESCAPE

1. Rae Kushner's testimonies were recorded by the Holocaust Center at Kean College in 1982 and by the USC Shoah Foundation in 1996; both were part of a movement to capture Holocaust oral histories while the survivors were still alive. For details of life in Novogrudok and in the Naliboki forest, before, during, and after the war, I have also relied on testimonies of Lisa Reibel, Jack Kagan, and Sonya Oshman; as well as records kept by the US Holocaust Memorial Museum and by Yad Vashem, the Israeli Holocaust memorial project. Three books provided important context: Nechama Tec's *Defiance* (New York: Oxford University Press, 2009), which later became the inspiration for the movie of the same name and was based on scores of interviews with survivors from a camp of Jewish partisans; Shalom Yoran's *The Defiant: A True Story of Jewish Vengeance and Survival* (New York: St. Martin's Press, 1996), a personal memoir of his own escape from the Nazis and time in the forest; and *The Miracle of Life: The Story of Rae and Joseph Kushner* (Chevy Chase, MD: E. Epstein, 1998), a book compiled by Rae's four children on the occasion of her 75th birthday. Two documentaries, *A Partisan Returns: The Legacy of Two Sisters* (Jewish Partisan Educational Foundation, 2008), written and directed by Mitch Braff, and *The Bielski Brothers* (History Channel, 1994), directed by

Arun Kumar and written by Kumar and David Herman, supplied additional information about this period.

2. All quotes from Lisa Reibel are from her testimony to Nancy Kislin of the Holocaust Resource Center at Kean College, held by the United States Holocaust Memorial Museum, December 17, 1987, https://collections.ushmm.org/search/catalog/irn502781.
3. All quotes from Jack Kagan are from his testimony to the Imperial War Museum, held by the United States Holocaust Memorial Museum, June 29, 1986, https://collections.ushmm.org/search/catalog/irn510829.
4. All quotes from Rae Kushner (except where noted) are from her testimony to Sidney Langer of the Holocaust Resource Center at Kean College, held by the United States Holocaust Memorial Museum, 1982, https://collections.ushmm.org/search/catalog/irn504520.
5. All quotes from Sonya Oshman are from her testimony to Bernard Weinstein of the Holocaust Resource Center at Kean College, held by the United States Holocaust Memorial Museum, February 17, 1988, https://collections.ushmm.org/search/catalog/irn504779.
6. Kushners, *Miracle of Life*, 28.
7. *Defiance*, directed by Edward Zwick (Santa Monica, CA: Bedford Falls Productions, 2008).
8. Tec, *Defiance*, 270.
9. Kushners, *Miracle of Life*, 12.
10. Tec, *Defiance*, 281.
11. Tec, *Defiance*, 284.
12. Kushners, *Miracle of Life*, 12–13.
13. Rae Kushner, testimony held by the USC Shoah Foundation, July 25, 1996, https://collections.ushmm.org/search/catalog/vha18937.

2. THE AMERICAN DREAM

1. Joseph Kushner died relatively young, and, though a prolific builder, he did not live a public life. For the details of his story, I am relying on Rae Kushner's testimonies and the Kushner family's 1998 book, *The Miracle of Life: The Story of Rae and Joseph Kushner* (Chevy Chase, MD: E. Epstein, 1998), stories of their experience the Kushners passed on; as well as records I obtained that were originally compiled by the Hebrew Immigrant Aid Society, which helped the Kushners immigrate and resettle in New York. The books Mark Wischnitzer's *Visas to Freedom: The History of HIAS* (Cleveland: World, 1956); Nechama Tec's *Defiance* (New York: Oxford University Press, 2009), and Edward Zwick's 2008 movie of the same name based on it; and Shalom Yoran's memoir of his life in the Polish forest during the war, *The Defiant: A True Story of Jewish Vengeance and Survival* (New York: St. Martin's Press, 1996), provided additional context, as did the 1994 History Channel documentary *The Bielski Brothers* and the Jewish Partisan Educational Foundation's 2008 short film *A Partisan Returns: The Legacy of Two Sisters*.
2. Kushners, *Miracle of Life*, 11.
3. Tec, *Defiance*, 112.
4. Tec, *Defiance*, 220.
5. Kushners, *Miracle of Life*, 89.
6. Wischnitzer, *Visas to Freedom*, 215.
7. Wischnitzer, *Visas to Freedom*, 218.
8. Kushners, *Miracle of Life*, 91.
9. Rae Kushner, testimony held by the USC Shoah Foundation, July 25, 1996, https://collections.ushmm.org/search/catalog/vha18937.
10. Kushners, *Miracle of Life*, page 13.

11. HIAS Case File, "Kushnier, Joseph and Raja," opened March 1949, obtained by author.
12. James Hughes, former dean of the Bloustein School of Planning and Public Policy, interviewed by author, August 2018.
13. Jared Kushner, interviewed by Jonathan Swan, *Axios on HBO*, season 2, episode 1, aired June 2, 2019.
14. Kushners, *Miracle of Life*, 95.
15. Richard Rothstein, *The Color of Law: A Forgotten History of How Our Government Segregated America* (New York: Liveright, 2018), 64–65.
16. Rothstein, *Color of Law*, 77.
17. The history of Kushner land purchases is based on an examination of deeds, mortages, trusts, and other records from the 1950s through the 1980s from New Jersey's Union, Middlesex, and Essex Counties, obtained by author.
18. Details of the Wilf family history are from Yad Vashem: https://www.yadvashem.org/museum/holocaust-history-museum/donors/wilf-family.html.
19. Indenture, made January 6, 1958, Middlesex County, Book No. 1506, page 428–32.
20. Kushners, *Miracle of Life*, 106.
21. Rae Kushner, testimony to Sidney Langer of the Holocaust Research Center at Kean College, held by the United States Holocaust Memorial Museum, 1982, http://collections.ushmm.org/search/catalog/irn504520.

3. LAND OF OPPORTUNITY

1. Gwenda Blair, *The Trumps: Three Generations That Built an Empire* (New York: Touchstone Books, 2001), 73.
2. Blair, *The Trumps*, 86.
3. Blair, *The Trumps*, 32.
4. Blair, *The Trumps*, 49.
5. Blair, *The Trumps*, 50.
6. Blair, *The Trumps*, 60.
7. Blair, *The Trumps*, 93.
8. Blair, *The Trumps*, 111–14.
9. Blair, *The Trumps*, 116–17.
10. Wayne Barrett, *Trump: The Deals and the Downfall* (New York: HarperCollins, 1992), 35.
11. Nina Burleigh, *Golden Handcuffs: The Secret History of Trump's Women* (New York: Gallery Books, 2018), 30–31.
12. *Brooklyn Daily Star*, June 1, 1927.
13. Barrett, *Trump*, 34.
14. Blair, *The Trumps*, 128.
15. Michael D'Antonio, *The Truth About Trump* (New York: St. Martin's, 2016), 28.
16. Barrett, *Trump*, 34.
17. Barrett, *Trump*, 35.
18. Barrett, *Trump*, 36.
19. Barrett, *Trump*, 39.
20. Richard Rothstein, *The Color of Law: A Forgotten History of How Our Government Segregated America* (New York: Liveright, 2018), 65.
21. Barrett, *Trump*, 42.
22. Thomas Grace testimony, *FHA Investigation: Hearings Before the Committee on Banking and Currency, United States Senate*, 83rd Congress, Second Session (July 1954), 1162–78, https://babel.hathitrust.org/cgi/pt?id=umn.31951d035843371;view=1up;seq=413.
23. Blair, *The Trumps*, 150.

24. David Barstow, Susanne Craig, and Russ Buettner, "Trump Engaged in Suspect Tax Schemes as He Reaped Riches From His Father," *New York Times*, October 2, 2018, https://www.nytimes.com/interactive/2018/10/02/us/politics/donald-trump-tax-schemes-fred-trump.html.
25. "Mass Building Lowering Cost, Builder Finds," *Brookyn Eagle*, January 29, 1939.
26. Blair, *The Trumps*, 184–85.
27. Burleigh, *Golden Handcuffs*, 36.
28. Burleigh, *Golden Handcuffs*, 38.
29. Blair, *The Trumps*, 159.
30. Blair, *The Trumps*, 224.
31. Barstow, Craig, and Buettner, "Trump Engaged in Suspect Tax Schemes."
32. "Beach Haven Ain't My Home (aka. 'Old Man Trump')," lyrics by Woody Guthrie, music by Johnny Irion (Mount Kisco, NY: Woody Guthrie Publications, Inc. [BMI], 2016; New York: Rte. 8 Music [ASCAP], 2016), https://www.woodyguthrie.org/Lyrics/Beach_Haven_Aint_My_Home.htm.
33. Barstow, Craig, and Buettner, "Trump Engaged in Suspect Tax Schemes."
34. Barstow, Craig, and Buettner, "Trump Engaged in Suspect Tax Schemes."
35. Susanne Craig, interviewed by Ilya Marritz, "Trump and Taxes: The Art of the Dodge," *Trump, Inc.*, October 24, 2018, https://www.wnycstudios.org/story/trump-inc-trump-taxes-art-dodge.
36. William F. McKenna testimony, *FHA Investigation: Hearings Before the Committee on Banking and Currency, United States Senate*, 83rd Congress, Second Session (July 1954), 17–18, https://babel.hathitrust.org/cgi/pt?id=umn.31951d035843371&view=1up&seq=33.
37. Fred C. Trump testimony, *FHA Investigation: Hearings Before the Committee on Banking and Currency, United States Senate*, 83rd Congress, Second Session (July 1954), 400, https://babel.hathitrust.org/cgi/pt?id=umn.31951d035843371&view=1up&seq=418.
38. Fred C. Trump testimony, *FHA Investigation*, 402, 420.
39. Barrett, *Trump*, 56.
40. Barrett, *Trump*, 67.
41. Barrett, *Trump*, 70.
42. Barrett, *Trump*, 86.
43. Barrett, *Trump*, 87.
44. Donald J. Trump with Tony Schwartz, *The Art of the Deal* (New York: Ballantine Books, 2015), 95.
45. "McCarthy-Welch Exchange," *American Rhetoric*, https://www.americanrhetoric.com/speeches/welch-mccarthy.html.
46. "U.S. Begins Calling Witnesses in Roy Cohn's Perjury Trial," *New York Times*, March 27, 1964; Richard Pearson, "Roy Cohn, Controversial Lawyer and McCarthy Aide, Dies at 59," *Washington Post*, August 3, 1986.
47. Trump, *The Art of the Deal*, 99.

4. THE FALL OF NEW YORK

1. *New York City's Economic Crisis: Hearings Before the Joint Economic Committee, Congress of the United States*, 94th Congress (September and October 1975), https://www.jec.senate.gov/reports/94th%20Congress/Hearings/New%20York%20City%27s%20Economic%20Crisis%20(758).pdf.
2. New York State Department of Labor, "New York City Manufacturing Jobs Since World War II," fig. in "NYC Manufacturing in Decline," *THIRTEEN*, https://www.thirteen.org/uncertainindustry-2007/uncategorized/nyc-manufacturing-in-decline/.

3. Kim Phillips-Fein, *Fear City: New York's Fiscal Crisis and the Rise of Austerity Politics* (New York: Metropolitan Books, 2017), 6.
4. Phillips-Fein, *Fear City*, 74–75.
5. Frank Van Riper, "Ford to City: Drop Dead," *New York Daily News*, October 30, 1975, https://www.nydailynews.com/new-york/president-ford-announces-won-bailout-nyc-1975-article-1.2405985.
6. Robert D. McFadden, "Abraham Beame Is Dead at 94; Mayor During 70's Fiscal Crisis," *New York Times*, February 11, 2001, https://www.nytimes.com/2001/02/11/nyregion/abraham-beame-is-dead-at-94-mayor-during-70-s-fiscal-crisis.html?pagewanted=1.
7. Lee Dembart, "Beame Reflects on His Service in City," *New York Times*, December 27, 1977, https://www.nytimes.com/1977/12/27/archives/beame-reflects-on-his-service-in-city-stepping-down-after-30-years.html.
8. Jeff Nussbaum, "The Night New York Saved Itself from Bankruptcy," *New Yorker*, October 16, 2015, https://www.newyorker.com/news/news-desk/the-night-new-york-saved-itself-from-bankruptcy.
9. Interview with Charles V. Bagli, long time *New York Times* real estate reporter, by author, December 2018.
10. Wayne Barrett, "Like Father Like Son," *Village Voice*, January 15, 1976.
11. US Securities and Exchange Commission, *The Financial Collapse of the Penn Central Company: Staff Report of the Securities and Exchange Commission to the Special Subcommittee on Investigations* (Washington, DC: Government Printing Office, 1972), https://fraser.stlouisfed.org/files/docs/historical/house/1972house_fincolpenncentral.pdf.
12. Wayne Barrett, *Trump: The Deals and the Downfall* (New York: HarperCollins, 1992), 93.
13. Barrett, "Like Father."
14. Barrett, *Trump*, 117–25.
15. Barrett, *Trump*, 124.
16. Donald Trump with Tony Schwartz, *The Art of the Deal* (New York: Ballantine Books, 2015), 134.
17. Alden Whitman, "A Builder Looks Back—and Moves Forward," *New York Times*, January 28, 1973, https://www.nytimes.com/1973/01/28/archives/a-builder-looks-backand-moves-forward-builder-looks-back-but-moves.html.
18. William E. Geist, "The Expanding Empire of Donald Trump," *New York Times Magazine*, April 8, 1984, https://www.nytimes.com/1984/04/08/magazine/the-expanding-empire-of-donald-trump.html.
19. Michael Cohen, testimony before the House Oversight and Reform Committee, 115th Congress (February 27, 2019).
20. Judy Klemesrud, "Donald Trump, Real Estate Promoter, Builds Image as He Buys Buildings," *New York Times*, November 1, 1976, https://www.nytimes.com/1976/11/01/archives/donald-trump-real-estate-promoter-builds-image-as-he-buys-buildings.html.
21. Richard Ravitch, interviewed by author, February 2019; Barrett, *Trump*, 148–51.
22. Barrett, *Trump*, 132.
23. Ivana Trump, *Raising Trump* (New York: Gallery Books, 2017), 40–41.
24. Trump, *Raising Trump*, 50–51.
25. Ivana Trump prenuptial agreement, 1977, the Wayne Barrett Papers, Dolph Briscoe Center for American History, the University of Texas at Austin; Barrett, *Trump*, 137.
26. Barrett, *Trump*, 137.
27. Frank Lynn, "Beame Finishes Third," *New York Times*, September 9, 1977, https://www.nytimes.com/1977/09/09/archives/beame-finishes-third-voter-turnout-is-a-record-in-one-of-citys.html.

28. Barrett, *Trump*, 146.
29. Barrett, *Trump*, 153.
30. Barrett, *Trump*, 130.
31. Charles V. Bagli, "A Trump Empire Built on Inside Connections and $885 Million in Tax Breaks," *New York Times*, September 17, 2016, https://www.nytimes.com/2016/09/18/nyregion/donald-trump-tax-breaks-real-estate.html, and additional information supplied to author by the NYC Department of Finance, January 2019.
32. Donald Trump with Charles Leerhsen, *Surviving At The Top* (New York: Random House, 1990), 38–39; Barrett, *Trump*, 97, 113–14.
33. Reagan for President, "Official Announcement," 4President.org, November 13, 1979, http://www.4president.org/speeches/reagan1980announcement.htm.
34. Jeffrey Toobin, "The Dirty Trickster," *The New Yorker*, May 23, 2008, https://www.newyorker.com/magazine/2008/06/02/the-dirty-trickster.
35. *Get Me Roger Stone*, directed by Dylan Bank, Daniel DiMauro, and Morgan Pehme (Los Gatos, CA: Netflix, 2017).
36. "NBC Evening News for 1981-04-30," Vanderbilt Television News Archive, https://tvnews.vanderbilt.edu/programs/516524; *Get Me Roger Stone*.
37. Roger Stone, interviewed by Wayne Barrett, 2004, Barrett Papers.
38. Toobin, "The Dirty Trickster."
39. Roy Cohn, interviewed by Stuart Scheftel, *Insight*, WNYC, December 21, 1982.
40. Ronald Reagan, "Address Before a Joint Session of the Congress on the Program for Economic Recovery," *The American Presidency Project*, February 18, 1981, https://www.presidency.ucsb.edu/documents/address-before-joint-session-the-congress-the-program-for-economic-recovery-0.
41. Steven R. Weisman, "Intentionally or Not, Tax Policy Is a Social Policy," *New York Times*, August 2, 1981, https://www.nytimes.com/1981/08/02/weekinreview/intentionally-or-not-tax-policy-is-a-social-policy.html.
42. Edward Cowan, "Reagan's 3-Year, 25% Cut in Tax Rate, Voted by Wide Margins in the House and Senate," *New York Times*, July 30, 1981, https://www.nytimes.com/1981/07/30/business/reagan-s-3-year-25-cut-in-tax-rate-voted-by-wide-margins-in-the-house-and-senate.html.
43. Joseph A. McCartin, "The Strike That Busted Unions," *New York Times*, August 2, 2011, https://www.nytimes.com/2011/08/03/opinion/reagan-vs-patco-the-strike-that-busted-unions.html.
44. Emily Bazelon, "Elizabeth Warren Is Completely Serious," *New York Times*, June 17, 2019, https://www.nytimes.com/2019/06/17/magazine/elizabeth-warren-president.html.
45. US Bureau of Labor Statistics, "Union Membership Rate 10.5 Percent in 2018, Down from 20.1 Percent in 1983," *The Economics Daily*, January 25, 2019, https://www.bls.gov/opub/ted/2019/union-membership-rate-10-point-5-percent-in-2018-down-from-20-point-1-percent-in-1983.htm.
46. Ronald Reagan, "The President's News Conference," *The American Presidency Project*, August 12, 1986, https://www.presidency.ucsb.edu/documents/the-presidents-news-conference-957.

5. THE BUSINESS OF DONALD TRUMP

1. Gerald Levy and Mike Bellinger, State of New York Commission on Government Integrity, memorandum of interview with Donald Trump, January 27, 1988, obtained by author.
2. Donald Trump, interviewed by Tom Brokaw in "A 33-Year Old Donald Trump Talks

NYC Real Estate in 1980," NBC News, posted December 21, 2015, https://www.msnbc.com/documentaries/watch/today-show-1980-with-donald-trump-589527619719.

3. Kenneth C. Crowe, "Long Voyage to Exploitation," *Newsday*, January 15, 1984.
4. Joseph Rodonich et al. v. House Wreckers Union Local 95 et al., 82 Civ. 5583 (S.D.N.Y.), trial testimony, November 18–December 2, 1985.
5. Edward I. Koch, *Mayor: An Autobiography* (New York: Simon & Schuster, 1984), 286–87.
6. Donald Trump with Tony Schwartz, *The Art of the Deal* (New York: Ballantine Books, 2015), 190–92.
7. Tony Gliedman to Ed Koch, memorandum, March 27, 1981, as cited in Koch, *Mayor*, 287.
8. FBI memorandum, April 27, 1982, obtained under the Freedom of Information Act and first reported by Jason Leopold in "'If You Keep Fucking With Mr. Trump, We Know Where You Live,'" *BuzzFeed News*, May 1, 2017, https://www.buzzfeednews.com/article/jasonleopold/if-you-keep-fucking-with-mr-trump-we-know-where-you-live#.cs19XbjNg9.
9. FBI memorandum, April 27, 1982.
10. Edward A. Gargan, "Is the City Building Its Tax Base or Eroding It?," *New York Times*, July 26, 1981, https://www.nytimes.com/1981/07/26/weekinreview/is-the-city-building-its-tax-base-or-eroding-it.html.
11. Trump-Equitable v. Gliedman, 87 A.D. 2d 12 (N.Y. App. Div. 1982), May 20, 1982, appellate decision of the Supreme Court of New York, First Department.
12. Trump, *Art of the Deal*, 191.
13. Gwenda Blair, *The Trumps: Three Generations That Built an Empire* (New York: Touchstone Books, 2001), 320.
14. Trump-Equitable Fifth Avenue Company v. Gliedman, 62 F (N.Y. 2d 539), July 5, 1984. Court of Appeals of the State of New York.
15. Trump, *Art of the Deal*, 191.
16. Mike McManus to Dodie Livingston, White House memorandum, October 3, 1983, as annotated by White House staff, obtained by author.
17. Tony Gliedman to Ed Koch, letter of resignation, February 26, 1986, the Wayne Barrett Papers, Dolph Briscoe Center for American History, the University of Texas at Austin.
18. Harry Berkowitz, "The Manager Behind the Mogul," *Washington Post*, September 23, 1989, https://www.washingtonpost.com/archive/realestate/1989/09/23/the-manager-behind-the-mogul/56c7cfba-261b-4c4b-a197–557f40ae4b89/.
19. Blair, *The Trumps*, 325.
20. Blair, *The Trumps*, 327.
21. Louise Story and Stephanie Saul, "Stream of Foreign Wealth Flows to Elite New York Real Estate," *New York Times*, February 7, 2015, https://www.nytimes.com/2015/02/08/nyregion/stream-of-foreign-wealth-flows-to-time-warner-condos.html.
22. Jerry Capeci, "Frank Perdue Meets the Godfather," *New York*, July 25, 1983.
23. Wayne Barrett, *Trump: The Deals and the Downfall* (New York: HarperCollins, 1992), 193–97.
24. Barrett, *Trump*, 203.
25. Robert I. Friedman, *Red Mafiya: How the Russian Mob Has Invaded America* (New York: Berkley, 2002), 213.
26. Donald Trump to Michael Critchley, September 15, 1986, the Wayne Barrett Papers, Dolph Briscoe Center for American History, the University of Texas at Austin.
27. John Connolly, "Pal Joey: What Do Donald Trump, Helicopters, the Federal Courts and Cocaine All Have in Common?," *Spy*, June 1991.
28. Barrett, *Trump*, 293.

6. THE GAMBLE

1. For the description of the night of his arrest, I am relying on Barrett's handwritten notes from that night, as found in the Wayne Barrett Papers, Dolph Briscoe Center for American History, the University of Texas at Austin, as well as recollections shared by Barrett prior to his death; the recollections of Timothy O'Brien, who was working with Barrett at the time; and details related in Wayne Barrett, *Trump: The Deals and the Downfall* (New York: HarperCollins, 1992).
2. Timothy L. O'Brien, *TrumpNation: The Art of Being Donald* (New York: Grand Central, 2016), 108.
3. O'Brien, *TrumpNation*, 135.
4. Andrea Bernstein, "A Personal Remembrance of Wayne Barrett," WNYC News, January 19, 2017, https://www.wnyc.org/story/personal-remembrance-wayne-barrett.
5. Former Trump associate, interview notes by Wayne Barrett, January 1991, the Wayne Barrett Papers, Dolph Briscoe Center for American History, the University of Texas at Austin.
6. Michael Checchio, "The Atlantic City Mob: Out of Casinos, In the Money," *Press of Atlantic City*, December 19, 1986.
7. Former Trump associate, Barrett interview, January 1991.
8. Wayne Barrett, *Trump: The Deals and the Downfall* (New York: HarperCollins, 1992), 252.
9. O'Brien, *TrumpNation*, 117.
10. Robert O'Harrow Jr., "Trump's Ties to an Informant and FBI Agent Reveal His Mode of Operation," *Washington Post*, September 17, 2016, https://www.washingtonpost.com/investigations/trumps-ties-to-an-informant-and-fbi-agent-reveal-his-modes-of-operation/2016/09/16/6e65522e-6f9f-11e6–9705–23e51a2f424d_story.html; State of New Jersey, Department of Law and Public Safety, Division of Gaming Enforcement, "Report to the Casino Control Commission," October 16, 1981.
11. Harry J. Diduck v. Kaszycki & Sons Contractors, Inc. et al., 83 Civ. 6346 S.D.N.Y., July 6, 1990, Daniel Sullivan testimony at trial.
12. Damon T. Taylor, Federal Bureau of Investigation, memorandum, September 22, 1981.
13. State of New Jersey, "Report to the Casino Control Commission," 96.
14. O'Harrow, "Trump's Ties to an Informant."
15. Brendan Byrne, interview notes by Wayne Barrett, January 1991, the Wayne Barrett Papers, Dolph Briscoe Center for American History, the University of Texas at Austin.
16. "Prominent Attorney Paddy McGahn Dies," *Press of Atlantic City*, August 1, 2000, https://www.pressofatlanticcity.com/prominent-attorney-paddy-mcgahn-dies/article_0718a0c6-16da-11e6-a79c-d7db22b60a3c.html.
17. Franklin Foer, "The Plot Against America," *Atlantic*, March 2018, https://www.theatlantic.com/magazine/archive/2018/03/paul-manafort-american-hustler/550925/.
18. Gwenda Blair, *The Trumps: Three Generations That Built an Empire* (New York: Touchstone Books, 2001), 533–34.
19. Matt Katz, "Trump, Self-Proclaimed Outsider, Was New Jersey Political Insider," WNYC News, June 2, 2016, https://www.wnyc.org/story/trump-self-proclaimed-outsider-began-new-jersey-political-insider/.
20. Former New Jersey elected official, interview notes by Wayne Barrett, January 1991, the Wayne Barrett Papers, Dolph Briscoe Center for American History, the University of Texas at Austin.
21. David Grandeau, interviewed by author, September 2016.
22. Richard L. Berke, "Prodded by Lobbying Group, G.O.P. Reveals $100,000 Donors," *New York Times*, January 24, 1989, https://www.nytimes.com/1989/01/24/us/prodded-by-lobbying-group-gop-reveals-100000-donors.html.

23. Charles V. Bagli, "Despite Recent Controversies, No Reelection Opponent Yet for Morgenthau," *New York Observer*, March 13, 1989.
24. State of New Jersey Department of Law and Public Safety, Division of Gaming Enforcement, "Report to the Casino Control Commission," April 7, 1987.
25. Donald Trump testimony before State of New York Commission on Government Integrity, *Hearing on Campaign Finance Practices of Citywide and Statewide Officials*, March 14, 1988.
26. Craig Unger, *House of Trump, House of Putin: The Untold Story of Donald Trump and the Russian Mafia* (New York: Dutton, 2018), 49–51.
27. Ivana Trump, *Raising Trump* (New York: Gallery Books, 2017), 164.
28. Former Trump associate, Barrett interview, January 1991.
29. Neil Barsky, "Trump, the Bad, Bad Businessman," *New York Times*, August 5, 2016, https://www.nytimes.com/2016/08/07/opinion/sunday/trump-the-bad-bad-businessman.html.
30. State of New Jersey Department of Law and Public Safety, Division of Gaming Enforcement, "Preliminary Report on the Financial Condition of the Donald J. Trump Organization Post-Restructuring," August 13, 1990.
31. Brendan Murphy, "Trump's Taj Mahal Casino to Enter 'Consensual' Bankruptcy," *United Press International*, November 16, 1990, https://www.upi.com/Archives/1990/11/17/Trumps-Taj-Mahal-casino-to-enter-consensual-bankruptcy/7010658818000/.
32. Abe Wallach, interviewed by author and Ilya Marritz, January 2018.
33. New Jersey Division of Gaming Enforcement, "Preliminary Report," August 13, 1990, 58–59.
34. Lisa Belkin, "Donald Trump's original apprentice, Louise Sunshine, recalls her 'magical' years and not-so-happy ending," *Yahoo News*, September 24, 2016, https://www.yahoo.com/news/donald-trumps-original-apprentice-louise-sunshine-recalls-her-magical-years-and-the-not-so-happy-ending-090040690.html; Wallach interview, January 2018.
35. David Barstow, Susanne Craig, and Russ Buettner, "Trump Engaged in Suspect Tax Schemes as He Reaped Riches From His Father," *New York Times*, October 2, 2018, https://www.nytimes.com/interactive/2018/10/02/us/politics/donald-trump-tax-schemes-fred-trump.html.
36. James Rowley, "Trump Agrees to Pay $750,000 Penalty to Settle Antitrust Lawsuit," *Associated Press*, April 5, 1988, https://apnews.com/54ea0dc590fc97d9e9e86c65336649a1.
37. State of New Jersey Department of Law & Public Safety, Division of Gaming Enforcement v. Trump Plaza Associates, No. 89-247 (O.A.L. July 2, 1991), https://www.washingtonpost.com/wp-stat/graphics/politics/trump-archive/docs/ccc-order--6-21-1991-fred-trump-fine.pdf; Michael Isikoff, "Trump Challenged Over Ties to Mob-Linked Gambler with Ugly Past," *Yahoo News*, March 7, 2016, https://www.yahoo.com/news/trump-challenged-over-ties-to-mob-linked-gambler-100050602.html.
38. "How Donald Trump's Father Once Bailed Out His Casino," *The Press of Atlantic City*, June 6, 1991, https://www.pressofatlanticcity.com/news/how-donald-trump-s-father-once-bailed-out-his-casino/article_934cb836-2c1d-11e6-8a13-173759856fe0.html.
39. Financial Crimes Enforcement Network, "FinCEN Announces Penalty Against Trump Taj Mahal Associates," news release, January 22, 1998, https://www.fincen.gov/news/news-releases/fincen-announces-penalty-against-trump-taj-mahal-associates.
40. David Grandeau, interviewed by author, September 2016. I have relied for these pages on two thousand pages of documents released by the New York State Temporary Commission on Lobbying in December 2000, including the deposition of Roger Stone and the interrogatory of Donald Trump, billing records, receipts, and other documents following an investigation into unlawful lobbying by Donald Trump and Roger Stone.

Parts of the story were first reported by me and my colleague Ilya Marritz in "A Front Group, a Lawsuit and a Private Investigator: How Trump Rigged the System to Delay Gambling in New York," WNYC News, October 20, 2016.

41. Tom Condon, "Trump Lures Big Money to a Small N.J. Election," *Hartford Courant*, July 16, 1998, https://www.courant.com/news/connecticut/hc-xpm-1998-07-16-9807160226-story.html.
42. J. Curtis Herge, letter to Lawrence M. Noble, "Affidavit of Donald J. Trump," June 26, 2000, as cited in http://online.wsj.com/public/resources/documents/Trump_Campaign_Finance_Affidavit_2000.pdf.
43. Conciliation agreement between Gormley for Senate Primary Election Fund and the Federal Election Commission, February 22, 2005, https://eqs.fec.gov/eqsdocsMUR/00002DD1.pdf.

7. THE DON OF SUBURBIA

1. Philip Roth, *The Plot Against America* (New York: Vintage, 2005), 2.
2. Rae Kushner testimony to Sidney Langer of the Holocaust Resource Center at Kean College, held by the United States Holocaust Memorial Museum, https://collections.ushmm.org/search/catalog/irn504520.
3. New Jersey land records on file in Union, Middlesex, and Essex Counties, 1950s–1980s, including deeds, mortgages, and trusts, obtained by author.
4. "To Wed Murray Kushner," *Hillside Times*, May 16, 1974.
5. Deed, dated February 17, 1981, Essex County, New Jersey, Book no. 410, 172, obtained by author.
6. Matt Katz, *American Governor: Chris Christie's Bridge to Redemption* (New York: Threshold Editions, 2016), 20.
7. US Department of Housing and Urban Development, Office of Policy Development and Research, *U.S. Housing Market Conditions Historical Data* (August 1998), tables 8A–8C, https://www.huduser.gov/periodicals/ushmc/summer98/histdat2.html.
8. Joseph Kushner, will dated October 11, 1982, Essex County, New Jersey, obtained by author.
9. Peter Grant, "Multifamily Affair: Kushner Aims to Be a Big-Time Player," *Wall Street Journal*, September 6, 2000, https://www.wsj.com/articles/SB968192153138618934.
10. Rae Kushner, testimony held by the USC Shoah Foundation Institute, July 25, 1996, https://collections.ushmm.org/search/catalog/vha18937.
11. Joanne McFadden, "Mountain View Maintains Mendham Tradition," *The Record*, June 27, 1993.
12. Ted Sherman, "Real Estate King Talks Softly But Carries a Long List of Friends," *Star Ledger*, December 22, 2002.
13. Elise Young and Jeff Pillets, "Sex, Money, Power, Betrayal, and Ruin," *The Record*, August 22, 2004 (special reprint section).
14. Calculated by the author with data from OpenSecrets.org.
15. "Remarks by President Bill Clinton at Democratic National Committee Reception Florham Park, New Jersey," *Federal News Service*, October 8, 1997.
16. FDIC consent decree, "In the Matter of The NorCrown Trust, Charles Kushner," FRB Dkt. No. 05-010-B-HC (February 10, 2005).
17. Robert Yontef v. Westminster Management, No. 2:03-cv-00504 (D.N.J. February 4, 2003), complaint.
18. Calculated by the author with data from New Jersey Election Law Enforcement Commission, elec.state.nj.us.
19. Young and Pillets, "Sex, Money, Power, Betrayal, and Ruin."

20. Grant, "Multifamily Affair."
21. Daniel Golden, *The Price of Admission: How America's Ruling Class Buys Its Way into Elite Colleges—and Who Gets Left Outside the Gates* (New York: Three Rivers Press, 2007), 23–48.
22. United States v. Richard Stadtmauer, 620 F.3d 238 (3d Cir. September 9, 2010).
23. *Stadtmauer*, 620 F.3d 238.
24. Some of the details from the Fontainebleau seders were first reported by Gabriel Sherman, "The Legacy," *New York*, July 10, 2009, http://nymag.com/news/features/57891/.
25. Kushner v. Kushner, No. C00155 (Hudson County Court, January 18, 2002); as reported in Ted Sherman, "The Family: Five Years of Bad Blood," *Star-Ledger*, July 14, 2004.
26. Robert Yontef v. Westminster Management, No. 2:03-cv-00504 (D.N.J., February 4, 2003), complaint.

8. ICARUS

1. Elise Young and Jeff Pillets, "Sex, Money, Power, Betrayal, and Ruin," *The Record*, August 22, 2004 (special reprint section).
2. Young and Pillets, "Sex, Money, Power, Betrayal, and Ruin."
3. Daniel Golden, *The Price of Admission: How America's Ruling Class Buys Its Way into Elite Colleges—and Who Gets Left Outside the Gates* (New York: Three Rivers Press, 2007), 45.
4. James E. McGreevey, "The Making of a Gay American," *New York*, September 14, 2006, http://nymag.com/news/politics/21340/.
5. Robert Yontef v. Westminster Management, No. 2:03-cv-00504 (D.N.J. February 4, 2003), complaint.
6. Kushner v. Kushner, No. C00155 (Hudson County Court, January 18, 2002); as reported in Ted Sherman, "The Family: Five Years of Bad Blood," *Star-Ledger*, July 14, 2004.
7. Young and Pillets, "Sex, Money, Power, Betrayal, and Ruin."
8. Young and Pillets, "Sex, Money, Power, Betrayal, and Ruin."
9. Federal Election Commission, Matter Under Review #5279: Bill Bradley for President, Inc., complaint, June 8, 2001, https://www.fec.gov/data/legal/matter-under-review/5279/.
10. Federal Election Commission, Matter Under Review #5279: Bill Bradley for President, Inc., first general counsel's report, May 29, 2002.
11. *Westminster Management*, No. 2:03-cv-00504, June 25, 2002.
12. Federal Election Commission, "Consolidated Response of Certain Respondents to 'Reason to Believe,'" in Matter Under Review #5279: Bill Bradley for President, Inc., September 23, 2002.
13. Federal Election Commission, "Condolidated Response," MUR #5279.
14. Federal Election Commission, "Response from Esther Schulder, Jacob Schulder, Jessica Schulder Orbach and Ruth Schulder," Matter Under Review #5279: Bill Bradley for President, Inc., November 4, 2002.
15. Tom McGeveran, "Port's Chairman Asks for Recusal on Bus Terminal," *New York Observer*, November 4, 2002, https://observer.com/2002/11/ports-chairman-asks-for-recusal-on-bus-terminal/.
16. Tom McGeveran, "G.O.P. Demands New Port Head Decline Post," *New York Observer*, January 6, 2003, https://observer.com/2003/01/gop-demands-new-port-head-decline-post/.
17. United States v. Charles Kushner, No. 2:04-cr-00580-JLL (D-N.J., July 12, 2004), criminal complaint.
18. *Kushner*, No. 2:04-cr-00580-JLL, criminal complaint.
19. *Kushner*, No. 2:04-cr-00580-JLL, criminal complaint.
20. George E. Jordan, "Kushner Sibling Rivalry Evolves to Legendary Proportions," *Star-Ledger*, January 18, 2004.

21. Emily Horton, "The Legacy of the 2001 and 2003 'Bush' Tax Cuts," *Center on Budget and Policy Priorities*, October 23, 2017, https://www.cbpp.org/research/federal-tax/the-legacy-of-the-2001-and-2003-bush-tax-cuts.
22. Samara R. Potter and William G. Gale, "The Bush Tax Cut: One Year Later," *Brookings Institution*, June 15, 2002, https://www.brookings.edu/research/the-bush-tax-cut-one-year-later/.
23. Rae Kushner, will dated September 26, 1996, Essex County, New Jersey, obtained by author.
24. *Kushner*, No. 2:04-cr-00580-JLL, criminal complaint.
25. Dafna Zucker, "Public May Get Discount Bank Options If Tender Fails," *Globes*, May 5, 2004, https://en.globes.co.il/en/article-793838.
26. Federal Election Commission, "Real Estate Developer to Pay $508,900 Civil Penalty to Federal Election Commission," news release, June 30, 2004, https://www.fec.gov/updates/real-estate-developer-to-pay-508900-civil-penalty-to-federal-election-commission/.
27. Gabriel Sherman, "The Legacy," *New York*, July 10, 2009, http://nymag.com/news/features/57891/.
28. Mike Kelly, "Kushner Proves Rich Not Smarter Than Rest of Us," *The Record*, July 14, 2004.
29. Chris Christie, press conference, July 14, 2004.
30. Christie press conference.
31. Chris Christie with Ellis Henican, *Let Me Finish: Trump, the Kushners, Bannon, New Jersey, and the Power of In-Your-Face Politics* (New York: Hachette, 2019), 251.
32. Ben Brafman, interviewed by author, August 2019.
33. Ben Brafman to author, email, August 2019.
34. Christie, *Let Me Finish*, 103.
35. *Kushner*, 2:04-cr-00580-JLL (D-NJ, August 18, 2004), criminal information.
36. "In the matter of the NorCrown Trust, Charles Kushner," FRB Dkt No. 05-010-B-HC, FDIC-04-224e, and FDIC-04-223k (Februay 2005).
37. "The Closing: Charles Kushner," interview by Lauren Elkies in *The Real Deal*, November 4, 2007, https://therealdeal.com/issues_articles/the-closing-charles-kushner/.
38. Rae Kushner from the testimony to Sidney Langer of the Holocaust Resource Center at Kean College, held by the United States Holocaust Memorial Museum, 1982, https://collections.ushmm.org/search/catalog/irn504520.
39. Elkies, "The Closing: Charles Kushner."

9. "A BRIDGE TO THE FUTURE"

1. "Giuliani Campaign Rally," C-SPAN, November 2, 1989, https://www.c-span.org/video/?9777-1/giuliani-campaign-rally.
2. Wayne Barrett, "The Case of the Missing Case: How a Trump Probe Died in Rudy's Office," *Village Voice*, October 12, 1993, https://www.villagevoice.com/2018/06/04/rudys-long-history-of-quashing-trump-probes/.
3. Barrett, "The Case of the Missing Case."
4. Ralph Blumenthal, "Dinkins Proposes Record Expansion of Police Forces," *New York Times*, October 3, 1990, https://www.nytimes.com/1990/10/03/nyregion/dinkins-on-crime-dinkins-proposes-record-expansion-of-police-forces.html.
5. Samuel M. Ehrenhalt, "Economic and Demographic Change: The Case of New York City," *Monthly Labor Review* 116, no. 2 (February 1993): 40–50, https://www.bls.gov/opub/mlr/1993/02/art4full.pdf.
6. "H.R. 3450 (103rd): North American Free Trade Agreement Implementation Act," November 20, 1993, *GovTrack*, https://govtrack.us/congress/bills/103/hr3450.

7. "Remarks by President Clinton, President Bush, President Carter, President Ford, and Vice President Gore in Signing of NAFTA Side Agreements," September 14, 1993, https://clintonwhitehouse6.archives.gov/1993/09/1993-09-14-remarks-by-clinton-and-former-presidents-on-nafta.html.
8. *Long Beach Press-Telegram*, October 1993, in Andrew Kaczynski, "Donald Trump Spoke Forcefully against NAFTA at a 1993 Business Conference," *BuzzFeed News*, February 29, 2016.
9. Bob Liff, "Giuliani Is No Friend of NAFTA," *Newsday*, November 9, 1993.
10. Gwen Ifill, "Clinton Vows Fight for His Health Plan," *New York Times*, January 26, 1994, https://www.nytimes.com/1994/01/26/us/state-of-the-union-the-overview-clinton-vows-fight-for-his-health-plan.html.
11. Carolyn Skorneck, "Clinton Says He Will Sign Welfare Overhaul; House Passes It," *Associated Press*, July 31, 1996, https://www.apnews.com/f11a3d867b896908c6c598e31fb94ff8.
12. Barbara Vobejda, "Clinton Signs Welfare Bill amid Division," *Washington Post*, August 23, 1996.
13. "Clinton's Speech Accepting the Democratic Nomination for President," *New York Times*, August 30, 1996.
14. Calculated by the author with data from the New York City Campaign Finance Board.
15. Donald J. Trump to the Honorable Rudolph Giuliani, letter, February 16, 1996, obtained by author; Randy M. Mastro to Donald J. Trump, letter, February 27, 1996, obtained by author.
16. Franz Leichter, news release, The Wayne Barrett Papers, Dolph Briscoe Center for American History, The University of Texas at Austin, June 8, 1995.
17. Daniel Bush, "Tortured Project Shows Trump 'Knows What Buttons to Push,'" *E&E News*, October 5, 2015, https://www.eenews.net/stories/1060025833.
18. Howard Glaser (@hglaser1), "Thread on genesis of @realDonaldTrump animosity to @NYGovCuomo -Cuomo blocked Trump 1990's attempt to siphon fed $$ for his luxury housing," Twitter, August 17, 2018, https://twitter.com/hglaser1/status/1030515682612572165 (unavailable as of October 10, 2019).
19. Donald J. Trump with Meredith McIver, *Trump: How to Get Rich* (New York: Ballantine Books, 2004), 141–42.
20. Elizabeth Kolbert, "Metro Matters; Liberal Party Has One Ideal: Its Survival," *New York Times*, May 14, 1998, https://www.nytimes.com/1998/05/14/nyregion/metro-matters-liberal-party-has-one-ideal-its-survival.html.
21. Wayne Barrett, "Peas in a Pod: The Long and Twisted Relationship between Donald Trump and Rudy Giuliani," *New York Daily News*, September 4, 2016, https://www.nydailynews.com/opinion/wayne-barrett-donald-trump-rudy-giuliani-peas-pod-article-1.2776357.
22. Charles V. Bagli, "A Trump Empire Built on Inside Connections and $885 Million in Tax Breaks," *New York Times*, September 17, 2016, https://www.nytimes.com/2016/09/18/nyregion/donald-trump-tax-breaks-real-estate.html?_r=0.
23. Angela Mosconi, "Trump Patriarch Eulogized as Great Builder," *New York Post*, June 30, 1999, https://nypost.com/1999/06/30/trump-patriarch-eulogized-as-great-builder/.
24. David Barstow, Susanne Craig, and Russ Buettner, "Trump Engaged in Suspect Tax Schemes as He Reaped Riches From His Father," *New York Times*, October 2, 2018, https://www.nytimes.com/interactive/2018/10/02/us/politics/donald-trump-tax-schemes-fred-trump.html.
25. Heidi Evans, "Inside Trumps' Bitter Battle: Nephew's Ailing Baby Caught in the Middle," *New York Daily News*, December 19, 2000, https://www.nydailynews.com/archives/news/trumps-bitter-battle-nephew-ailing-baby-caught-middle-article-1.888562.

26. New York State Department of Labor, "Local Area Unemployment Statistics Program: New York State, Labor Market Regions, Metropolitan Areas, Counties, and Municipalities of at Least 25,000 Population," https://labor.ny.gov/stats/laus.asp.
27. Calculated by the author with data from NYU Furman Center, January 2019.
28. "A Brief History of the Glass-Steagall Act," *Dēmos*, https://www.demos.org/sites/default/files/publications/glass-steagall-history_Demos.pdf; Arthur E. Wilmarth Jr., "The Road to Repeal of the Glass-Steagall Act," *Wake Forest Journal of Business and Intellectual Property Law* 17, no. 4 (Summer 2017): 441–548, https://scholarship.law.gwu.edu/cgi/viewcontent.cgi?article=2556&context=faculty_publications.
29. "Statement by President Bill Clinton at the Signing of the Financial Modernization Bill," November 12, 1999, U.S. Department of the Treasury Press Center, https://www.treasury.gov/press-center/press-releases/Pages/ls241.aspx.
30. "Financial Services Bill Signing," C-SPAN, November 12, 1999, https://www.c-span.org/video/?153587-1/financial-services-bill-signing.
31. Hillary Clinton US Senate bid announcement, State University of New York, Purchase, February 6, 2000, taped by author.
32. Dan Barry and Abby Goodnough, "Errors Turn Fund-Raising Coup Into Embarrassment for Giuliani," *New York Times*, August 12, 1999, https://www.nytimes.com/1999/08/12/nyregion/errors-turn-fund-raising-coup-into-embarrassment-for-giuliani.html.
33. Knut Royce, "FBI Tracked Alleged Russian Mob Ties of Giuliani Campaign Supporter," Center for Public Integrity, December 14, 1999.
34. Calculated by author with data from the New York City Campaign Finance Board.
35. Caleb Melby and Keri Geiger, "Behind Trump's Russia Romance, There's a Tower Full of Oligarchs," *Bloomberg Businessweek*, March 16, 2017, https://www.bloomberg.com/news/articles/2017–03–16/behind-trump-s-russia-romance-there-s-a-tower-full-of-oligarchs.
36. NYC Department of Finance, Automated City Register Information System (ACRIS), December 12, 2001, block 1340, lot 1347, 3407/2295.
37. Calculated by author with data from OpenSecrets.org.
38. "Clinton Victory Speech," C-SPAN video, November 7, 2000, https://www.c-span.org/video/?160369–1/clinton-victory-speech.
39. Roger Stone, interviewed by Wayne Barrett, 2004, Barrett Papers.
40. The Committee to Take Back Our Judiciary v. Florida Elections Commission, No. 02-4672 (2003), https://www.doah.state.fl.us/ROS/2002/02003613%20Amended%20RO.PDF.

10. ESCAPE FROM NEW JERSEY

1. Jared Kushner, "2014 Undergraduate Commencement II - Hofstra University," YouTube, posted by Hofstra University, June 4, 2014, https://www.youtube.com/watch?v=wAoXCIeeTYI.
2. Jared Kushner, interviewed by George Gurley in *The Kingdom of New York: Knights, Knaves, Billionaires, and Beauties in the City of Big Shots*, ed. *The New York Observer* (New York: HarperCollins, 2009), 338–39.
3. "30 Fawn Dr, Livingston, NJ 07039," property listing, *Zillow*, March 21, 2019, https://www.zillow.com/homedetails/30-Fawn-Dr-Livingston-NJ-07039/38665056_zpid/.
4. Photograph of Senator Robert G. Toricelli with "Jacob Schulder of West Orange, Gared Kushner of Livingston, and his father, Charles Kushner," by Ed Hill, *The Record*, February 20, 1997.
5. Calculated by author with data from OpenSecrets.org.

6. Federal Election Commission, Matter Under Review #5279: Bill Bradley for President, Inc., referral, June 8, 2001, https://www.fec.gov/data/legal/matter-under-review/5279/.
7. Naomi Zeveloff, "How Jared Kushner Became a Teenage Hero—and Learned to Be a Zionist," *Forward*, January 26, 2017, https://forward.com/news/israel/361090/how-jared-kushner-became-a-teenage-hero-and-learned-to-be-a-zionist/.
8. Daniel Golden, *The Price of Admission: How America's Ruling Class Buys Its Way into Elite Colleges—and Who Gets Left Outside the Gates* (New York: Three Rivers Press, 2007), 45–46.
9. Alan E. Wirzbicki, "2,055 Admitted to Class of 2003," *Harvard Crimson*, April 5, 1999, https://www.thecrimson.com/article/1999/4/5/2055-admitted-to-class-of-2003/.
10. Federal Election Commission, "Consolidated Response of Certain Respondents to 'Reason to Believe,'" in Matter Under Review #5279: Bill Bradley for President, Inc., September 23, 2002.
11. Matt Viser, "Jared Kushner Got His Start as Somerville Landlord," *Boston Globe*, June 22, 2017, https://www.bostonglobe.com/news/politics/2017/06/22/the-apprentice-real-estate-rookie-jared-kushner-snapped-somerville-properties-but-also-made-mistakes/4Y3VWYsNqJO3TAtfKfBSKJ/story.html.
12. Jared Kushner, "2014 Undergraduate Commencement II - Hofstra University."
13. The story of Jared Kushner's Massachusetts land transactions is based on an examination of deeds, mortgages, and trusts from Southern Middlesex land records, available at http://www.masslandrecords.com/MiddlesexSouth/.
14. Jared Kushner, "2014 Undergraduate Commencement II - Hofstra University."
15. Viser, "Somerville Landlord."
16. Judy Maltz, "Hundreds of Thousands in Donations Tie Kushners and Trump to Chabad Movement," *Haaretz*, January 10, 2017.
17. Drew C. Pendergrass, "Becoming Jared Kushner," *Harvard Crimson*, March 9, 2017, https://www.thecrimson.com/article/2017/3/9/jared-kushner-undergrad/.
18. "Jared Kushner Speaks at Chabad House at Harvard, 2003," YouTube, posted by JTA News, January 27, 2017, https://www.youtube.com/watch?v=56S3cBvAr9Q.
19. *The New York Observer, Kingdom of New York*, 234.
20. *The New York Observer, Kingdom of New York*, 338.
21. Jared Kushner, "2014 Undergraduate Commencement II - Hofstra University."
22. Gabriel Sherman, "The Legacy," *New York*, July 10, 2009, http://nymag.com/news/features/57891/.
23. Chris Christie with Ellis Henican, *Let Me Finish: Trump, the Kushners, Bannon, New Jersey, and the Power of In-Your-Face Politics* (New York: Hachette, 2019), 248.
24. *The New York Observer, Kingdom of New York*, 338.
25. *The New York Observer, Kingdom of New York*, 338.
26. *The New York Observer, Kingdom of New York*, 338.
27. Katharine Q. Seelye, "Developer's Son Acquires The New York Observer," *New York Times*, July 31, 2006, https://www.nytimes.com/2006/07/31/business/media/31observer.html.
28. Sherman, "Legacy."
29. *The New York Observer, Kingdom of New York*, 338–39.
30. *The New York Observer, Kingdom of New York*, 339.
31. Jared Kushner, "2014 Undergraduate Commencement II - Hofstra University."
32. United States v. William E. Baroni Jr. and Bridget Anne Kelly, No. 2:15-cr-00193-SDW (D-N.J.), September 23, 2016, David Wildstein trial testimony.
33. Jared Kushner to David Wildstein, email, released during *Baroni* trial.
34. Jeff Pillets, "Doing Time the Easy Way; Disgraced Kushner Has Chauffeur, Job, Furloughs," *The Record*, June 19, 2006.

35. William Grimes, "Four Seasons, Lunch Spot for Manhattan's Prime Movers, Moves On," *New York Times*, July 8, 2016, https://www.nytimes.com/2016/07/10/nyregion/four-seasons-lunch-spot-for-manhattans-prime-movers-moves-on.html.
36. Paul Laurie/PMC, "Jared Kushner and Peter Kaplan Present the Relaunch of the New York Observer Website," April 18, 2007, Patrick McMullan Company, https://www.patrickmcmullan.com/events/5b3ef4fb9f92906676448199/.

11. ENTRÉE

1. *Late Night with Conan O'Brien*, season 14, episode 116, guest Ivanka Trump, aired March 16, 2007.
2. Ivanka Trump, *The Trump Card: Playing to Win in Work and Life* (New York: Touchstone, 2009), 19–22
3. Donald J. Trump with Tony Schwartz, *The Art of the Deal* (New York: Ballantine Books, 2015), 72.
4. Tony Schwartz, email correspondence with author, January 28, 2019.
5. Trump, *Trump Card*, 21.
6. Ivanka Trump (@ivankatrump), "She's a builder! (I think it's safe to say some things are genetic . . .)," Instagram, October 2, 2013, https://www.instagram.com/p/e9yCyxikJh/.
7. Trump, *Trump Card*, 38.
8. Trump, *Trump Card*, 36.
9. Ivana Trump, *Raising Trump* (New York: Gallery Books, 2017), 167.
10. Trump, *Trump Card*, 52.
11. Ivanka Trump, interview in Jamie Johnson, *Born Rich*, HBO, January 19, 2003.
12. "Ivanka Trump," interview by Lloyd Grove, *Portfolio.com*, November 10, 2008, https://www.entrepreneur.com/article/198386.
13. "Ivanka on What Growing Up Trump Was Like | The Oprah Winfrey Show | Oprah Winfrey Network," originally aired February 20, 2009, posted to YouTube by the Oprah Winfrey Network April 11, 2016, https://youtu.be/lsusrsuMuV0.
14. Trump, *Trump Card*, 72.
15. Documents sourced from NYC Department of Finance, Automated City Register Information System (ACRIS).
16. Trump, *Trump Card*, 93.
17. Emily Jane Fox, *Born Trump: Inside America's First Family* (New York: HarperCollins, 2018), 248.
18. Charles V. Bagli, "Due Diligence on the Donald," *New York Times*, January 25, 2004.
19. Trump attorney and the *New York Times*, correspondence, 2004, obtained by author.
20. Patrick Radden Keefe, "How Mark Burnett Resurrected Donald Trump as an Icon of American Success," *New Yorker*, December 27, 2018, https://www.newyorker.com/magazine/2019/01/07/how-mark-burnett-resurrected-donald-trump-as-an-icon-of-american-success.
21. Keefe, "Mark Burnett."
22. Franklin Foer, "How Kleptocracy Came to America," *Atlantic*, March 2019, https://www.theatlantic.com/magazine/archive/2019/03/how-kleptocracy-came-to-america/580471/.
23. "The Donald Interviews The Kids | Forbes," YouTube, posted by *Forbes*, October 30, 2006, https://www.youtube.com/watch?v=Vc0k1CMl6_o.
24. Trump, *Trump Card*, 57.
25. Mike McIntire, Megan Twohey, and Mark Mazzetti, "How a Lawyer, a Felon and a Russian General Chased a Moscow Trump Tower Deal," *New York Times*, November 29, 2018, https://www.nytimes.com/2018/11/29/us/politics/trump-russia-felix-sater-michael-cohen.html.

26. Tom Hamburger, Rosalind S. Helderman, and Dana Priest, "In 'Little Moscow,' Russians Helped Donald Trump's Brand Survive the Recession," *Washington Post*, November 4, 2016, https://www.washingtonpost.com/politics/in-little-moscow-russians-helped-donald-trumps-brand-survive-the-recession/2016/11/04/f9dbd38e-97cf-11e6-bb29-bf2701dbe0a3_story.html; Nathan Layne, Ned Parker, Svetlana Reiter, Stephen Grey, and Ryan McNeill, "Russian Elite Invested Nearly $100 Million in Trump Buildings," *Reuters*, March 17, 2017, https://www.reuters.com/investigates/special-report/usa-trump-property/.
27. United States v. Michael Sheferovsky, 1:00-mj-01058 (E.D.N.Y. 2000).
28. United States v. Felix Sater, 1:98-cr-01101-ILG (E.D.N.Y. 1998), letter filed with the court, March 21, 2011.
29. Sater gave multiple interviews describing these events; see Anthony Cormier and Jason Leopold, "Trump Moscow: The Definitive Story of How Trump's Team Worked the Russian Deal During the Campaign," *BuzzFeed News*, May 17, 2018, https://www.buzzfeednews.com/article/anthonycormier/trump-moscow-micheal-cohen-felix-sater-campaign; "Trump Business Associate Felix Sater Speaks Out on Russia Ties," interview by Chris Cuomo, CNN, March 16, 2018 https://www.youtube.com/watch?v=rdFmBd9BXKs; and "Trump Associate Felix Sater Speaks Out," inteview by Chris Hayes, MSNBC, March 16, 2018, http://www.msnbc.com/transcripts/all-in/2018-03-16.
30. Matt Apuzzo and Maggie Haberman, "Trump Associate Boasted That Moscow Business Deal 'Will Get Donald Elected,'" *New York Times*, August 28, 2017, https://www.nytimes.com/2017/08/28/us/politics/trump-tower-putin-felix-sater.html.
31. Heather Vogell, with Andrea Bernstein, Meg Cramer, and Peter Elkind, "Pump and Trump," ProPublica, October 17, 2018, https://features.propublica.org/trump-inc-podcast/trump-family-business-panama-city-khafif/.
32. *The Apprentice*, season 5, episode 15, "Decision Time," aired June 5, 2006 on NBC.
33. Observer Staff, "The Afternoon Wrap: Wednesday," *New York Observer*, January 3, 2007, https://observer.com/2007/01/the-afternoon-wrap-wednesday-8/.
34. "The Closer," *New York Daily News*, September 27, 2007, https://www.nydailynews.com/life-style/real-estate/closer-article-1.245321.
35. Melissa Grace, "Cheers, Jeers for Donald Trump's SoHo Condominium Hotel," *New York Daily News*, September 20, 2007, https://www.nydailynews.com/news/money/cheers-jeers-donald-trump-soho-condominium-hotel-article-1.245948.
36. Charles V. Bagli, "Real Estate Executive With Hand in Trump Projects Rose From Tangled Past," *New York Times*, December 17, 2007, https://www.nytimes.com/2007/12/17/nyregion/17trump.html.
37. Charles V. Bagli, interviewed by author, December 2018.
38. *The Apprentice*, season 6, episode 1, "To Have and Have Not," aired January 7, 2007 on NBC.
39. Trump, *Trump Card*, 187.
40. Judy Klemesrud, "Donald Trump, Real Estate Promoter, Builds Image as He Buys Buildings," *New York Times*, November 1, 1976, https://www.nytimes.com/1976/11/01/archives/donald-trump-real-estate-promoter-builds-image-as-he-buys-buildings.html.
41. "Ivanka Trumps All," *Stuff Magazine*, September 2006 (cover).
42. Ivanka Trump, "Executive Branch Personnel, Public Financial Disclosure Report," OGE Form 278e (Washington, DC, Office of Government Ethics, 2018 [filed May 15, 2018]).
43. Phoebe Eaton, "Ivanka Trump: The New Queen of Diamonds," *Harper's Bazaar*, September 24, 2007, https://www.harpersbazaar.com/celebrity/red-carpet-dresses/a207/ivanka-trump-diamonds-1007/.
44. George Gurley, "Trump Power: Ivanka Trump," *Marie Claire*, January 29, 2007, https://www.marieclaire.com/career-advice/tips/a105/ivanka-trump/.

45. Trump, *Trump Card*, 222.
46. Ben Schreckinger, "DOJ Sues Ivanka's Ex-Business Partner for Massive Fraud," *Politico Magazine*, August 17, 2018, https://www.politico.com/magazine/story/2018/08/17/ivanka-trump-business-partner-justice-department-lawsuit-moshe-lax-219369.
47. PageSix.com staff, "Ivanka Observed," *New York Post*, April 20, 2007.
48. Richard Johnson, "No More Lies," *New York Post*, May 4, 2007, https://web.archive.org/web/20070510011038/http://www.nypost.com/seven/05042007/gossip/pagesix/no_more_lies_pagesix_.htm.
49. Jo Piazza, "Fashion Dish: Poor showing for Nicky Hilton," *New York Daily News*, September 10, 2007, https://www.nydailynews.com/entertainment/gossip/fashion-dish-poor-showing-nicky-hilton-article-1.242974.
50. "Jared Kushner," *New York Post*, September 28, 2007.
51. Ruth La Ferla, "Introducing the Ivanka," *New York Times*, December 27, 2007, https://www.nytimes.com/2007/12/27/fashion/27IVANKA.html.
52. Gabriel Sherman, "The Legacy," *New York*, July 10, 2009, http://nymag.com/news/features/57891/.
53. PageSix.com Staff, "Sightings . . . Sightings . . . ," *New York Post*, August 10, 2008, https://pagesix.com/2008/08/10/sightings-sightings-29/.
54. PageSix.com Staff, "Shiksa No More," *New York Post*, October 29, 2008, https://pagesix.com/2008/10/29/shiksa-no-more/.
55. "Interview with Ivanka Trump," *Portfolio*, 2008, quoted in Heather Vogell, Andrea Bernstein, Meg Cramer, and Peter Elkind, "Pump and Trump," *Trump, Inc.*, October 17, 2018, https://www.wnycstudios.org/story/trump-inc-pump-trump-panama.
56. Inti Pacheco, Manuela Andreoni, Alex Mierjeski, and Keenan Chen, "Trump Org: A Magnet for Dirty Businessmen," *Univision News*, February 26, 2018, https://www.univision.com/univision-news/latin-america/trump-org-magnet-for-dirty-businessmen.
57. The Trump Organization "Baja Project" Cases, No. BC409651 (Cal. Super. July 20, 2012), fourth amended complaint, exhibit 67, "From the Desk of Ivanka Trump," *Trump Baja News* 3 (September 2007).
58. "Ivanka Trump Speaks Out," YouTube, posted by CBS, March 14, 2009, https://www.youtube.com/watch?v=M-2ELTUvIhA.
59. Ivanka Trump (@IvankaTrump), Twitter, July 16, 2009, https://twitter.com/IvankaTrump/status/2668887612.
60. Ivanka Trump, interviewed by Leonard Lopate, *The Leonard Lopate Show*, October 13, 2009, https://www.wnyc.org/story/59336-the-trump-card/.

12. A FLOOD OF MONEY

1. New York City Department of Finance, Automated City Register Information System, (ACRIS), deed recorded November 20, 2006.
2. Jason Maloni (spokesman for Paul Manafort), email correspondence with author, March 23, 2017.
3. Andrew E. Kramer, "Out of Siberia, a Russian Way to Wealth," *New York Times*, August 20, 2006, https://www.nytimes.com/2006/08/20/business/yourmoney/20oligarch.html.
4. Franklin Foer, "The Plot Against America," *The Atlantic*, March 2018, https://www.theatlantic.com/magazine/archive/2018/03/paul-manafort-american-hustler/550925/.
5. "The Global Intelligence Files," email sent August 15, 2007 to intelligence@stratfor.com, released on May 29, 2013, https://wikileaks.org/gifiles/docs/54/5467826_humint-russia-my-night-with-deripaska-part-i-.html, cited in Foer, "The Plot."
6. Foer, "The Plot."
7. Jeff Horwitz and Chad Day, "Before Trump Job, Manafort Worked to Aid Putin," *Asso-*

ciated Press, March 22, 2017, https://www.apnews.com/122ae0b5848345faa88108a03de40c5a.

8. United States v. Paul Manafort Jr., No. 1:18-cr-00083 (E.D. Va. August 21, 2018), Exhibit EE-FF at 104, ID#2586, document #153-2, filed July 26, 2018.
9. "Profile: Ukraine's ousted President Viktor Yanukovych," *BBC News*, February 28, 2014, https://www.bbc.com/news/world-europe-25182830.
10. *Manafort*, Exhibit EE-FF at 93, ID#2575.
11. United States v. The Premises Located Alexandria, Virginia, 22314, No. 1:17-sw-00449 (E.D. Va. August 21, 2018), application for a search warrant, filed July 5, 2017; United States v. Paul Manafort Jr., transcript of proceedings held on August 6, 2018, document #231, filed August 13, 2018.
12. Calculated by the author with data from NYU Furman Center, February 2019.
13. Jonathan Chait, "Going for Gold," *New Republic*, May 21, 2001, https://newrepublic.com/article/87096/going-gold.
14. Samara R. Potter and William G. Gale, "The Bush Tax Cut: One Year Later," *Brookings Institution*, June 15, 2002, https://www.brookings.edu/research/the-bush-tax-cut-one-year-later/.
15. Joseph E. Stiglitz, "The Economic Consequences of Mr. Bush," *Vanity Fair*, November 7, 2007, https://www.vanityfair.com/news/2007/12/bush200712.
16. Alex Blumberg, Adam Davidson, Ira Glass, "The Giant Pool of Money," *This American Life*, episode 355, May 9, 2008, https://www.thisamericanlife.org/355/transcript.
17. Guy Chazan, "In Russia, a Top Rabbi Uses Kremlin Ties to Gain Power," *Wall Street Journal*, May 8, 2007, https://www.wsj.com/articles/SB117858672536595256.
18. William Neuman, "With Backing from an Israeli Billionaire, a Developer Finds Opportunities in Disparate Places," *New York Times*, February 6, 2005, https://www.nytimes.com/2005/02/06/realestate/with-backing-from-an-israeli-billionaire-a-developer-finds.html.
19. United States v. Prevezon Holdings Ltd. et al., 1:13-cv-06326 (S.D.N.Y. 2017).
20. Neuman, "With Backing."
21. Zev Chafets, "The Missionary Mogul," *New York Times Magazine*, September 16, 2007, https://www.nytimes.com/2007/09/16/magazine/16Leviev-t.html.
22. David Barstow, Susanne Craig, and Russ Buettner, "Trump Engaged in Suspect Tax Schemes as He Reaped Riches From His Father," *New York Times*, October 2, 2018, https://www.nytimes.com/interactive/2018/10/02/us/politics/donald-trump-tax-schemes-fred-trump.html.
23. Jon Greenberg, "Hillary Clinton Says Donald Trump Rooted for the Housing Crisis," *PolitiFact*, September 26, 2016, https://www.politifact.com/truth-o-meter/statements/2016/sep/26/hillary-clinton/hillary-clinton-says-donald-trump-rooted-housing-c/.
24. People of the State of New York by Eric T. Schneiderman v. Trump Entrepreneur Initiative LLC, 2014 NY Slip Op 30305(U) (N.Y. March 1, 2016), complaint, filed August 24, 2013.
25. *Trump Entrepreneur Initiative*, complaint.
26. Donald Trump, interviewed by Deborah Solomon, 2009, tape supplied to author.
27. Michael Crowley, "Trump and the Oligarch," *Politico Magazine*, July 28, 2016, https://www.politico.com/magazine/story/2016/07/donald-trump-2016-russian-ties-214116.
28. eTN Editor, "Executive Talk: Donald Trump Jr. Bullish on Russia and Few Emerging Markets," *eTurboNews*, September 15, 2008, https://www.eturbonews.com/9788/executive-talk-donald-trump-jr-bullish-russia-and-few-emerging-ma.
29. Sam Roberts, "Homes Dark and Lifeless, Kept by Out-of-Towners," *New York Times*, July 6, 2011, https://www.nytimes.com/2011/07/07/nyregion/more-apartments-are-empty-yet-rented-or-owned-census-finds.html.
30. Calculated by the author with data from NYU Furman Center, February 2019.

31. Cindy Rodriguez, "As Bloomberg Built Affordable Housing, City Became Less Affordable," WNYC News, July 9, 2013, https://www.wnyc.org/story/304422-new-york-remade-city-more-desirable-ever-also-too-expensive-many.

13. THE INITIATION

1. Raakhee Mirchandani, "The 50 Most Powerful Women in NYC," *New York Post*, June 1, 2008, https://nypost.com/2008/06/01/the-50-most-powerful-women-in-nyc/.
2. Dominic Rushe, interviewed by author, July 2017.
3. Charles V. Bagli, "Real Estate Executive with Hand in Trump Projects Rose from Tangled Past," *New York Times*, December 17, 2007, https://www.nytimes.com/2007/12/17/nyregion/17trump.html.
4. Some of the reporting in this chapter originally appeared in an article I wrote with Jesse Eisinger, Justin Elliott, and Ilya Marritz, "How Ivanka Trump and Donald Trump, Jr., Avoided a Criminal Indictment," published on October 4, 2017, by the *New Yorker*, ProPublica, and WNYC. It was based on interviews with twenty people familiar with the investigation, dozens of former city and state officials, court records, land records, data maintained by the New York State Board of Elections, filings with the New York Attorney General's office and the New York City Bureau of Standards and Appeals, and other public documents. We were not able to review copies of the emails that were the focal point of the inquiry and relied on the accounts of multiple individuals who had seen them. https://www.wnyc.org/story/ivanka-donald-trump-jr-close-charged-felony-fraud/.
5. *The Apprentice*, season 5, episode 15, "Decision Time," aired June 5, 2006, on NBC.
6. Bernstein et al., "How Ivanka Trump and Donald Trump, Jr., Avoided a Criminal Indictment."
7. Ivanka Trump, interviewed by Cynthia McFadden, *ABC News Nightline*, October 13, 2009.
8. Calculated by the author with data from New York State Board of Elections.
9. Frank Lynn, "Cuomo and Abrams Tell Ethics Panel of Fund-Raising," *New York Times*, March 11, 1989.
10. Bernstein et al., "How Ivanka Trump and Donald Trump, Jr., Avoided a Criminal Indictment."
11. Palmer Gardens LLC v. Bayrock/Sapir Organization LLC, No. 1:10-cv-05830 (S.D.N.Y.), second amended complaint, document 14, filed November 30, 2010.
12. Elizabeth A. Harris, "Fifteen Buyers File Lawsuit Against Trump Soho Project," *New York Times*, August 2, 2010, https://www.nytimes.com/2010/08/03/nyregion/03trump.html.
13. Adam Leitman Bailey to Cyrus R. Vance, Jr., letter, November 2, 2011, obtained by author.
14. Daniel Geiger, "The Brouhaha Behind the Ground Zero Mosque Introduced Adam Leitman Bailey to the World. So What's Next for Real Estate's Most Public Attorney?" *New York Observer*, February 21, 2012, https://observer.com/2012/02/the-brouhaha-behind-the-ground-zero-mosque-introduced-adam-leitman-bailey-to-the-world-so-whats-next-for-real-estates-most-public-attorney/.
15. Bernstein et al., "How Ivanka Trump and Donald Trump, Jr., Avoided a Criminal Indictment."
16. Calculated by author from records of New York State Board of Elections.
17. Bernstein et al., "How Ivanka Trump and Donald Trump, Jr., Avoided a Criminal Indictment."
18. Jesse Eisinger, "Manhattan District Attorney Says He'll No Longer Accept Contributions from Lawyers with Cases before Him," ProPublica, January 23, 2018.

14. "TO SPEND WITHOUT LIMIT"

1. "Unemployment Rate in Stark County, OH," Federal Reserve Bank of St. Louis, https://fred.stlouisfed.org/series/OHSTAR1URN.
2. Center for Responsive Politics, "Election 2010 to Shatter Spending Records as Republicans Benefit from Late Cash Surge," OpenSecrets.org, October 27, 2010, https://www.opensecrets.org/news/2010/10/election-2010-to-shatter-spending-r/.
3. Chris Cillizza, "How Citizens United Changed Politics, in 7 Charts," *Washington Post*, January 22, 2014, https://www.washingtonpost.com/news/the-fix/wp/2014/01/21/how-citizens-united-changed-politics-in-6-charts/.
4. Jane Mayer, *Dark Money: The Hidden History of the Billionaires Behind the Rise of the Radical Right* (New York: Anchor Books, 2017), 257.
5. Mayer, *Dark Money*, 231.
6. Mayer, *Dark Money*, 235.
7. David D. Kirkpatrick, "A Quest to End Spending Rules for Campaigns," *New York Times*, January 24, 2010, https://www.nytimes.com/2010/01/25/us/politics/25bopp.html.
8. Citizens United v. Federal Election Commission, 558 U.S. 310 (2010), https://casetext.com/case/citizens-united-v-federal-election-comn.
9. "Text: Obama's State of the Union Address," *New York Times*, January 27, 2010, https://www.nytimes.com/2010/01/28/us/politics/28obama.text.html.
10. Heather Vogell, with Andrea Bernstein, Meg Cramer, and Peter Elkind, "Pump and Trump," ProPublica, October 17, 2018, https://features.propublica.org/trump-inc-podcast/trump-family-business-panama-city-khafif/.
11. "Trump Ocean Club Panama," YouTube, posted by The Trump Organization, July 11, 2011, https://www.youtube.com/watch?v=BMSlAb4RD7M.
12. "Trump Ocean Club Panama," YouTube.
13. "Ivanka Trump," interview by Lloyd Grove, *Portfolio.com*, November 10, 2008, https://www.entrepreneur.com/article/198386.
14. "Trump Ocean Club Panama," YouTube.
15. Ken Silverstein, "Narco-a-Lago: Money Laundering at the Trump Ocean Club Panama," *Global Witness*, November 2017, https://www.globalwitness.org/en/campaigns/corruption-and-money-laundering/narco-a-lago-panama/#chapter-0/section-1.
16. Newland International Properties, Inc., offering memorandum for Trump Ocean Club International Hotel and Tower, Panama, for Bear, Stearns and Co., Inc., November 2007, obtained by author.
17. Vogell et al., "Pump and Trump."
18. Vogell et al., "Pump and Trump."
19. "Ivanka Trump visits Trump International Hotel & Tower, Toronto," YouTube, posted by Trump International Hotel & Tower Toronto, July 24, 2008, https://www.youtube.com/watch?v=9z5590CHoFM.
20. Sarbjit Singh v. Donald John Trump Sr., No. C60787, [2016] ONCA 747.
21. *Donald John Trump Sr.*, No. C60787, [2016] ONCA 747.
22. Tom Burgis, "Tower of Secrets: The Russian Money behind a Donald Trump Skyscraper," *Financial Times Magazine*, July 11, 2018, https://www.ft.com/trumptoronto.
23. "Billionaires 2010: #773 Alexander Shnaider," *Forbes*, March 1, 2010, https://www.forbes.com/profile/alexander-shnaider/#22d9eddd7c1c.
24. Mark MacKinnon, "Searching for Boris Birshtein," *Globe and Mail*, December 29, 2018, https://www.theglobeandmail.com/canada/investigations/article-boris-birshtein-investigation/.
25. Tom Burgis, "Tower of Secrets."
26. Robert Cribb et al., "How Every Investor Lost Money on Trump Tower Toronto (but

Donald Trump Made Millions Anyway)," *Star* with *Columbia Journalism Investigations*, October 21, 2017, https://www.thestar.com/news/world/2017/10/21/how-every-investor-lost-money-on-trump-tower-toronto-but-donald-trump-made-millions-anyway.html.

27. Heidi Brown and Nathan Vardi, "Man of Steel," *Forbes*, March 28, 2005, https://www.forbes.com/forbes/2005/0328/132.html#181708702fc0.
28. Burgis, "Tower of Secrets."
29. Rob Barry, Christopher S. Stewart, and Brett Forrest, "Russian State-Run Bank Financed Deal Involving Trump Hotel Partner," *Wall Street Journal*, May 17, 2017, https://www.wsj.com/articles/russian-state-run-bank-financed-deal-involving-trump-hotel-partner-1495031708.
30. Donald J. Trump, "Executive Branch Personnel Public Financial Disclosure Reports," OGE Form 278e, (Washington, DC, Office of Government Ethics [filed June 22, 2015 and May 15, 2018]).
31. "Grand Opening of Trump International Hotel & Tower®," YouTube, posted by Cision Canada, April 17, 2012, https://www.youtube.com/watch?v=jMs_WrN63PQ.
32. Tara Perkins, "Trump Talks Up Toronto Tower," *Globe and Mail*, April 17, 2012.
33. Cribb et al., "How Every Investor Lost."
34. Mark DeCambre, "Schwarzman Likens Bam to Hitler over Taxes," *New York Post*, August 17, 2010, https://nypost.com/2010/08/17/schwarzman-likens-bam-to-hitler-over-taxes/.
35. Mayer, *Dark Money*, 254.
36. Ilya Marritz, "Obama Saved New York by Saving Wall Street. But.," WNYC News, January 17, 2017, https://www.wnyc.org/story/obama-and-new-york-city-economy/.
37. Russ Choma, "The 2012 Election: Our Price Tag (Finally) for the Whole Ball of Wax," *OpenSecrets.org*, March 13, 2013, https://www.opensecrets.org/news/2013/03/the-2012-election-our-price-tag-fin/.
38. Center for Responsive Politics, 2012 Outside Spending, Federal Election Spending, by Group, https://www.opensecrets.org/outsidespending/summ.php?cycle=2012&chrt=V&disp=O&type=U.
39. Ivanka Trump, interviewed by Piers Morgan, *Piers Morgan Tonight*, February 9, 2012.
40. Calculated by the author with data from Federal Election Commission.

15. LICENSE

1. Federal Election Commission, Matter Under Review #6462: Donald J. Trump et al., first general counsel's report, January 25, 2013.
2. Caleb Melby, "Guns, Girls and Sex Tapes: The Unhinged, Hedonistic Saga of Billionaire Stewart Rahr, 'Number One King of All Fun'," *Forbes*, September 17, 2013, https://www.forbes.com/sites/calebmelby/2013/09/17/guns-girls-and-sex-tapes-the-saga-of-billionaire-stewart-rahr-number-one-king-of-all-fun/#3e523fc53f86.
3. Michael Cohen, interviewed by Amy Walter and Jonathan Karl, *ABC News*, March 11, 2011.
4. Trump Tower press conference, March 10, 2011, audiotape from WNYC archives.
5. Many of the details of Cohen's background were first reported in the story I wrote with my WNYC colleague Ilya Marritz, "The Company Michael Cohen Kept," *Trump, Inc.*, April 18, 2018, https://www.wnycstudios.org/story/trump-inc-podcast-company-michael-cohen-kept.
6. House Permanent Select Committee on Intelligence, *Deposition of: Michael Cohen*, (Washington, DC: February 28, 2019) 12, https://docs.house.gov/meetings/IG/IG00/20190520/109549/HMTG-116-IG00-20190520-SD002.pdf.
7. United States v. Michael Cohen, No. 1:18-cr-00602 (S.D.N.Y.), unredacted search warrant dated April 8, 2018, Exhibit 2 – 18MAG 2969., document #43-1, filed March 19, 2019.

8. "Michael Cohen Testimony Before House Oversight Committee," February 27, 2019, *C-SPAN*, https://www.c-span.org/video/transcript/?id=57772.
9. "Michael Cohen Testimony."
10. *Morning Joe*, "Emily Jane Fox: Michael Cohen Says Trump Is Like His Father," aired April 10, 2018.
11. *Deposition of: Michael Cohen*, February 28, 2019, 22.
12. Trump Tower press conference, March 10, 2011.
13. Adam Davidson, "Trump's Business of Corruption," *New Yorker*, August 14, 2017, https://www.newyorker.com/magazine/2017/08/21/trumps-business-of-corruption.
14. Trump Tower press conference, March 10, 2011.
15. Gregory Krieg, "14 of Trump's Most Outrageous 'Birther' Claims—Half from After 2011," CNN, September 16, 2016, https://www.cnn.com/2016/09/09/politics/donald-trump-birther/index.html.
16. "Trump: Obama Birth Certificate Needs Truth Test," YouTube video, posted by the Associated Press, April 27, 2011, https://www.youtube.com/watch?v=f6hsm81VXKY.
17. Barack Obama, "C-SPAN: President Obama at the 2011 White House Correspondents' Dinner," April 30, 2011, https://www.c-span.org/video/?c4667818/president-obama-2011-white-house-correspondents-dinner.
18. First general counsel's report, MUR #6462.
19. Jane Mayer, *Dark Money: The Hidden History of the Billionaires Behind the Rise of the Radical Right* (New York: Anchor Books, 2017), 110.
20. Wayne Barrett, *Trump: The Deals and the Downfall* (New York: HarperCollins, 1992), 242.
21. Christopher Rowland, "Deadlock by Design Hobbles Election Agency," *Boston Globe*, July 7, 2013, https://www.bostonglobe.com/news/nation/2013/07/06/america-campaign-finance-watchdog-rendered-nearly-toothless-its-own-appointed-commissioners/44zZoJwnzEHyzxTByNL2QP/story.html?s_campaign=sm_tw.
22. Ellen L. Weintraub, "Trump's Pick for White House Counsel Is Wrong for the Job," *Washington Post*, December 9, 2016, https://www.washingtonpost.com/opinions/i-worked-with-trumps-pick-for-white-house-counsel-he-doesnt-care-about-corruption/2016/12/09/76f0793c-bcac-11e6-94ac-3d324840106c_story.html.
23. Matthew S. Petersen, "Statement of Reasons," MUR #6462, February 22, 2017.
24. James V. Grimaldi and Mark Maremont, "Donald Trump Made Millions from Multilevel Marketing Firm," *Wall Street Journal*, August 13, 2015, https://www.wsj.com/articles/trump-made-millions-from-multilevel-marketing-firm-1439481128.
25. Multiple videos posted to YouTube, March 21, 2011.
26. Donald J. Trump, "Executive Branch Personnel Public Financial Disclosure Report," OGE Form 278e (Washington, DC, Office of Government Ethics [filed June 22, 2018]).
27. Grimaldi and Maremont, "Trump Made Millions."
28. Jane Doe v. The Trump Corporation et al., No. 1:18-cv-09936 (S.D.N.Y.), amended complaint, document #77, filed January 31, 2019.
29. *The Trump Corporation et al.*, No. 1:18-cv-09936-LGS (S.D.N.Y.).
30. *The Apprentice*, season 11, episode 4, "Off the Hook," aired March 27, 2011.
31. Ivanka Trump, *The Trump Card: Playing to Win in Work and Life* (New York: Touchstone, 2009), 240.
32. *The Trump Corporation et al.*, motion to dismiss, document #83, February 21, 2019.
33. *The Trump Corporation et al.*, order denying motion to dismiss, document #97, filed July 24, 2019.
34. Maggie Haberman and Alexander Burns, "Donald Trump's Presidential Run Began in an Effort to Gain Stature," *New York Times*, March 12, 2016, https://www.nytimes.com/2016/03/13/us/politics/donald-trump-campaign.html.

35. Claude Solnik, "Questions Spread over Payment at Trump Rallies," *Long Island Business News*, June 19, 2015, https://libn.com/2015/06/19/questions-spread-over-payment-at-trump-rallies-3/.
36. Calculated by the author with data from New York State Board of Elections.
37. Jon Swaine, "FBI Looked Into Trump Plans to Build Hotel in Latvia with Putin Supporter," *The Guardian*, March 29, 2018, https://www.theguardian.com/world/2018/mar/29/trump-fbi-hotel-latvia-investigation-russia-links.
38. Baltic International Bank, "Donald Trump John Jr. Told about Their Family Business at the Conference Hosted by Baltic International Bank," news release, May 30, 2012, https://www.bib.eu/en/news/05/30/donald-trump-jr-attends-bib-annual-conference.
39. "Interview with Donald Trump Jr. (Riga, 19 May 2012)," YouTube, posted by Otkritij Gorod, November 7, 2012, https://www.youtube.com/watch?v=AO1Wv5E8wpA.
40. Jon Swaine and Scott Stedman, "Revealed: Russian Billionaire Set Up US Company before Trump Tower Meeting," *Guardian*, October 18, 2018.
41. Adam Davidson, "Donald Trump's Worst Deal," *New Yorker*, March 5, 2017, https://www.newyorker.com/magazine/2017/03/13/donald-trumps-worst-deal.
42. "Corruption Perceptions Index 2012," *Transparency International*, https://www.transparency.org/cpi2012/results.
43. Davidson, "Donald Trump's Worst Deal."
44. Ivanka Trump (@ivankatrump), "I'm in Baku, Azerbaijan . . . and will reveal why next week! In the meantime, check out this cityscape view from my balcony!" Instagram video, October 22, 2014, https://www.instagram.com/p/udVmt8CkFf/?hl=en.
45. Michael Isikoff and David Corn, *Russian Roulette: The Inside Story of Putin's War on America and the Election of Donald Trump* (New York: Twelve, 2018), 5.
46. Luke Harding, *Collusion: Secret Meetings, Dirty Money, and How Russia Helped Donald Trump Win* (New York: Vintage Books, 2017), 234.
47. Isikoff and Corn, *Russian Roulette*, 6.
48. Jeremy Diamond, "Exclusive: Video Shows Trump with Associates Tied to Email Controversy," CNN, July 13, 2017, https://www.cnn.com/2017/07/12/politics/video-trump-relationships-russian-associates/index.html.
49. United States General Accounting Office, *Report to the Ranking Minority Member, Permanent Subcommittee on Investigations, Committee on Governmental Affairs, United States Senate; Suspicious Banking Activities: Possible Money Laundering by U.S. Corporations Formed for Russian Entities* (Washington, DC: US General Accounting Office, October 2000), https://www.gao.gov/new.items/d01120.pdf.
50. Raymond Bonner, "Laundering of Money Seen as 'Easy,'" *New York Times*, November 29, 2000, https://www.nytimes.com/2000/11/29/business/laundering-of-money-seen-as-easy.html.
51. Isikoff and Corn, *Russian Roulette*, 17.
52. Konrad Putzier, "Hotel Trio Aims to Bring Manhattan to Moscow," *Real Estate Weekly*, November 12, 2013, https://rew-online.com/2013/11/hotel-trio-aims-to-bring-manhattan-to-moscow/.
53. Donald J. Trump (@realDonaldTrump), Twitter, November 11, 2013, https://twitter.com/realDonaldTrump/status/399939505924628480.
54. Special Counsel Robert S. Mueller III, *Report on the Investigation into Russian Interference in the 2016 Presidential Election*, vol. 1 (Washington, DC: US Department of Justice, March 2019), 68.
55. Mueller, *Report on the Investigation*, vol. 1, 113.

16. OTHER PEOPLE'S MONEY

1. David Yassky, interviewed by author, March 2019.
2. Eliot Spitzer, interviewed by author, March 2019.
3. Jared Kushner, interviewed by George Gurley in *The Kingdom of New York: Knights, Knaves, Billionaires, and Beauties in the City of Big Shots*, ed. *The New York Observer* (New York: HarperCollins, 2009), 338–39.
4. Lisa Chase, interviewed by author, June 2018.
5. David Carr, "At Peter Kaplan's Funeral, Mourning the Master of the Masters," *New York Times*, December 3, 2013, https://www.nytimes.com/2013/12/04/nyregion/at-peter-kaplans-funeral-mourning-the-master-of-the-masters.html.
6. Kyle Pope, "The Jared Bubble: What My 18 Months as Jared Kushner's First Editor Taught Me about the Trump Family and the Press," *Columbia Journalism Review*, Fall 2017, https://www.cjr.org/special_report/cjr-kyle-pope-jared-kushner-observer.php.
7. "Behind the Bricks: A Sneak Peek at Residential Development in NY," YouTube, posted by 92nd Street Y, April 1, 2016, https://www.youtube.com/watch?v=t4C7_WBf1.
8. Jesse M. Keenan, "666 Fifth Avenue, New York, NY: A Case Study," New York: Columbia University and the Center for Urban Real Estate, 2013, http://www.cacq.com/images/site_images/666%20Fifth%20Ave_Case%20Study.pdf.
9. David Kocieniewski and Caleb Melby, "Kushners' China Deal Flop Was Part of Much Bigger Hunt for Cash," *Bloomberg*, August 31, 2017, https://www.bloomberg.com/graphics/2017-kushners-china-deal-flop-was-part-of-much-bigger-hunt-for-cash/.
10. Moody's Investors Services, "Wachovia Bank Commerical Trust, Commerical Mortgage Pass-Through Certificates, Series 2007-C31," May 3, 2007, 18, obtained by author.
11. Moody's Investors Services, "Wachovia Bank," 17.
12. Trepp Loan Property Detail, "GECMC 2007-C1: 666 Fifth Avenue – A Note," obtained by author.
13. Kocieniewski and Melby, "Kushner's China Deal."
14. Kocieniewski and Melby, "Kushner's China Deal."
15. Trepp Loan Property Detail, "GECMC," 5.
16. Elizabeth Spiers, "The Big Dick Mack Story," *Elizabeth Spiers*, July 7, 2016, https://web.archive.org/web/20160712144349/http://www.elizabethspiers.com/the-big-dick-mack-story/.
17. Sarah Ellison, "How Jared Kushner Became Donald Trump's Mini-Me," *Vanity Fair*, July 7, 2016, https://www.vanityfair.com/news/2016/07/jared-kushner-donald-trump-mini-me.
18. Trepp Loan Property Detail, "GECMC," 5.
19. Kocieniewski and Melby, "Kushner's China Deal."
20. David M. Levitt, "Kushner Reworks Debt on NYC's 666 Fifth Ave. with Vornado," *Bloomberg*, December 16, 2011, https://www.bloomberg.com/news/articles/2011–12–16/kushner-refinances-record-setting-manhattan-tower-as-vornado-takes-a-stake.
21. Kocieniewski and Melby, "Kushner's China Deal."
22. Kushner Companies promotional booklet, 2018, obtained by author.
23. Alec MacGillis, "Jared Kushner's Other Real Estate Empire in Baltimore," *New York Times Magazine*, May 23, 2017, https://www.nytimes.com/2017/05/23/magazine/jared-kushners-other-real-estate-empire.html.
24. Brad Berton, "Kushner Comes Back," *Multifamily Executive*, October 15, 2012, https://www.multifamilyexecutive.com/business-finance/transactions/kushner-comes-back_o.
25. Oshrat Carmiel, "NYC Apartment Investors Seek Big Returns by Buying Small," *Bloomberg*, March 20, 2013, https://www.bloomberg.com/news/articles/2013-03-20/nyc-apartment-investors-seek-big-returns-by-buying-small.

26. Kim Barker, "Behind New York's Housing Crisis: Weakened Laws and Fragmented Regulation," *New York Times*, May 20, 2018, https://www.nytimes.com/interactive/2018/05/20/nyregion/affordable-housing-nyc.html.
27. Carmiel, "NYC Apartment Investors."
28. Jesse Drucker, "Bribe Cases, a Jared Kushner Partner and Potential Conflicts," *New York Times*, April 26, 2017, https://www.nytimes.com/2017/04/26/us/politics/jared-kushner-beny-steinmetz.html.
29. Rey Mashayekhi, "Israeli Investors Retreated from NYC Real Estate in 2016: Report," *Commercial Observer*, March 30, 2017, https://commercialobserver.com/2017/03/israeli-investors-retreated-from-nyc-real-estate-in-2016-report/.
30. World Bank, "Israel," *World Bank Open Data*, accessed August 13, 2019, https://data.worldbank.org/country/israel.
31. Drucker, "Bribe Cases."
32. MacGillis, "Other Real Estate Empire."
33. Bernard Condon, "Kushner Cos. Filed False NYC Housing Paperwork," *Associated Press*, March 18, 2018, https://apnews.com/002703e70347481cb993027d04f543cc.
34. Jared Kushner, remarks at TerraCRG Commercial Realty Group's "Only Brooklyn. The Brooklyn Real Estate Summit," May 6, 2014, https://www.youtube.com/watch?v=vrduuwybf8w.
35. "Behind the Bricks," YouTube.
36. "Jared Kushner and LIVWRK In Contract to Buy Big Gowanus Property," *Brownstoner*, June 18, 2014, https://www.brownstoner.com/real-estate-market/jared-kushner-and-livwrk-in-contract-to-buy-big-gowanus-property/.
37. Jonathan Van Meter, "Ivanka Trump Knows What It Means to Be a Modern Millennial," *Vogue*, February 25, 2015, https://www.vogue.com/article/ivanka-trump-collection-the-apprentice-family.
38. The Editors, "Sick Politics," *New York Observer*, January 22, 2013, https://observer.com/2013/01/sick-politics/.
39. The Editors, "It's the Economy, Silly," *New York Observer*, February 19, 2013, https://observer.com/2013/02/its-the-economy-silly/.

17. THE MERGER

1. Donald J. Trump and the Trump Organization v. Eric T. Schneiderman, complaint to the New York State Joint Commission on Public Ethics (JCOPE), filed December 2, 2013.
2. *Eric T. Schneiderman*, JCOPE complaint, 11.
3. Calculated by the author with data from OpenSecrets.org, NJ Elect, and New York State Board of Elections campaign finance databases.
4. *Eric T. Schneiderman*, JCOPE complaint, 20.
5. "ANOTHER big day for the Zuckerbergs: Newlyweds attend wedding of New York's gay power couple (and fellow Facebook founder)," *Daily Mail*, July 2, 2012.
6. *Eric T. Schneiderman*, JCOPE complaint, 22.
7. People of the State of New York by Eric T. Schneiderman v. Trump Entrepreneur Initiative, Index No. 451463/2013, complaint, August 24, 2013.
8. David Grandeau, interviewed by author, September 2016.
9. William D. Cohan, "Big Hair on Campus," *Vanity Fair*, December 3, 2013, https://www.vanityfair.com/news/2014/01/trump-university-fraud-scandal.
10. Donald J. Trump (@realDonaldTrump), Twitter, December 3, 2013, https://twitter.com/realDonaldTrump/status/407838490056196096.
11. Michael Craig, "The Politics and Power of A.G. Schneiderman," *New York Observer*, February 25, 2014, https://observer.com/2014/02/the-politics-and-power-of-a-g-schneiderman/.

12. Jane Mayer and Ronan Farrow, "Four Women Accuse New York's Attorney General of Physical Abuse," *New Yorker*, May 7, 2018, https://www.newyorker.com/news/news-desk/four-women-accuse-new-yorks-attorney-general-of-physical-abuse.
13. Ravi Somaiya, "A New York Observer Article Brings a Spat in Trump's Orbit," *New York Times*, February 26, 2014, https://www.nytimes.com/2014/02/27/business/media/a-new-york-observer-article-brings-a-spat-in-trumps-orbit.html.
14. Andrew Kaczynski, "Newspaper Denies Attorney General Profile Is Donald Trump's Revenge," *BuzzFeed News*, February 25, 2014, https://www.buzzfeednews.com/article/andrewkaczynski/observer-denies-attorney-general-profile-is-donald-trumps-re.
15. Michael Kranish and Jonathan O'Connell, "Kushner's White House Role 'Crushed' Efforts to Woo Investors for NYC Tower," *Washington Post*, September 13, 2017, https://www.washingtonpost.com/politics/kushners-white-house-role-crushed-efforts-to-woo-investors-for-nyc-tower/2017/09/13/723a9732-82c8-11e7-ab27-1a21a8e006ab_story.html.
16. Kranish and O'Connell, "Kushner's White House Role."
17. John Schmid, "Deutsche Bank Linked to Auschwitz Funding," *New York Times*, February 5, 1999, https://www.nytimes.com/1999/02/05/news/deutsche-bank-linked-to-auschwitz-funding.html; Dave Davies, interview with David Enrich, "Deutsche Bank Is the 'Rosetta Stone' to Unlock Trump Finances, Journalist Says," *Fresh Air*, May 9, 2019, https://www.npr.org/2019/05/09/721723204/deutsche-bank-is-the-rosetta-stone-to-unlock-trump-finances-journalist-says.
18. David Enrich, "A Mar-a-Lago Weekend and an Act of God: Trump's History with Deutsche Bank," *New York Times*, March 18, 2019, https://www.nytimes.com/2019/03/18/business/trump-deutsche-bank.html.
19. Andrea Bernstein and Heather Vogell, "Trump and Deutsche Bank: It's Complicated," *Trump, Inc.*, May 22, 2019, https://www.wnycstudios.org/story/trump-inc-trump-deutsche-bank-its-complicated.
20. Donald J. Trump et al. v. Deutsche Bank Trust et al., No. 026841/2008, Supreme Court of the State of New York, County of Queens, complaint, filed November 3, 2008.
21. Jacqueline S. Gold, "Duo Make Private Bank Jewel in B of A's Crown," *American Banker*, March 24, 1999, https://www.americanbanker.com/news/duo-make-private-bank-jewel-in-b-of-as-crown.
22. Monte Burke, "How Ivanka Trump Got the Doral Resort (and the Blue Monster) for a Bargain Basement Price and Had a Baby at the Same Time," *Forbes*, March 6, 2013, https://www.forbes.com/sites/monteburke/2013/03/06/how-ivanka-trump-got-the-doral-resort-and-the-blue-monster-for-a-bargain-basement-price-and-had-a-baby-at-the-same-time/#1ee04841525d.
23. Drew Harwell, "Why America Fell Out of Love with Golf," *Washington Post*, March 5, 2015, https://www.washingtonpost.com/news/wonk/wp/2015/03/05/why-america-fell-out-of-love-with-golf/.
24. Motion to approve entry of sale in connection with Doral Golf Resort & Spa, document #732, filed October 18, 2011, MSR Resort Golf Course LLC, No. 11–10372-shl, (Bankr. S.D.N.Y.).
25. Bernstein and Vogell, "Trump and Deutsche Bank."
26. Carl Gaines, "Deutsche Bank's Rosemary Vrablic and Private Banking's Link to CRE Finance," *Commercial Observer*, February 6, 2013, https://commercialobserver.com/2013/02/deutsche-banks-rosemary-vrablic-and-private-bankings-link-to-cre-finance/.
27. Enrich, "Mar-a-Lago Weekend."
28. Jonathan O'Connell, David A. Fahrenthold, and Jack Gillum, "As the 'King of Debt,' Trump Borrowed to Build His Empire. Then He Began Spending Hundreds of Millions in Cash," *Washington Post*, May 5, 2018, https://www.washingtonpost.com/politics/as-the

-king-of-debt-trump-borrowed-to-build-his-empire-then-he-began-spending-hundreds-of-millions-in-cash/2018/05/05/28fe54b4-44c4-11e8-8569-26fda6b404c7_story.html.

29. Enrich, "Mar-a-Lago Weekend."
30. Bill Littlefield, "A Day (and a Cheeseburger) with President Trump," WBUR, May 5, 2017, https://www.wbur.org/onlyagame/2017/05/05/james-dodson-donald-trump-golf.
31. US General Services Administration, "GSA Selects the Trump Organization as Preferred Developer for DC's Old Post Office," news release, February 7, 2012, https://www.gsa.gov/about-us/newsroom/news-releases/gsa-selects-the-trump-organization-as-preferred-developer-for-dcs-old-post-office.
32. Stephen M. Ryan and James W. Kim, McDermott, Will and Emery, protest binder, filed with GSA, April 16, 2012, made available under the Freedom of Information Act.
33. Jonathan O'Connell, "How the Trumps Landed the Old Post Office Pavilion," *Washington Post*, August 17, 2012, https://www.washingtonpost.com/business/how-the-trumps-landed-the-old-post-office-pavilion/2012/08/17/54cbf1da-bbdd-11e1–9134-f33232e6dafa_story.html.
34. Jan deRoos, HVS Professor of Hotel Finance and Real Estate at the Cornell SC Johnson College of Business, analysis supplied to author, March 2019.
35. Aram Roston, documents obtained for *BuzzFeed News*, from his FOIA appeal: Exhibit G. Form of Ownership Affidavit / Organizational Chart, Affidavit Composition of Tenant (Trump Old Post Office, LLC), n.d., https://www.documentcloud.org/documents/3000979-Exhibit-G-After-FOIA-APPEAL.html.
36. Caleb Melby and David Kocieniewski, "Debt, Conflict and Vacancy Imperil Kushners' Times Square Dream," *Bloomberg*, June 25, 2019, https://www.bloomberg.com/graphics/2019-kushner-times-square-property-development/.
37. Consent order, January 30, 2017, In the Matter of Deutsche Bank AG and Deutsche Bank AG New York Branch, New York State Department of Financial Services.
38. Consent order, Deutsche Bank.
39. David Enrich, interviewed by author for *Trump, Inc.*, April 2019.
40. David Enrich, Jesse Drucker, and Ben Protess, "Trump Sought a Loan During the 2016 Campaign. Deutsche Bank Said No.," *New York Times*, February 2, 2019, https://www.nytimes.com/2019/02/02/business/trump-deutsche-bank.html.
41. David Enrich, "Deutsche Bank Staff Saw Suspicious Activity in Trump and Kushner Accounts," *New York Times*, May 19, 2019, https://www.nytimes.com/2019/05/19/business/deutsche-bank-trump-kushner.html.
42. Jared Kushner, interviewed by Jonathan Swan, *Axios on HBO*, season 2, episode 1, June 2, 2019.
43. Ivanka Trump (@ivankatrump), "Kisses from St. Petersburg!" Instagram, February 1, 2014, https://www.instagram.com/p/j4OmmbCkKk/?hl=en.
44. Ellie Hall, Susie Armitage, and Chris Geidner, "Here's the History Behind the Trumps, the Russian Pop Singer, and His Billionaire Father," *BuzzFeed News*, July 12, 2017, https://www.buzzfeednews.com/article/ellievhall/the-russian-connection.
45. Ivanka Trump (@ivankatrump), "Thank you @mamasinthebuilding for an unforgettable four days in Russia!, " Instagram, February 5, 2014, https://www.instagram.com/p/kBmFGdCkP4/.
46. Calculated by the author with data from OpenSecrets.org; Max de Haldevang, "Major GOP Donor Len Blavatnik Had Business Ties to a Russian Official," *Quartz*, January 22, 2019, https://qz.com/1521847/major-gop-donor-len-blavatnik-had-business-ties-to-a-russian-official/.
47. Stephanie Baker, Irina Reznik, and Katya Kazakina, "Billionaire Ally of Putin Socialized with Kushner, Ivanka Trump," *Bloomberg*, August 18, 2017, https://www.bloomberg

.com/news/articles/2017-08-18/billionaire-ally-of-putin-socialized-with-kushner-ivanka-trump.

48. Miriam Elder, "New York Observer Stands By Journalist Who Smeared Kremlin Foes," *BuzzFeed News*, March 2, 2015, https://www.buzzfeednews.com/article/miriamelder/new-york-observer-stands-by-journalist-who-smeared-kremlin-f.

18. THE INFOMERCIAL

1. "VOTE IVANKA! The Trump in Charge of a Growing American Dynasty," *Town and Country*, February 2016 (cover).
2. Nikki Schwab, "Donald Trump Peppers CPAC Speeches with Humblebrags," *US News*, March 6, 2014, https://www.usnews.com/news/blogs/washington-whispers/2014/03/06/donald-trump-peppers-cpac-speeches-with-humblebrags.
3. Chuck Todd, *Meet the Press*, NBC News, January 25, 2015.
4. United States v. Internet Research Agency et al., No. 1:18-cr-00032-DLF (D.C. 2018), indictment, document #1, filed February 16, 2018; Greg Myre, "'Putin's Chef' Has His Fingers in Many Pies, Critics Say," NPR, January 30, 2019, https://www.npr.org/2019/01/30/685622639/putins-chef-has-his-fingers-in-many-pies-critics-say.
5. Financial Crimes Enforcement Network, "FinCEN Fines Trump Taj Mahal Casino Resort $10 Million for Significant and Long Standing Anti-Money Laundering Violations," news release, March 6, 2015, https://www.fincen.gov/news/news-releases/fincen-fines-trump-taj-mahal-casino-resort-10-million-significant-and-long.
6. "Donald Trump presidential campaign announcement," C-SPAN, June 16, 2015, https://www.c-span.org/video/?326473-1/donald-trump-presidential-campaign-announcement.
7. "Polls: 2016 Republican Presidential Nomination," *RealClearPolitics*, 2016, https://www.realclearpolitics.com/epolls/2016/president/us/2016_republican_presidential_nomination-3823.html.
8. "Michael Cohen Testimony Before House Oversight Committee," February 27, 2019, *C-SPAN*, https://www.c-span.org/video/transcript/?id=57772.
9. Andrew McCabe, interviewed by Andrea Bernstein and Heather Vogell in "Former FBI Deputy Chief Andrew McCabe and Trump, Inc. Compare Notes," *Trump, Inc.*, May 29, 2019, https://www.wnycstudios.org/story/trump-inc-former-fbi-director-andrew-mccabe-compare-notes.
10. House Permanent Select Committee on Intelligence, *Deposition of: Michael Cohen* (Washington, DC: February 28, 2019), 28, https://docs.house.gov/meetings/IG/IG00/20190520/109549/HMTG-116-IG00-20190520-SD002.pdf.
11. "Cohen Testimony Before House Oversight."
12. House Permanent Select Committee on Intelligence, *Part 2, Deposition of: Michael Cohen* (Washington, DC: March 6, 2019), 68, https://assets.documentcloud.org/documents/6019075/HMTG-116-IG00-20190520-SD001-1.pdf.
13. Donald Trump, interviewed by John Sweeney in "Donald Trump Sued Over Failed Florida Deal," BBC, July 8, 2013, https://www.bbc.com/news/av/uk-23205781/donald-trump-sued-over-failed-florida-deal.
14. "Interview of: Donald J. Trump, Jr.," testimony before Senate Judiciary Committee, September 7, 2017, US Senate, https://www.judiciary.senate.gov/imo/media/doc/Trump%20Jr%20Transcript_redacted.pdf.
15. Search Warrant in the Matter of the Search of Four Premises and Two Electronic Devices, case No. 18-MAG 2969 (S.D.N.Y.), April 8, 2018.
16. Azeen Ghorayshi, Emma Loop, Jason Leopold, and Anthony Cormier, "These Secret Files Show How the Trump Tower Moscow Talks Unfolded while Trump Heaped Praise

on Putin," *BuzzFeed News,* February 5, 2019, https://www.buzzfeednews.com/article/azeenghorayshi/trump-tower-moscow-the-secret-files-cohen-sater-putin.

17. Heather Vogell, Andrea Bernstein, and Meg Cramer, "Trump's Moscow Tower Problem," *Trump, Inc.*, March 21, 2019, https://www.wnycstudios.org/podcasts/trumpinc/episodes/trump-inc-trump-moscow-tower-problem.
18. Trump Acquisition, LLC, and I.C. Expert Investment Company, letter of intent, October 28, 2015, included in the "Trump Moscow" documents obtained by *BuzzFeed News,* 163–69.
19. Ghorayshi et al., "These Secret Files."
20. "Third Republican Primary Debate - Main Stage - October 28 2015 on CNBC," YouTube, posted by US Presidential Debates, January 28, 2016, https://www.youtube.com/watch?v=wpCOloV3DZk.
21. Luke Harding, *Collusion: Secret Meetings, Dirty Money, and How Russia Helped Donald Trump Win* (New York: Vintage Books, 2017), 310.
22. Michael Cohen and Felix Sater, email correspondence, October 2015, included in the "Trump Moscow" documents obtained by *BuzzFeed News,* 69, 202.
23. "Cohen Testimony Before House Oversight."
24. United States v. Michael Cohen, No. 1:18-cr-00850 (S.D.N.Y.), criminal information, November 29, 2018.
25. Special Counsel Robert S. Mueller III, *Report on the Investigation into Russian Interference in the 2016 Presidential Election,* vol. 1 (Washington, DC: US Department of Justice, March 2019), 72–73.
26. Mueller, *Report,* vol. 1, 70.
27. Mueller, *Report,* vol. 1, 76.
28. Jeff Horwitz, "Trump Picked Stock Fraud Felon as Senior Adviser," *Associated Press,* December 4, 2015, https://apnews.com/29c255c0b69a48258ecae69a61612537.
29. Vogell et al., "Trump's Moscow Tower Problem."
30. Michael Cohen to Felix Sater, text message, December 30, 2015, included in the "Trump Moscow" documents obtained by *BuzzFeed News,* 231.
31. *Cohen,* November 29, 2018, criminal information.
32. Mueller, *Report,* vol. 1, 75.
33. Felix Sater to Michael Cohen, text message included in the "Trump Moscow" documents obtained by *BuzzFeed News,* 242.
34. United States v. Netyksho et al., No. 1:18-cr-00215 (D.C.), indictment, document #1, filed July 13, 2018, https://www.justice.gov/file/1080281/download.
35. Steven Bertoni, "Exclusive Interview: How Jared Kushner Won Trump the White House," *Forbes,* November 22, 2016, https://www.forbes.com/sites/stevenbertoni/2016/11/22/exclusive-interview-how-jared-kushner-won-trump-the-white-house/#4313d1413af624.
36. Patrick Healy and Michael Barbaro, "Donald Trump Calls for Barring Muslims from Entering U.S.," *New York Times,* December 7, 2015, https://www.nytimes.com/politics/first-draft/2015/12/07/donald-trump-calls-for-banning-muslims-from-entering-u-s/.
37. Gabriel Sherman, "Operation Trump: Inside the Most Unorthodox Campaign in Political History," *New York,* April 3, 2016, http://nymag.com/intelligencer/2016/04/inside-the-donald-trump-presidential-campaign.html.
38. "Read Jared Kushner's Prepared Remarks," *New York Times,* July 24, 2017, https://www.nytimes.com/interactive/2017/07/24/us/politics/document-Read-Jared-Kushner-s-Statement-to-Congressional.html.
39. Mueller, *Report,* vol. 1, 103–4.
40. Kushner Companies, "660 Fifth Avenue," promotional booklet, obtained by author.
41. "Transcript: Donald Trump's Foreign Policy Speech," *New York Times,* April 27, 2016,

https://www.nytimes.com/2016/04/28/us/politics/transcript-trump-foreign-policy.html.

42. "Jared Kushner's Prepared Remarks."
43. Indictment, *Netyksho*.
44. Mueller, *Report*, vol. 1, 81.

19. BIG CAVIAR

1. Paul Manafort, "TPs for Trump Conversation," February 2016, published in "Read the Job Application Memo Manafort Sent to Trump," *New York Times*, October 31, 2007, https://www.nytimes.com/interactive/2017/10/31/us/politics/document-manafort-trump-application.html.
2. Special Counsel Robert S. Mueller III, *Report on the Investigation into Russian Interference in the 2016 Presidential Election*, vol. 1 (Washington, DC: US Department of Justice, March 2019), 135.
3. "TPs for Trump Conversation."
4. Paul Manafort, interviewed in *Get Me Roger Stone* directed by Dylan Bank, Daniel DiMauro, and Morgan Pehme (Los Gatos, CA: Netflix, 2017).
5. Glenn Thrush, "To Charm Trump, Paul Manafort Sold Himself as an Affordable Outsider," *New York Times*, April 8, 2017, https://www.nytimes.com/2017/04/08/us/to-charm-trump-paul-manafort-sold-himself-as-an-affordable-outsider.html.
6. Alexander Burns and Maggie Haberman, "Donald Trump Hires Paul Manafort to Lead Delegation Effort," *New York Times*, March 28, 2016, https://www.nytimes.com/politics/first-draft/2016/03/28/donald-trump-hires-paul-manafort-to-lead-delegate-effort/.
7. Mueller, *Report*, vol. 1, 135.
8. *In the Matter of Section 36(3) of the Exempted Limited Partnership Law, 2014, and in the Matter of Pericles Emerging Market Partners, L.P.*, Cause No. FSD 0131 of 2014, (Grand Court of the Cayman Islands, Financial Services Division, December 9, 2014), 12.
9. Franklin Foer, "The Plot Against America," *Atlantic*, March 2018, https://www.theatlantic.com/magazine/archive/2018/03/paul-manafort-american-hustler/550925/.
10. Mueller, *Report*, vol. 1, 77.
11. Michael Cohen, testimony before US House Oversight and Reform Committee, February 27, 2019, https://www.c-span.org/video/?458125-1/michael-cohen-president-trump-he-racist-con-man-cheat.
12. Felix Sater to Michael Cohen, text message, May 4, 2016, included in the "Trump Moscow" documents obtained by *BuzzFeed News*, 258–65.
13. Chris Christie with Ellis Henican, *Let Me Finish: Trump, the Kushners, Bannon, New Jersey, and the Power of In-Your-Face Politics* (New York: Hachette, 2019), 244.
14. Christie, *Let Me Finish*, 251.
15. Ashley Parker and Alan Rappeport, "Donald Trump Has Delegate Majority for Republican Nomination, The A.P. Says," *New York Times*, May 26, 2016, https://www.nytimes.com/2016/05/27/us/politics/donald-trump-republican-nomination.html.
16. US House Oversight Committee Report, *Corporate and Foreign Interests Behind White House Push to Transfer U.S. Nuclear Technology to Saudi Arabia*, (Washington, DC: House Oversight Committee, July 2019), 14–16.
17. Tom Barrack and Yousef al Otaiba, email correspondence, obtained by author.
18. Donald Trump Jr. and Rob Goldstone, email correspondence, June 3–8, 2016, released by Donald Trump Jr. (@DonaldJTrumpJr) on Twitter July 11, 2017, published in "Read the Emails on Donald Trump Jr.'s Russia Meeting," *New York Times*, July 11, 2017,

https://www.nytimes.com/interactive/2017/07/11/us/politics/donald-trump-jr-email-text.html.

19. United States General Accounting Office, *Report to the Ranking Minority Member, Permanent Subcommittee on Investigations, Committee on Governmental Affairs, United States Senate; Suspicious Banking Activities: Possible Money Laundering by U.S. Corporations Formed for Russian Entities* (Washington, DC: US General Accounting Office, October 2000), https://www.gao.gov/new.items/d01120.pdf.
20. Mueller, *Report*, vol. 1, 67–68.
21. Mueller, *Report*, vol. 1, 184.
22. Felix Sater to Michael Cohen, text message, June 9, 2016, included in the "Trump Moscow" documents obtained by *BuzzFeed News*, 266.
23. Ellen Nakashima, "Russian Government Hackers Penetrated DNC, Stole Opposition Research on Trump," *Washington Post*, June 14, 2016, https://www.washingtonpost.com/world/national-security/russian-government-hackers-penetrated-dnc-stole-opposition-research-on-trump/2016/06/14/cf006cb4-316e-11e6-8ff7-7b6c1998b7a0_story.html.
24. "Campaign Chair Denies Financial Relationship between Trump and Russia," YouTube, from *CBS This Morning*, season 5, episode 179, aired July 27, 2016, posted by Daily Kos, June 15, 2018, https://www.youtube.com/watch?v=e0WudY0RM1I.
25. Ken Kurson, "Breaking: Key Bridgegate Figure to Accept Guilty Plea," *Observer*, July 5, 2016, https://observer.com/2016/07/breaking-key-bridgegate-figure-to-accept-guilty-plea/.
26. Anti-Defamation League, "ADL Urges Donald Trump to Reconsider 'America First' in Foreign Policy Approach," news release, April 28, 2016, https://www.adl.org/news/press-releases/adl-urges-donald-trump-to-reconsider-america-first-in-foreign-policy-approach.
27. Dana Schwartz, "An Open Letter to Jared Kushner, From One of Your Jewish Employees," *New York Observer*, July 5, 2016, https://observer.com/2016/07/an-open-letter-to-jared-kushner-from-one-of-your-jewish-employees/.
28. Jared Kushner, "The Donald Trump I Know," *New York Observer*, July 6, 2016, https://observer.com/2016/07/jared-kushner-the-donald-trump-i-know/.
29. Jose A. DelReal, "Kushner's Cousins Say Family Holocaust Stories Should Have Been Off-Limits in Trump Defense," *Washington Post*, July 7, 2016, https://www.washingtonpost.com/news/post-politics/wp/2016/07/07/kushners-cousins-say-family-holocaust-stories-should-have-been-off-limits-in-trump-defense/.
30. Mueller, *Report*, vol. 1, 137
31. "Transcript: Donald Trump at the G.O.P. Convention," *New York Times*, July 22, 2016, https://www.nytimes.com/2016/07/22/us/politics/trump-transcript-rnc-address.html.
32. Special Counsel Robert S. Mueller III, *Report on the Investigation into Russian Interference in the 2016 Presidential Election*, vol. 2 (Washington, DC: March 2019), 19.
33. Mueller, *Report*, vol. 1, 138–39.
34. Guy Faulconbridge, Anna Dabrowska, and Stephen Grey, "Toppled 'Mafia' President Cost Ukraine Up to $100 Billion, Prosecutor Says," *Reuters*, April 30, 2014, https://www.reuters.com/article/us-ukraine-crisis-yanukovich/toppled-mafia-president-cost-ukraine-up-to-100-billion-prosecutor-says-idUSBREA3T0K820140430.
35. Mueller, *Report*, vol. 1, 140.
36. United States v. Paul Manafort Jr., No. 1:17-cr-00201 (D.C. 2017), transcript of sealed hearing, February 4, 2019.
37. Mueller, *Report*, vol. 1, 141.

20. DIRT

1. Andrew E. Kramer, Mike McIntire, and Barry Meier, "Secret Ledger in Ukraine Lists Cash for Donald Trump's Campaign Chief," *New York Times*, August 14, 2016, https://www.nytimes.com/2016/08/15/us/politics/paul-manafort-ukraine-donald-trump.html.
2. *United States v. Roger Jason Stone, Jr.*, Case No. 1:19-cr-00018-ABJ (D.C., January 24, 2019), indictment.
3. Special Counsel Robert S. Mueller III, *Report on the Investigation into Russian Interference in the 2016 Presidential Election* (Washington, DC: US Department of Justice, March 2019), vol. 1, 54.
4. David A. Fahrenthold, "Trump Recorded Having Extremely Lewd Conversation about Women in 2005," *Washington Post*, October 8, 2016, https://www.washingtonpost.com/politics/trump-recorded-having-extremely-lewd-conversation-about-women-in-2005/2016/10/07/3b9ce776-8cb4-11e6-bf8a-3d26847eeed4_story.html.
5. *Roger Jason Stone, Jr.*, indictment, 9.
6. Michael Barbaro and Megan Twohey, "Crossing the Line: How Donald Trump Behaved With Women in Private," *New York Times*, May 14, 2016, https://www.nytimes.com/2016/05/15/us/politics/donald-trump-women.html.
7. "Ivanka Trump 'bothered' by NYT story on her father," YouTube, from *CBS This Morning*, season 5, episode 118, aired May 17, 2016, posted by CBS This Morning, May 18, 2016, https://www.youtube.com/watch?v=DNQPeT0ZFRQ.
8. Ivanka Trump (@IvankaTrump), "Shop Ivanka's look from her #RNC speech: http://bit.ly/29Qj7dE #RNCinCLE," Twitter, July 22, 2016, https://twitter.com/IvankaTrump/status/756492146484580352.
9. Nicole Puglise, "How Ivanka Trump Used the Republican Convention as a Fashion Show," *The Guardian*, July 23, 2016, https://www.theguardian.com/us-news/2016/jul/23/ivanka-trump-republican-convention-fashion.
10. "Transcript of the Second Debate," *New York Times*, October 10, 2019, https://www.nytimes.com/2016/10/10/us/politics/transcript-second-debate.html.
11. "Watch Ivanka Trump at Fortune's MPW Summit," *Fortune*, October 19, 2016, http://fortune.com/video/2016/10/19/ivanka-trump-mpw-summit/.
12. Ronan Farrow, "Donald Trump, a Playboy Model, and a System for Concealing Infidelity," *New Yorker*, February 16, 2018, https://www.newyorker.com/news/news-desk/donald-trump-a-playboy-model-and-a-system-for-concealing-infidelity-national-enquirer-karen-mcdougal.
13. Aaron Blake, "The Trump–Michael Cohen Tape Transcript, Annotated," *Washington Post*, July 24, 2018, https://www.washingtonpost.com/news/the-fix/wp/2018/07/24/the-trump-michael-cohen-tape-transcript-annotated/.
14. "Michael Cohen Testimony Before House Oversight and Reform Committee," C-SPAN, February 27, 2019, https://www.c-span.org/video/transcript/?id=57772.
15. United States v. Michael Cohen, No. 1:18-cr-00602 (S.D.N.Y.), criminal information, filed August 21, 2018, 16.
16. "Cohen Testimony Before House Oversight," February 27, 2019.
17. Mueller, *Report*, vol. 1, 149.
18. Michael Lewis, *The Fifth Risk* (New York: W. W. Norton, 2018), 21.
19. Chris Christie, *Let Me Finish: Trump, the Kushners, Bannon, New Jersey, and the Power of In-Your-Face Politics* (New York: Hachette, 2019), 7.
20. Christie, *Let Me Finish*, 8.
21. Mueller, *Report*, vol. 1, 146.
22. Mueller, *Report*, vol. 1, 156–59.
23. "Read Jared Kushner's Prepared Remarks," *New York Times*, July 24, 2017, https://www

.nytimes.com/interactive/2017/07/24/us/politics/document-Read-Jared-Kushner-s-Statement-to-Congressional.html.

24. "Kushner's Prepared Remarks."
25. Mueller, *Report*, vol. 1, 160.
26. "Kushner's Prepared Remarks."
27. Mueller, *Report*, vol. 1, 161.
28. "Kushner's Prepared Remarks."
29. David Filipov, Amy Brittain, Rosalind S. Helderman, and Tom Hamburger, "Explanations for Kushner's Meeting with Head of Kremlin-Linked Bank Don't Match Up," *Washington Post*, June 1, 2017, https://www.washingtonpost.com/politics/explanations-for-kushners-meeting-with-head-of-kremlin-linked-bank-dont-match-up/2017/06/01/dd1bdbb0-460a-11e7-bcde-624ad94170ab_story.html.
30. Mueller, *Report*, vol. 1, 161–62.
31. "Kushner's Prepared Remarks."

21. TRUMP, INC.

1. "Interview of: Glenn Simpson," testimony before US Senate Judiciary Committee, August 22, 2017, https://www.documentcloud.org/documents/4345537-Fusion-GPS-Simpson-Transcript.html.
2. Christopher Steele, "Company Intelligence Report 2016/080; US Presidential Election: Republican Candidate Donald Trump's Activities in Russia . . . ," memorandum, June 20, 2016, https://www.documentcloud.org/documents/3259984-Trump-Intelligence-Allegations.html, released with Ken Bensinger, Miriam Elder, and Mark Schoofs, "These Reports Allege Trump Has Deep Ties to Russia," *BuzzFeed News*, January 10, 2017, https://www.buzzfeednews.com/article/kenbensinger/these-reports-allege-trump-has-deep-ties-to-russia.
3. Michael Isikoff and David Corn, *Russian Roulette: The Inside Story of Putin's War on America and the Election of Donald Trump* (New York: Twelve, 2018), x.
4. Masha Gessen, "The Putin Paradigm," *New York Review of Books*, December 13, 2016, https://www.nybooks.com/daily/2016/12/13/putin-paradigm-how-trump-will-rule/.
5. Andrea Bernstein, Ilya Marritz, and Eric Umansky, "Trump's 'No Conflict Situation,'" *Trump, Inc.*, February 7, 2018, https://www.wnycstudios.org/story/no-conflict-solution-trump-inc.
6. Jonathan Lemire, "What Was in those Folders at Donald Trump's Press Conference?," *Boston Globe*, January 12, 2017, https://www.bostonglobe.com/news/politics/2017/01/12/what-was-those-folders-donald-trump-press-conference/BVq5qgRjAKk2rpICgQEOTN/story.html.
7. Zephyr Teachout, interviewed by author and Ilya Marritz, January 2018.
8. James Comey, *A Higher Loyalty: Truth, Lies, and Leadership* (New York: Flatiron Books, 2018), 258.
9. Gessen, "The Putin Paradigm."
10. Susanne Craig, Jo Becker, and Jesse Drucker, "Jared Kushner, a Trump In-Law and Adviser, Chases a Chinese Deal," *New York Times*, January 7, 2017, https://www.nytimes.com/2017/01/07/us/politics/jared-kushner-trump-business.html.
11. Emily Rauhala and William Wan, "In a Beijing Ballroom, Kushner Family Pushes $500,000 'Investor Visa' to Wealthy Chinese," *Washington Post*, May 6, 2017, https://www.washingtonpost.com/world/in-a-beijing-ballroom-kushner-family-flogs-500000-investor-visa-to-wealthy-chinese/2017/05/06/cf711e53-eb49-4f9a-8dea-3cd836fcf287_story.html.
12. Jared Kushner, "Executive Branch Personnel, Public Financial Disclosure Report" OGE Form 278e, (Washington, DC, Office of Government Ethics, 2018 [filed May 15, 2018]), 2.

13. United States v. W. Samuel Patten, No. 1:18-cr-00260 (D.C.), criminal information, filed August 31, 2018.
14. Ilya Marritz and Justin Elliott, "Trump's Inauguration Paid Trump's Company—With Ivanka in the Middle," ProPublica, December 14, 2018, https://www.propublica.org/article/trump-inc-podcast-trumps-inauguration-paid-trumps-company-with-ivanka-in-the-middle.
15. Emily Jane Fox, "'I Am Disgusted': Behind the Scenes of Trump's Increasingly Scrutinized $107 Million Inauguration," *Vanity Fair*, February 7, 2019, https://www.vanityfair.com/news/2019/02/behind-the-scenes-of-trumps-107-million-inauguration.
16. Marritz and Elliott, "Trump's Inauguration."
17. Sharon LaFraniere, Maggie Haberman, and Adam Goldman, "Trump Inaugural Fund and Super PAC Said to Be Scrutinized for Illegal Foreign Donations," *New York Times*, December 13, 2018, https://www.nytimes.com/2018/12/13/us/politics/trump-inauguration-investigation.html.
18. United States v. Stephen M. Calk, 1:19-cr-0366 (S.D.N.Y), May 21, 2019, indictment.
19. Marritz and Elliott, "Trump's Inauguration."
20. Craig Timberg, Rosalind S. Helderman, Andrew Roth, and Carol D. Leonnig, "In the Crowd at Trump's Inauguration, Members of Russia's Elite Anticipated a Thaw between Moscow and Washington," *Washington Post*, January 20, 2018, https://www.washingtonpost.com/politics/amid-trumps-inaugural-festivities-members-of-russias-elite-anticipated-a-thaw-between-moscow-and-washington/2018/01/20/0d767f46-fb9f-11e7-ad8c-ecbb62019393_story.html.
21. "The Inaugural Address," The White House, January 20, 2017, https://www.whitehouse.gov/briefings-statements/the-inaugural-address/.
22. Noah Bookbinder, Citizens for Responsibility and Ethics in Washington, "Re: Jared Kushner's Potential Conflict of Interest from Cadre," letter to Hon. Walter M. Shaub Jr., July 6, 2017, https://s3.amazonaws.com/storage.citizensforethics.org/wp-content/uploads/2017/07/06023725/OGE-Letter-Kushner-7-6-17.pdf.
23. Charles Kushner and Laurent Morali, interviewed by Will Parker and Konrad Putzier in "Kushner, Unfiltered," *Real Deal*, June 1, 2018, https://therealdeal.com/issues_articles/kushner-unfiltered/.
24. Justin Elliott and Al Shaw, "White House Power Player Jared Kushner is Keeping Parts of His Real Estate Empire," ProPublica, February 24, 2017, https://www.propublica.org/article/white-house-power-player-jared-kushner-keeping-parts-of-real-estate-empire.
25. Jesse Drucker, Kate Kelly, and Ben Protess, "Kushner's Family Business Received Loans after White House Meetings," *New York Times*, February 28, 2018, https://www.nytimes.com/2018/02/28/business/jared-kushner-apollo-citigroup-loans.html.
26. Telis Demos and Erica Orden, "Citi Says Kushner Cos. Loan Was 'Completely Appropriate,'" Wall Street Journal, March 21, 2018, https://www.wsj.com/articles/citi-says-kushner-cos-loan-was-completely-appropriate-1521644913.
27. Drucker, Kelly, and Protess, "Kushner's Family Business."
28. Kristina Webb, "Comparing Dinners: What Trump and Obama served Xi on Visits to U.S.," *Palm Beach Post*, April 12, 2017, http://postonpolitics.blog.mypalmbeachpost.com/2017/04/12/comparing-dinners-what-trump-and-obama-served-xi-on-visits-to-u-s/.
29. Ivanka Trump (@IvankaTrump), "Very proud of Arabella and Joseph for their performance in honor of President Xi Jinping and Madame Peng Liyuan's official visit to the US!," Twitter, April 7, 2017, https://twitter.com/i/web/status/850488492828360704.
30. Ivanka Trump (@ivankatrump), "Very proud of Arabella and Joseph for their performance in honor of President Xi Jinping and Madame Peng Liyuan's official visit to the United States. 欢迎 (welcome)!," Instagram, April 7, 2017, https://www.instagram.com/p/BSmgFKIl2M6/.

31. Erika Kinetz, “Ivanka’s Biz Prospers as Politics Mixes with Business,” *Associated Press*, April 19, 2017, https://apnews.com/d9e34f23a64947d99e4a7d757012c509.
32. Anjali Kamat, “Political Corruption and the Art of the Deal,” *New Republic*, March 21, 2018, https://newrepublic.com/article/147351/political-corruption-art-deal; Andrea Bernstein, Eric Umansky, and Anjali Kamat, “Former Indian Official: Donald Trump Jr. Pushed ‘Blatantly Illegal’ Project, *Trump, Inc.*, March 21, 2018, https://www.wnycstudios.org/podcasts/trumpinc/episodes/trump-inc-podcast-former-indian-official-donald-trump-jr-pushed-blatantly-illegal-project.
33. “Hyderabad: Ivanka Trump Energetic Speech Live From HICC | Global Entrepreneurship Summit,” YouTube, posted by RAJ News Telugu, November 28, 2017, https://www.youtube.com/watch?v=dmFn1A969MI.
34. Bernstein, Umansky, and Kamat, “Former Indian Official.”
35. “Ivanka Trump: ‘We’re Going to Deliver Historic Tax Reforms & It’s Going to Happen Before Christmas,’” YouTube, from *Fox and Friends* episode dated December 18, 2017, posted by Fox News Insider, December 18, 2017, https://www.youtube.com/watch?v=kZfnFBJkfkQ.
36. Ivanka Trump interview, *Fox and Friends*, aired December 21, 2017.
37. Jesse Drucker and Alan Rappeport, “The Tax Bill’s Winners and Losers,” *New York Times*, December 16, 2017, https://www.nytimes.com/2017/12/16/business/the-winners-and-losers-in-the-tax-bill.html.
38. Kim Soffen and Reuben Fischer-Baum, “10 Key Takeaways from the Republican Tax Bill,” *Washington Post*, December 20, 2017, https://www.washingtonpost.com/graphics/2017/business/tax-bill-overview/.
39. James Tankersley, “Budget Deficit Jumps Nearly 17% in 2018,” *New York Times*, October 15, 2018, https://www.nytimes.com/2018/10/15/us/politics/federal-deficit-2018-trump-tax-cuts.html.

22. “A TERRIBLE SITUATION”

1. إيلي حنا, “رجال ابن سلمان في مكاتب ‘فريق الظل’ الأميركي,” *Al Akhbar*, December 6, 2018, cited in David D. Kirkpatrick, Ben Hubbard, Mark Landler, and Mark Mazzetti, “The Wooing of Jared Kushner: How the Saudis Got a Friend in the White House,” *New York Times*, December 8, 2018, https://www.nytimes.com/2018/12/08/world/middleeast/saudi-mbs-jared-kushner.html.
2. David D. Kirkpatrick, “The Most Powerful Arab Ruler Isn’t M.B.S. It’s M.B.Z.,” *New York Times*, June 2, 2019, https://www.nytimes.com/2019/06/02/world/middleeast/crown-prince-mohammed-bin-zayed.html.
3. Dexter Filkins, “A Saudi Prince’s Quest to Remake the Middle East,” *New Yorker*, April 2, 2018, https://www.newyorker.com/magazine/2018/04/09/a-saudi-princes-quest-to-remake-the-middle-east.
4. Kirkpatrick, “Most Powerful Arab Ruler.”
5. Special Counsel Robert S. Mueller III, *Report on the Investigation into Russian Interference in the 2016 Presidential Election*, vol. 1 (Washington, DC: US Department of Justice, March 2019), 151–56.
6. United States v. George Aref Nader, Case No. 1:18-mj-196, criminal complaint, filed under seal, April 19, 2018, unsealed June 3, 2019.
7. Erik Prince, testimony before US House of Representatives, Permanent Select Committee on Intelligence, Washington, DC, November 30, 2017, https://docs.house.gov/meetings/IG/IG00/20171130/106661/HHRG-115-IG00-Transcript-20171130.pdf.
8. Mueller, *Report*, vol. 1, 156.
9. House Oversight Committee Report, *Corporate and Foreign Interests Behind White*

House Push to Transfer U.S. Nuclear Technology to Saudi Arabia (Washington, DC: House Oversight Committee, July 2019).

10. Kirkpatrick et al., "The Wooing of Jared Kushner."
11. Shane Harris, Carol D. Leonnig, Greg Jaffe, and Josh Dawsey, "Kushner's Overseas Contacts Raise Concerns as Foreign Officials Seek Leverage," *Washington Post*, February 27, 2018, https://www.washingtonpost.com/world/national-security/kushners-overseas-contacts-raise-concerns-as-foreign-officials-seek-leverage/2018/02/27/16bbc052-18c3-11e8-942d-16a950029788_story.html.
12. Kirkpatrick et al., "The Wooing of Jared Kushner."
13. Secretary Rex Tillerson, interviewed by Committee on Foreign Affairs, US House of Representatives, Washington, DC, May 21, 2019, https://foreignaffairs.house.gov/_cache/files/e/7/e7bd0ed2-cf98-4f6d-a473-0406b0c50cde/23A0BEE4DF2B55E9D91259F04A3B22FA.tillerson-transcript-interview-5-21-19.pdf.
14. Filkins, "Saudi Prince's Quest."
15. Filkins, "Saudi Prince's Quest."
16. David D. Kirkpatrick, "The Kingdom and the Kushners: Jared Went to Riyadh. So Did His Brother," *New York Times*, March 21, 2019, https://www.nytimes.com/2019/03/21/world/middleeast/kushner-saudi-arabia.html.
17. David Kocieniewski and Stephanie Baker, "Kushner's Cadre in Talks with Saudi-Backed SoftBank Fund," *Bloomberg*, May 22, 2018, https://www.bloomberg.com/news/articles/2018-05-22/kushners-cadre-startup-said-to-seek-saudi-backed-softbank-funds.
18. Filkins, "Saudi Prince's Quest."
19. Adam Entous and Evan Osnos, "Jared Kushner Is China's Trump Card," *New Yorker*, January 19, 2018, https://www.newyorker.com/magazine/2018/01/29/jared-kushner-is-chinas-trump-card.
20. Entous and Osnos, "China's Trump Card."
21. Harris et al., "Kushner's Overseas Contacts."
22. Tillerson interview, May 21, 2019.
23. Laura Strickler, Ken Dilanian, and Peter Alexander, "Officials Rejected Jared Kushner for Top Secret Security Clearance, But Were Overruled," *NBC News*, January 24, 2019, https://www.nbcnews.com/politics/donald-trump/officials-rejected-jared-kushner-top-secret-security-clearance-were-overruled-n962221.
24. Ivanka Trump, interviewed by Abby Huntsman in "Ivanka Trump Talks White House Security Clearance Controversy," *ABC News*, February 8, 2019, https://abcnews.go.com/Politics/video/ivanka-trump-talks-white-house-security-clearance-controversy-60938538.
25. House Oversight and Reform Committee Chairman Elijah E. Cummings, letter to Counsel to the President Pat Cipollone, April 1, 2019, https://oversight.house.gov/sites/democrats.oversight.house.gov/files/2019-04-01.EEC%20to%20Cipollone-WH%20re%20Security%20Clearances%201.pdf.
26. Staff of the Committee on Oversight and Reform, "Summary of Interview with White House Whistleblower on Security Clearances," memorandum, April 1, 2019, https://oversight.house.gov/sites/democrats.oversight.house.gov/files/2019-04-01.Memo%20on%20Whisteblower%20Interview%202.pdf.
27. Katie Rogers, Maggie Haberman, and Nicholas Fandos, "Ex–White House Official Says No One Pressured Him to Overturn Security Clearance Recommendations," *New York Times*, May 2, 2019, https://www.nytimes.com/2019/05/02/us/politics/carl-kline-security-clearance.html.
28. Jared Kushner, interviewed by Laura Ingraham, *Ingraham Angle*, aired on Fox News April 1, 2019.

29. David Ignatius, "How the Mysteries of Khashoggi's Murder Have Rocked the U.S.-Saudi Partnership," *Washington Post*, March 29, 2019, https://www.washingtonpost.com/opinions/global-opinions/how-the-mysteries-of-khashoggis-murder-have-rocked-the-us-saudi-partnership/2019/03/29/cf060472-50af-11e9-a3f7-78b7525a8d5f_story.html.
30. Joyce Lee and Dalton Bennett, "The Assassination of Jamal Khashoggi," *Washington Post*, April 1, 2019, https://www.washingtonpost.com/graphics/2019/world/assassination-of-jamal-khashoggi-documentary/.
31. Kirkpatrick et al., "Wooing of Jared Kushner."
32. "Jared Kushner full interview with Van Jones," CNN, October 22, 2018, https://www.cnn.com/videos/politics/2018/10/22/jared-kushner-full-interview-citizen-by-cnn-van-jones-vpx-sot.cnn.

23. AMERICAN OLIGARCHY

1. Zach Everson, interviewed by author, July 2019.
2. Steven L. Schooner and Daniel I. Gordon, "GSA's Trump Hotel Lease Debacle," *Government Executive*, November 28, 2016, https://www.govexec.com/excellence/promising-practices/2016/11/gsas-trump-hotel-lease-debacle/133424/.
3. Kevin Terry to Donald Trump Jr., letter, March 23, 2017, released pursuant to the Freedom of Information Act.
4. Steven L. Schooner, interviewed by author, March 2019.
5. Office of Inspections and Office of Inspector General, *Evaluation of GSA's Management and Administration of the Old Post Office Building Lease* (Washington, DC: US General Services Administration, January 16, 2019), JE-19-002 (redacted), https://www.gsaig.gov/sites/default/files/ipa-reports/JE19-002%20OIG%20EVALUATION%20REPORT-GSA%27s%20Management%20%26%20Administration%20of%20OPO%20Building%20Lease_January%2016%202019_Redacted.pdf.
6. Robert Maguire, interviewed by author, January 2018.
7. Ilya Marritz, Meg Cramer, and Katherine Sullivan, "How a Nigerian Presidential Candidate Hired a Trump Lobbyist and Ended Up in Trump's Lobby," *Trump, Inc.*, February 27, 2019, https://www.wnycstudios.org/podcasts/trumpinc/episodes/trump-inc-nigerian-presidential-candidate-hired-trump-lobbyist-trumps-lobby.
8. Dino Grandoni and Juliet Eilperin, "Three Trump Cabinet Members Attended Mining Lobbyist Meeting at Trump International Hotel," *Washington Post*, October 5, 2017, https://www.washingtonpost.com/news/energy-environment/wp/2017/10/05/three-trump-cabinet-members-attended-mining-lobbyist-meeting-at-trump-international-hotel/.
9. Ilya Marritz, Justin Elliott, and Zach Everson, "Romanian Prime Minister Is Staying at Trump's D.C. Hotel," *Trump, Inc.* March 25, 2019, https://www.wnycstudios.org/podcasts/trumpinc/episodes/trump-inc-nigerian-presidential-candidate-hired-trump-lobbyist-trumps-lobby.
10. Office of Inspector General, US General Services Administration, *Review of GSA's Revised Plan for the Federal Bureau of Investigation Headquarters Consolidation Project* (August 27, 2018), 19, https://www.gsaig.gov/sites/default/files/audit-reports/Review%20of%20GSA%27s%20Revised%20Plan%20for%20the%20FBI%20HQ%20Consolidation%20Project%20REDACTED%20-%20508%20compliant.pdf.
11. Office of Inspector General, *Review of GSA's Revised Plan.*
12. Ivanka Trump, "Executive Branch Personnel Public Financial Disclosure Report," OGE Form 278e (May 15, 2018 and May 14, 2019); Donald J. Trump, "Executive Branch Personnel Public Financial Disclosure Report," OGE Form 278e (May 15, 2018 and May 15, 2019).

13. Desmond Butler and Tom LoBianco, "The Princes, the President and the Fortune Seekers," Associated Press, May 21, 2018, https://apnews.com/a3521859cf8d4c199cb9a8567abd2b71/The-princes,-the-president-and-the-fortune-seekers.
14. David D. Kirkpatrick and Mark Mazzetti, "How 2 Gulf Monarchies Sought to Influence the White House," *New York Times*, March 21, 2018, https://www.nytimes.com/2018/03/21/us/politics/george-nader-elliott-broidy-uae-saudi-arabia-white-house-influence.html.
15. Justin Elliott, "Trump's Patron-in-Chief," ProPublica, October 10, 2018, https://features.propublica.org/trump-inc-podcast/sheldon-adelson-casino-magnate-trump-macau-and-japan/.
16. Justin Elliott and Ilya Marritz, "Trump Inauguration Chief Tom Barrack's 'Rules for Success'—*Trump, Inc.* Podcast," ProPublica, February 20, 2019, https://www.propublica.org/article/trump-inc-podcast-trump-inauguration-chief-tom-barrack-rules-for-success.
17. Bradley Hope, Tom Wright, and Rebecca Davis O'Brien, "U.S. Probing Whether Malaysian Fugitive Laundered Funds to Pay Chris Christie and Trump Lawyer," *Wall Street Journal*, August 29, 2018, https://www.wsj.com/articles/u-s-probing-whether-malaysian-fugitive-laundered-funds-to-pay-chris-christie-and-trump-lawyer-1535535000.
18. Isaac Arnsdorf, "The Shadow Rulers of the VA," ProPublica, August 7, 2018, https://www.propublica.org/article/ike-perlmutter-bruce-moskowitz-marc-sherman-shadow-rulers-of-the-va.
19. Lisa Friedman, "The Investigations That Led to Scott Pruitt's Resignation," *New York Times*, April 18, 2018, https://www.nytimes.com/2018/04/18/climate/scott-pruitt-epa-investigations-guide.html.
20. Rachana Pradhan and Dan Diamond, "Federal Auditor Calls for Recouping $341K Tom Price Spent on Flights," *Politico*, July 13, 2018, https://www.politico.com/story/2018/07/13/tom-price-auditor-travel-685778.
21. Juliet Eilperin, Josh Dawsey, and Darryl Fears, "Interior Secretary Zinke Resigns amid Investigations," *Washington Post*, December 15, 2018, https://www.washingtonpost.com/national/health-science/interior-secretary-zinke-resigns-amid-investigations/2018/12/15/481f9104-0077-11e9-ad40-cdfd0e0dd65a_story.html; David Leonhardt and Ian Prasad Philbrick, "Trump's Corruption: The Definitive List," *New York Times*, October 28, 2018, https://www.nytimes.com/2018/10/28/opinion/trump-administration-corruption-conflicts.html.
22. Coral Davenport, "Interior Dept. Opens Ethics Investigation of Its New Chief, David Bernhardt," *New York Times*, April 15, 2019, https://www.nytimes.com/2019/04/15/climate/bernhardt-interior-department-ethics-investigation.html.
23. Mike McIntire, Sasha Chavkin, and Martha M. Hamilton, "Commerce Secretary's Offshore Ties to Putin 'Cronies,'" *New York Times*, November 5, 2017, https://www.nytimes.com/2017/11/05/world/wilbur-ross-russia.html.
24. Dan Alexander, "Lies, China and Putin: Solving the Mystery of Wilbur Ross' Missing Fortune," *Forbes*, June 18, 2018, https://www.forbes.com/sites/danalexander/2018/06/18/lies-china-and-putin-solving-the-mystery-of-wilbur-ross-missing-fortune-trump-commerce-secretary-cabinet-conflicts-of-interest/#42df47377e87.
25. Sarah Chayes, *Thieves of State: Why Corruption Threatens Global Security* (New York: W. W. Norton, 2016).
26. Sarah Chayes, interviewed by Andrea Bernstein in "Elliott Broidy's All-Access Pass," *Trump, Inc.*, September 26, 2018, https://www.wnycstudios.org/story/trump_inc_elliott_broidy_rise_fall.

24. JUSTICE

1. Robert S. Mueller III, *Report on the Investigation into Russian Interference in the 2016 Presidential Election*, vol. 2 (Washington, DC: US Department of Justice, March 2019), 78.
2. Mueller, *Report*, vol. 2, 50–51.
3. Mueller, *Report*, vol. 2, 86–87.
4. Mueller, *Report*, vol. 2, 114–18.
5. Michael S. Schmidt, "Obstruction Inquiry Shows Trump's Struggle to Keep Grip on Russia Investigation," *New York Times*, January 4, 2018, https://www.nytimes.com/2018/01/04/us/politics/trump-sessions-russia-mcgahn.html.
6. United States v. Michael Cohen, No. 1:18-cr-00602 (S.D.N.Y.), unredacted search warrant dated April 7, 2018, exhibit 6 – 18MAG 2958., document #43-6.
7. Mueller, *Report*, vol. 2, 154.
8. Mueller, *Report*, vol. 2, 147.
9. Mueller, *Report*, vol. 2, 146.
10. George Stephanopoulos, "Exclusive: Michael Cohen says family and country, not President Trump, is his 'first loyalty,'" *ABC News*, July 2, 2018, https://abcnews.go.com/Politics/michael-cohen-family-country-president-trump-loyalty/story?id=56304585.
11. US Department of Justice, "Grand Jury Indicts 12 Russian Intelligence Officers for Hacking Offenses Related to the 2016 Election," news release, July 13, 2018, https://www.justice.gov/opa/pr/grand-jury-indicts-12-russian-intelligence-officers-hacking-offenses-related-2016-election.
12. United States v. Victor Borisovich Netyksho et al., Case 1:18-cr-00215-ABJ (D.C., July 13, 2018), https://www.justice.gov/file/1080281/download.
13. "Remarks by President Trump and President Putin of the Russian Federation in Joint Press Conference," The White House, July 16, 2018, https://www.whitehouse.gov/briefings-statements/remarks-president-trump-president-putin-russian-federation-joint-press-conference/.
14. United States v. Paul Manafort, No. 1:18-cr-00083 (E.D. Va.), transcript of trial proceedings held on July 31, 2018 at 27, ID# 3478, document #206, filed August 6, 2018.
15. *Manafort*, No. 1:18-cr-00083 (E.D.Va.), transcript of trial proceedings held on August 1, 2018 at 6, ID# 3155, document #203, filed August 6, 2018.
16. *Manafort*, No. 1:18-cr-00083 (E.D.Va.), transcript of trial proceedings held on August 1, 2018.
17. Nathan Layne and Karen Freifeld, "Trump Defends Ex-Aide Manafort as Jury Ends Second Day of Deliberations," *Reuters*, August 17, 2018, https://www.reuters.com/article/us-usa-trump-russia-manafort/trump-defends-ex-aide-manafort-as-jury-weighs-verdict-idUSKBN1L20Z6.
18. "Juror in the Paul Manafort trial speaks out," *Fox News @ Night with Shannon Bream*, *Fox News*, August 22, 2018, https://video.foxnews.com/v/5825647815001/#sp=show-clips.
19. United States v. Michael Cohen, No. 1:18-cr-00602 (S.D.N.Y.), transcript of plea proceedings held on August 21, 2018, document #7, filed September 14, 2018.
20. United States v. Roger Jason Stone Jr., No. 1:19-cr-00018 (D.C.), indictment, filed January 24, 2019.
21. *Cohen*, No. 1:18-cr-00602 (S.D.N.Y.), transcript of sentencing proceedings held on December 12, 2018.
22. "Full Transcript of Mueller's Statement on Russia Investigation," *New York Times*, May 29, 2019, https://www.nytimes.com/2019/05/29/us/politics/mueller-transcript.html.
23. Anonymous US government official to Richard Burr (chairman of the Senate Committee on Intelligence) and Adam Schiff (chairman of the House Permanent Select Committee on Intelligence), letter, August 12, 2019 (hereafter referred to as "whistle-blower report").

24. Oliver Bullough, *Moneyland: The Inside Story of the Crooks and Kleptocrats Who Rule the World* (New York: St. Martin's Press, 2019), 8.
25. Andrea Bernstein, Ilya Marritz, Katie Zavadsky, and Jake Pearson, "Ukraine," *Trump, Inc.*, October 2, 2019, https://www.wnycstudios.org/podcasts/trumpinc/episodes/trump-inc-ukraine.
26. Kurt Volker, testimony before the House Committee on Foreign Affairs, Permanent Select Committee on Intelligence, and Committee on Oversight, Washington, DC, October 3, 2019.
27. Eliot L. Engel, Adam B. Schiff, and Elijah E. Cummings to members of the Intelligence, Oversight and Reform, and Foreign Affairs committees, letter, October 3, 2019.
28. Donald J. Trump to Volodymyr Zelensky, memorandum of telephone conversation, July 25, 2019, https://www.whitehouse.gov/wp-content/uploads/2019/09/Unclassified09.2019.pdf.
29. Whistle-blower report, 4.
30. Engel et al., letter, October 3, 2019.
31. Engel et al., letter, October 3, 2019.
32. Volker testimony, 10.
33. Caitlin Emma and Connor O'Brien, "Trump Holds Up Ukraine Military Aid Meant to Confront Russia," *Politico*, August 28, 2019, https://www.politico.com/story/2019/08/28/trump-ukraine-military-aid-russia-1689531.
34. Engel et al., letter, October 3, 2019.
35. Russell Wheeler, "Appellate Court Vacancies May Be Scarce in Coming Years, Limiting Trump's Impact," *Brookings Institution*, December 6, 2018, https://www.brookings.edu/blog/fixgov/2018/12/06/trump-impact-on-appellate-courts/.
36. Adam Liptak and Maggie Haberman, "Inside the White House's Quiet Campaign to Create a Supreme Court Opening," *New York Times*, June 28, 2018, https://www.nytimes.com/2018/06/28/us/politics/trump-anthony-kennedy-retirement.html.
37. "Presidential Economic Address," February 28, 2017, C-SPAN, https://www.c-span.org/video/?424147-1/president-trump-addresses-joint-session-congress.
38. Brett M. Kavanaugh, Supreme Court nominee confirmation hearing, Senate Judiciary Committee, Washington, DC, September 5, 2018, C-SPAN, https://www.c-span.org/video/?c4754538/user-clip-senator-kamala-harris-questions-scotus-nominee-judge-brett-kavanaugh-day-2.
39. Reuters, "More than 20 Million Viewers Watched Kavanaugh Hearing on TV," *NBC News*, September 28, 2018, https://www.nbcnews.com/pop-culture/tv/more-20-million-viewers-watched-kavanaugh-hearing-tv-n914946.
40. United States Senate Committee on the Judiciary, Brett M. Kavanaugh Supreme Court Justice hearing, September 27, 2018.

EPILOGUE

1. Pool Report, White House Press Pool, written by Josh Dawsey of the *Washington Post*, July 12, 2019, emailed to author from White House Press Pool.
2. "Immigration Chief: 'Give Me Your Tired, Your Poor Who Can Stand On Their Own 2 Feet,'" Rachel Martin, NPR, August 13, 2019, https://www.npr.org/2019/08/13/750726795/immigration-chief-give-me-your-tired-your-poor-who-can-stand-on-their-own-2-feet.
3. Thomas Kaplan, "How the Trump Campaign Used Facebook Ads to Amplify His 'Invasion' Claim," *New York Times*, August 5, 2019, https://www.nytimes.com/2019/08/05/us/politics/trump-campaign-facebook-ads-invasion.html.
4. Rae Kushner, testimony to Sidney Langer of the Holocaust Research Center at Kean College, held by the United States Holocaust Memorial Museum, 1982, https://collections.ushmm.org/search/catalog/irn504520.

5. Jared Kushner, interviewed by Jonathan Swan, *Axios on HBO*, season 2, episode 1, aired June 2, 2019.
6. Ivanka Trump, interviewed by *Axios*'s Mike Allen, C-SPAN, Washington, DC, August 2, 2018, https://www.c-span.org/video/?449294-1/ivanka-trump-remarks-education-workforce.
7. Rae Kushner, testimony held by the USC Shoah Foundation Institute, July 25, 1996, https://collections.ushmm.org/search/catalog/vha18937.
8. The Kushner Family and Ellen Robinson Epstein, *The Miracle of Life: The Story of Rae and Joseph Kushner* (Chevy Chase, MD: E. Epstein, 1998), 13.
9. Hannah Arendt, *The Origins of Totalitarianism* (New York: Harcourt/Harvest Books, 1976), 277.
10. Hannah Arendt, "Truth and Politics," *New Yorker*, February 25, 1967, https://www.newyorker.com/magazine/1967/02/25/truth-and-politics.
11. Marc Kushner, "Why the buildings of the future will be shaped by . . . you," lecture, TED, Vancouver, Canada, March 2014, https://www.ted.com/talks/marc_kushner_why_the_buildings_of_the_future_will_be_shaped_by_you?language=en.
12. Arendt, *Origins of Totalitarianism*, vii.
13. Richard J. Bernstein, "The Origins of Totalitarianism: Not History, but Politics," *Social Research* 69, no. 2 (Summer 2002): 381–401.
14. Tony Kushner, interviewed by Andrea Bernstein in "Tony Kushner on His New Play, Unions, Forgiveness and Mark Ruffalo," *WNYC News*, March 11, 2011, https://www.wnyc.org/story/117969-wnycs-andrea-bernstein-interviews-playwright-tony-kushner/.

INDEX